Rebel Angel

Rebel Angel

The Life and Times of
Annemarie Schwarzenbach

Padraig Rooney

polity

First published in 2025 by Polity Press

Epigraph to Chapter 4 reproduced with the generous permission of the Truman Capote Literary Trust.

Polity Press
65 Bridge Street
Cambridge CB2 1UR, UK

Polity Press
111 River Street
Hoboken, NJ 07030, USA

ISBN-13: 978-1-5095-6629-7

A catalogue record for this book is available from the British Library.

Library of Congress Control Number: 2024940082

Typeset in 11.5 on 14 Adobe Garamond
by Fakenham Prepress Solutions, Fakenham, Norfolk NR21 8NL
Printed and bound in Great Britain by CPI Group (UK) Ltd, Croydon

The publisher has used its best endeavours to ensure that the URLs for external websites referred to in this book are correct and active at the time of going to press. However, the publisher has no responsibility for the websites and can make no guarantee that a site will remain live or that the content is or will remain appropriate.

Every effort has been made to trace all copyright holders, but if any have been overlooked the publisher will be pleased to include any necessary credits in any subsequent reprint or edition.

For further information on Polity, visit our website:
politybooks.com

Contents

Figures

Acknowledgements

I am indebted to the following for invaluable help with research: Stephanie Cudre-Mauroux, Christa Baumberger, Rudolf Probst, Sabrina Friederich, Kristel Roder at the Swiss Literary Archives in Bern; Thomas Bruggmann and Alexis Schwarzenbach at Zentralbibliothek Zurich; Dinah Berner at Monacensia im Hildebrandhaus-Literaturarchiv in Munich; Heidrun Fink at the Deutsches Literaturarchiv Marbach, Marbach am Neckar; archivists and librarians at Basel University Library for access to the Otto Kleiber and Carl Burchardt papers; Martin Waldmeier at Zentrum Paul Klee in Bern for his knowledge of Schwarzenbach's photographs; Maren Richter, document curator at Obersalzberg, for agreeing to talk to me about Maria Daelen; Patrick Moser at Historisches Museum Basel for his knowledge of Switzerland during wartime; Carole Bonstein Archive, Geneva.

Alexander Rankin and Laura Russo welcomed me at the Howard Gottlieb Archival Research Center, Boston University; archivists at Washington University in St. Louis for the Robert Newton Linscott papers; archivists at the Harry Ransom Humanities Research Center, University of Texas at Austin for permission to consult the Carson McCullers papers.

Many people provided assistance in the writing of this book. Roger Perret, scholar and editor of Schwarzenbach's work, shared valuable documents. Schwarzenbach's biographer and editor in French, Dominique Laure Miermont-Grente, took time to answer my questions. Thomas Blubacher on a sunny day in Rheinfelden fleshed out the career of Ruth Landshoff-Yorck. Carlos Dews kindly read my manuscript with his expert eye for Carson McCullers. Sarah Schulman also read the manuscript and provided a much-needed boost. Aine Keenan brought to bear her enthusiasm and considerable knowledge of Ella Maillart. Todd D. Smith, Executive Director of the Bechtler Museum of Modern Art in Charlotte, NC, commissioned voiceovers of my Schwarzenbach translations. Brian Ferrari shared his knowledge of cabaret singer Spivy le Voe, not to be confused with Victoria Spivey. Elsa Fischer in Bern and Hilary Cole in Basel sent clippings from Swiss newspapers. Kirsten Jaehde helped with German translation. To all of them, many thanks.

Introduction

In 2018 the *New York Times* published an obituary of Annemarie Schwarzenbach some seventy-five years after her untimely death. The Swiss author's stock was up and a desire to correct the dead-white-male bias of historical reporting led the obituarist to wonder what lay behind this resurgence of interest: gay cult figure, androgynous glamour, the romance of trustafarian travel, drugs and an early death?

All of the above. Schwarzenbach was 'a beautiful but troubled soul', as the *Times* obituary put it, well aware of the effect she had on men and women. There lies the crux, between physical beauty and trouble of soul. She struck Nobel laureate Thomas Mann as an 'extraordinarily pretty' boy. Several years later, by which time morphine had made its mark, he called her 'a ravaged angel'. Another Nobel laureate, Roger Martin du Gard, referred to her 'inconsolable angelface'. A stable of Weimar writers worked her androgynous effect into their fictional characters. Women and men stood in awe of her beauty, on the ski slope, in cafés and nightclubs. This youthful otherworldly effect – spoiled innocence, fallen angel – hasn't gone out of fashion and exerts a similar pull on a modern audience. *Those whom the gods love die young.* Schwarzenbach died in her own bed during a war when millions less fortunate suffered horrific deaths, when her friends found themselves scattered to the winds of exile, barely escaping with their lives. Her life played out against the rise of the Nazis and the German diaspora in France and New York. Between one war and another, Schwarzenbach burned brightly, as we like to gloss such tragic romantics, in 'a world of cocktails and cigarettes, sleepers and sleek limousines', as critic Carl Seelig eulogized her. She reported in journalism and fiction on the disorder of the decade, the rise of fascism and the allure of travel. Being Swiss cushioned her movements, as did wealth, looks and a diplomatic marriage. Cursed by restlessness, the arc of her short life nonetheless did not bend towards fulfilment. Quite the contrary: drugs, schizophrenic episodes, and an inability to be still all fractured her sense of self and eventually her writing.

The twenty-first-century mode latches onto rebels like Schwarzenbach as precursors to our own identity politics. Her illness, addictions and lesbianism get reconfigured as symptoms of social and parental oppression: she becomes a victim in the 'live fast, die young' club. This remaking was already nascent in the generation after the First World War, cropping their hair, shooting up and tuning out in the dives of Berlin and Montparnasse, blaming their elders for the tribulations of the Great War. Schwarzenbach's glamour-girl image, her queerness, sometimes obscures her role as a political rebel against the rise of fascism. This entanglement of meme and content, image and politics, photography and writing, is central to her life. Interest in her writing and photos is inextricable from her visual appeal, as her earlier biographer, Charles Linsmayer, pointed out. Schwarzenbach's cult, her short, glamorous, tragic life, her pretty face, have all tended to upstage the writing.[1] This biography attempts to redress that balance.

The face undoubtedly helped. Schwarzenbach was memorably photographed, in particular by Marianne Breslauer, whose portrait of 'the writer Annemarie Schwarzenbach' appeared in the October 1933 edition of Berlin's *Uhu* magazine and over the following century has come to shape an aesthetic, an infinitely marketable lesbian look, *noli me tangere*, disaffected cool. Schwarzenbach in turn wielded her Rolleiflex throughout her travels and many of these photographs were published in magazines in her lifetime. The visual record foregrounds her cars, the steamships, exotic wastelands, bedraggled refugees and young fascists of the thirties; Persia, Afghanistan, Russia, the underbelly of the United States: trouble spots still in the headlines. She joins the sorority of female explorers of the Middle East, breaking the bounds of gender while not straying too far from the colonial hotel and the diplomatic bag. Constantly writing, observing and responding to her tarnished times with great intelligence, style and political engagement, she managed to fall on the right side of history despite her Nazi-sympathizing family. For a decade between the wars, she seemed to be at the centre of the zeitgeist, to try hard to overcome her addiction and her psychological frailty. She was more than just a pretty face.[2]

*

At the start of the coronavirus pandemic in March 2020, just before countries closed their borders and went into lockdown, I was skim-reading three decades of diaries in the Monacensia Library in Munich, where the Mann family archives are preserved. Thomas Mann's children, Erika and Klaus, both gay, had been close friends of Annemarie all her adult life and she was welcomed at the family dinner table. The diaries belonged to opera singer Emmy Krüger, Renée Schwarzenbach's friend – girlfriend, lover, lady's companion? Krüger transcribed her diaries in pencil, for the most part, onto tiny three inch by two inch pages folded between the original diary covers in a cramped, evenly flowing hand, using up all the available space. They were difficult to make out in German. I was wearing white gloves and wielding a magnifying glass, Google translate open on the laptop beside me, with a view out the window onto the linden trees fronting the Isar river and the Englischer Garten. The evenness of the hand, the sameness of the writing instrument and the detached pages, slipped between card and leatherette covers year after year, gave the transcription away – copied out some time after the war. I was anticipating the *annus miserabilis* 1933, when Krüger sang at Hitler's behest in Munich. But the 1933 diary was missing. When I pointed this out, the archivist shrugged her shoulders as though she'd encountered such lacunae before. Diaries are like families: working up their best stories, trimming the embarrassments, putting on a brave, made-up face to the world in different layers of reality: fact, myth, history, fiction, lie. Krüger's diaries and their elisions illustrate the difficulty of seeing clearly the progress of National Socialism in the twenties and thirties long after the apotheosis of the movement and its defeat.

The politics of memory proceeds by selective amnesia, and homosexual memory in families, more often than not, takes the same primrose path. Tampering with the written record occurred on the afternoon of Annemarie's death when Renée burned her daughter's diaries and correspondence, including letters from Erika and Klaus Mann, Erich Maria Remarque, Carson McCullers, her husband Claude Clarac as well as countless girlfriends and confidants. This too was an attempt to set the record *straight*, not just about Annemarie but also her fraught relationship with her mother. After the war, when traveller Ella Maillart wished to publish her account of a journey with Annemarie to Kabul,

The Cruel Way, Renée insisted on disguising her daughter's name and on editorial oversight. Throughout history, family and inheritance law has sidelined homosexual relationships in the name of propriety – and property – while the written record has been winnowed, sanitized if not outright gone up in flames. The Nazis were past masters at this too.

Schwarzenbach took an early definitive stance against National Socialism. In Munich I'd arranged to meet Dr. Maren Richter, historian and curator at the Obersalzberg Memorial and Educational Center at Berchtesgaden, Hitler's mountain fastness. We discussed German resistance, in particular Annemarie's friends Maria Daelen, Albrecht Haushofer and others in the context of Operation Valkyrie, the failed assassination of the Führer in 1944. Daelen had a long affair with Wilhelm Furtwängler, chief conductor of the Berlin Philharmonic, whose own career and allegiance remain contested. Schwarzenbach's resistance was not simply a matter of good and bad Germans but of coming to terms with the complexity of responses to National Socialism as it evolved over twenty years among family and friends. Hitler's promise to make Germany great again appealed to all sorts of people but not to socialists, communists, the writers and artists of Weimar's cultural renaissance, many of whom were Jewish and gay in both senses of the word. This was Annemarie's tribe and she ran with it early. Her friend and fellow exile Klaus Mann describes her as 'one of these peculiar sham-émigrés',[3] but her political stance was extraordinarily brave and unwavering in the face of her staunch family, their early fundraising on Hitler's behalf, and their militaristic bent.

*

Schwarzenbach first attracted attention in Switzerland with the publication in Zurich of her novel *Friends of Bernhard* (1931) when she was twenty-three. Her second book, *Lyric Novella* (1933), its Berlin publication overshadowed by Hitler's accession to power, employs the device of transmuting lesbian experience into heterosexual narration: changing the pronouns. A third novel, set in an Austrian ski resort, *Flucht nach oben*, resurfaced after her death and was published in 1999. A collection of short stories, *Bei diesem Regen*, and a biography of a mountaineer, *Lorenz Saladin: Ein Leben für die Berge*, garnered some attention during her lifetime.

A combination of politics, family disapproval, restlessness and sheer gumption led to Schwarzenbach's decade of travel through the Middle East, Persia, Afghanistan, the Soviet Union, the Baltic states, three times to the United States and a final trip to the Belgian Congo during the war. *Pace* Disraeli, for her the East became a career: she got three or four books out of it, a useful husband, thousands of photos and a sense of self, her own private Araby. 'She was restless and her quest for happiness had given way to a quest for tranquillity', writes her friend Ruth Landshoff-Yorck. Throughout her travels she wrote for Swiss newspapers and magazines (German outlets being denied her) on topics ranging from modernization in Ankara, archaeological digs, female education in Persia, the first Soviet Writers Conference in Moscow, to politics in the Balkan States, race and labour issues in the Rust Belt and the American South, development in the French Congo. In the United States her journalism became more hard-hitting, radical, observant – her editor, Otto Kleiber at Basel's *National-Zeitung*, thought it unsuitable for the 'women's pages'. Her tendency was to see the bread-and-butter writing she did as exactly that, filling the gaps between inspiration. She wrote quickly, with little revision, in a mode that became increasingly self-involved. While her youthful talent as a fiction writer might have been realized had she lived, journalism, travel, addiction and mental instability were her enemies of promise. By the time of her death, nonetheless, Schwarzenbach had a body of work and a reputation in Switzerland as a brave, intrepid, idiosyncratic writer, albeit one you might not want your daughter to meet or emulate, a reputation that has only grown in the eighty years since.

This first account in English of Schwarzenbach's life and times has taken me to the edge of my linguistic abilities, encompassing research in German and French in Basel, Bern, Boston, Lausanne, Marbach, Munich and Zurich, much of it undertaken during half-terms, in the intervals of lockdowns or between six and eight in the morning, before homeroom kicked in. *Rebel Angel* has benefited from earlier biographies by Areti Georgiadou, Dominique Laure Miermont, Charles Linsmayer and Alexis Schwarzenbach, and from the pioneering editing and research of Roger Perret, Walter Fähnders and Dominique Laure Miermont, among others. Three Schwarzenbach titles have been translated into English by Lucy Renner Jones and Isabel Fargo Cole, published by Seagull

Books. Citations from Schwarzenbach's original German manuscripts in the Swiss Literary Archives, from the Schwarzenbach family archives in Zentralbibliothek Zurich and from her work published by Lenos Verlag are my English translations alone.

1

Cocoon

Moreover, he is a prey to numerous maladies ... and the fibre of his cocoon reflects such disorders.[1]

Frank R. Mason, *The American Silk Industry and the Tariff*

Cantilevered over the cash machines at the junction of 32nd Street and Park Avenue in New York is a distinctive bronze clock. On the hour, the figure of Zarathustra waves a wand and a slave swings a hammer against the cocoon at his feet, from which emerges the Queen of Silk bearing a tulip. This elaborate timepiece, ornamented with mulberry leaves, represents the mythical origin of silk in Persia, as well as being a nod to Swiss timekeeping. 470 Park Avenue is still called the Schwarzenbach Buildings, commemorating the family that brought the silk business to America.

In Switzerland, sericulture owes its exploitation to the Huguenots, many of whom were weavers fleeing French oppression. Along the shores of Lake Zurich, the cottage industry expanded with mechanization during the nineteenth century – black taffeta, derived from the Persian word for 'twisted' or 'woven', became the Zurich speciality. Factories sprang up outside the lake villages of Adliswil and Horgen, and silk was exported all over Europe and to the growing American market. By the end of the nineteenth century, Zurich boasted the second-largest silk production in the world, rivalled only by Japan.

Schwarzenbachs are attested around the lake at least since the fifteenth century. Founded in 1828, the Schwarzenbach silk firm was based in Thalwil, about twelve kilometres south of Zurich. Johannes Schwarzenbach had intended that his elder son August should take over the business and the younger son Robert was destined for a plantation career in Java, then a Dutch colony. The Java project fell through and in 1859 Robert was dispatched to New York where he established a branch of the family business. The American Civil War brought tariffs – imports of raw silk to the United States quadrupled between 1860 and 1870, and fortunes were made. Johannes died suddenly of congenital heart failure, Robert Schwarzenbach returned to Zurich, and together with August they transformed the family firm into one of the great industrial fortunes of the nineteenth century with branches in London, Paris, Lyon, Berlin, Milan and New York. Berlin's *Volkszeitung* dubbed Robert the 'silk king of the world'. He built an imposing mock-Elizabethan residence facing the lake at Rüschlikon to match – it had one of the first tennis courts in Switzerland.

At the firm's height, it employed 28,000 workers, providing a local library and teetotal restaurant, a raft of improving evening classes along the lines of the Women's Institute in Britain. Following the Franco-Prussian war of 1871, Alsace was incorporated into the German Empire under Bismarck. The Germans encouraged Swiss investment and a Schwarzenbach factory opened at Huningue right on the border with Basel, taking advantage of cheaper labour and lower tariffs. That inveterate wanderer D.H. Lawrence left his native England in 1912 and, travelling south along the shore of the lake at Zurich, noted the immigrant labour: 'they were all workers in the factory – silk, I think it was – in the village. They were a whole colony of Italians, thirty or more families.'[2]

In 1904, Robert Schwarzenbach died, like his father, of heart trouble, and the business passed to the sons. Alfred was the first member of this industrialist family to pursue further education, studying law in Berlin and Leipzig and graduating *magna cum laude*. Alfred's repertoire as a gentleman of the industrial elite included hunting in Baden, Pears Soap, London tailors and stays at Claridge's. He was characterized by mildness and an ability to conciliate in his often tempestuous family. After a short period in a Paris bank, he returned to oversee the family firm. The greater part of its wealth stemmed from the expanding American market, where labour was cheap and profits continued to climb. Erected in 1912, the Schwarzenbach Buildings on Park Avenue testify today to this solidity and opulence. By 1928 there were 4,445 Schwarzenbach looms in the United States and a total of 3,977 in Switzerland, Germany, France and Italy combined.[3] With the Wall Street Crash the price of silk fell over the following years and so 1928 can be considered the apogee of this most successful family business.

On her mother's side, Annemarie Schwarzenbach descended from military stock. Her grandmother, Clara Wille, who survived her by three years, was the daughter of Friedrich Wilhelm Graf von Bismarck, a young cavalry officer ennobled for his part in Napoleon's Russian campaign. Bismarck's second marriage to a woman forty-one years his junior produced two children: August and the long-lived Clara, born in 1851. Following an idyllic childhood on the shores of Lake Constance, August joined a Baden regiment but sided with the Prussians in the wars of 1870 when Germany became united under a third cousin, Otto von Bismarck. Annemarie Schwarzenbach's mother was not inclined to underestimate this swashbuckling aristocratic heritage.

Clara, for her part, first spotted Ulrich Wille in Rome in the winter of 1868. They took to the floor at Berlin's society balls and were engaged to be married. It was a glittering world of dancing, social calls and garrison life, all in the middle of a conflict that would unify Germany, bring on two world wars and redraw the map of Europe over the coming century. Ulrich Wille hailed from a literary and political family with origins in La Sagne, a village in the canton of Neuchâtel close to the present border with France. The family name had been the more French Vuille, and the change to Wille as well as Ulrich's birth in Hamburg in 1848 indicate political affiliations. His father, François, a liberal journalist, had fled Frankfurt following the failed 1848 revolution, a swathe of revolts across European states attempting to free themselves from aristocratic autocracy. François was a forty-eighter in exile in Switzerland, based on the shore of Zurich's lake at Mariafeld, where he and his wife Eliza, from a Hamburg shipping family, hosted a literary salon. Gottfried Keller, Arnold Böcklin, Franz Liszt and Richard Wagner were some of the luminaries hosted by the Willes. Their son Ulrich inherited the chip on the shoulder that comes with political exile, the stubbornness of the revolutionary and an appreciation for pan-European culture that he would hand on to his grand-daughter. Despite his cultivated upbringing, Ulrich was a child of the garrison, German unification and imperial might. Like Clara, he had somewhat tenuous connections to the Swiss Federation into which neither of them had been born.

Annemarie Schwarzenbach's mother, Renée, born in 1883, was the youngest in a family of three boys and a girl. Renée enjoyed sledding on the Dolder, picnicking on the shores of the lake with like-minded debutantes and their young pretenders. Her father climbed the ranks of the military, from division commander to colonel on the eve of the First

World War. He dabbled in municipal and state politics and developed a reputation for siding with Prussian militarism to the chagrin of Switzerland's French-speaking confederates. Renée's brothers made good marriages; the Wille-von Bismarcks could count on military cachet but were neither of old Zurich stock nor particularly rich. The two daughters – Renée and Isi – could expect to marry well by virtue of name and standing.[4]

It was a horsey childhood as befits a military family at the end of the age of cavalry, when Sisi of Austria proudly saddled up and the Transvaal was part of the holdings of empire. Just as her daughter Annemarie would be among the first generation of motoring women to take to the road, so Renée's overriding passion all her life was for horses, emblematic of her father's rank as head of cavalry and of her nineteenth-century aristocratic entitlement. Her uncle August von Bismarck had a large house and stables at Freiburg, abutting the Black Forest, where Renée liked to ride. She rode astride: no side-saddle for her.[5] Her youngest son, Hasi, went on to win a silver medal for horse riding in the 1960 Rome Olympics. Renée liked to take the reins and all biographical accounts agree on her formidable character, almost a caricature of German military rectitude: hierarchy, discipline, horsemanship. This assertive streak derived from her father but also from the habits of dressage.

Her three older brothers brought their friends to the house and the teenage Renée's emotional weather ran to stormy. If the boys were horsey, all the better. At age fourteen she fixed up a darkroom under the eaves at Mariafeld and began to develop her own photographs, snapping horses and people with equal passion. She attended the Villa Yalta girls school in Zurich. Though never much bothered by academics, she took to tennis and violin practice, *Tannhäuser* and drama, especially enjoying male roles. In some off-stage photos she smokes a pipe. Her affections were showered on young men and girls alike. Bursts of feeling confided to her diaries and snapped in the photographic record stem from unbridled pash, romantic fantasy and a delight in imbroglio for its own sake.[6] Around 1900 the sixteen-year-old Renée moved on from ecstatic outpourings about Lily Fierz to the twenty-one-year-old Inez Rieter, while simultaneously swooning over Richard Vogel, a lieutenant pushing thirty. All her life, Renée was able to divide her romantic attention between men and women.

Her parents sent her to the Villa Béatrix finishing school in Geneva to tame her character, a move she would employ with her own recalcitrant daughter when the time came. Boarding school brought out Renée's head girl propensities and succeeded in sharpening her penchant for special friendships – '*Ich schwärme fur Sie!*' ('I've got a crush on you!') was the refrain of her girl-filled diaries. She liked to project herself as rebellious and daring – in manner if not in politics and economics. Conventionally unconventional, she rarely strayed from the strictures of her upbringing and class. Her biographer and grand-nephew, Alexis Schwarzenbach, teases out the particular quality of her love for women too easily subsumed under what used to be thought of as 'going through a phase'. Renée's long phase carried over into an accommodating marriage, running parallel to a thirty-year relationship with the diva Emmy Krüger.

> Although Renée's first sexual experience occurred at boarding school, it would be wrong to dismiss her love for Claire Thon as merely a 'special friendship'. … Hand in hand, however, went the conviction that the acme of personal happiness belonged in traditional marriage.[7]

On her last night at boarding school, all three roommates' beds were joined together and there was champagne, and over the rest we draw a veil.

It was a class and time when education didn't much get in the way of picnics on the lake island of Lützelau or a tumble on the Dolder snow, either of which might lead to a marriage proposal. Parents kept a wary eye, estimating monetary worth and emotional valence. Renée met Alfred Schwarzenbach in the course of a courtesy call she made to the family home at Rüschlikon across the lake in the summer of 1903. She'd had her eye on him since February and Alfred's youngest sister Olga might have acted as intermediary. They belonged to a similar social set, though the Schwarzenbachs were immensely richer than the Willes. Renée returned home across the lake in the Schwarzenbach motorboat and the two families eventually gave their imprimatur to an engagement.

Alfred and Renée were married in Meilen on 11 February 1904. The lake was stormy and it rained but cleared for the wedding breakfast at Mariafeld. The happy couple departed on a seven-week honeymoon beginning in the Bellevue Hotel in Bern, where they returned on occasion over the years for anniversaries to the same bridal suite high above the Aar River. For the first nine years of their marriage, they occupied an elegant villa with garden and stables on Parkring in Zurich-Enge, next door to Alfred's Aunt Mathilde in the Villa Ulmberg. Their first son, Robert, or Robuli as he was known, was born at midnight on 15 December 1904 and a second child, Suzanne, in 1906. When Robuli was a year old, his mother worried about his lack of progress in speech. Speech never really developed and doctors speculated over the years as to the probable cause; there appeared to be no problem with hearing or vocal cords. Autism, in hindsight, seems likely, although at the beginning of the last century the condition was little known and tended to be misdiagnosed as idiocy or hydrocephalus. The Zurich psychiatrist Carl Jung was to hand at the Burghölzli Clinic. By age six, her first child showed little if any development of speech and was cared for henceforth in a clinic for handicapped children in southern Germany, with visits home to Bocken. Robuli required specialist treatment and care for the rest of his life.

By 23 May 1908, when Mina Renée Annemarie Schwarzenbach was born, the parents might have been hoping for a second son. It was a sultry Saturday turning to snow overnight, obscuring the mountains at the end of the lake. A difficult birth, a nine-pound child. A fourth child in 1911 – Alfred (Freddy) and a fifth two years later in 1913 – also a boy, Hans (Hasi) – assured the patriarchal line. At the time of Freddy's birth, the six-and-a-half-year-old Robuli still showed little sign of communicating normally – and so on Freddy's shoulders rested the family inheritance and his father's name.

*

Hilary Mantel, discussing Princess Diana, a fourth girl in a family wanting a male heir, posits the theory that 'unwanted or superfluous children have difficulty in becoming embodied; they remain airy, available to fate, as if no one has signed them out of the soul store'.[8] While Renée was a loving mother, very present in the lives of her five wanted children, her attention could be uneven as Mantel suggests can be the case in sprawling aristocratic families. Renée herself had wanted to be a boy when she was a child. Robuli's difficulties preoccupied her

Robert-Ulrich (Robuli), Suzanne, Annemarie, Alfred (Pedy) and baby Hans (Hasi)
Schwarzenbach, 16 August 1915. Photo by Renée Schwarzenbach-Wille
Courtesy of Zentralbibliothek Zürich

to the detriment of her relationship with her second child Suzanne, who got on better with her father. With the birth of Annemarie, the mother's favouritism became evident. Annemarie took to horse riding and rode all her life; Suzanne did not. 'Annemarie always won people over, as I stood by. Unnoticed', Suzanne recalled.[9] Mantel's phrase 'difficulty becoming embodied' describes Annemarie's lifelong sense of herself as occupying a female carapace or grappling with a split between body and soul, a split to which we might now put a different name.

As a society lady with decided musical tastes, Renée frequented the company of female artistes – singers, actresses – to a degree that would have caused scandal to a married man. In 1910, two years after Annemarie's birth, she encountered Emmy Krüger, a twenty-four-year-old opera singer from Frankfurt, performing for the first time at the Stadttheater in Zurich. Renée was twenty-seven, a mother of three (soon to be four). She embarked on a relationship with the singer which endured for over three decades.

Renée clearly championed Emmy's singing career, followed her from performance to performance, and sought to influence casting decisions where she could. She liked to take control and to get her way. Her strong-willed character made her compelling as a society hostess and dovetails into her attraction to right-wing politics. 'Renée arrived – what a miracle to experience such friendship?'[10] Krüger's diary records time and again. Krüger was career-minded, given to enthusiasms, slights and exclamation marks, somewhat preening and kitsch, like the opera world itself. As the children grew, she took a vicarious delight in their doings. As Renée's relationship with her deepened, the singer had her own room in the Schwarzenbach home and was invited to family events. Krüger's widowed mother at times visited Bocken for prolonged periods; her ashes rested there in the extensive gardens. Renée shuttled between Zurich and Munich for musical events and Emmy became the live-in diva that the children came to know as mama's friend, later referred to by Annemarie as 'die Dame Krüger'. Alfred, for his part, displayed 'a baffling tolerance towards his wife's love affairs with other women, clearly setting him apart from other bourgeois family men of the time'.[11] It was an unusual ménage, papered over with propriety, extraordinary for the time and place.

Renée seems to have been aware of Annemarie's boyish or tomboyish tendencies from an early age, and to have played with them. The photographic record shows Annemarie as child and adolescent adopting at Renée's instigation a number of masculine alter-egos: Knaben Fritz, der Rosenkavalier or an accordion-playing sailor. Just as she named her horses after Wagner figures, Renée enjoyed photographing her daughter in theatrical costumes drawn from opera and dressing her children up for special occasions. For the golden wedding anniversary of Ulrich and Clara Wille at Mariafeld, Annemarie was got up as Richard Wagner, the favourite composer of her mother and her mother's friend. This transvestite tendency,

**Annemarie in her much-loved lederhosen, July 1918. Photo by Renée
Schwarzenbach-Wille**
Courtesy of Zentralbibliothek Zürich

though occasional, nonetheless reveals Renée's opera-buff and subli-
mated lesbian character. She understood the theatricality of costume
expressing different selves through role play, an understanding she
passed on to her always savvily-dressed daughter:

> Annemarie's dressing up in boy's or male clothes was confined to special
> occasions, while her day-to-day attire was similar to that of girls her age. Her
> hair, however, she kept cut short, and already by age seventeen she sported
> the side-parted Eton crop which characterized her perfectly androgynous look
> as an adult.[12]

As an adult undergoing treatment for addiction, Annemarie remembered the airless atmosphere of her mother's love:

> She spoils me with her love. She brought me up as a boy, and like a child prodigy. She knows all my feelings like her own, those she has never followed through on. But she has misinterpreted me ever since I was thirteen, and no longer her pageboy.[13]

In an early text, Annemarie describes her awareness of older women in a memory from childhood suffused with feverishness and desire:

> Attractive women used to visit our house long ago when I was very young. They sat with mother and drank tea from blue china cups. When I presented myself, they held me close and caressed me. And their pale hands gave off a scent, tender and sweet, that lingered long after in the nursery. I sat still and breathed it in. … But I felt that something was wrong, and cried to myself. Whenever I encountered beautiful women, injustice, the sense of wrong, returned.[14]

In October 1912 the family moved to Bocken along the lakeshore in Horgen, to a large baroque house built in 1688, with extensive parkland, stables and dependencies. From the topmost floor it had a view south across the lake to the Alps. To the east, it overlooked Meilen and the Wille home at Mariafeld. To the north Zurich city. Alfred and Renée turned Bocken into a family home of extraordinary splendour, epitomizing the wealth and culture of the nineteenth-century industrial bourgeoisie brought into the turbulence of the twentieth century. Here Renée maintained her salon of musicians, composers and artists, fed and watered by a crew of servants, and kept an eagle-eyed welcome over the comings and goings of her youngest daughter's motley friends. Her hospitality reached its high point in a garden party for three hundred invitees of the theatre, musical and artistic worlds on 25 June 1921 on the occasion of the Zurich Festival, when guests were ferried from the city down the lake to Bocken. Nobel literature laureate Gerhart Hauptmann and future laureate Hermann Hesse were present. Later musical invitees were Kurt Weill and Wilhelm Furtwängler.

For the children, too, it was a playground: horses, pigs, hens, the nearby lake, skiing and sledding on the hills rising towards the

Sihlwald behind the house. With her coeval cousin, Gundalena Wille, Annemarie raced around the grounds on her bicycle – no hands. She attended the local primary school for a brief three weeks in 1916 before being withdrawn due to scarlet fever, following which she was privately tutored.

*

Annemarie Schwarzenbach considered a musical career until mid-adolescence, when her enthusiasm went over to writing. Renée captioned a snap of her daughter with her new music teacher: 'Annemarie with her love, Fraulein Fischer'[15] and from an early age the prodigy's piano playing won plaudits. By age eleven her playing drew the attentions of the Zurich Festival conductor Arthur Nikisch – Renée stage-managing both festival and daughter. As a teenager, she played Schumann's *Concerto for Piano* with aplomb. Music was cherished in the family: her aunt Mathilde had hosted a salon and maintained friendships with musicians and writers. Clara Wille gave Annemarie for her 1925 confirmation a signed copy of Wagner's piano music which was thought to have come down from Annemarie's great-grandmother, Eliza Wille.[16] Ella Maillart remembered that Annemarie would gravitate towards a piano on the rare occasions that she found one en route to Afghanistan. 'When she played she became a whole other person. But you know, on our way to Kabul there were few opportunities to play piano.'[17]

Besides music, Renée cultivated an interest in photography. She liked to dress up the teenage Annemarie and the invariably sullen cast of the model prefigures the unsmiling, posed demeanour Annemarie adopted in the many photographs of her as an adult. In other snaps, a nine-year-old Annemarie is dressed in lederhosen bought in Bavaria on one of Renée's visits to Emmy Krüger.[18] This was the young Annemarie's favourite attire so much so that she once attended church in it and was promptly ejected by the pastor.[19] Perhaps conscious of her gapped teeth, she refrained from smiling in photographs and adopted what her biographer Areti Georgiadou calls her 'aristocratically suffering facial expression'. Ella Maillart describes Annemarie putting forth 'a charm that acted powerfully on those who are attracted by the tragic greatness of androgyny'.[20] Annemarie's characteristic and studiedly androgynous look had its origins in the costume cupboard of childhood.

Following a diagnosis of scarlet fever in 1916, Annemarie's siblings were packed off across the lake to grandmother Clara at Mariafeld and the patient confined to Bocken. Quarantined for many months, mother and daughter recuperated at the spa waters in Rheinfelden. Perhaps as a consequence of this exclusive maternal care, Annemarie developed a propensity for illness – real, attention-getting and imaginary – that was to become a recurring feature in her life and writing. She was home-tutored until the age of fifteen, unlike her older sister Suzanne who attended the Zurich Freie Gymnasium and stayed in the city during the week in the Villa Schönberg with her uncle Ulrich Wille and his wife Inez. Annemarie, however, was enrolled at the Götz-Azzolini private school in Zurich. 'Mama always found the local Frei Gymnasium terrible even though I got on fine there',[21] recalled Suzanne.

Emmy Krüger noticed early that Annemarie was rebellious, describing in April 1921 the 'dark paths' down which Annemarie was treading, causing anxiety to her parents. Annemarie revealed to Krüger's mother that she hoped to become a writer.[22]

> As a child I had a tendency to write everything down, all that I saw and did, experienced and felt. When I was nine, I wrote my first novel in a school exercise book. And since I knew that nine-year-olds aren't taken seriously by adults, I made the hero eleven years old.[23]

Her decidedly rebellious, anti-fascist cast of mind and body had its origins in the 1920s. Mother and daughter subscribed to two diverging views of the German world – Nazi reaction and Weimar freedom – as they played out to disastrous consequences over the decade. A number of the architects of the Nazi blueprint were guests at Bocken and her grand-parents' house at Meilen as Annemarie was growing up. Her mother's involvement with the Wagner Festival at Bayreuth stoked Renée's Teutonic heart. As early as October 1920, Munich political geographer and former major-general Karl Haushofer remarked on her enthusiasm for a restoration of German might. A military strategist and orientalist, Haushofer is credited with disseminating German *Lebensraum*, expansionism by another name, first developed by zoologist Friedrich Ratzel at the turn of the century.[24] Haushofer had taught and become friends with Rudolf Hess, soon to be Hitler's right-hand man. Hess studied for a semester at the ETA, Zurich's prestigious technical institute, in 1922. Haushofer introduced Hess to Renée and the student was an occasional guest at Bocken. By the time of Hitler's accession to power, the German Consul-General in Zurich was able to confidently relay Renée's support for the new regime to his superiors in Berlin: 'Frau Schwarzenbach, in particular, enthusiastically advocates National Socialism at every opportunity.'[25]

Dr. Emil Gansser, a chemist working for Siemens, orchestrated Hitler's two-day fundraising visit to Switzerland in August 1923. Gansser was a keen Nazi supporter, a guest at Bocken well-connected to the chemical and pharmaceutical industries. Hitler stayed at the Gotthard Hotel on Bahnhofstrasse and visited Ully Wille, Renée's brother, at his Villa Schönberg, where Wagner had written most of *Tristan and Isolde*, a connection Hitler would have appreciated.[26] He had been coached to tone down his anti-semitic harangue among the rich Swiss burgers, and not to stuff his face on the canapés. A strong, stable Germany was in Switzerland's economic interest and perhaps the ranting little man of humble origins in Bavaria could provide that. Bolshevism in Russia had put the fear of God into the righteous and thrifty Swiss elect. Hitler paid calls on bankers and silk manufacturers, met Schaffhausen industrialist Ernst Homberger, dined at the Baur au Lac, and gave a rallying speech at Ully's Villa Schönberg. The evening before his departure, along with Dr. Gansser, Hitler dined with General Wille in Meilen. Clara noted in her diary: 'Hittler [*sic*] is an exceptionally likeable man. When he speaks, he is really overawing; he speaks wonderfully.'[27] Hitler later sent the General and Clara Wille an autographed copy of his book *Mein Kampf* in recognition of the hospitality he had benefited from in Zurich.[28] Historian Alexis Schwarzenbach, based on a letter from his grandfather Hans, believes Hitler also visited Bocken on this occasion and that funds might have passed from Alfred Schwarzenbach to Hitler's fledgling National Socialism as it took wing.[29]

Renée's musical culture inclined towards the Wagnerian and so she was fertile ground for the pop philosophy of National Socialism. The Bayreuth Wagner Festival had become a reactionary symbol of Germany's former pre-eminence and adopted the kitsch cultural values that Hitler and his nationalists espoused. King Ludwig of Bavaria's patronage gave the festival a certain high camp among camp followers. Siegfried Wagner, the composer's son, Ludwig's godson and festival director, had an ambisexual air about him camouflaged by his wife, Winifred. They married when Siegfried was forty-seven and Winifred seventeen and an English orphan. She became a close friend of Adolf Hitler – her four children knew him as Uncle Wolf. The Wagner Festival opened again in 1924 after a ten-year hiatus; the green hill at Bayreuth had turned distinctly brown and looked towards Germany's mythological past in all its papier mâché glory. The writer Joseph Roth saw through this Wagnerian flummery: 'They put up some Wagnerian scenery and give foreigners an operatic song and dance of their politics of vulgar expediency.'[30] Many of the organizers were Nazi supporters and Renée, Emmy and the Schwarzenbach girls were annual acolytes. Siegfried and Winifred Wagner, in turn, were invited to Bocken throughout the postwar decade. The Wagners' potent mix of pan-German *völkisch* myth, high musical culture and anti-semitism chimed with Emmy's costume jewellery mind. Renée's advocacy paid off when Emmy was invited to sing at the festival in August 1924 and in succeeding years.

In August 1924 Renée travelled from Switzerland in a chauffeured car with her mother Clara, her daughters Suzanne and sixteen-year-old Annemarie for the fortnight at Bayreuth. Three generations of the Wille-Schwarzenbach clan were not alone among women from the upper echelons of society and men of a certain stamp who cultivated Wagner's music. Since the 1880s the festival had been a discreet meeting place for homosexuals during the high summer, for like-minded spirits.[31] Siegfried's personal assistants for nearly a quarter century were a lesbian couple.[32] Bayreuth had also become a gathering place for the old war-bedraggled German nobility to lick its wounds and lament its downfall. While Siegfried himself could not be seen to be political, there was no mistaking the message of the festival programme that year: 'Foreigners, especially the racially less northern types, have no real connection with the art of Richard Wagner – at least not the *real* Bayreuth connection.'[33] Opening night was a performance of *Die Meistersinger*, directed by Siegfried, in a theatre decorated with the colours of the Wilhelmine Reich. At its conclusion there was a speech about foreign threats and then the audience spontaneously sang all three verses of the national anthem.[34] Musicologist Kurt Singer described the new Bayreuth public of 1924: 'nationalistic and conservative right

Emmy Krüger in Rheinfelden, July 1916. Photo by Renée Schwarzenbach-Wille
Courtesy of Zentralbibliothek Zürich

down to their swastikas, cheering uncritically. … No more than ten non-Aryans attending.'[35]

Photographs of the Schwarzenbach girls at Bayreuth show their cygnet-necked beauty and the New Woman fashions of the day. Suzanne, turning eighteen, will marry the following year. Annemarie had just finished a year at the Götz-Azzolini school in Zurich and was beginning to write her first articles for the *Wandervogel* magazine. Grown tall and willowy, over the course of three summer visits to Bayreuth she must have turned a few heads. In *Lyric Novella* her male narrator recalls the theatricality of the festival:

I remembered at the Bayreuth Festival often seeing a special kind of scene change: ... mist rose up, diffused by coloured lights, then it grew dense, flowed together in whitish streams and formed walls that became ever more impenetrable behind which the scene sank imperceptibly. Then all was still: the mist dispersed, the stage reappeared and a new landscape emerged, gently tinged with a new light.[36]

Renée was back again at Bayreuth in August 1925 with husband and family in tow, Annemarie tanned from two weeks in Thun where she had taken dance classes.[37] The King of Bulgaria, Prince Hohenlohe and the Countess Schlippenbach graced the festival, and Hitler was there for the first time following an early release from prison. Emmy Krüger played Sieglinde and afterwards the party leader kissed her hand, praised her singing and made remarks about the 'Jew Schorr' who had shared the stage with her in the Walkyrie.[38] In a letter to her grandmother Clara, Annemarie likewise praised Emmy's singing and appearance but also enthused over Friedrich Schorr, whom Hitler had, according to Emmy, disparaged, and whom Clara too had dismissed as 'a total Jew'.[39] The casual anti-semitism of the older Wille-Schwarzenbach women took a more virulent stamp with Emmy Krüger. Schorr was one of the great bass-baritones of his time and this spectacle of likes and dislikes underscores how anti-semitism operated in German cultural life in the lead-up to the Nazi reign: race trumped talent as the noose tightened. The spurious notion of the *Kulturkammer* re-emerged (it had first strutted on the German stage under Bismarck), somewhat like a later generation's 'no platforming', where artists and the public subscribed to a collective agreement as to what constitutes German, no 'foreigners' allowed. For German read 'Aryan spirit' and for foreign read 'Jewish'. Musicologist Kurt Singer lost his job in 1933, emigrated to Amsterdam, was interned in Westerbork and deported to Theresienstadt, where he perished. Schorr saw the writing on the wall early and emigrated to the United States in 1931. Annemarie would soon witness the dismantling of whole generations of artistic achievement in Germany, as books were burned and artists were prevented from working. In 1925 the Wagners hosted the Schwarzenbach family and in turn made their way to Bocken for a two-week September stay. The crowning moment of Emmy Krüger's career at Bayreuth came in 1927 in her role as Isolde. The

Schwarzenbach women were back again in force that year to support her.[40]

*

Nineteen-year-old Suzanne Schwarzenbach married thirty-four-year-old engineer Torgny Öhman on 22 October 1925. She was the first of the family to escape the tensile threads of the cocoon. The groom had been a friend of the family since Suzanne was four and the Schwarzenbachs had visited the Öhmans in Sweden on a number of holidays. Suzanne had become romantically involved during her teens. Annemarie was bridesmaid. The marriage of the first daughter of one of Zurich's richest men was celebrated with all pomp and circumstance at Bocken. The newly-marrieds departed to live near Stockholm.

Annemarie too was beginning to rustle her wings, and the relationship between mother and daughter grew more fraught and contentious with adolescence. Renée could role play and control the child but, as her growing daughter began to stretch the limits of propriety, there were clashes about the company she kept. In a photograph from September

Annemarie, age 16, serving at a hunting party, October 1924. Photo by Renée Schwarzenbach-Wille
Courtesy of Zentralbibliothek Zürich

1925 showing the Wagners at Bocken, Trud Widmer, 'a friend and admirer of Renée and Emmy' who lived nearby on the lake, is suggestively holding Annemarie's hand.[41] The gesture and Annemarie's look give the photograph a defiant edge, clearly aimed at the photographer. The teenager had just been confirmed by Pastor Ernst Merz, with whom she had struck up a friendship and a confiding correspondence. In a letter to Merz, Annemarie described being sent to boarding school at Fetan 'for moral and health reasons' and mentions an unhappy love for an unnamed woman.[42] Writing to Jacqueline Nougarède, a friend from their time at the Sorbonne, Annemarie makes fond reference to this early love:

> Madame Riedel's singing in the Corso is a great success! Mme. Riedel is the woman I fell in love with when I was a child of sixteen or seventeen, and maybe she was the best friend I ever had. I loved her passionately, and she loved me, and it was very beautiful. Now she goes around with a Portuguese woman whom I like as well, whose daughter is roped in as 'a friend of mine' – it's funny.[43]

While Annemarie appears to have embarked on a more open expression of her lesbianism, Renée seems more closeted; scant record remains of her ever having thought about her relationship with Emmy in such terms. The omission is both surprising and revealing. That an adult woman in mannish clothes and seen by others as mannish, would conduct a lifelong relationship with another woman, spend holidays together apart from her husband, frequent the opera world with all its knowing ambivalence, cultivate bisexual and homosexual friends and acquaintances in the theatre world and not reflect deeper on this relationship seems strange, even wilful. Perhaps Annemarie's emerging frankness presented a threat to her mother's airbrushed notion of herself in relation to Emmy. Friends and reliable witnesses to Annemarie's later instability were clear that 'the big drama in her life, I believe, was with her mother'. Ella Maillart's view echoed those of Marianne Breslauer and Margot von Opel, all three close friends:

> young, talented, charming, attractive, nonetheless deeply sad and depressed by her unfortunate relationship with her mother, whom she loved and admired while at the same time recognized as the root of her eternal restlessness.[44]

Annemarie confronted this contentious relationship a decade later when undergoing treatment in Prangins Sanatorium under Dr. Forel:

> She deliberately isolated me in order to keep me by her side; and ignores the fact that she finally drove me further away than needs be. She understood I was 'lesbian' early on.[45]

The sins of the mother were visited on the daughter for all to see, and Renée didn't like what she saw. Distancing herself from Renée's control became Annemarie's life work.

A key advocate for Annemarie's first writings was Pastor Ernst Merz whom she met in the autumn of 1924 at a Swiss Wandervogel gathering. The twenty-eight-year-old pastor and the sixteen-year-old Annemarie struck up a conversation that continued in letters for the rest of Annemarie's life.[46] Merz was impressed by Annemarie's lively intelligence

Annemarie during spring break from school, 1926. Photo by Renée Schwarzenbach-Wille
Courtesy of Zentralbibliothek Zürich

and attracted to her androgynous beauty. He carefully nurtured her soulfulness and encouraged her first writing. In the young pastor she found a kindred spirit and a confidant. 'All I want to do is wander – from world to world, and don't want to stop until I finally bow down to God's pardon and find the source of purity',[47] she wrote to him from boarding school in 1926. Her fervour and piety are surprising in light of the worldly background from which she issued.

Merz was connected to the 'circle around the poet Stefan George (1868–1933) and acquainted Schwarzenbach with his works'.[48] George's poetry was mystical and classical and he and his followers espoused a good deal of Greek posturing which obfuscated a controlling paederastic nature. His charismatic aura attracted acolytes. When the National

Annemarie with Pastor Ernst Merz during her time in the Wandervogel, 1925. Photo by Renée Schwarzenbach-Wille
Courtesy of Zentralbibliothek Zürich

Socialists attempted to co-opt George as the poet of their cause, he exiled himself to Switzerland, where Merz, also mystical and homosexual, encountered him and his following of young, good-looking hangers-on. 'But George is so deeply rooted, earthy, brilliantly one of a kind and therefore inexplicable', Annemarie wrote to Merz from Paris in 1929.[49] She was not alone in being seduced by the 'king of a secret Germany' whose aristocratic sense of life and half-hidden erotic world responded to her own. 'There were many who found it seductive; it was a fresh wind in the stuffy atmosphere of the universities, and an exciting alternative to the routine cant of the politicians.'[50]

Pastor Merz had something of the worker-priest about him, and espoused socialist ideals. Despite such proletarian and anti-militaristic sympathies, he was welcomed at Bocken and invited to officiate at family events. Renée too maintained an occasional correspondence with him over many years. Perhaps she recognized the pastor's good faith and stabilizing influence on her wayward daughter. At his urging, Annemarie wrote three articles for the *Wandervogel* magazine during 1925 and 1926: her first published writing. In Christopher Isherwood's *Goodbye to Berlin*, a Wandervogel youth declares: 'Women are no good, … They spoil everything. They haven't got the spirit of adventure.' In 'The Question of Girls' (1925),[51] Annemarie tackled this marginalized role in the predominantly male if not outright homosexual ethos of the Wandervogel and urged her female readers to look beyond the romantic trivia of campfire singalongs:

> In discussion no girl was really able to express her opinion, or hold her own. That the boys are far superior to us in games is not surprising. But in general we girls are not inferior to the boys. I mean, girls between the ages of fifteen and twenty-one have nothing to fear from the dominance of the male sex. But in the Wandervogel they do. There are a hundred reasons for this state of affairs, but no excuse.[52]

Her article went on to disparage girls for a lack of gumption and solidarity, for a frivolous cast of mind.[53] Her two further pieces concerned the role of the individual in society and the virtue of solitude. Merz's influence – the George mystique, solidarity with the workers, the triad of socialism, spirituality and sexuality – played itself out in Annemarie and found echoes. Her juvenalia for the *Wandervogel* magazine and also her first article for the *Neue Zürcher Zeitung (NZZ)* – '*Stellung der Jugend*' ('Youth Today') – strike a minor note for her generation's moment between the wars: the struggle between fascism and communism, the nationalistic jingoism of her mother doing battle with Annemarie's liberal ethos. 'Have we not had enough of arguing with our fathers, and always the same sticking points … to each his world. A generation flies its flag and youth is always victorious. The future is ours.'[54]

Fetan, a boarding school founded in 1793, sits high in a remote valley of south-eastern Switzerland, hemmed in by the Austrian and Italian borders. The *Hochalpinen Töchterinstitut Ftan*, to give it its full bluestocking title, was popular with international parents and afforded opportunities for winter sports within motoring distance of Zurich, Austria and glitzy St. Moritz. Here sporty daughters from well-to-do families gained some Alpine sheen and were kept out of harm's way.

In the Piper travel guide to Switzerland, Annemarie described the approach to her alma mater:

> Villages here perch on the sunny south-facing terraces … The boarding school is a splendid, much-loved institution overlooking the village, housing about eighty students: international, more or less sporty, sort-of studious, leading enviable lives …[55]

Ernst Merz later summed up his correspondence with the seventeen-year-old:

> It wasn't easy for her to leave home, the lake and the city, but she mucked in and quickly adapted to her new situation. … She described most of her peers as smug and empty-headed. She wrote on Sunday mornings in bed, surrounded by books and exercise books, given to musings, confiding her conflicting feelings of guilt and purity, her belief that only by force of personality could she overcome her sense of being a sinner.[56]

This paints a fairly typical picture of an intelligent girl finding her feet at boarding school. Annemarie's distinctive short hairstyle irritated her schoolmates and no doubt her superior manner irked too. Her

Fetan classmate Mady Hosenfeldt and Annemarie, August 1926. Photo by Renée Schwarzenbach-Wille
Courtesy of Zentralbibliothek Zürich

androgynous appearance and trouble with a girlfriend at Bocken signal Annemarie's awareness of where her desires lay, and consequent guilt. Likewise, her 'rapport' with her maths teacher had its Colette-style erotic element as related by Klaus Mann in his diary.[57] Like her mother, Annemarie soon began to participate in school plays and costume parties, to hanker after girls, and to perfect her skiing.

Annemarie's interests at Fetan emerge in letters to her uncle Georg Reinhart, Winterthur businessman and oriental art collector. He knew writers and artists such as Rilke, Hermann Hesse, Ludwig Kirchner and Karl Geiser. Her correspondence reveals the bleakness of her environment and perhaps an early orientalist tendency:

> 1 November 1925. Could you send some incense sticks to this horrible freezing kip? I'm trying really hard to make it liveable. Annemarie.

Uncle Georg replied:

> Your wish is my command. In the two separate packets you'll find:
> 1. Seven Chinese joss sticks (without holder)
> 2. Seven Indian joss sticks (with holder)
> 3. A small bronze Indian pot
> 4. A sitting Vishnu figurine in alabaster (painted)
> 5. An etching of two musicians

The packages were wrapped in red Chinese rice paper, including a figurine of Visnu brought from Benares. A grateful Annemarie wrote to thank him:

> I like it here so far so good but the girls are dim. Most seem to have no interest in anything, are lazy as sin and busy themselves with their bits of studies and their little friends. There's a couple of nice Germans I like, and not just because they've got something original about them.[58]

One of the nice Germans at Fetan was Sabine Nagel but she proved resistant to Annemarie's attentions. Her teachers, on the other hand, found her intelligent and deep but she was a spirit in search of an exit and couldn't wait to leave the confines of school to discover the world. Suzanne had married and moved to Sweden; family life was quickening. A peer recalled that Annemarie 'wanted to get out of there as soon as she could ... to meet people, see the world, and be done with school-girls'.[59] Finishing her sophomore year with top marks,[60] she spent the summer back at Bocken, swimming at Trud Widmer's lakefront house in Kilchberg. Here a school friend from Fetan, Mady Hosenfeldt, enters the photographic record preserved by the voyeuristic Renée, and the two models in their one-piece bathing suits radiate a wistful knowingness for the camera.[61]

The cloistered atmosphere of boarding school made its way into Annemarie's first novel, *Friends of Bernhard*, written quickly at age twenty-three while completing her studies at university. Bernhard is an adolescent in Paris, a shoe-in for Annemarie herself, and ambivalent about his studies:

> … in Bernhard's double life, school doesn't really figure alongside music, his true passion. However, he's not a bad student, understands quickly, works hard and is attentive to his teachers. In fact, it depends on the teacher, especially in maths where he didn't understand anything at first and was banging his head against a wall until a new young teacher turned up …[62]

Mother and daughter, [1930?]. Photo by Renée Schwarzenbach-Wille
Courtesy of Zentralbibliothek Zürich

Another character in the novel, Christina, is a trouble-maker at a Swiss boarding school and the director, a Swiss Miss Brodie, takes a kindly interest. Christina's roommate is Jolie, 'a small girl with the look of a Japanese' who falls for bad-girl Christina's charm:

> Jolie suddenly opened wide her slanted Japanese eyes, flashing anger or fear, it was hard to tell. She gripped the windowsill with two tiny hands and in a hard, loud voice said: 'But I love Christina.'

In correspondence with Dominique Schlumberger, a Fetan alumna and future heiress to the Schlumberger mining fortune, Annemarie is suggestive without being explicit about their alma mater. A cousin of Jacqueline's shared a room with Sabine Nagel, one of the nice Germans 'who is really very interesting. Did your cousin never mention her?'[63] Besides hints about her affections, Annemarie's letters inform us that she was reading Tacitus, Livy, Horace, and Voltaire in French. Later, she recalled taking some caffeine-based remedy at night in order to stay up and work longer.[64] She read and worked hard at Fetan and, in correspondence at least, was sad to leave. Matriculating in November 1927, she entered Zurich University.

Twenty-year-old Annemarie's letter to Ernst Merz on 6 August 1928 expresses a clear-eyed view of her lesbianism. Her coming out implies a deepening of the relationship between pastor and schoolgirl over the preceding four years. She might have divined his own hidden sexuality behind the mystical socialism, while at the same time leaving him with no illusions about where her own desires lay. Like Annemarie's husband-to-be Claude Clarac, Merz had fallen for her androgynous spell to the extent of wanting to marry her, as his 1928 diary indicates. She perhaps wanted to lay Merz's affections to rest: 'Knowing that you are of independent mind, I feel I can tell you … that I can only love women with an authentic passion.'[65] This decisive statement for a twenty-year-old illuminates the degree of calculation in her later decision to marry Clarac:

> Besides, what you termed the lesbian world in your letter is so looked down on. Somehow, I've come to realize that people think of it in lurid terms: furtive vice, dirty and degrading. 'Unnatural.' Since I know this is not your view, I can admit to warm, strong feelings of affection and burning friendship, all my

young yearning, directed only towards women. Only women inspire in me real passion. I might feel camaraderie and trust for males and young men, in terms of working with them, but as soon as they come on to me as a 'woman', I switch off to the point of disgust. Maybe this is despicable, unnatural, but it's my true nature. And if I were to squeeze into the mould of what others call natural, it would be against my will, which strikes me as equally despicable.[66]

This, of course, is a coming-out letter, a confession addressed to a friend and kindred soul, written from Sweden where the family was on holiday.

Gundalena Wille, Annemarie, Renée, Suzanne, Hasi and Pedy, 7 July 1921. Photo by Renée Schwarzenbach-Wille
Courtesy of Zentralbibliothek Zürich

Annemarie might have begun to feel the pressure, the unsubtle push towards heterosexual rules of engagement. Merz knew in the deep heart's core whereof she wrote. That there are not more such letters is due to winnowed archives, families keen to tidy away inconvenient truths and thereby own the story. Annemarie faced the facts of her situation, anticipating the marrying game – 'the mould of what others call natural' – while standing outside herself to look at the connotations of 'the lesbian world'. She has begun to wriggle free from the silk cocoon.

2

Women on the Left Bank

I would rather give a healthy boy or a healthy girl a phial of prussic acid than this novel.

James Douglas, *Sunday Express*, 19 August 1928, reviewing
The Well of Loneliness

Term at Zurich University commenced in the second week of November 1927 and Annemarie opted to study history, philosophy and literature. She didn't pass unnoticed in the corridors and was aware of her effect on fellow students, for the most part male, earning her the moniker 'her royal highness',[1] confirming the impression of distance, even haughtiness, she had cultivated at Fetan, a princess manner she could play up. She attended lectures with her cousin Gundalena Wille and these *jeunes filles bien rangées* turned heads.

Perhaps her choice of history stemmed from a liking to stand back from events: 'I find that history explains things, provides answers and a measure of clarity. You can see the cause and effect of events, the limitations and greatness of human affairs, how relative human values are.'[2] She studied under Karl Meyer, Ernst Gagliardi and Professor Carl J. Burckhardt. Burckhardt hailed from the same patrician Basel family that had produced the author of *The Civilization of the Renaissance in Italy* (1860), whose face graces the Swiss thousand franc note. His descendant moved fluently between positions as High Commissioner at the League of Nations, President of the Red Cross, periods in academia and diplomacy. Annemarie's correspondence with Burckhardt[3] reveals his usefulness to her but also a pedagogic and friendly rapport. Gagliardi, for his part, writing about Bismarck at the time of Annemarie's matriculation, would have been aware of her family's connection to the statesman. Karl Meyer ('*homo alpinus* and admirably diligent')[4] later supervised Annemarie's doctoral thesis on the history of the Lower Engadine. She was in good academic hands, and her writing for the *NZZ* at the end of her student years cut a dash.

Besides Pastor Merz, fellow student Albrecht Haushofer was nursing aspirations and sending her romantic verse in September 1929. Haushofer, son of geo-strategist Karl Haushofer, first encountered Annemarie when he visited Bocken in the company of fellow student Rudolf Hess. Annemarie's interests in history and the orient were fed by Haushofer senior – former military attaché to Tokyo, a widely respected authority on the Far East. He sent Annemarie copies of his books and she accompanied the Haushofers and her grandmother Clara Wille on an outing to the Rigi. Hindsight has tarred Haushofer senior with the Nazi brush but in the late twenties the import of his mish-mash of clashing civilizations, *Lebensraum* and involvement in German–Japanese rapprochement had yet to reach its apotheosis.[5] Albrecht Haushofer, the son, was also an orientalist and traveller. His politics, however, increasingly diverged from that of his father's generation and by 1935 or so he had established contact with anti-Nazi elements in Germany. Half-Jewish, a *Mischling*, he was implicated in a plot against Hitler, and the Gestapo kept a close eye on him thereafter. Haushofer was interned in Moabit Prison in Berlin and shot by the SS as the Russians entered the city in the last days of the war. In one of the seventy-nine sonnets found in the inside pocket of his overcoat after his death, he writes: 'I should have earlier recognized the call of duty / I should have more loudly called the devil out; / I reined my judgement in for far too long.'[6] These *Moabit Sonnets*, disinterred in the nick of time, have since come to represent his affirmation of the human spirit at the edge of the grave.

Grandmother Clara's view of Albrecht Haushofer confirmed her grand-daughter's diffidence: 'Annemarie is right – he's not the man for her!'[7] Her letters to him from Paris reveal little about her life there. At the time of her dissertation, she sought help with sources and maps, and was coyly deprecating when her thesis was finally submitted. By the time she contacted Haushofer in Berlin, where he lived, it was already several months into her stay in the capital and she was recovering from overindulgence in alcohol and perhaps drugs. Learning of her death shortly before his own, he wrote a sonnet in her memory, haunted by both their ghostly presences:

> Today you were here,
> So young, intact, so weirdly close,

*Like then when we were first apart
and stars burned bright and clear.*[8]

*

Few rites of passage rival a year in Paris at age twenty and Annemarie headed to the Sorbonne for a two-semester sandwich course during her second year at Zurich. For a lesbian who was already fairly clear about the object of her desires, the prospect of being away from home must have held untold possibilities. After two years closeted at boarding school in the Engadine, and a year in the small university town that was Zurich, where all the best families knew each other, in October 1928 Annemarie packed her bags, excited by the relative anonymity that Paris offered. She had been reading Claudel and Gide, admiring the latter's courage and his questioning of morality: 'Do you think there is such a thing as morality?' she enquired of Dominique Schlumberger. 'For me it's just habit, invented by boring and cowardly people.'[9] In Paris she hoped to take riding classes in order to participate in the 1929 show-jumping competitions, like her mother and brother.[10] The city's attractions, however, proved a turning point for this horsey daughter of good family expected to marry into society. That old boulevardier Joseph Roth describes the Paris of the twenties he had roistered in since the end of the First World War:

> … it was midnight when the doors of Paradise were opened, and one went down to one's damnation. One loses one's bearings as well: all the Montmartre sky with its colorful sins of advertising, the terrestrial honking of terrestrial car horns in the rue Pigalle.[11]

Annemarie was enrolled to study philosophy, history and psychology while staying at the newly-founded Foyer International des Étudiantes facing the Luxembourg Gardens. The Latin Quarter's student cafés and bars, the more up-market Coupole in Montparnasse, and nebulous artists' studios became the stamping ground of her early writing:

> There's a wide-angle view out across the roofscape of Montparnasse, the green treetops of the Luxembourg gardens behind which rise the towers of Saint Sulpice. … I am at home here, in a manner of speaking: a room with books, desk and sofa bed.[12]

Accompanied to Paris by her cousins Jutta and Gundalena Wille, she was not entirely free of family. Among the international residents Annemarie made friends easily, some of whom stuck by her during the coming decade. A fellow graduate of Fetan, Dominique Schlumberger, lived at home on rue Las-Cases in the 7th arrondissement and was studying physics and mathematics at the Sorbonne. There was an excursion to Fontainebleau and a picnic in Chantilly with the Wille girls, Schlumberger, Jacqueline Nougarède and a Russian friend of Annemarie's, Tania Doukhovetzky, who was also staying at the Foyer. Annemarie's French was fluent and this group of mostly wealthy young women, well connected and urbane, formed a cushion against the harsher realities of student life.

Another friend encountered at the Foyer was Maria Daelen. Brought up largely by her father, a metallurgic engineer, Maria's early life was turbulent following her parents' divorce when she was two. Her mother, Katharina von Oheimb, one of thirty-six female parliamentarians in the Reichstag, was liberal, socialist and feminist in outlook. Maria inherited her mother's anti-Nazi sympathies as well as her feminist streak. She had attended a private girls school in Wiesbaden and studied medicine in Hamburg and Munich. From November 1929 to November 1930, she practised in the West End Hospital in Berlin, where for a time she shared her apartment with Annemarie. 'The friends were very free with each other; friendship and love could merge. Maria's sexual inclinations went in many directions.'[13]

Daelen was one of a number of older bisexual or lesbian women to whom Annemarie turned in the course of her life, often in times of illness. Both lived under the shadow of forceful mothers, seeking attention and approval.[14] Maria was striking-looking, strong-jawed and photogenic; her photograph had appeared in Berlin society magazines, hands on hips wearing a doctor's white coat. She was friends with a number of the up-and-coming German female photographers of the day – in particular, Marianne Breslauer, whose seminal photographs of Annemarie would later do so much to propagate the Swiss writer's image. Maria was well aware how deliberately Annemarie could project a little-boy-lost look: Maria's nickname for her was Enzio.[15] While practising medicine in Berlin, she nonetheless belonged to the city's beau monde by virtue of birth and wealth. Invited to Bocken as one of Annemarie's

Paris friends, Maria created a positive impression on grandmother Clara and initially on the wary Renée.

While her relationship with Maria was likely exploratory at this stage, and with the Russian Tania also, correspondence with other female friends sometimes hangs back in the shadows. Annemarie looked at women with desire, modulated in different social contexts, ambiguous in correspondence. Writing to Nougarède and Schlumberger, there is no overt lesbian expression but a teasing testing of limits. To Nougarède she described the Engadin region of Switzerland as 'this little corner of the world which I love the way you love a beautiful woman'.[16] Later, when Annemarie met and fell in love with Erika Mann, she described her to Nougarède as 'one of the most delicious women I have ever met'.[17] Annemarie signed off as 'Arthur' in a letter mentioning the screenwriter Vollmoeller – perhaps a reference to Arthur Rimbaud? When Nougarède announced her engagement, Annemarie sent 'hearty congratulations' and wrote that it is 'so difficult for me to imagine you married'.[18] Their correspondence tailed off as Annemarie's new, more risqué lesbian and homosexual friends came to the fore and as Nougarède's marriage got underway.

Dominique Schlumberger's marriage too distanced her from Annemarie's more adventurous friends. In an early letter, Annemarie admits to finding the film actress Elizabeth Berguer attractive, especially in the 1929 film *Fräulein Else*, and seems to hint at other crushes. In 1929 Schlumberger was writing film journalism at about the time Annemarie approached the *NZZ* with her own book reviews.[19] Annemarie's January 1929 encounter with Karl Vollmoeller, then working with Sternberg and Jannings on *Blue Angel* (1930), was instrumental in Schlumberger gaining a position as intern on the set in Berlin, where she relocated in 1930.[20]

Many of Annemarie's relationships with women project a degree of one-sided imagining and ambiguity. Fluidity characterizes her New Woman friends of the thirties, often already married, subsuming their bisexuality or lesbianism behind a carapace, choosing discretion over being out. As with male homosexuals, lesbians took camouflage in heterosexual marriage. Sexual acquiescence and economic dependence were, and often still are, of course, linked in heterosexual life. Such marriages kept parents happy and, if the spouse was also homosexual,

Annemarie picnicking in the Foret de Chantilly with Dominique Schlumberger, 1929
Courtesy of Zentralbibliothek Zürich

there could be some freedom to play away. Many lesbians in Annemarie's circle of friends chose the route of marriage, or were coerced into it, or fluidly moved between heterosexual and homosexual lifestyles, as a two-way closet door. It was fashionable ('chic') to be thought lesbian or to pretend to be lesbian in the 1920s, and to be footloose and fancy-free in Paris and Berlin between the wars lent itself to experimentation.[21]

Letters home only tell half the story, letters to friends often camouflage and paint a picture. Writing to Ernst Merz at Christmas, Annemarie is vague:

> I never wrote to you from Paris. I penned little work there, apart from the numerous college notebooks that I filled with lecture notes ... I've already gained a lot of experience. I met many people – I confess that I was quite confused by so much accommodating and pampering – maybe I got too caught up in it at the beginning.[22]

*

Returning to Paris after Christmas at home and New Year skiing in St. Moritz, she picked up her pen again and took as subject matter nightlife among a coterie of young people, raffish characters, students, émigré Russians and social-climbing dancers:

> A bright studio with a naked lady, a smoke-hazed bar with a small girl trembling under a spotlight, or Nicolas with the sweet smile who dances the tango with me or perhaps Madeleine stretched out under a woollen blanket, whom Marcel kissed …[23]

She evolved her characteristic way of looking, disguising or sublimating her sexual interest by adopting the persona or observing eye of a 'young man … with a handsome child's face', a gender-bending formula employed in her first novel, *Friends of Bernard*. Changing the pronouns smuggled gay affections into the straight world of fiction, a fairly standard procedure for homosexual writers of the period. At times she hints at her own closeted state and the camouflage resorted to by women in order to pass in society:

> I know other women who have draped so many veils around their souls that their face has become a mask, and life throbs behind it, as though threatening to suddenly flare up and scorch the veils.[24]

Paris, like Berlin, was awash with Russian émigrés. A Russian family saga morphing into a historical romance exercised Annemarie at the time.[25] The story features Russian cafés and an excursion out of Paris to the forest, as well as an émigré family: Natasha, a singer who left St. Petersburg aged fifteen, eight-year-old Nikolai and their mother. 'Nikolai wanted to be a General, or sometimes maybe the chamberlain of the little Tsarevich, or king of Poland.'[26] The Russians like to sit in the Luxembourg gardens and watch the children playing with toy boats. A girl encountered in a library leads the uncertain narrator to Natasha:

> Natasha is tall, slim and sophisticated. You can spot her from a mile away standing on the street, with her easy-going face, a face like a protective wall behind which tiredness, a little weakness, quick flashes of disappointment peep out.[27]

Five years older than Annemarie, Tania Doukhovetzky had attended the Notting Hill and Ealing High School for girls in England and was now resident at the Foyer International. 'Tania is not happy and she will never be happy because she doesn't want to be.'[28] This hint of depression or something awry in Tania's personality is borne out by correspondence from Renée and others. Tania's influence on Annemarie's early fiction as well as her presence at Bocken during the summer of 1929 suggest some degree of romantic involvement.

The male student narrator of a second story dated 1929 has an engaging, lyrical way with description: 'I read through half of the night. In the evening we go for a walk on the boulevards, drink coffee and grenadine that is sweet and bright red, and when we get home I forget to be tired. The street lamps shine like moonlight into my room.'[29] This tentative flâneur encounters a director called Hochberg, apparently based on the screenwriter Vollmoeller, who frequents the Coupole's bohemian crowd. Hochberg 'read my work, made some corrections and put it aside again'.[30] The director tells the student the story of Lena, a dancer of Polish-Jewish origin who made her name in Berlin:

> Hochberg tells how she showed up from somewhere back east, a little Polish Jew in a red velvet dress. Just the little red dress was all she had. And Lena sat up in all the Berlin cafés and made a name for herself. She was petite and attractive. Not very different from today, except that she was trim and now she has filled out, strong with broad shoulders. She was dark even then. I think she must have a drop of gypsy blood. Pure Jews don't have those eyes. By the way, her eyes were this incredible blue ...[31]

Lena marries three times, becomes rich from her first two husbands, and accompanies the director to Paris where she leads a bohemian life, painting and hanging around the Coupole. 'Lena put the men and the dance school behind her and traipsed around all the studios in Montparnasse and fell in love with nobody.'[32] This intriguing story within a story implies the author's familiarity with the Montparnasse scene. 'He comes to the Coupole every night to see Lena... So at midnight to *La Jungle*, the *Bal des Quat'zarts*.'[33] La Jungle was an African-themed jazz bar and the Bal des Quat'zarts was an infamous annual arts students' carnival where the dancers mislaid their clothes as the night wore on and licentiousness was on the menu.

Annemarie intercuts this account of bar-crawling with a description of Sorbonne life:

> Students scurry on the stairs. The Sorbonne courtyard is bleary after rain. Out on the street two students are holding forth and handing out leaflets … A blond woman sits at the bar, sipping now and again from her drink and detaining one of the students by the nape. She is pale and approachable. More students come in after their lectures, immediately ordering coffee and tartines and hilariously reading out snatches of their notes to each other.[34]

A third story is set again among the Russians. This time the protagonist is called Madeleine, an émigrée who left Russia as a teenager, and a character called Marcel. Marcel attempts to introduce the narrator to a baby-faced gigolo: '"You look so nice together with your baby-faces. Madeleine has a weakness for them." Madeleine laughed at the whole table. "How wicked you are", she said, "but how true – both of them are cute with their baby-faces."'[35] The story comes to an end with a stroll through the Latin Quarter to the river: 'I walk down the Boulevard St. Michel, where students are sitting out on the terraces drinking coffee and eating croissants. I cross the bridge from Place St. Michel towards Notre Dame …'[36]

These early writings about Paris show the twenty-two-year-old responding to young people in cafés, bars, attics and dancehalls. Her baby-faced male narrator is after the girls but, as Annemarie admitted to Erika Mann, this was merely a device: '*I fully understand that the boy is not really a boy.*'[37] The Russian diaspora of the Left Bank and the jazz age provide a fevered sexuality. They also show a tug-of-war between the safe student world and the lure of a nighttime pleasure.

Shari Benstock underlines this need for discretion in her seminal account of lesbian women in Paris between the wars, *Women of the Left Bank*. 1928 was the year Virginia Woolf published *Orlando*, inspired in part by Woolf's affair with the cross-dressing Vita Sackville-West. The two writers courageously took a stand on the grounds of freedom of speech in favour of a novel that was causing scandal on both sides of the English Channel – *The Well of Loneliness*:

> All London, they say, is agog with this. Most of our friends are trying to evade the witness box; for reasons you may guess. But they generally put

43

it down to the weak heart of a father, or a cousin who is about to have twins.[38]

The Well of Loneliness was quickly removed from circulation amid a flurry of immorality charges while Pegasus Press in Paris attempted to circumvent English censorship and create a *succès de scandale*. The French edition sold well, especially at the Gare du Nord news stand beside the *Flèche d'Or* deluxe express train to London.[39] The obscenity trial of November 1928 echoed the Wilde trials of 1895 and gave a foretaste of the Chatterley ban some thirty years later: English prudery was in its element. Much of the medical establishment of the day echoed the legal view of lesbianism as an illness for which a 'cure' was needed. Because of the adverse publicity *The Well of Loneliness* had garnered, people began to question romantic friendships between women, to look askance at school girl crushes in novels and to regard spinster school teachers with suspicion.[40] Gertrude Stein, Adrienne Monnier, Djuna Barnes and Sylvia Beach, all members of what Radclyffe Hall calls 'the miserable army' in Paris, were left in no doubt about the implications of this legal defeat.

Alexis Schwarzenbach has traced a copy of the German 1929 translation of *The Well of Loneliness* in the student library of Zurich University, and also a copy in the library at Bocken.[41] It is quite likely that Annemarie read it either in French or German, soon after her return from Paris, and so was aware of its implications for her own coming out both in life and in fiction.

The Foyer International was a short walk from a number of lesbian salons and bars in Montparnasse. *Le Monocle*, the most popular and notorious of them, was located at 60 Boulevard Edgar Quinet and owned by Lulu de Montparnasse (not to be confused with Kiki). In the rue de Lappe behind Place de la Bastille, *Les Trois Colonnes* was frequented by corner boys and ephebes alike. In Klaus Mann's 1932 novel, *Vanishing Point*, his protagonist accompanies a character called Annemarie there after meeting her in Montparnasse. 'The romantically tricked-out little bar was enchanting and lively. Boys in caps, girls with bright scarves around their necks looked like an Apache chorus in an operetta.'[42]

While there is no firm indication of Annemarie's wanderings at this time, there is no reason to think, given her lively circle of friends and her

Annemarie with Hélène d'Oliveira, 1927
Courtesy of Zentralbibliothek Zürich

own explorer's curiosity, that she didn't venture out to sample the city's nightlife.

*

A few weeks before the end of her two semesters in Paris, writing to Merz, Annemarie sounds a vague note about the changes it has wrought:

> I will be leaving Paris in a few weeks. It has been good here, I learned a lot and stored away some feelings to savour later. It was here that I slowly sloughed off the last vestige of childhood, everything has become weightier, more responsible, deeper. There is also a new powerful urge to aim higher.[43]

Accompanying her home from Paris in June 1929 was the Russian exile Tania, who spent the summer at Bocken, and benefited from the care and attention paid by Annemarie's family to their disturbed house-guest. A doctor at Bocken treated her during her three-month stay, and both Renée and Annemarie appear to have been helping her out (and Tania's mother) with sums of money. Renée was of the opinion that the illness was hysterical, attention-seeking, describing the patient as '*la reine douloureuse*' and blaming her for ruining Annemarie's health, always a source of concern. By September Tania had returned to Paris, with a sigh of relief all round.

> You've no idea the worries I've had with Annemarie's 'special friendships' – but she eventually *always* makes good friends – and then there's Vollmoeller and his crowd! – Poor Annemarie has such bad taste! Tania is not a bad girl – but she is suffocating her friend![44]

In January 1929, during the Christmas holidays between semesters in Paris, Annemarie had encountered screenwriter Karl Vollmoeller in Badrutt's Palace Hotel in St. Moritz. Whether she sought him out or he pursued her is moot: they met in the lobby. Certainly Annemarie was as capable as the next writer of networking to advance her career; and Vollmoeller always had an eye for a pretty girl, the younger the better. This meeting widened her circle to writers and cinema people, and precipitated a family row about what Renée called her '*amitiés différentes*'.[45] Vollmoeller had co-authored the screenplay of the highly successful *Blue Angel* and was intimate with the world of Montparnasse cafés and the figure of Lena Amsel, all of which caused concern to Annemarie's bourgeois family and began to make its way into her writing. His disreputable private life was well known in the opera world where Renée's diva Emmy Krüger, always ready to be holier than thou, sniffed the wind.

Renée's disapproval of Vollmoeller strained the atmosphere at Bocken following her daughter's return from Paris. Annemarie's association with him went against Renée's need to control and her innate bourgeois tendency to observe the proprieties. While some friends found favour with Renée – Maria Daelen initially, the art historian Hannah Kiel, Jacqueline Nougarède – others fell foul. It was not just a matter of Annemarie asserting herself; guests too became aware of Renée's overbearing manner, as Annemarie recognized: 'These slow oppressive days, misunderstandings, slights, wounded sentiments, nerves, biting one's tongue. Do you remember dinner at Bocken? Afterwards you admitted: "It's the atmosphere. I'm suffocated." Sometimes I too am smothered.'[46]

Pretty or handsome celebrities who die young tend to become the stuff of legend. Dancers, however, leave a light trace on history and Lena Amsel is remembered these days, if at all, for what others wrote about her, as the twenties came to an expensive crash. Writers Klaus Mann, Wilhelm Speyer, Ruth Landshoff-Yorck and Annemarie all traced Amsel's Polish-Jewish origins, her burst of frenzied celebrity in decadent Berlin – short, fast, scattering ash – as a meteoric metaphor for the Weimar Republic itself. Perhaps too she appears spectre-like behind Waugh's ditzy party girl Agatha in *Vile Bodies* (1930). Amsel's death in a car accident in Paris on 2 November 1929, a taffeta and rhinestone princess bursting into flames, brought that decade to an abrupt close, as the Wall Street Crash seemed to bring an end to the roar and folly of the twenties.

Lena Amsel had been a protégé of Vollmoeller who likely encouraged Annemarie to look her up in Paris. Certainly, in November 1929, Annemarie took up the figure of Amsel, like many others, in her writing. Ruth Landshoff-Yorck, another protégé of Vollmoeller, remembered Amsel's early appearance in Berlin's *Wintergarten* in 1917:

> She could not dance a farthing. Dressed in a yellow gown she was making steps intended to show her up as a seductive female, and towards the end two enormous negroes came on stage and gathered her in their four huge arms to carry her away while she wiggled her legs.[47]

Amsel and Landshoff-Yorck's careers mirror each other. Both were teenagers advanced by Vollmoeller. They frequented the trendy Café des Westens in Berlin, where Jean Ross, aka Sally Bowles, lunched with Isherwood, Spender and Aaron Copeland in 1931. Both were Jewish girls married into German nobility – the most lucrative of Amsel's three marriages was to Hugo Graf von Moy – whose palace still sits on the corner of Odeonsplatz in Munich. Her first marriage to an Argentinian riding instructor lasted three months and her last liaisons were with surrealist Louis Aragon and Swiss sculptor André Lasserre. Both women were able to conduct their lives thanks to wealthy husbands, Vollmoeller's largesse and their own *schtick*. They emerged from the Berlin street and café life Vollmoeller knew so well:

She always came back to him, telephoned from somewhere, he rescued her, sent money or tickets or picked her up in his car, and she promised she would be faithful and never was.[48]

Amsel moved from cabaret to screen in the early twenties, working with the then unknown Marlene Dietrich. Annemarie and Landshoff-Yorck in their writing are drawn to Amsel as the epitome of the Polish Jew who has danced her way out of her origins. 'Lena had come from Lodz, a fact most ambitious girls would have kept secret.'[49] In a bar called the Tabarin, she encounters a compatriot from the Lodz of her past, from a culture that would be decimated in the coming decades:

> 'Don't you recognize me, little Lenachen? ... Uncle Fränkel from Lodz? You don't know your kind old Uncle Fränkel any more, Lenchen?' He stood modestly still as Lena fell on his neck and embraced him. ... girls were certainly not born in order to become dancers, but to be the future mothers of youthful Jews who got to study, to study ...[50]

Klaus Mann's character Greta Valentin, a former dancer, in *Vanishing Point* (1932) follows the same narrative arc of celebrity and accidental death:

> The village deep in Poland, the sadness of the ghetto. A small ugly girl with the big eyes who gets swept up by a stable boy – what was she called then? Not yet Greta – and ran off with him to Warsaw; cursed by her father (father in a kaftan and ringlets), the eternally suffering mother (mother with wig and worried, sallow beaky face); what does the girl live on – the girl who's not yet Greta – in the city of Warsaw? Who does she sleep with, and who teaches her the rudiments of dance?[51]

Greta has the same child-like, ingenue quality that Vollmoeller liked: the country girl given her start in the metropolis. Writer Stefan Grossmann also remembered Amsel sitting in Berlin's Café des Westens:

> ... she had the look of a child, and spoke for the most part Polish and a bit of German, and was the sweetheart of a very young novelist-poet who, soon after he picked up this slender waif, had to defend his actions in a court of law

because his beloved was not yet sixteen. The young poet died suddenly, just about the time Lena had picked up enough German to kick start her career.[52]

Berlin at the time was awash with such aspiring performers, girls and boys living hand to mouth in the hope of stardom or the next role, their looks quickly fading on the porous border between street, cabaret stage and silver screen.

By 1927 Amsel was living in Paris, in two rooms in the Hotel Raspail not far from the cafés and bars of Montparnasse. Man Ray photographed her and she had ended an affair with Louis Aragon. She drove a blue Bugatti 'with a clumsily painted bird on the door', and had recently taken up painting. Her dance-cabarets of preference were the Coupole, the Jungle and the Grand Écart. On 1 November 1929 Amsel was in Le Grand Écart on rue Fromentin with Kiki of Montparnasse – a small, mirrored, atmospheric bal-dancing that attracted an eclectic fashionable crowd. The painter André Derain invited her to his studio at Barbizon outside Paris. The next day, in their separate Bugattis, they drove back to the city with Florence Pitron as Lena's passenger. Both cars drove at speed and in some accounts appeared to be racing each other. Amsel's Bugatti skidded on the slippery road, overturned and caught fire. Both women died horribly burned in the conflagration.

Annemarie's *Pariser Novelle II*, written shortly after Amsel's death, memorializes the dancer. Her self-made persona was attractive to a writer like Annemarie: spirited, glamorous, denizen of bar and cabaret, motorcars and speed, tragic death. Annemarie's description suggests more than just hearsay:

> Lena left in her wake men and dancing lessons, hung around the studios of Montparnasse and fell in love with nobody. Her three marriages had exhausted her. Lena shuddered with disgust when she recalled them. What she wanted now was sun, trees, flowers, fine company to pass the time of day with and lie out on the summer grass. Every Saturday she drove off, trailer in tow, heading for the horizon's *dolce far niente* …[53]

Amsel dances on in a handful of largely forgotten novels and memoirs of the day, and in porcelain figurines made of her in Pierrot costume, which occasionally turn up on vintage sites. She was a Weimar product:

an underage Jewish nobody from Poland, with a little-girl face, picked up by older men for her 'childlike' looks and willing manner and launched onto the cabaret stage – Dietrich and Sally Bowles hail from the same circus ring. Amsel couldn't really dance but knew how to put on a show. She worked the punters with gamine coquettishness, part-soubrette, part-Puck. Her success tells us more about the lust of her audience than her abilities, and also demonstrates that gender exploitation was hardwired into the worlds of cinema and stage right from the start.

At the conclusion of her year at the Sorbonne, Annemarie returned to tame little Switzerland, having encountered a freewheeling range of new women and well-connected men – film journalist Dominique Schlumberger, surgeon Maria Daelen, screenwriter Vollmoeller, and through him the dancer Lena Amsel. Alfred Schwarzenbach, despite the coming storm, gave her a new car, a green Dodge Victory Brougham – the Victory marking the tenth anniversary of the Allies' triumph over the Boche – in recognition of her hard work and her coming of age.

3

Breaking the Threads

… she seemed to vacillate; she was man; she was woman; she knew the secrets, shared the weaknesses of each.

Virginia Woolf, Orlando

The Schwarzenbach firm was much invested in America and the stock market crash of November 1929 alarmed Alfred. Travelling to New York in the early months of 1930 in an attempt to sort out the firm's affairs, he returned dispirited in May. The Schwarzenbach parents, invested in respectability as much as in the American silk market, were also exercised by Annemarie's frequentations at this time. Until she turned twenty-one, she was legally and financially under her father's thumb; Switzerland would not extend the vote to women for another forty years and all sorts of restrictions kept the patriarchy in charge, particularly where wealth, family allowance and inheritance were concerned. Her parents might still have entertained hopes that her 'special friendships' were a passing phase and that her character might yet be tamed by a good husband. Renée and Alfred did not turn a blind eye to Annemarie's increasingly free and easy lifestyle. Her initial contact with screenwriter Karl Vollmoeller in St. Moritz led to her meeting his long-time protégé Ruth Landshoff and their circle of mondaine friends. At the same time, Annemarie got to know Erika and Klaus Mann, children of Nobel laureate Thomas Mann based in Munich. Here, the sabre-rattling of the National Socialists was beginning to exploit Weimar decadence and its perceived Jewish under-pinnings – the Manns were half-Jewish. Annemarie straying into high bohemia led to friction at home. The German political struggle between left and right – with Jews and Communists as scapegoats – against a background of economic decline was mirrored in the generational tug-of-war at the heart of the Schwarzenbach family.

Glamour attached to Annemarie early on; friends were aware of her patrician, well-heeled background and her beauty was incontrovertible.

Masculine dress, swanky cars, easy travel, luxury hotels and skiing only went so far to gloss over her psychological vulnerability. 'Every friend became a nurse to her',[1] wrote Ruth Landshoff, and the pattern had already begun of crying on women's shoulders and bemoaning her family and fate, a situation others might have viewed as enviable. Annemarie felt free to invite her girlfriends home, to introduce them to her mother and to show them the splendour of summer at Bocken. This was initially the case with Tania Doukhovetzky, Maria Daelen, Hanna Kiel, Erika Mann and many others. The daughter's relative openness, and the hospitality of her mother, would suggest some acknowledgement – on both mother and daughter's part – of the nature of these affections. Annemarie was always capable of frantically moving from one context to another, with different sets of friends in different countries, not necessarily knowing each other. This nurtured a mystique – the girl who motors up the drive and disappears as quickly in a cloud of exhaust, as Landshoff-Yorck noted: 'Annemarie had many reputations – different ones in different places and with different persons – and only some of them were bad.'[2]

Besides new friendships, her return from Paris marked the beginning of an intense period of work. By November 1929, Annemarie was following a timetable of thirty-four classes a week, some until seven in the evening. She left Bocken at 7.30 in the morning in her new car and often wrote between lectures at her father's city office. She sent a short story called 'Erik'[3] and a film review of Sergei Eisenstein's work to the features editor of the *NZZ*, Eduard Korrodi. He was encouraging, inviting her to the newspaper to learn the practical side of journalism. She reviewed the best-selling 1929 children's novel *Emil and the Detectives* by Erich Kästner.[4] This was the beginning of a professional relationship with Zurich's leading newspaper under Korrodi's guiding hand. Following a two-week holiday with her parents in Rome in February 1930, she sent Korrodi a travel sketch which he rejected. However, by the spring of 1930 an essay on contemporary youth had appeared, setting itself up to address the perennial question of what young people want and how they see themselves differently from their elders. Posed by dramatists such as Wedekind and Hasenclever before the war, this question was back with a vengeance after it; a generation had come to adulthood for whom the First World War was noises off, whereas it had been the defining event of their parents' lives. Annemarie's newspaper writings fashioned her as a voice of the coming generation, and the *NZZ* readership doubtless knew her as a scion of a prominent Zurich family.

The Wille-Schwarzenbach family viewed Annemarie's education and publishing beginnings according to their lights. Her mother thought Annemarie should study music, while 'grandmother sees me as a well brought up young lady at a finishing school etc. Right now they let me be, and I get on with work.'[5] The widening gulf between Annemarie's politics and her family's militaristic-capitalist mindset is evident from a September 1929 letter to Jacqueline Nougarède:

> You know I have very deep-seated anti-militarist ideas, very 'modern', independent, anti-everything class-based, aristocratic in the bad sense of the term, and *for* whatever is simple, free, open – and you must have noticed at Meilen that such ideas are contrary to those of my family. ... because it would be much easier to bend to the habits of my social class.[6]

A suitor from a literary family, Claude Bourdet, studying engineering in Zurich, has left an impression of Annemarie's social class and the elegant musical world at Bocken on 31 May 1930:

> There was a garden-party concert at 5.30, a German female quartet performed Boccherini, Scarlatti, Pergolesi and Handel, with vocals by a friend of Madame Schwarzenbach who had sung at the Wagner Festival in Paris ...
>
> Afterwards there was supper at little tables spread out in the park and people helped themselves from an enormous buffet catered by the Baur au Lac. This was followed by dancing to a band composed of three big Zurich burghers, bankers or business people, playing six hands at the piano, two Sunday violinists scratching away, the cellist thumping his instrument ...[7]

Annemarie's relationship with Bourdet, future French Resistance hero and co-founder of *Le Nouvel Observateur*, blossomed into friendship. His account of her to his mother, the writer Catherine Pozzi, shows he was smitten:

> She was a tall young girl, at once delicate and athletic, with a gawky or masculine manner; her voice was low and soft, a bit husky, or *hesitant* ... Dominique had told me that I would like her – I was blown away on the first

Claude Bourdet
Agence France-Presse © AFP

day, struck miserable like someone who knows he will never win over that which he most wants. Her family, … their legendary wealth in Switzerland, and above all her beauty, her culture, her easy-going expression, all of which left me forlorn like a beached fish in her wake.[8]

As with Albrecht Haushofer, Annemarie was careful to keep the relationship mostly epistolary. Contact with Bourdet seems to have fizzled out by the end of the decade.

Alfred Schwarzenbach had stepped into the breach to enlighten Annemarie on Vollmoeller's reputation.[9] Writing to Dominique Schlumberger in Berlin, where she was helping on the set of *Blue Angel*, Annemarie qualified somewhat her initial enthusiasm for the old roué:

I have neither more nor less trust in him than previously – you champion him so much and I know full well that he can be charming and kind, that he is intelligent and that I love him – but I believe nonetheless that there is some truth to the things Papa said. And even if I don't really care – it's still the case that Papa does, and I can only freely meet up again with V. when I have my independence; in other words when I have left home, with a job, the right to live independently.[10]

Vollmoeller was a small, rather unassuming-looking man with a large forehead and a prominent chin that gave him the look of Punch, between which perched a pair of granny glasses. A charming and erudite talker, he drove a huge white Austro-Daimler while Ruth Landshoff was still riding her bike to school. He bought her a custom-made Megola motorcycle on which she rode around in overalls and then an Adler Standard 6 Cabriolet with black leather seats, just about the time when any self-respecting it-girl in Berlin was photographed at the wheel of her own car.[11] What Vollmoeller liked was an ephebe quality, attracted as he was to *le fruit vert*: 'Peter [Vollmoeller] had too often said how much he liked youth in a girl and to me it seemed that youth for him stopped soon after seventeen … With him, with Peter, I knew I was both girl AND boy …'[12]

It was this androgynous quality that drew him to Annemarie.

[He] had returned from Switzerland and said he had found a new girl … 'She comes from a big house on the edge of the Zurich lake. Her parents have a lot of money. She does not get along with her mother. I found her in St. Moritz. She wants to meet you. She has read some of your poems.'[13]

Annemarie's correspondence shows that she was aware of how this well-connected couple might be useful to her writerly ambition. She wrote to Ernst Merz about Vollmoeller's enthusiasm for Stefan George: 'I met a friend of George in St. Moritz (that ephemeral happy-go-lucky mountain town) called Karl Vollmoeller, who convinced me that George is the only true, natural blessed-by-fate genius and maestro there is.'[14]

The Schwarzenbach family base for winter holidays was Suvretta-Haus, one of the leading hotels of St. Moritz. In 1919 Nijinski gave his last ever major performance in the hotel's ballroom – his swansong. Evita Peron, King Farouk of Egypt and the Shah of Persia have at one time or another slept easy in its beds, and among its literary guests it counted Thomas

Mann, Hermann Hesse and Mann's publisher and Ruth Landshoff's uncle Samuel Fischer.

The hotel forms the setting for Annemarie's *To See a Woman / Eine Frau zu sehen*, a short story remarkable for articulating a lesbian point of view in the same year as the publication of *The Well of Loneliness* and Virginia Woolf's *Orlando*. In this coming-out story Annemarie abandons the costume party of the heterosexual world and gives the reader a convincing picture of a twenty-year-old negotiating her sexual needs in a Belle Époque hotel:

> To see a woman: for a second only, a mere glance, only to lose her again somewhere down a dark corridor, behind a door that I cannot permit myself to open – but to see a woman and to feel in that same instant that she had spotted me too, her eyes lingering inquiringly as if meeting on the brink of the unknown ...[15]

The closed social world of the wealthy is Annemarie's backdrop, where women whisper and conspire, men vie for their attention and where an undercurrent of lesbian desire parries the feints and thrusts of the heterosexual mating game. 'I have already cautioned you how perilous it is to flout society's judgement of this woman and how dangerous it is to cast aside the moral boundaries erected to uphold the necessarily strict conventions ... I urge you to weigh carefully and be circumspect.'[16]

While Annemarie touted around her other fiction at this time, she kept back this much franker story, suggesting a degree of auto-censure on her part and awareness of the narrative tricks that would make her stories 'pass' – the technique of straightwashing. The date on the typescript – 24 December 1929 – places its genesis close to Annemarie's first encounter with Ruth Landshoff at the end of 1929 or January 1930 in St. Moritz.

> Annemarie was very pretty. Her head was a Donatello David head, her blonde hair was smooth and cut like a boy's. Her blue eyes dark and slow moving, her mouth childish and soft, with shyly parted lips. She wore a skirt and a boy's shirt and a blue blazer and she was not afraid of my dog.[17]

Vollmoeller and Landshoff had been leading a charmed life for many years: 'Winter months in St. Moritz in the Palace never really for long.

Fall in the Salzkammergut. Summer starting in the South of France, finishing in Venice. Trips all around Europe. A few days, a few weeks in Amsterdam, in Basel, in Paris, in Vienna, in Salzburg. Once at least every year in Nice in the Ruehl or the Negresco.'[18] Harry Graf Kessler in his diary refers to Vollmoeller's ground-floor flat behind the Brandenburg Gate as 'Harem on the Pariser Platz', whose visitors occasionally had to enter and leave by the window. Film director Géza von Cziffra mentions in his memoirs the revolving door of Vollmoeller and Landshoff's bedroom:

> She was pretty and charming, endowed with many talents of body and, fortuitously, mind. Both men and women loved her, and she responded in kind. … She had a way of picking up young girls, sorting them out, and the chosen ones landed up in Vollmoeller's bed who then after an interlude passed them on to his friends. Like a second-hand car. When Vollmoeller with Landshoff and two or three pretty girls in tow turned up for five o'clock tea in the Eden Bar, people used to whisper: 'The Vollmoellers are out on a test-drive!'[19]

Matters came to a head in September 1930 when Annemarie, against her parents' wishes, drove to Venice to join Vollmoeller and Landshoff in the Palazzo Vendramin, a luxuriously appointed canalside hideaway of marble floors, coffered ceilings, grand fireplaces surmounted by stucco work. The palace had been Richard Wagner's last residence, where he died in 1883. In Venice Ruth rubbed shoulders with the Princesse de Polignac, of Proust fame, and with the Marchesa Luisa Casati, who kept a pair of cheetahs on a leash and sometimes a live snake as a necklace, with a black manservant in tow. The Princess, née Winnaretta Singer, the American sewing-machine heiress, was a grande dame of the Belle Époque put out to grass in the inter-war years. She had married not one but two princes, the second the penniless Prince Edmond de Polignac, conceived in prison, homosexual and in need of a steady income: the pope blessed their union. Like Christa Winsloe, whom Landshoff also knew, Singer was lesbian, in yet another society *mariage blanc* with European nobility – 'the union of the lyre and the sewing machine' as Madame Émile Blanche wagged.

A sequence of photos taken by Vollmoeller on this occasion shows Annemarie in white drawstring pants and linen shirt, looking boyish, with

Ruth Landshoff and Annemarie, photographed by Karl Vollmoeller, Palazzo Vendramin, Venice, September 1930
Deutsches Literaturarchiv (DLA) Marbach

Landshoff mooning at her. (Other photos in the archive show Landshoff nude, as well as a topless sequence taken of Josephine Baker; Vollmoeller was quite the shutterbug.)[20] Among those present were the photographer and model Doris von Schönthan, who later joined the French Resistance, Ursula von Zedlitz, half-English, half-German translator and writer, and the Princesse de Polignac herself. This was a smart, eclectic sisterhood. Returning via Munich, Annemarie unwisely spilled the beans to Emmy Krüger – who might be expected to be in awe of the Wagner connection but whose reaction no doubt was conveyed to Bocken:

> She sullies her parents' name in this filth! Was in Venice with Vollmoeller and his ladies – and the shamelessness of the goings-on made my blood freeze. She is sick – insane, as I said years ago – I see no good future for this child. I do pity Renée and Alfred.[21]

Annemarie herself told her mother, the parents drew a line in the sand and she was grounded for the duration. While her behaviour may have been in question, it was the infamous reputation of the principal players that was at issue. In a letter to Erika Mann, whom Annemarie had just met in Munich, she gave her account of her mother's reaction:

> I told Mama all about Venice, since it's pointless anyway … Mama threw everything back at me, namely, that if I continue to have anything to do with Vollmoeller and R. (as was the previous bone of contention), my parents will cut me off, that I am also degrading myself and – above all, that I hand a personal triumph (cue violin strings) to those in the Palace for having gone there to spite my parents' express opposition.[22]

This, of course, is a standard parent–child dispute about disreputable friends leading youth astray. Nonetheless, a breach had been opened and the financial screws tightened. Annemarie was beginning to encounter like-minded friends – politically devil-may-care, sexually polymorphous, reputationally dubious, connected to the moneyed end of the arts – who would prove helpful to her writing ambitions but also peel back the respectable veneer of heterosexual life. All of them in the coming years would feel the pinch of fascism and be obliged to seek the path of exile. The good-girl destiny mapped out for Annemarie had taken a turn towards high bohemianism, Weimar decadence and political resistance.

*

Returning from Venice via Munich in September 1930, Annemarie met Erika Mann for the first time. Klaus, Erika's brother, also became a good friend to Annemarie some months later. Annemarie was twenty-three and had been writing fiction with increasing seriousness since she was seventeen. Her association with the Mann siblings precipitated *Friends of Bernhard*, a first novel written quickly in the same year and published in June 1931 to some acclaim. The Manns constituted her most enduring friendships in a lifetime of emotional ups and downs, when many were uprooted and exiled or grew tired of her rich-girl antics and stormy personal weather.

She introduced herself in a letter to Erika as an aspiring writer and was invited to call at the Mann villa on Poschinger Strasse. The siblings had been in the limelight for a number of years, basking in reflected glory from their father, awarded the Nobel Prize for Literature in December

1929. Annemarie must have known too, from Ruth Landshoff and perhaps from other mutual acquaintances on the daisy chain, that Erika was lesbian and made no bones about it. 'I didn't know her before. She turned up in Munich and contacted me to arrange to meet. She wanted to be a writer and was interested in my brother Klaus's and my writing, and in her own as well, and wanted to talk about work. And so she came to my parents' house, Thomas and Katia Mann.'[23]

Thomas Mann, for his part, noted in his diary following Annemarie's visit: 'Strangely, if she were a boy, then she would have to be considered extraordinarily pretty', a comment typical of his gender-bending and of his own interest in boys. Mann was being fêted as the *grand homme*, the representative voice of his fractious country, a role he was always happy to fulfil with adroit grandiloquence.

Erika and Klaus Mann, 1927. Photo by Edward Wasou
Image courtesy of Wikimedia Commons

The Manns – parents and six children – were variously Bavarian bohemians, 'villa proletariat', or thoroughly bourgeois in habits of body and mind. They were a long way from the Prussian militarism of the Wille side of Annemarie's family. In the villa that Thomas Mann had built from the proceeds of his best-selling *Buddenbrooks*, each child had a personalized silver napkin ring. Erika was almost three years older than Annemarie and had behind her a half-career in the theatre, a spurious marriage to the rising actor of the day, Gustav Gründgens, and a harum-scarum world tour with her brother, in the course of which they had met the glamour-pusses of German Hollywood, traded on family celebrity, and finangled a book contract. She had the dark shiny Pringsheim eyes on her mother's Jewish side of the family, a dramatic chic mannishness and her own car. We get a glimpse of her allure for Annemarie in a short film clip dating from 1928, in which this *Dichterkind* promotes a forth-coming trip to Morocco, courtesy of Hapag-Lloyd Cruises who were footing the bill.[24] Dressed as a ship's guide or bellhop, in shirt, tie and mariner's cap, Erika radiates charm; winning face, the suit a size too big like a boy at high school graduation. At the time Annemarie fell for her, Erika was making a name for herself as a writer of articles and children's stories. Klaus also wrote, with a knack for publicity, but with more depth and verve than his sister. Jean Cocteau, knowing a thing or two about shallowness himself, described their posturing as 'a drama of frivolity'.[25] They were a kind of German literary brat pack.

That there was more to their meeting than dinner with the parents and a chat about writing is clear from the correspondence. The young people went to the Simplicissimus cabaret in Munich, the centre of bohemian life and a place to let one's hair down,[26] with Fred Pasternek, a mutual friend from Zurich, joining them.[27] Munich was an artistic and royal city, a Renaissance court gathering the peoples of the south-west, Bavaria and its hinterland. As V.S. Pritchett puts it, the German language here 'has less of the sergeant-major in it'.[28] Munich became a key stopping-off place for Annemarie over the next two years. She became acquainted with the writers, theatre people and painters around the Mann family. Upper Bavaria, with its lakes and proximity to the Austrian ski stations, was only half a day's drive from Switzerland.

Back home in Bocken, Annemarie had found her match. She addressed Erika as 'My big brother Eri, whom I love so much.'[29] This cosy acolyte vein continued in subsequent letters where it is clear that Annemarie has found refuge from rows with her parents sparked by the Venice visit. 'I talked to Father. Your long and kind-hearted letter helped me to put my case reasonably well. It was still very bitter.'[30] While Annemarie gave her parents her side of the story, Erika seems to have intervened on her behalf with Emmy Krüger in Munich. 'Too bad you are not here now to say a few words in my favour. You did that so well with Emmy Krüger – really fabulously decent of you.'[31] The Schwarzenbach parents exercised tough love and forbade Annemarie from travelling for the winter.

Annemarie was at pains to present herself to Erica as industrious. 'Today I've already written ten pages of what might become a novel, if I have enough patience and talent.'[32] The novel, *Friends of Bernhard*, grew apace and was completed in a two-month burst of intense writing. She saw it as an amplification of her Paris stories about young people café-hopping around the Left Bank and as a token of new-found friendship, an ambisexual roman à clef. Leaving the university library at nine or ten in the morning, she repaired to her father's quiet Zurich office where she wrote 'two, four, six hours at a stretch'.[33] Annemarie saw her short novel echoing Cocteau's *Les enfants terribles*. Signing off her letters to Erika with 'Your child A', she had found an alternative family, allies against her biological one. Cocteau's notion of youth living apart from parents, in a licentious clique, made its way into the new novel, and reflected Annemarie's own desire to put some distance between herself and her family:

> I think the boy Bernhard will be a similar 'type', but treated with more care, since he is just 17 and a typical 'younger brother', also he will at least have no opportunity to *strike an attitude*, which in the Parisian stories came off so suspiciously girlish (and, as some people noted, 'perverse' – as if such a loaded word could be bandied about so carelessly!)[34]

Annemarie sees herself as a child, the young brother, to Erika's older role; there is yearning but not much contentment. This gives pause to speculate, as Annemarie's first biographer does, how fulfilling the relationship may have been between the two young people. Erika had behind her one brief marriage to Germany's premier gay actor, Gustaf Gründgens, and another unconsummated one to England's gay poet, W.H. Auden, coming up. How deep did Annemarie's affair with Erika go? Lacking Erika's side of the correspondence, we don't know how recip-rocated nor how embodied Annemarie's feelings were.

A month into the two women's friendship, Annemarie had arranged a speaking engagement for Erika and Klaus at Zurich's Federal Polytechnic School in December, for an honorarium of 300 Swiss francs plus travel expenses. Writing from the student union, telephoning Erika, using fellow student Fred Pasternek as go-between, she was able to keep her connection with the Manns alive while being confined to Zurich.

Her correspondence with Erika provides a glimpse of a fairly packed day-to-day life. In October she entertained three Spanish princelings for lunch at Bocken and returned with them in her Victory to university lectures, escorted by police outriders.[35] On a later occasion she was stopped because of no lights and she took pride in being addressed by

Thea Frenssen and Annemarie, Bocken 1932
Courtesy of Zentralbibliothek Zürich

the policeman as 'young man'. She was nervous about her first public reading at the end of October at the Lyceum Club in Zurich, a women's club. Later in the term she drove up to the Dolder Grand for coffee with German ice-skating champion Thea Frenssen, finding common cause as women in a man's world: 'sometimes the only woman braving it out among fifteen men ... as she does'.[36] Frau Frenssen appears later in January 'frightfully graceful' on the skating rink at Suvretta-Haus in St. Moritz, where Annemarie joined her. Swooning after a duchess at the races in Geneva in November, Annemarie (riding a horse called Lady Lough) gives way to camp banter.[37] Her letters occasionally provide glimpses of how lesbian desire operated. The gilded world of hotels, celebrity and royalty, harking back to the nineteenth century, living on at the races in the twentieth, is at odds with her later image as a rebel defending the downtrodden. These were not the horses of Franz Marc's *Der Blaue Reiter* movement but the old Wilhelminian nags out for a late run before being put to pasture. Annemarie sits astraddle diverging worlds; her letters to Erika were written at Bocken and from the student union, but also from the Baur en Ville Hotel in Zurich and the Beau-Rivage Hotel in Geneva. While the Mann siblings, too, enjoyed a gilded youth, it was no match for Annemarie's. Their nickname for her was Princess Miro.

Erika's first two-day visit to Bocken passed off well with Renée. The daughter of the Nobel laureate knew how to comport herself and had her feet more on the ground than Annemarie, who was inclined to be flighty. The Manns gave their by-now standard talk on young German writers, with which they had regaled the American lecture circuit the year before. Annemarie was aware at this second meeting in the flesh that her ardour was not matched by Erika's, whose girlfriend at this time was the Munich actress Therese Giehse. While Annemarie initially wanted exclusive claim on Erika's affections, the more pragmatic and older Erika let her down gently – by August 1931, Annemarie mentions 'Frau Giehse' in the correspondence.

Shortly before meeting Annemarie, Klaus had been rehearsing his play *The Siblings* at the Münchner Kammerspiele, where it opened and quickly flopped in November 1930. Annemarie had wanted to travel to Munich for the première on 12 November but her father kiboshed the idea.[38] Klaus, too, was gay and grew close to Annemarie even as Erika was pulling away. He had just turned twenty-three, and already had behind him an aborted engagement to Pamela Wedekind, daughter of the playwright and a childhood friend. He had published short stories, children's stories, a novel about Alexander the Great and a play featuring lesbian lovers. The quintessential flâneur and littérateur, Klaus was at home in Europe's cities by night and day. 'Bliss it may have been then to be alive', writes Anthony Heilbut, 'to prowl the world's capitals in pursuit of drugs and pretty boys, to party with Garbo and commune with Gide.'[39] Klaus's description of his youth in Munich, Berlin and Paris gives a flavour of the libertine atmosphere that drew Annemarie to the Mann children and allowed her to feel more at home with them than in gnomic Zurich:

> ... we want narcotics and kisses to forget our wretchedness. Let's go to bed with each other! Or fool around in the parks if there are no beds. Boys with girls, boys with boys, girls with girls, men with girls and boys, women with men or boys or girls or tamed little panthers – what's the difference? Let's embrace each other! Let's dance![40]

Klaus's rackety life in hotels on both sides of the Atlantic became a model for Annemarie, whose own life was soon to turn peripatetic. He epitomizes the revolt against the generation of the fathers, in aesthetic, political and sexual matters, characterized by inter-war youth, as historian Peter Gay has identified: 'When we think of Weimar, we think of modernity in art, literature, and thought; we think of the rebellion of sons against fathers: Dadaists against art, Berliners against beefy philistinism.'[41] Annemarie was ripe for this agenda and her encounters with Erika and Klaus in Munich and Zurich accentuated a revolt already underway. As power shifted from Weimar to the National Socialists, these children of the revolution were instrumental in combating fascism and lending their voices to the German diaspora in opposition to Hitler.

*

Annemarie's supervisor for her doctoral thesis in history[42] was Karl Meyer, a specialist in the Middle Ages attached to the university and to Zurich's technical institute, ETH. He held firmly against National Socialism, at the time growing contentious across the border in Bavaria.

Her chosen area of research was the history of the Upper Engadine in the Middle Ages and the early Modern Era and she went about it with typical zeal. She knew the region well from her school days in Fetan but also from frequent visits to St. Moritz. While she researched in the cantonal archives in Chur, the geographer Albrecht Haushofer helped with maps and Professor Burckhardt loaned her books.

The small community under study was the Romansh-speaking Rhaetian people of the canton of Graubunden in south-east Switzerland. Annemarie took issue with the one-sided view of the Engadine as part of the German sphere of influence, seeing it as a cultural crossroads between Latin and Germanic cultures, what we might now call a 'liminal space' – the Engadine mountain world literally straddling Roman *limes*. In contesting a German-centric view, she was up against political nostrums – *Volk*, *Rassenkunde* (the pseudo-science of race) – then gaining currency among faculty and students in German universities. Five years after the Locarno Treaty which had settled national borders, a disgruntlement with foreigners deciding its fate had resurfaced in Germany.

She had sufficient belief in Burckhardt's judgement and influence to show him her early stories and sketches – a confidence not misplaced since Burckhardt forwarded her work to the editor of Amalthea. This Vienna-based publishing house at the time acted as a counter-offensive to the rise of Bolshevik influence. By 6 February 1931, she knew her novel *Friends of Bernhard* had been accepted and slated for publication in June.

Alfred's grounding was no longer in force. Staying once more at Suvretta-Haus, she expected Vollmoeller to be in his usual residence at Badrutt Palace in St. Moritz, but he was ill. Ruth Landshoff had married David Graf Yorck von Wartenburg in December 1930, a society marriage much put about in the magazines, though, curiously, Annemarie makes no mention of it.

Her dissertation submitted and university requirements met in April 1931, Annemarie had reached the end of her studies. One of her last assignments was on Georg Trakl, an Austrian poet who had, like Annemarie, a troubled relationship with drugs and died of a cocaine overdose in a military hospital at the beginning of the First World War, age twenty-six. Annemarie had moved into Zurich in order to better concentrate on her work for her finals. As light relief she walked in the garden and read

Thomas Mann's essays. She drove to Munich with Valerie Korrbrunner, from there to Paris with Hanna Kiel, both of them staying somewhat indisposed at the Hotel Matignon, and then south to the Riviera for a long weekend to meet up with Klaus Mann who was enjoying the late spring weather. Her years of wanderlust had begun.

*

The Mann siblings were under contract to write *The Riviera Book* in the Piper travel series, capitalizing on their knowledge of the newly fashionable south of France.[43] When Korrodi showed Annemarie the 'sulphur yellow' cover illustration by Walter Trier, he had enough confidence in her to ask her to co-write the proposed Swiss volumes of this new automobile-friendly guidebook. Annemarie quickly took to the travel writing genre, which she would make her own over the coming decade. Hanging around Suzie's Bar in Bandol at Pentecost and in Sanary-sur-Mer, she wrote '*Brief von der Côte d'Azur*'[44] (Letter from the Côte d'Azur) which appeared in the *NZZ* in June. She tried out a Sunday supplement style, name-dropping and trend-spotting, presenting a chic Riviera for her readership.

In Sanary, beginning to become a watering hole for the German anti-Nazi diaspora, she met car enthusiast and young writer Sybille Bedford – then known as Sybille von Schoenebeck. Bedford describes the exhilaration of being alive with wheels at the end of the third decade of the twentieth century:

> Cars were cheap enough, manageable enough, worked well enough to be bought and used with insouciance. One could take a chum, a girl, a suitcase, set out on a fine morning, start in the cool of night, *comme le coeur vous en dise*. ... Suddenly there was choice; the world had opened up, even the world twenty miles beyond one's doorstep.[45]

Futurism and speed defined the new decade. Annemarie's life was beginning to pick up momentum, shuttling between Paris, Zurich, Venice and Nice. Klaus Mann's novel *Treffpunkt im Unendlichen* (1932) – 'Vanishing Point' – written quickly in the summer of 1931, introduces a character called Annemarie. The narrator first spots her in a carriage of the Berlin–Paris express:

The young girl was called Annemarie and was apparently heading to Paris to train as a fashion illustrator. She had been brought up by an aunt who had tried to palm her off – the girl's parents had disappeared in South America – and had left her with a monthly allowance of one hundred and fifty marks.[46]

The girl crosses his path again a year later, at the end of the novel, in the Dôme café in Montparnasse:

He noticed she had become leaner in the face, her mouth fuller, and also more tarted up than before. Her watery-blue eyes were brightly shadowed – dove-grey shadows, thought Sebastian. The grey dress somewhat tight and rather worn. But the bright red neckerchief set it off jauntily. 'She has learned', thought Sebastian. 'Yes indeed. She's gone to bed, in the meantime, with quite a few men, some for money, others for pleasure. My guess is about twenty or thirty. Last time I met her, she was still a virgin …'.[47]

Klaus's fictional Annemarie is a cypher for change, for the frenzy of the Weimar interlude. They drink a few Pernods and end up in a dancehall in the rue de Lappe. She has learned to drink cherry brandies and cognacs. She beds a sailor. There was a vogue among women in the 1920s for the marine look, as Sybille Bedford recalled: 'she wore sailor trousers, and a little scarlet singlet that left bare the back and the athletic arms, shells on her ears and more shells about her neck'.[48] In planning what to wear for the Munich carnival in February, Annemarie informed Erika that a sailor suit 'is decidedly my favourite suit for such occasions and the costume most suitable for any eventuality!!'[49]

Klaus wasn't the only writer at the time rendering Annemarie in fiction, an indication of her effect on men and women alike. In *Die Goldene Horde* (1931), Wilhelm Speyer imagines her as a fifteen-year-old runaway from school called Annemarie, who joins a travelling circus as a performer. Richard, a classmate, is charged with finding her:

A year ago, she had been a rather unremarkable schoolgirl whom nobody paid any attention to … a petite child, nimble and unpretentious; there was a slight oriental cast to her complexion that suited the circus; black, closely cropped hair but not too short, parted on the side.[50]

A second Speyer novel, *Sommer in Italien* (1932), captures a more overtly lesbian figure. The narrator and his friend Dorothy encounter a young writer of unsettling beauty, 'a lovely Sappho adept' together with a brother and sister nicknamed 'the children', who entertain the company with rapid-fire, sharply enunciated repartee: 'they worshipped at the altar of the clipped syllable, to which they paid divine service'. The witty infamous siblings are clearly Erika and Klaus, who affected this manner of speaking, and the attractive lesbian is Annemarie in this roman à clef. Speyer fell under her charm until he too realized that she wasn't interested.

Returning to Bocken from her French travels in mid-June, Annemarie became embroiled in another parental row. In Bavaria the National Socialists were on the march and squabbling with Communists. The Nazis were anathema to Annemarie's new friends, many of whom came from assimilated Jewish families, whereas Renée's politics had become emboldened. She had followed Hitler's rise through the Munich beer halls and was largely sympathetic to his message of restoring German might following the humiliation of the Treaty of Versailles. Like many genteel Nazis, Renée tempered her views where the violence and excesses of Hitler's followers were concerned, disapproving of their coarse Jew-baiting. Her accusation of 'moral depravity'[51] levelled at Annemarie at this time was no doubt coloured by politics but also showed Renée turning a blind eye to the larger depravity gaining ground across the border. 'Where do I belong? *Why don't Papa or Mama actually speak to me?*'[52] was Annemarie's response to these recriminations. She took refuge with Erika, holidaying at Walchensee in the Bavarian Alps, where politics was very much on the menu and where most likely Annemarie first met Erika's girlfriend Therese Giehse. The writer Bruno Frank, a neighbour and friend of the Mann family, was also there. Renée became infuriated at the leftist, Jewish and lesbian company her daughter was keeping. Annemarie's letter home flaunts a certain defiant tone, mentioning Frank's view that Nazi politics was 'to blame'[53] for the recent brawls in Bavaria. The knives were out.

*

Begun in September of the previous year and finished in two months, *Freunde um Bernhard* (*Friends of Bernhard*) was published in spring

1931 by Almathea Verlag. Annemarie's letter to Albrecht Haushofer downplays its completion:

> ... only a thick manuscript of a short novel, which I'm not sure you would be all that interested in: adolescent characters, blunt and 'human' in their needs, insecure and immature they certainly are.[54]

Despite this modesty, she was anxious about its reception. Annemarie sketched her characters for Erika: 'The youngster Gert, cowardly, insecure and impressionable. Christina and her handsome brother Leon – I wonder if you will like Christina, she's quite a strange creature – unscrupulous but forgivable ... I think my deepest sympathy goes out to Gert, this cowardly, hideous boy.'[55] Bernhard's friends are arty, willowy young men, feisty women and protective adults. Just turned seventeen, he has the face of a child, and is a music student in Paris whose favourite composer is Bach.

The setting is the Latin Quarter, with excursions to Berlin and Lugano, the way-stations of the young, idle rich. Annemarie's bright studios and hazy bars seem a bohemian leftover from a nineteenth-century novel, unreal and already out of date by the end of the *années folles*, with their burnt sugar smell of 'Crêpes Suzette'.[56] Bernhard's friends talk about love but the novel's englamoured relationships don't succumb to passion and remain curiously sexless; there's no oil paint on the sheets. The novel recalls Klaus Mann's first play, *Anja and Esther*, about the polymorphously perverse affections of four boys and girls loosely based on his sister Erika, Pamela Wedekind, Ricki Hallgarten and himself. Annemarie's young characters are similarly self-regarding, cushioned by art and money.

While all her characters are young, they don't quite break free of their autobiographical moorings. Following a row about who's got the most talent, Gert returns to Berlin and the siblings head to Florence. Gert begins to reminisce about their time in the south, evoking chianti bottles, donkeys and hotel balconies:

> In an osteria smelling of olive oil and salami, they had grilled fish. That night Leon drank a lot of wine. The straw-covered bottle sat on the table, the cloth stained. They were sitting out on the terrace and street sounds rose from below.

A cat roamed the tables with a mewling cry and they slipped him pieces of bread and pasta and Gert took him in his arms and stroked his marmalade fur.[57]

In Paris, Bernard feels abandoned by his friends and by the older somewhat louche men and women who have taken him under their wing. Betsy, an American in Europe and a musician like him, is heading home, as many did when the bottom had fallen out of the economy in 1929. In the novel's final pages Bernhard wanders a Latin Quarter quay alone, observing the schoolboys whose ranks he has now left:

It must be five, class over, a tide of little boys in black school smocks crossed the junction noisily, their grimy berets sitting well back on small heads, on a shock of dark mussed hair. They whistle and throw stones. A few knots of quieter boys make their way, chatting among themselves like the middle schoolers they are. They're pallid, grey-skinned around the eyes. Bernhard watches them as they go.[58]

Erika pointed out to Annemarie the novel's similarity with André Gide's *Counterfeiters*: 'You must be right, but it must have been subconscious, since I haven't read *The Counterfeiters* for many years. And now I see that it has a character called Bernard. Oh oh!'[59]

Ruth Landshoff summed up this first novel's reception:

Her first book was published and got benevolent notices in Austria and Germany and rapturous ones in Switzerland. In that book only a few passages showed her dignified and delightful prose. Most of it was about the intricate pattern of difficulties among a group of certain young people who most probably were fashioned after real life persons. Everyone was terribly sensitive.[60]

The 'clicking latch of a *roman à clef*', as Julian Barnes calls it, is heard only by those in the know, and time throws the key away. Annemarie's young people have been let loose in the props room and are trying on the costumes. The camped-up transvestite quality of her characters recalls girls playing princes and courtiers in a school performance. She had found a way to write herself into men or boys who liked other boys or who were indeterminate. Women dressing as men had long been a way to gain entrance to the wider world: it provided a hitherto forbidden entrée to Georges Sand; when nineteenth-century female factory workers discovered that male workers were paid double the wages of women, they disguised themselves accordingly; Virginia Woolf's *Orlando* enacts the same conceit. Colette, Missy, Marlene Dietrich and Mae West all played with such theatrical gender-bending. Areti Georgiadou, Annemarie's biographer, picks up this motif of disguise, of drag:

> The literary device of the androgynous young protagonist or narrator allows the author to insinuate herself without having to pretend to herself as a woman. Their very boyishness gives them licence to behave as the author wishes and, though ostensibly male, they never become virile. They remain

Annemarie before driving to Berlin, 19 September 1931. Photo by Renée Schwarzenbach
Courtesy of Zentralbibliothek Zürich

young, innocent and sexually indeterminate, representing an unfallen state –
an idealized child as an incarnation of utopia, an expression of the desire for
original purity.[61]

By August 1931 Annemarie was well underway with her next book,
titled *Autumn Departure*, a manuscript that has been lost. In the same
month she spent two days in Salzburg with Erika and worked in a breezy
house style on the *Piper Guide to Switzerland*. Professor Burckhardt
proposed some research work in Berlin, giving an air of legitimacy to
Annemarie's move there in September. It was a city that had been in her
sights for some time.[62] Renée agreed to let her go on condition that she
stay at a cousin's house in Frohnau. She photographed her departing
daughter with one foot on the running board, hand on the car door
handle, ready for the road. Dr. Annemarie Schwarzenbach at twenty-
three is wearing her good-girl outfit – sleeveless v-neck sweater over a
white blouse, wrap-around skirt covering the knees, sheer stockings,
Mary-Janes with Cuban heels and a narrow strap, not yet dusty from
driving. She could be heading off to the convent but instead she is a
young novelist with her sights set on Berlin.

4

Closet of Selves

'Well, really, darling', she said, because I was clearly puzzled, 'if it's not about a couple of old bull-dykes, what the hell is it about?'[1]

Truman Capote, *Breakfast at Tiffany's*

The premiere of a steamy lesbian boarding school drama, *Mädchen in Uniform* (*Girls in Uniform*), took place at the Gloria Palast in Berlin on the evening of 27 November 1931. The director of its all-female cast, Leontine Sagan, had pulled off a first that still resonates with a queer cinema audience a hundred years later. The setting is a school in Potsdam for the daughters of Prussian army officers and nobles. Fourteen-year-old motherless new girl Manuela von Meinhardis falls for a beautiful teacher, Frau von Bernburg. The teacher crosses a line by giving the girl one of her petticoats; pash becomes passion. A school performance turns to anarchy when the servants spike the punch and Manuela drunkenly declares her love. The film's psychodrama ends with Manuela's attempted suicide foiled by last-minute schoolgirl solidarity.

Christa Winsloe, Baroness von Hatvany, a Munich-based friend of the Mann family and well known in the lesbian subculture of both cities, wrote the successful play on which the film was based. Erika Mann had a minor part in the film. The leading actress who played the besotted teen, twenty-three-year-old Hertha Thiele, recalled half a century later:

The whole of *Mädchen in Uniform* was set in the Empress Augusta boarding school, where Winsloe was educated. Actually there really was a Manuela who remained lame all of her life after she threw herself down the stairs. She came to the premiere of the film. I saw her from a distance, and at the time Winsloe told me, 'The experience is one which I had to write from my heart'. Winsloe was a lesbian. She was not even sixteen when she married Baron von Hatvanyi.[2]

Despite the film's taboo-breaking, by November 1931 Prussian family values and militarism were back for a return fight following a decade of Weimar hanky-panky. The balance of German power had shifted towards the right and pugilists were emboldened. Many of the cast of *Mädchen in Uniform* were Jewish and forced to slip from public and professional life as the decade advanced. Director Leontine Sagan left Berlin shortly afterwards for England and then South Africa, while her first film was banned under the Nazis. Christa Winsloe, exiled in France, joined the Resistance and died in 1944. Emilia Unda, playing the headmistress, was a Latvian Jew who died in Berlin in 1939. Walter Supper, the film's assistant director, refused under Nazi pressure to divorce his Jewish wife. When it was clear she would be arrested – he shot her, himself and his dog rather than face separation. Walter Froelich, the film's producer and senior artistic director, joined the National Socialists and became president of the film corporation under Goebbels. Two years after the premiere of *Mädchen in Uniform*, all that Weimar high-jinks disappeared with the snap of a garter strap.[3]

Hertha Thiele strips away the social veneer of this select group of theatre people, the lesbian sisterhood which packed the neo-baroque cinema on the Kurfürstendamm:

> Christa Winsloe did not really have to confront social ostracism because she was very well-off. At the time of the Weimar Republic whoever had money could allow themselves everything. It was the same if you were in a high position. Therese Giehse, who had quite a reputation at the Munich Kammerspiele, and Erika Mann, no-one gave a damn what they did. It would have been different if it had been some poor devil.[4]

At the end of that first screening of *Mädchen in Uniform* there was silence for a minute before tumultuous applause broke out. Thiele describes the production team and cast as 'sitting there like lame ducks'. They were sitting ducks in more ways than one.

*

Arriving late to the party in September 1931, Annemarie spent just over a year in Berlin. She had hopes of establishing herself as a writer but a combination of illness, restlessness and political change meant that she never quite settled in the German capital. Her feeling of achievement and purpose was justified: academic honours, a first novel published and well received, some journalism work, a circle of well-connected literary friends. However, in a letter to Erika from Berlin, Annemarie mentions a 'nervous breakdown'[5] – though this may have been exhaustion from the previous year of writing, study and travel. A sense of a soul adrift haunts her letters at this time, as vagabonding and emotional instability begin to take hold. The promise of sexual liberation that the city held for so many was stymied by her own demons.

After two weeks with her cousin's family in the garden suburb of Berlin-Frohnau, Annemarie found her bearings and moved into an apartment on Hohenzollernstrasse, south of the city in Zehlendorf. Presumably it was more *Sturmfrei* – where the landlady didn't object to visitors – than her cousin's home from home.

Sybille Bedford described Berlin on the cusp of National Socialism:

> It was, one must realise, less than a year before Hitler came to power. There *was* an ominous feeling about the country (I am sure this is not mere hindsight); in Berlin people appeared to be both restless and resigned, waiting for *anything* to happen, revolution from the extreme left or right, and in either case a cataclysmic breakdown of the social order.[6]

Klaus Mann's diary allows us to track Annemarie's movements during this period when the two nighthawks deepened their relationship. The Manns shared a flat with others on Rankestrasse; the artist Eva Herrmann, socialite Doris von Schönthan and Klaus's friend Willi Luschnat joined the party. Herrmann, an artist known for her caricaturing style, soon became part of the German diaspora in Sanary-sur-Mer where she was a close friend of Bedford. Doris von Schönthan, also a friend of Bedford's, has been described as tall, slender and fragile in the 1920s flapper mode, somewhat nerve-racked, or as thin, witty, forgetful and ditzy. An orphan, adopted by dramatist and impresario Franz von Schönthan, she made her name as a model, photographer and twenties girl about town. Like her friend Ruth Landshoff, and others in Annemarie's Berlin circle, she was of Jewish or part-Jewish origin. Herrmann, Bedford and Landshoff were all lesbian to varying degrees. Klaus Mann described his boyfriend Willi Luschnat, sometimes identified as a dancer: 'We had fun together: he was a nice enough chap; good-natured, lazy, naive. His vitality refreshed me, and I was amused by his amazing ignorance.'[7]

The neophyte Annemarie couldn't have been in better hands than Klaus's, who had written from experience about the city's gay underworld as far back as his first novel, *The Pious Dance* (1926), and had worked there as a drama critic. They kicked off the weekend at the Katakombe, a cabaret catering to an arty clientèle. Klaus and Erika had been on the radio in the morning, went for lunch with the publisher Max Fischer, and got back on the airwaves again in the evening, talking up their recent Moroccan trip. They dined with Annemarie at the Taverne, a working-class bar, and continued their *Dielen-Bummel* – pub-crawl – to the Jockey Bar in Charlottenburg, which saw the likes of Gide, Cocteau and Marlene Dietrich cavorting at its tables. The pianist Ernst Engel mixed jazz and classical numbers, there was a regulation black dancer and 'a little blond sailor girl dancing on the grand piano and belting out chansons and songs in a thin voice with bold gestures'.[8] Later still, Klaus accompanied Annemarie to Ariane, a new lesbian bar, where there were 'lesbian complications' which Klaus doesn't elucidate.[9] Erika apparently called it a night, leaving Klaus to escort Annemarie; all that brotherly love in the women's letters seems not to have materialized. This *beau monde* party of writers' children, flappers and their hangers-on began the evening in the modish cabaret world with its already well-established performative codes where 'the men are women / and the women men'.[10] The night ended in a new lesbian bar, with Annemarie leading the way.

Contemporary written accounts of gay nightlife in Berlin between the wars are hard to come by. Ruth Landshoff gives a flavour:

A bar in the Friedrichsgracht [sic], a lovely part of old Berlin, where the guests were often criminals. … Here we met occasionally young boys who had run away from reform school and we helped them stay out and sometimes helped hide them. … And Johnny's night club became together with the Jockey our private playground.[11]

On 19 October Klaus took tea with Annemarie and the artist Baron Rudolf von Ripper, an adventurer who had travelled to Syria and China and was married to 'Mopsa' Sternheim. Mopsa and Ripper were morphine users, as was Klaus. He had taken opium with Cocteau in

Paris, overdosed on hashish in Morocco with Erika and it wasn't long before Annemarie's casual drug use escalated.

The Mann circle remained circumspect in their private lives, not confiding much to diaries and letters and expressing their sexuality in the shadows. Bourgeois convention ruled, at least by day. The society women among Annemarie's friends, many belonging to or married into German nobility, had good reason to cloak their desires. They kept up chic respectable appearances: promoting writing careers, navigating the world of the arts, visits to family and being fashionable together. They had much to lose by attracting scandal – as some of them learned to their cost. Many had family funds or were married to wealthy men. They were not a bohemian crowd – more *jeunesse dorée*, with all the privilege that entailed in a Berlin marked by deflation and now economic depression. The precise degree of openness about sexuality among these good-time girls is hard to estimate. Male homosexuality remained illegal under Paragraph 175 of the German code and blackmail was an ever-present threat; lesbianism was not on the statute books. Willi, Klaus's boyfriend, is without surname in the diary; nonetheless, the relationship went deep and Klaus sought out the ex-Brownshirt after the war. Annemarie didn't write directly about her Berlin lesbian experience, except for glancing references in letters to Erika, just as she never mentioned in writing nor advocated directly for female suffrage in Switzerland. Her fiction played peek-a-boo with the closet and her journalism only became overtly political later on. Annemarie may also have been wary of her mother reading her letters; a woman who burns your letters when you're dead is likely to read one or two of them while you're still alive. Ruth Landshoff's memoirs, written decades after the war, take up this ontological question: how does maturity and moral tidiness look back at youth?

> Sordid … It depends who is looking at it. Or when. I looking at it then sideways not giving it a thought felt flattered, special, recognized. Today I wrinkle my nose. How horrid. Today I say how horrid these parties. Booze and cocaine. Call girls and trade boys. Or do I say that? No, I don't. I have become older but not a moralist in the bourgeois sense.[12]

Besides the Jockey and the Ariane, the lesbian bars Annemarie frequented were located around Nollendorfplatz in Berlin West. The

Maly und Igel kept its corner door discreetly open for six years at Lutherstrasse 16 with a sign that said 'Closed for Private Party'. It was selective and well established by the time Annemarie made her entrance and met Maly, one of the Jewish owners, and Ingel, her partner. The club seated about sixty customers, featured hot jazz and a dance floor with flashing red lights. It was a 'favourite hangout for lesbian artists, intellectuals, singers, stage actresses, and film stars. Lesbians working for Max Reinhardt's theatre organizations often stage birthday celebrations here.'[13] The actress Louise Brooks recalled its denizens as 'a choice of feminine or collar-and-tie lesbians'.[14]

Erika returned to Munich leaving Annemarie to explore Maly und Igel, where she had become a regular.[15] By the end of October and ten days sick in bed, Annemarie was well aware that all-night binges, alcohol and sentimental liaisons had taken their toll. She refers to 'the whole passionate affair with Ursula'[16] as a contributing cause of her breakdown but she had never been strong and illness was to dog her for the rest of her days.

*

Rheinsberg lies on a lake about an hour's drive north-west of Berlin. Frederick the Great built a castle here and the town's faded grandeur – parkland, contemplative walks, garrison buildings, monuments to imperial glory – might seem reactionary as the locale for a literary retreat. On the evening of 8 November 1931, a Sunday, Annemarie drove in the dark from Berlin and took a room at the lakeshore Hotel Fürstenhof, with its deep trellised balconies in the spa style. In three weeks here she dashed off her second published book, *Lyric Novella*. Like its male narrator, she was attempting to get over an infatuation for a Berlin barmaid, as remembered by Ruth Landshoff: 'She was wildly attracted to a girl who served drinks at a little bar because that girl, Ursula, was entirely without principles in a rather serious and sulky manner.'[17] Ursula appears to have worked at Ariane, where Klaus mentioned some 'lesbian complication' in his diary for 18 October. Annemarie acknowledged that the affair – infatuation, two-night stand? – was complicated:

> Besides, I have no idea now what will become of it, everything is quite awkward, and Klaus has things much easier with his young chap [Willi].

Ursula came back here twice, it turned out quite friendly, and occasional visits to Ariane will no longer cost me an arm and a leg. But we will see, something just has to give, Ursula, or me, or the others.[18]

On arrival at Rheinsberg she slept fourteen hours, cried a bit, and reconciled herself to not having her way, suffering through the typical 'infatuation of a seventeen-year-old',[19] as described to Erika, who had become both shoulder to cry on and mother-nurse.

There is another contender, however, a second Ursula, mentioned in correspondence at this time: twenty-six-year-old Ursula von Hohenlohe-Oehringen, née Ursula von Zedlitz. London-born and bilingual, *this* Ursula was a society wife whose husband, a German prince born in Madrid, was fifteen years her senior. They married in January 1928 and divorced without issue in February 1931. At the time she met Annemarie in Venice, Ursula was working as a journalist. Annemarie calls her a 'very clever child' despite Ursula harbouring reservations about Annemarie's own writing. Both Erika and Ursula thought Annemarie was 'totally pampered' and self-indulgent.[20] Annemarie's princess manner boded ill for future relationships. Which of the two Ursulas did Annemarie fall for, precipitating the writing of *Lyric Novella*? Perhaps the fictional barmaid Sibylle is a conflation of both real-life infatuations.

There was a good deal of soul-searching at Rheinsberg; about writing, but also about the emotional impasse in which the author felt trapped. *Friends of Bernhard* had been an exploration of the 'seventeen-complex', a phrase Annemarie uses at least twice to mean her emotional immaturity, but perhaps also her daughterly role vis-à-vis older women. That she was well aware of her youthful appearance is clear from a comment in a later letter to Anita Forrer: 'You know, I have always resisted growing up and becoming adult, with the result that it shows: although I now no longer have a youthful or baby face, and don't behave like a child either, most people are tempted – if they like me – to see me as younger, half-treating me as a child.'[21] At twenty-three she needed to move beyond teenage infatuation into the more give-and-take affairs of the heart.

It was 'colder than a gravedigger's ass in the damp autumn woods'[22] around Rheinsberg. *Lyric Novella* is a winter's tale, executed quickly on impulse. (In the same months she wrote another novel, now lost, titled

Aufbruch im Herbst.) The surviving novella follows a nameless twenty-year-old foreign affairs student as he shuttles between a well-to-do Berlin world (servants, diplomatic reception, aristocratic antecedents, snazzy car) and cabaret nightlife (the promise of sex, drugs, *Verbrecherkneipen* or thieves dens). He finds himself infatuated with a chanteuse called Sibylle. Her lack of interest in him makes him seem pathetic, the archetypal romantic john caught in the machinations of an older, more experienced woman working a nightclub. *Lyric Novella*'s chief disguise is our old friend gender-flipping, masquerade or veiling.[23] Writing to a critic after the novella's publication, Annemarie made her veiling clear: 'the twenty-year-old hero is not a hero, not a young man, but a young woman'.[24] This is a lesbian affair, the pronouns switched, with some implausibility in its drama.

The narrative moves at speed between apartments and bars in nocturnal Berlin and a quiet village where our lovelorn student has gone to ground. Like Annemarie, the narrator is proud of his wheels and not without rich-boy smugness. 'I paid a third of it with my earnings, and my father paid for the other two thirds.' Where these 'earnings' come from is not explained. Littered with hints and double-entendres, Annemarie's recent literary and lesbian acquaintances in Berlin appear in disguise. A friend called Magnus, ill in bed, seems to have a more than perfunctory relationship with the concierge's son: 'a pale and thin boy of about eighteen years of age who cooks and tends to all Magnus' needs'. The boy is solicitous; Magnus maternal; 'They say *Du* to each other'.[25] This couple appears to be based on Klaus Mann and his teenaged Willi. Another character, Frau von Niehoff – no hope there – provides a shoulder to cry on and a key to her apartment. She is unsatisfactorily married, with a child, like her real-life counterpart, Edith von Schmidt-Pauli, one of those older, married-to-power women willing to listen to Annemarie's angst. Schmidt-Pauli's husband was a writer and Nazi flunkey in the propaganda ministry, who would later cause Annemarie some difficulty.[26] A photo of the beloved chanteuse above the narrator's desk shows her 'wearing short trousers and an open-neck shirt with a bold check pattern. Her pale face was exaggeratedly lit, making it almost look like a mask.'[27] Sibylle is cruel, 'a very female cruelty: that was often said to warn me'. When she sings, she is like 'a Gothic angel except a trace more boyish because of her narrow hips'. Sibylle takes the narrator to a working-class gay bar with purple wallpaper and an underworld atmosphere:

> Apart from us there was only one other couple sitting at a table in the room: the man was tall and grossly fat, and the woman had black curly hair like a Negress, and was heavily made-up. She was the only woman here besides Sibylle, but Sibylle said she was a man in drag.[28]

Sibylle doesn't quite cohere as a character, and appears to have more in common with the barmaid than with the princess Ursula. 'Nothing holds us together but I am steeped in her presence' describes an infatuation, a crush, but when pressed towards a physical rapport, the narrator does little more than wax lyrical. Towards the end of this eighty-page novella it suddenly emerges that Sybille has a child, whose father is a drug dealer, and she wants money or stability. '"You have to do something for me", she said. "I only thought of it today. You have to sign that you will provide for the child."' This is clearly a shake-down and throughout there are intimations of dominance and power. Sibylle is not putting out and the narrator realizes that 'she didn't love me and it was as painful as if I'd already lost her'. The astute reader will already have come to this conclusion long before.

Lyric Novella is written in a kind of *style blanc* that would gain distinction in the work of Albert Camus after the war, though he borrowed his short, declarative sentences and affectless rhetoric from the hard-boiled Americans: James Cain's *The Postman Always Rings Twice*, Hemingway and Chandler. Annemarie too had been reading Hemingway, as Klaus Mann pointed out in his review of the novella.[29]

There is another level to this novella, one hinted at through choice of setting, though never named by Annemarie's protagonist. Kurt Tucholsky had published *Rheinsberg* in 1912, a short novel about a romantic couple, Wolfie and Claire, who escape for a weekend to the countryside. The novel proved a great success, is still in print over a century later, and has become a touchstone for young love but also for a romantic prelapsarian Germany, against which Annemarie's unhappy tale ironically plays. Like other aspects of her difficult second book, this correspondence with Tucholsky's better-known work seems undercooked.

*

Annemarie had been in Rheinsberg for a productive and restful three weeks. Back in Berlin in December, she played golf with art historian Hanna Kiel and resumed a busy social life in the company of writers and journalists Roby Frey, Hansi Sturm, Doris von Schönthan and Mopsa's husband, Rudolph von Ripper – known as Jack Ripper. Letters to Erika are angst-filled (*himmelangst*, underlined twice), full of soul-searching, taking rejection by Ursula von Hohenlohe as a bitter lesson learnt, and no longer believing 'that there is such a thing as happy love, it is always hideous, disillusioning and infinitely lonely'.[30]

Annemarie renewed contact with Maria Daelen, towards whom she gravitated when needing a shoulder to cry on. Daelen lived in Berlin-Charlottenburg and specialized in surgery, a field almost exclusively ring-fenced by men. The two friends frequented a similar social clique of well-to-do women, shared a liking for cars (Maria drove a red Ford Cabriolet) and were attracted to each other. Maria provided sympathy and medical care but, as with other friends, in the long run she grew tired of Annemarie's neediness, alcohol and drug intake.

Maria had a remarkable personality. And Annemarie fell in love with her in Berlin. … she was also someone who was very kind to Annemarie and helped her immensely, and then she too lost patience. Just like everybody else.[31]

Returning to Bocken for Christmas, Annemarie went out of her way to Munich to join the Mann family for dinner. Klaus had read and reviewed her *Friends of Bernhard* favourably. After barely two months in Berlin, she had sampled the nightlife, drunk too much, fallen in love, completed a novella and another book was underway. At home, Annemarie resumed her old pursuits: riding with mother and brother Hasi, visiting grandmother Clara, listening to the new portable gramophone and welcoming royalty. The Schwarzenbachs entertained two Spanish infanta-in-exile, Beatrix and Maria Christina, living partly in Lausanne following the proclamation of the Second Spanish Republic in April 1931. Princess Beatrix, then twenty-two, brought out Annemarie's best courtly manner. Renée no doubt got an edited account of life in Berlin. 'When I talked to her on the phone this morning, she was kind of upset because Fair-Enough didn't make the race. So, of course, she said I am morally unbalanced. It's always the same thing. As soon as something is wrong with the horses, she remembers how bad I am.'[32]

Despite her disapproval, Renée travelled on 10 January 1932 to St. Gallen with Hanna Kiel for a reading at a women's club from Annemarie's lost novel. Kiel, art historian in a lesbian circle, moved to Florence when Hitler came to power and remained there for the rest of her life; Renée was rooting for the Führer: driver and passenger were singularly ill-matched. Annemarie's reading went well but she was again coming down with a headache, sore throat and flu. This did not prevent her skiing in Arosa with Ursula von Hohenlohe, Kiel and others, staying in the Chalet Canols in Lenzerheide-am-See for most of January. She was keen to have Erika visit but Erika was nursing her own illness and perhaps wanted to pull back from Annemarie's intensity.

Back in Berlin after a restorative month in the mountains, Annemarie began reviewing film for the *NZZ*: Jean Cocteau's obscure, experimental *Blood of a Poet* (1932), *Battleship Potemkin* (1925), as well as Viktor Turin's 1929 documentary about Soviet railway workers, *Turksib (Turkistan to Siberia)*.[33] Russian films were enjoying a vogue at the beginning of the thirties and Annemarie's choice signals her interest in documentary, in the Soviet experiment, as well as in exotic travel: all portending the direction her writing and life would take. In January she weighed up various destinations – Persia, Mexico, Spain – with Hanna and Erika.[34] She visited the studios of UfA, the German film production company in the Berlin suburb of Babelsberg.[35] Her writing about film indicates she had thought about the importance of showing rather than telling, spotting its influence on Hemingway, with implications for her own writing:

> A writer such as Hemingway employs a very similar technique. He doesn't write: 'the man was very disappointed' but rather describes the man's body language, for example: 'he got up and left the room'. Such descriptions are interchangeable with a shooting script.[36]

Why did she not review the premier lesbian film of the period, *Mädchen in Uniform*? A glancing reference in a letter suggests she 'suffered agonies' watching it – perhaps from embarrassment at seeing her desires embodied on celluloid.[37] The film may simply have been too close to the bone.

In January Annemarie moved into Maria Daelen's apartment ('*provisorisch*') and after some weeks, into her own apartment nearby. Their friendship had evolved into an affair and quickly reverted to friendship. Annemarie was busy with research for the Piper guide in and around Lugano, and both Hanna Kiel and Maria Daelen accompanied her on these motoring trips from Berlin. Maria visited Bocken for the first time in late March and appears to have passed muster with Renée, who appreciated and was reassured by the doctor's friendship with her daughter.

German politics had begun to curtail freedoms and her stifling home life had awakened Annemarie's wanderlust. In January she wrote to Erika: 'I think one should quit Europe and the beaten path for a while.'[38] Later that month, Nazi stormtroopers broke up a Munich pacifist meeting where Erika was speaking, and the press mounted a vicious campaign of calumny against the whole Mann family. Writing from Bocken, Annemarie felt that her mother drained all the energy from her and the prospect of travel had become all the more an escape from suffocation at home. She was only twenty-four in the spring of 1932 when she joined Klaus and Erika, together with their childhood friend Ricki Hallgarten, in planning a journey overland to Persia. Grandmother Clara mentioned in her diary that Annemarie had switched 'her enthusiasm for all things modern to archeology'.[39] She researched their Persian trip with her usual thoroughness, sorting finances, visas and typhus shots, reading up on the Balkans, planning their route. This set the template for Annemarie's later journeys: travel as an escape from the domestic, in the footsteps of the legendary oriental travellers.

Ricki Hallgarten, however, was a different matter:

> The project of our Persian journey was just one of our devices to cheat Riki out of his suicide. We persuaded him to embark with us on an expedition with two cars ... Annemarie, 'the Swiss child', would join us. Wasn't it a grand, exciting idea? To get rid, for a while, of the whole mess here at home![40]

Departure was set for May 5. Klaus was feeling under the weather: in January he had tried morphine and cocaine in order to compare their effects, and had smoked opium with Cocteau. On May 4 they scheduled a press shoot advertising their trip for the Bavarian film company Emelka. The next day, after lunch – with Annemarie and Eva Herrmann present – Frau Mann took a phone call from Ammersee, where Riki kept a lakeside studio. He had shot himself in the heart, leaving a note that she should be contacted. The following day Erika and Klaus went to see the body and remarked on the blood stains all over the bedroom 'like the scattered fragments of a mysterious pattern – a last message, a warning, the writing on the wall'.[41] With the benefit of hindsight, Klaus in his memoirs couldn't help seeing his friend's suicide as a precursor of 'coming disasters'.

The oriental jaunt was off and the three remaining young people headed south to Venice. Munich actor Herbert Franz ('Babs') joined them.[42] They descended on the Hotel Metropole and changed to the Hotel des Bains on the Lido, where Mann senior had two decades earlier set *Death in Venice* on the eve of the First World War: 'its iridescent twilight, the Moorish dream of its architecture, the wistful song from the Grand Canal'.[43] The weather was momentarily hot and they enjoyed gondola and boat trips, *gelato* and *trattoria*, visits to museums and dressing up for dinner in the sumptuous hotel. It was here that Annemarie celebrated her twenty-fourth birthday.

Photographs, mostly taken by Babs, show the trio somewhat sombrely mugging at the camera. Annemarie's sharp fashion sense, youthful looks before morphine hardened her features, the draw of her peculiarly cold, affectless stare propagated her glamour decades later. In one Venice snap she sits scrunched between the Manns like a cosseted child in this chosen family, luggage at their feet, the stocky boatman at the tiller behind. Both Klaus and Erika are smoking, kitted out in summer whites. Erika's arm drapes over Annemarie's slight shoulder, the Swiss child slumped in her seat in a striped blazer and frock. She eyeballs the photographer with narrowed unsmiling eyes. In another snap Erika is draped around her once more rather precariously on the arm of a rattan chair, whereas Annemarie adopts the same defiant look, cigarette in hand, too cool to smile.

Klaus recalled Annemarie's rage in Venice when newspapers reported Blackshirts slapping Arturo Toscanini in Bologna; the sixty-four-year-old had refused to conduct the fascists' anthem '*Giovinezza*'. 'How could they dare to slap his face? Those dirty fascists, I mean! Toscanini's face! Think of it! And why? Because he didn't feel like conducting their lousy anthem! Oh! It's outrageous! Sickening, that's what it is.'[44] Toscanini had

Erika Mann, Annemarie, Klaus Mann, Venice 1932
Monacensia Literary Archive and Library, Munich

visited Bocken in 1924 and conducted a memorial concert for Siegfried
Wagner in Bayreuth in 1930, but broke with the festival's pro-fascist
atmosphere the following year. Annemarie's solidarity with Toscanini
put her at odds with views at home; Italy's fascism had helped keep
Schwarzenbach affiliate factories in Milan free of labour disputes.

After ten warm days in Venice, the terrible trio with Babs in tow drove
north in convoy. The Manns' car broke down and after a farewell drink
with Annemarie in the garage, she returned to Switzerland via Milan
while the Manns crossed the Julian Alps. They stopped for red wine in
the marketplace at Trent. The car broke down again south of Bolzano

and Klaus admired the handsome grease monkey in the garage. By the time they reached Munich, the newspapers were full of von Papen installed as the new Chancellor and Klaus's foreboding had intensified.

The shine had gone off Berlin for Annemarie and for many others whose lives and livelihoods were now threatened.[45] The halcyon days were over, and Annemarie turned to the idea of writing and travelling as lodestones in time of crisis. Ill again with fever, she read up on the origins of European culture in Mycenae, Knossos and the Sumerian sites of Ur and Kish.[46] She researched the Asian holdings in the Ethnological Museum in Berlin.[47] At about this time she met ethnographer and traveller Leo Matthias whose 1931 book *Griff in den Orient* recounted his experiences in Turkey, illustrated with his own photos – perhaps he urged her to travel to Persia.[48] She was itching to be on the move, research providing intellectual as well as romantic fodder for her wanderlust. Writing to Erika, Annemarie had become disillusioned with the city: 'I now know exactly what you loathe about Berlin and the blindness of the people here.'[49] She returned to her dislike of Berlin and Berliners later in the year – 'how tedious and standoffish the people here are'.[50] The *Berliner Schnauze* – the snarky tone, bringing down all pretensions – was not to her taste. Vladimir Nabokov, another patrician in exile at this time, felt a similar antipathy – and one wonders how much wealth and social class played into Annemarie's dealings with people.

Driving north from Munich, Klaus described a Germany 'terrorized by brutality bordering on hysteria, the whole country riven and dulled by a vulgar bloody-mindedness'.[51] The three of them – Erika, Klaus and Annemarie – planned a trip to Finland, where Klaus was pursuing a romantic interest. Swastika armbands adorned the Hitler Youth in the Stralsund harbour bars. Relieved to board the ferry to Rügen, these young cosmopolitans noted the charm of southern Sweden's open spaces, the dearth of alcohol and profusion of pastry shops, while Josephine Baker was regaling the Scandinavians with her banana dance.

They boarded the night ferry to Helsinki, Erika supervising the loading of her car. Young binge-drinking Swedes, lively with hard liquor, were on board. After an eighteen-hour crossing, the three friends rested and dined at Helsinki's premier Hotel Kämp. Erika and Klaus noted its pre-revolution atmosphere preserved in amber: palm court, jovial porter, fin-de-siècle ditties, droskies waiting. It was like one of their father's stories about aristocratic decline, with pretty boys cavorting in the lobby.[52] Reading Gide's *Corydon*, a seminal gay text, on the ferry, Klaus anticipated his reunion with the handsome, dapper Hans Aminoff, who had turned men's heads in Paris and was himself weighing up marriage and/or homosexuality.

At Pekkala, a charming estate on a peninsula in a landscape of lakes, they were guests of Aminoff's distinguished family. Klaus's diary for the summer doesn't give much away: 'Tendresse pour Hans'[53] seems not much after a long journey over land and sea. They embarked on a motorboat excursion through the lacustrine landscape. In the evening there was gramophone music; Annemarie played Bach and Chopin on the piano. It was a hot, stormy northern summer and they bathed in the dark lakes under a bright sky, eating crayfish and lingonberries. On 29 July Annemarie and Hans's sister, Ingrid, headed back early to Helsinki.

From this harum-scarum trip north, Klaus was inspired to write *Flucht in den Norden*, a novel telling the story of a homosexual relationship tricked out as a heterosexual one; Annemarie wasn't the only one veiling her desire. He gives his character Johanna Annemarie's androgynous features: 'She ran like a boy finally escaping from school. Her hair, flopping over her forehead, was cut like a boy's. From a distance she could be taken for a young man in the sixth form. Below her linen skirt her knees were bare.'[54] Johanna plays Bach on the piano. The manuscript's dedication 'To H.A., in memory of summer 1932' disappears in the published novel, by which time Aminoff had married and fathered a child, Antonia.[55] Klaus paid a second poignant visit to Pekkala, returning from the Moscow Writers Conference at the end of August 1934. Aminoff had morphed into another married homosexual taking his pleasure on the side. Folded away as a heterosexual love story, a bittersweet homosexual affair glimmers behind it like the northern lights.[56]

*

Biographies of Annemarie date her introduction to morphine to October 1932. Her family might have become aware as early as November of the previous year of drugs and excessive drinking. Her cousin in Berlin-Frohnau had difficulty keeping track of her movements.[57] A Berlin correspondent of Professor Burckhardt informed him in veiled terms of Annemarie's drug use. References to drugs and drug deals occur in *Lyric Novella* and while Annemarie's morphine use intensified in the autumn of 1932, she may have been dabbling over the course of the previous year. Ella Maillart noted Annemarie asking: 'How can a drug tried out of curiosity ever harm me?'[58] Ruth Landshoff recalled being 'in the part of the city where Mopsa lived and I proposed we go to her for refreshment. That is when Annemarie met Mopsa and I wish she hadn't.'[59] Mopsa Sternheim and her husband Jack Ripper were notorious users and Annemarie herself confirms this introduction to the drug that was to irreparably mark her life. 'With the arrival of Mopsa on the scene all hell broke loose.'[60] She liked Mopsa – an attractive, bisexual, larger-than-life character. Annemarie's later 1935 account to Dr. Forel confirms this context:

> The patient became a morphine addict in 1932 through a friend of Erika Mann's, Ms. Thea Sternheim, who also belonged to the group around [Pamela] Wedekind. Another friend, Annette Kolb, introduced her to Thea Sternheim, whom Erika Mann had seriously warned her about for fear she might become addicted. In November 1932, she injected herself with Eukodal, which had an immediate euphoric effect. At this time, she only took Eukodal 'socially'.[61]

Maria Daelen, like Erika, knew that Mopsa was bad news. 'For the first time she was tasting life without protection and without interference',[62] is how Ruth Landshoff describes Annemarie. By January 1933 Annemarie predicted correctly that morphine would 'ruin' her and was determined not to succumb.[63]

Journalist Adolph Stein, using the pen name Rumpelstilzchen, had brought the Berlin drug underworld to the attention of his suburban and provincial readers as early as 1920:

> At Alexanderplatz, which was next to the police station, morphine was easily obtainable in amounts 'not just enough for a few injections, but enough to send an entire small town to the grave'. Nine out of ten waiters in Berlin's cafes solicited cocaine orders from their customers, as other revellers openly snorted the powder in well-lit booths. Opium balls

were available for sale on the street and in hidden establishments. Glue, hashish, chloral hydrate, and marijuana rounded out the highs and lows. Indispensable party props for erotic amusement were the syringe and the hand mirror.[64]

Klaus used codewords and abbreviations in his diaries to cloak his drug consumption. Eukodal (Eu/Euka/Euca) was a morphine-based medicine, produced by Merck in Darmstadt, that doctors might prescribe, known as *Schwesterchen morphine*, morphine's little sister. The key code word in Klaus's diaries is *genommen*, meaning 'taken'. On the June 1931 evening he spent with Annemarie on the Eden Bar roof terrace, he noted that he took three doses of Eukodal and morphine. We don't know if Annemarie partook.

> She lived dangerously. She drank too much and never went to bed until late in the morning. ... I went to visit her. A bottle of vermouth was standing next to her manuscript. I was shocked. She had the gramophone playing while she wrote. I was even more shocked.[65]

Annemarie confirms that she wrote best while listening to music on an empty stomach with a little alcohol to hand.[66] The first volume of the Piper guide to Switzerland had gone to press and she was turning out pieces for a second volume, focused on north and west Switzerland. Journalism and hack work kept her busy, without feeding her imagination, and she ended 1932 'with no visible result, feeling rather sad and convinced that I can only half-cope with life'.[67]

Ruth Landshoff introduced Annemarie to the Berlin photographer Marianne Breslauer some time in 1932. Their encounter led to a joint motoring trip around northern Spain in spring 1933 but also to Breslauer's iconic series of photographs of Annemarie, taken at the Ullstein studio in Berlin, which fixed a particular image of the young Swiss writer for posterity. Man Ray had mentored Breslauer in Paris, encouraging her to find her own path in the direction of photojournalism and portraiture. In Berlin she photographed her 'New Woman' friends – as much a social movement as a revolution in feminine style. The style was a long way from the reality of rural and working women, some 1.5 million of whom were employed in greater Berlin, a third of them in the garment industry.

Breslauer's photographs did much to advertise and aestheticize the new look for a particular social class.

Breslauer's sitters – Lisa von Cramm, Maud Thyssen, Ruth von Morgen and Margot Lind – had in common aristocratic or celebrity marriages that reflect the political imbroglios of the day. Lisa von Cramm was married to tennis champion Baron Gottfried von Cramm, the clay king of Roland Garros in 1934. Lisa was grand-daughter of the Jewish banker Louis Hagen, a connection that played into Hitler's vengeance towards her famously anti-Nazi husband (he had openly called Hitler

Inge Westendarp, Margot Lind and Lisa von Cramm, 1936. Photo by Annemarie Schwarzenbach
Courtesy of Swiss Literary Archives and Wikimedia Commons

'the failed little house painter'). Annemarie had already noticed the seventeen-year-old Lisa's striking looks in St. Moritz two years earlier.[68]

Baroness Maud von Thyssen-Bornemisza's real name was Else Zarske Feller, and combinations thereof. She had married into one of Germany's oldest blueblood families:

> She became for a while a Charell girl of course and after that a mannequin at Strasser's. I was astonished at the speed of her development. … Her best friends at that time were the two Cramms, the tennis player and his charming dark little wife Lisa von Dobeneck, a cousin of the Potsdam Hagens, my favourite weekend people.[69]

In 1935 Baroness Maud was in the passenger seat beside Prince Alexis Mdivani when his car overturned, decapitating him and severing her tongue. Ruth Landshoff describes Maud Thyssen as 'great friends with Annemarie and had her to stay for months in Lugano [Baron Thyssen's house] and made her work well'.[70]

Margot Lind, a third member of this glamour group, would become emotionally involved with Annemarie a couple of years later in Switzerland. Annemarie herself photographed this clique of women in trousers, plus fours, blazers and rolled-up sleeves. Most of these society women are remembered today for the photographs that Marianne Breslauer and Annemarie took of them. Beauty was their calling card.

Breslauer, a baptized Protestant like her parents, was classified as Jewish under Nazi racial laws. She looked back on pre-war Berlin from exile in Switzerland many years later: 'We all dressed alike: masculine, short hair, styled to look like lesbians without actually being so.'[71] Annemarie 'had the same effect on me as she had on everybody: that curious mix of male and female. She reminded me of the image I have of the Angel Gabriel in Paradise. … Not at all like a real human being, but more like a work of art.'[72]

Breslauer's 'work of art' did much to propagate Annemarie's androgynous beauty and affectlessness. Her look chimed with the traumatized aesthetic of the Bauhaus: stripped down, disengaged, clean lines, low on make-up. A full-page portrait of 'the writer Annemarie Schwarzenbach' appeared in the October 1933 edition of *Uhu* magazine, photo credit withheld because of race laws. Annemarie looks sideways, lower lip plump, eyes sultry. From the start of her career her looks helped convey the troubling ambiguity of her writing.

*

Home always gave Annemarie a fresh perspective on away, and shuttling between independence and maternal care had become a coping mechanism. In Bocken there was horse riding and jumping, decorating the Christmas tree with her brother Hasi, and the prospect of skiing at New Year. Renée, apprised by family members, despaired at the company her daughter kept in Berlin. In early October Annemarie had read an extract from her forthcoming *Lyric Novella* as well as an account of her Finnish travels on Radio Zurich. Grandmother Clara read the final proofs at Christmas 1932,[73] and so the Wille-Schwarzenbach clan were in no doubt about nocturnal goings-on. *Lyric Novella* was due out in Berlin in March. Maria Daelen came on a visit and Renée continued to think of her as a stabilizing influence. Annemarie's cousins, Elizabeth and Gundalena Wille, resident in Berlin at this time, championed Daclen as 'really superb for Annemarie, shielding her from too many indiscriminate friendships'.[74] Renée thought that Annemarie needed to be protected from herself as her own worst enemy while tending to blame her daughter's nefarious friends for leading her astray. Clearly there were concerns at home about her alcohol and drug use.

At the beginning of January 1933, Annemarie and Maria were staying at Suvretta-Haus in St. Moritz. The two women attended the ball-themed 'Plantation Night' in Rüschlikon, with its Revelries on the Mississippi – Tombola, Cotillons, Pete Carona and his band,[75] and by 25 January they were back in Berlin where Maria had to get up for work whereas Annemarie spent the evening with Klaus at the Jockey Club. Despite her earlier determination, she accompanied Klaus to Friedrichstrasse in search of drugs. They returned to Annemarie's flat in Charlottenburg to shoot up. The night's revels ended at five in the morning.[76] On 10 February she was back with the Manns in Munich (the parents were away) and there was more morphine. A week later she wrote to Claude Bourdet from Hotel Zürser Hof in the Arlberg, pleading illness for neglecting him: 'after the flu and quite a bit of fever I left for the Arlberg with my friend Maria Daelen (doctor and a thoroughly charming woman). I'm making good progress with my skiing – and am writing a novel.'[77]

Flucht nach oben is in many ways Annemarie's best and most sustained piece of writing. It had to wait for publication until 1997, following its rediscovery in the archives of Zurich's Central Library. Like all of her work, it was written quickly, apparently in one draft, seizing the moment in the 'interlacing and overlapping of real and fictional experiences'.[78] Her characters, a group of skiers, act out an allegory of Germany's dilemma in spring 1933 in a luxury hotel above the world – the '*oben*' of the title.

Francis von Ruthern, son of a Prussian junker, is flicking through his expired passport. 'It was filled with the stamps of forgotten South American border crossings … at the time Mussolini was already in power and the Italians hated the Germans. A foreign army occupied the Ruhr. The German mark had fallen through the floor.'[79] He encapsulates the inter-war generation Annemarie belonged to: well-to-do minor German nobility, somewhat at a loose end, fond of travel and sports: golf, tennis, horse-riding and skiing. Francis's emotional entanglements are really Annemarie's lesbian affections transposed to a heterosexual milieu. This prodigal is vying for the favour of Countess Adrienne Vidal with a ski instructor called Andreas Wirz. Wirz is a smuggler ne'er-do-well, picked up at sixteen by a sugar daddy ('a rich Englishman') and deposited on the first rung of society's slippery ladder. Wirz's daemonic frustration exerts a fascination: his sexual ambiguity and predatory social climbing make him a gothic character. He befriends the countess's 12-year-old son Klaus, as well as Matthisel the hotel groom, and the author contrasts his nefarious motivations with the more cultured and cavalier Francis. The battle between these forces – uppity lowlife and returned prodigal – forms an allegory of German politics: old money ill-gotten in colonial lands fighting it out with the quasi-criminal underdog.

Like her earlier work, the ski novel has an intriguing roman à clef quality. Francis's brother commits suicide, echoing the fate of Ricki Hallgarten. The female characters seem like Annemarie's friends in motley – blond, pretty horsewomen married to absent rich husbands. Wirz thinks of them as 'elegant, soft and stupid, playing at being sporty, falling for the ski instructors as though they were film stars or bullfighters'.[80] Adrienne Vidal, the countess divorced at twenty, spends her time shuttling first class between spas and ski stations, her son in tow. Esther von M.[81] equally parcels out her days between skiing in the morning and 'luncheon, skating, tea, the bar, changing her clothes, dinner, bar again, dancing until midnight'. She's a rags-to-riches girl from a small town – the name Esther intimates her Jewish origins. A life of wagons-lits ensues: Hamburg, Berlin, Paris and London. 'None of [her friends] seemed to hold it against her that she had married old Herr von M., and at a stroke his fortune, which meant that now she was much richer than all her friends combined.' Someone whispers in her ear one day: 'There is no shame in having been poor … Beauty is capital.'[82] Annemarie has observed the material girls of Weimar Berlin and the reader sees that Wirz is not alone in climbing the social ladder.

Francis's memory of South America anticipates Annemarie's own exoticism, at a time when she was seeking to leave Europe:

> … there were pretty Indian girls hardly out of childhood, with their fetching animal-like eyes and soft smiles. The most graceful of these lookers, these smart and lively girls, were the young *mestizos*, half-Indian, half-Creoles, down by the port. Almost all were raised in town in awful high-rise projects while downstairs sailors and longshoremen came and went, the bars opened round the clock and the gramophone screeched out plaintive fado. Other girls lived at the outskirts of town, where the streets petered out into dirt tracks bordered by windowless one-story huts.[83]

This world of sex tourism, haciendas, praying Indians and thick-lipped mulattoes, now so totally out of kilter with the careful literary politics of cultural appropriation, contrasts with the elegant ski stations and their grand hotels: both worlds are Annemarie's stamping grounds:

> The low chimneys of the Palace Hotel emitted grey wisps of smoke. The evening meal was being prepared, soup and fish, meat, salad, dessert – for a hundred and fifty guests … and for the young people waiting for her in the bar. She could see them in her mind's eye, the boys from Paris and Berlin, from England and Holland.[84]

Both topographies, established early in Annemarie's life and writing, illustrate the tug-of-war between her glamorous Europe and a Shangri-La elsewhere. Behind the airbrushed coolness of Marianne Breslauer's society women – von Cramm, von Morgen, Grafin Yorck von Wartenburg – lies a world of wealth and privilege but also social climbing. Annemarie's shuttling between the well-heeled Weimar leisure class (none of these women seem to do a day's work) and an orientalist, exotic elsewhere has become her signature tune. In *Flucht nach oben* the quasi-colonial mindset dogging Annemarie's travels during the coming decade is already in place.

The typescript of *Flucht nach oben* is dated 'Le Lavandou, 10 May 1933'. Just before departing for Spain, she read an extract to Klaus, who had recently written a lacklustre review of her *Lyric Novella*.[85] He thought this new novel 'really good; significant progress – her adorable development'. The manuscript languished in the files of Swiss publisher Oprecht and perhaps caution prevented the publication of this allegory in the months after Hitler came to power. Annemarie does not seem to have pushed unduly for its publication. Travel was on her mind rather than staying put; the lure of the exotic won out.

Few in Annemarie's circle of friends harboured illusions about the import of Nazi policies. Already in 1932, in the Carlton Tea Room in Munich, under paste chandeliers and potted palms, Klaus had eavesdropped on Hitler talking about Therese Giehse, his sister's girlfriend and a family friend. Hitler 'stuffed himself with strawberry tartlets', three of them, Klaus observed, noting how flabby and pasty this dictator-in-the-making was, with his 'silly little moustache'. Hitler's party planned to join the audience in Munich's Kammerspiele nearby, where Giehse was to perform, Hitler refusing to countenance her Jewishness: 'After all, I know the difference between a German artist and a Semitic clown.'[86]

Erika too felt the heat. Pressure from functionaries, fractious audiences and personal threats followed her Peppermill cabaret from Munich into exile in Zurich. Klaus wrote in his diary for 30 January 1933: 'News that Hitler is Chancellor. Shock. Never thought it would come to this.'[87] The burning of the Reichstag on the night of 27–28 February gave spurious legitimacy to arrests, reprisals and political repression. Erika drove to Switzerland to join her parents on 12 March. Klaus boarded the night train from Munich to Paris. Both knew they were in the Nazi crosshairs.

As a Swiss national, Annemarie was spared the consequences suffered by her more high-profile friends. She too had her brush with Hitler in the foyer of the Berlin Opera House. The Führer-in-waiting walked past her, close enough for her to regret not having a revolver to shoot him.[88]

This *esprit d'escalier* is typical of her.[89] When Hitler became Chancellor, we find her riding in the Tiergarten 'in the company of Frederician soldiers, as colourful and upright as porcelain figurines'.[90] She couldn't have chosen a more *Kaiserlich* setting.

Her time in Berlin had been productive for her writing but it had also nurtured a need to escape, not so much the city, more so the psychological tensions of her character which were already manifest in drinking and drug taking followed by spells of illness. At the end of *Lyric Novella*, published and damned the month Hitler became Chancellor, Annemarie employed a wistful device which became characteristic. 'And I feel like going away from this place', the narrator states. 'I think about the sea. It's not far. In just a few hours, I could be on the Baltic Coast. I would look at the ships in the harbour, and the sailors.'[91] For well over a year she had been daydreaming of the desert and the steppe, where the cares of the world fell away. Those who were beginning to fall foul of Hitler's thugs – Jews, homosexuals, non-Aryans, communists, mixed-race children in the Rhineland territories – did not have the luxury of such an orientalist safety valve. What they needed was a passport, a boat, a train heading west. Following the political upheavals of 1933, Annemarie's illnesses and addictions began to mount as she became a traveller in the grand manner, not settling anywhere for long.

5

Pilgrim Soul

But the gods have eternity in their hand, and we must hasten, for our time is short.

Gertrude Bell, *Persian Pictures*

While Annemarie and the Mann siblings had aligned themselves early against Germany's National Socialists, the political reality found fertile ground at Bocken. The Schwarzenbach-Wille clan had followed the progress of the failed little house painter almost from the start, since his two-day fundraising visit to Switzerland in August 1923. Family reactions varied widely, from decorous accommodation and wait-and-see to outright enthusiasm or absolute horror. It was a family with business interests and employees on both sides of the Atlantic and therefore little inclined to entertain left-leaning ideas ascendant between the wars, a threat to the marriage of accumulated wealth and patrician prestige that the Schwarzenbach-Wille alliance represented. Alfred's business eye saw how right-wing politics kept socialism in check while disrupting his supply lines. In June 1933 Erika Mann informed her father about Alfred's view of the seismic shift across the border in Germany:

> Annemarie has just received a letter from her papa, wherein he writes that no one should trouble themselves about the petty undoubted excesses that come in the wake of the Hitler movement, … As long as their capitalist pockets are lined, their allegiance is clear.[1]

Alfred's Jewish customers in the garment trade in Germany were no longer in business.[2] Erika was correct in thinking that he judged politics in business terms, moral scruples falling into place behind the profit motive; in this he was no different from thousands of others.

Grandmother Clara, like General Wille, was inclined to characterize Hitler as an anti-semitic demagogue – a conclusion not difficult to reach. In 1923 the General had found Hitler unpromising.[3] While Emmy Krüger railed in no uncertain terms against Jews such as Bruno Walter, and others who she imagined had stymied her career, Clara held fire, whether through gentility or distaste we don't know. In a short text about morality and politics, she is inclined to draw a line between them: 'a person who meddles in politics abandons integrity and must obey other dictates than those central to his nature'.[4] Snobbery about Hitler's social origins made her wait and see, an equivocation she shared with much of the German aristocracy.[5]

Two of her children, however, were fervent Hitlerites. Renée had scant sympathy for German refugees in Zurich, those 'colourless internationalists' – especially the Manns. By April 1933, a sizeable diaspora had crossed the border into Switzerland, 'all of them cowards, all with their boots more or less dirty'.[6] By dirty boots she meant communist rabble-rousers, perhaps also by implication Jewish. Looked at more closely, the individual cases are tragic. Maria Daelen's head of surgery department in Westend Hospital in Berlin, Professor Arthur Meyer, shot his Jewish wife and then himself following the Nazi triumph.[7] On 7 April 1933 the so-called Aryanization regulations came into force, whereby Jews were removed from their jobs and from access to education. Renée's antipathy to refugees was of a piece with her aggressive nationalism; right-wing, equestrian-aristocratic, used to getting its way. Erika Mann, in a letter to Eva Herrmann, described Renée as a 'staunch Nazi' who viewed Germans in exile as 'communist refugee scum'.[8]

In Germany and Switzerland families were divided about the Nazis. As new medical policy regarding race, eugenics and euthanasia began to take hold, Maria Daelen's opposition as a practising doctor of necessity became muted, as did her feminist mother's. Inner exiles were afraid to speak out. Daelen's family gave credence to the new regime and many joined the party after 1933 while Maria's own allegiance was clear: 'I've never been more interested in politics than I am now; but only negatively, because my whole mind and heart stands in clear opposition to today's Germany.'[9] Ruth von Morgen, a mutual friend of both Daelen and Annemarie, had a son in Nazi uniform. Edith von Schmidt-Pauli, on whom Annemarie had based the character of Frau von Niehoff in *Lyric Novella*, was married to writer, journalist and Nazi apologist Edgar von Schmidt-Pauli, the man responsible for withdrawing the German section from International PEN. Many of Annemarie's recent Berlin friends were assimilated Jews attached in one way or another to the city's literary, cultural and entertainment circles. While her own opposition to Hitler was clear from the start, her women friends in Berlin were more circumspect.

At Christmas 1932 she cashiered the green Victory Dodge and acquired a swanky new car (daddy again), a Mercedes Mannheim, all sleek lines, fold-down roof and leather upholstery. At the same time her parents began to tighten the purse strings, aware of her excesses in Berlin but also of uncertain times ahead. This didn't stop her in mid-January meeting up with Mopsa, going all out for a night on 'the best French cognac', Maria Daelen ministering to the consequences, and then crashing the new car into a Berlin tram.[10]

Marianne Breslauer and Annemarie had long wanted to embark on a three-week tour of Spain, Breslauer to take photographs and Annemarie to drive and write up their travels. It wasn't until May 1933 that they departed, blown south by the political tail wind in Berlin. Annemarie was instrumental in putting Breslauer in touch with Lily Abegg of the Academia Photo Agency who was keen on the project.[11] Abegg was the Yokohama-born daughter of a Swiss silk merchant and for many years East Asia correspondent for the *Frankfurter Zeitung*. A political science graduate, career journalist and photographer, Abegg was drawn towards Asia and epitomized Annemarie's canny network skills and her drift towards travel writing. Abegg and Annemarie had shared an apartment in Berlin for a brief period. Breslauer, Abegg and Annemarie were exemplary of women travelling, writing and photographing between the wars. All three were branded by Nazi power.

Spain conjured up Hemingway's *The Sun Also Rises* (translated into German as *Fiesta*) and his stripped-down style had already influenced Annemarie's own writing. Journalism sharpened observation and trimmed the fat off Annemarie's sentences, as it had with Hemingway's when he was Paris correspondent for *The Toronto Star*. Her writing became less confessional, more observant and 'authenticity came to the fore'.[12] Like Abegg, Martha Gellhorn, Margaret Bourke-White and Dorothy Thompson, Annemarie was reporting in a man's world with the added underlying awareness of a lesbian reporting in a straight world.

Work was mixed with pleasure. Motoring south in her repaired car, Annemarie made a pit stop to visit the German literary exiles gathered in Sanary-sur-mer ('Berlin-on-Sea') and other towns along the Riviera. Klaus, knowing he was on Nazi lists, had escaped a hostile Munich in the nick of time. His life assumed its peripatetic pattern, a restlessness Annemarie's soon echoed. He wrote on hotel letterhead notepaper, faded by Mediterranean sunlight, in the blue hours between carousing on the waterfront and a café breakfast. Christopher Isherwood at this time recommended Klaus's work to his publishers, Jonathan Cape, and wrote to Klaus about his subject matter and style, akin to Isherwood's own: 'I don't know of any other writer who can describe hotels and waiters and railways as well as you can.'[13] By May 1933 the Mann family was beginning to consider more permanent exile. Klaus with his mother was prospecting for a house and went to look at a villa – '*La tranquille*' – which the Manns rented and settled into until late September.[14] Thomas Mann, leaving the house-hunting to others, was stoic about the move:

Klaus Mann. Photo by Annemarie Schwarzenbach
Courtesy of Swiss Literary Archives and Wikimedia Commons

... the awareness that an era in my life has come to an end, and the recognition that I must find a new basis for my existence. Despite the rigidly set ways of my fifty-eight years.[15]

By December, however, Mann was able to write: 'I almost feel more attached to Sanary: my small stone terrace in the evening, sitting in the wicker chair and watching the stars.'[16]

Erika and Therese Giehse, for their part, were ensconced in Les Roches Fleuries in Aiguebelle-Le Lavandou, 'directly above the sea with a touch of Honolulu ... cute plant-covered terraces giving directly onto the beach'.[17] Annemarie joined them on 3 May and a week later moved to the Hotel de la Tour in Sanary-sur-Mer. It was on this visit that she and Klaus battened down on the idea for *Die Sammlung*, the pre-eminent, short-lived German magazine which gave voice to literary exiles. Was it her idea or was it his? Three weeks beforehand, in correspondence with Klaus, she had suggested doing something in opposition to political events. At the same time she wrote from Hamburg to Claude Bourdet:

... could we – you, me, Erika, Klaus and others – start a review, an independent monthly for young Europeans, ... with French articles translated or bilingual in German and French. Private funding.[18]

'Private funding' meant her own contribution, and in this way Annemarie joined the parish of wealthy women in the thirties and forties who kept modernism in funds: the writer Bryher, Winifred Ellerman, who had inherited a shipping fortune; bookseller and publisher Sylvia Beach who bankrolled James Joyce; philanthropist and art collector Peggy Guggenheim.

By 4 May their project had taken shape as a bilingual review slated to appear in July or August. Annemarie offered the role of French editor to Bourdet, Klaus appending his endorsement.[19] *Die Sammlung* (*Compilation, Omnibus*), ran from September 1933 to August 1935, published by Querido in Amsterdam with significant financial support from Annemarie. She sought funding from her uncle Georg Reinhart, as she had earlier in Berlin for a film project, but to no avail. Reinhart doubted readership would extend much beyond German-speaking Switzerland, and had reservations about Klaus Mann's editorship.[20]

Klaus's diary for 3 May 1933 notes simply: 'Annemarie and a newspaper – her, me, Claude Bourdet. A great opportunity, hopefully.'[21] In its short run *Die Sammlung* published a sterling diaspora of German writers, as well as work from Hemingway and Huxley, Cocteau and Gide.

Erika too found a stage for resistance. Following a curtailed opening in Munich in January 1933, she had taken her cabaret *The Peppermill* on the road. They performed in Holland, Basel, Bern and elsewhere in Switzerland, excoriating the Nazis across the border in the Reich, braving hecklers and threats to her life. While Klaus and Annemarie conceived *Die Sammlung*, Thomas Mann enjoyed watching the stars, his German royalties still being paid.

> ... this particular wave of refugees was in an exceptionally privileged position – unlike the thousands, the millions of fugitives to come, they were not hounded (for the time being) and they were not destitute. They had been unable to bring any money but they went on earning an adequate if diminished living from their translation rights.[22]

During the second week of May, the German Student Union instigated book burnings in university towns across the country. A harbinger of hardened attitudes to freedom of expression, book burning was also a foretaste of populism tipping over into violence, by no means its last outing in the century to come. Joseph Roth watched as 'the smoke of our burned books rises into the sky, we German writers of Jewish descent must acknowledge above all that we have been defeated'.[23]

Thomas Mann took his time deciding whether to resist the barbarians while Hauptmann capitulated to the new regime and suffered the censorship of his earlier books. Many of the Sanary exiles – Heinrich Mann and Klaus, Brecht, and Roth himself – saw their books burned and their publication prospects go up in smoke, a reminder that exile, among other deprivations, meant loss of readership. In Berlin, students sacked and burned the library of Magnus Hirschfeld's Institute of Sex Research, witnessed by Christopher Isherwood. 'They arrived in trucks, early in the morning, playing a brass band ... they spent the morning pouring ink over carpets and manuscripts and loading their trucks with books.'[24] In order to avoid a similar fate, the Warburg Institute's famously rich, multi-disciplinary library relocated from Hamburg to

London in the nick of time in 1933. Throughout Germany, intellectual inquiry closed down in goose step with Nazi policy.

*

Picking Marianne Breslauer up at the train station in Montpellier in mid-May, Annemarie motored south across the Pyrenees into Catalonia. Wherever her white Mercedes Mannheim pulled in, with its attractive driver and passenger, admirers gathered round. In Girona they visited the Moorish baths – *Los Baños Árabes* – at the foot of the cathedral, and above Barcelona the eleventh-century Abbey of Montserrat. Swiss resident Piet Meyer showed the two women the town and a transvestite show. Annemarie liked to smoke Chesterfields at the wheel, drove at speed and with assurance.[25] Her travelling eye was often drawn to schoolchildren but also to the plight of girls in education. 'For Spanish girls there are hardly any good schools: they are taught deportment and their prayers. But all that goes by the wayside in the small country towns of northern Spain where the young girls between fourteen and twenty are as cheeky, loud and sassy as nowhere else.'[26]

There were only men on the streets at night, playing billiards and dominoes in the cafés. The two women travelled west along the slopes of the Pyrenees close to the French border, through Puigcerda and Seo de Urgel, enjoying driving on the white, hairpinning, almost deserted roads. In the austere Aragonese towns they encountered gypsies with wild hair, dirty hands and eyes as dark as castanets; nomadic life took hold of Annemarie's imagination:

> They overwhelmed us like wolves, we weren't even able to take photographs … And here in the small working-class towns of the western Pyrenees all we come across is the lone woman with a nursing child who wants to read our fortune, just like in Paris or Berlin.[27]

They visited Loyola for its association with the Jesuits. In Pamplona and San Sebastian they followed in Hemingway's footsteps. There were no bulls – it was not the season – but they stayed in the Hotel Quintana where Hemingway's Americans fraternized with bullfighters. Annemarie wrote not so much as a reporter but in the more personalized *feuilleton* style familiar to continental newspaper readers, what Joseph Roth called 'saying true things in half a page'.[28] Her Spanish *feuilletons* take on local colour with no pretensions to profundity:

> Pamplona is animated and cheerful, the cafes lively, and the big pelota courts host professional games and players every afternoon. Inveterate gamblers lose as much here as in Monte Carlo or at the Auteuil racetrack. We're staying at the Hotel Quintana where the matadors put up and negotiate their next engagements with their agents.[29]

Under the editorship of Otto Kleiber, Annemarie contributed to Basel's *National-Zeitung*. Arnold Kübler, editor of the large-format *Zürcher Illustrierte* magazine took Annemarie's Spanish pieces, with photos by Breslauer, for issues in September and October,[30] and in this way began a fruitful relationship. *Zürcher Illustrierte*, however, published Breslauer's photos under the 'aryanized' name 'M. Brauer', and so is guilty of falling into step with anti-semitic regulations in Germany.[31] Germany's reach across the Swiss border could have devastating effect on circulation figures.[32] Throughout the coming decade Annemarie published in all the major Swiss illustrated magazines and newspapers which came of age while German publishing across the border toed the line.

Breslauer fared less well. 'The Nazis were in power, the press in Germany was the same, and the Academia Agency no longer saw any possibility of publishing my photos, unless I agreed to adopt the name Annelise Brauer.'[33] Breslauer stuck to her principles. 'You need to remember that in 1933 we had no doubts about what was going to happen, or what could happen later.'[34] It was many decades before her photographs of Annemarie Schwarzenbach and of their motor flight through northern Spain came to light once more.

In Paris on magazine business, Klaus and Annemarie were much thrown together. They met Max Wolf, a freelance Swiss correspondent for the *Manchester Guardian* who later operated underground in Germany and sneaked out the minutes of the Reichstag trial hidden in a basket of fruit. Annemarie had arranged to meet Catherine Pozzi, the mother of Claude Bourdet. Her father, Dr. Samuel Pozzi, celebrated surgeon and gynaecologist, had been a friend to Sargent, Henry James and Montesquiou, as well as half of Paris, particularly the female half. His daughter, a woman of letters in her own right, knew Rilke, Valéry and Jean Paulhan, director of the *Nouvelle Revue française*. Annemarie and Klaus were keen to have Paulhan's support for *Die Sammlung* and Catherine Pozzi was curious to meet her son's correspondent. She espied the darker side of Annemarie's makeup:

> What a beauty! If she had her teeth seen to, she would be well and away above most of the beauty queens. We got on very well. … A gracious cast to her serious face. But she has a pained look, as though keeping her troubles in check. She's preoccupied by finding a role – all well and good – but I feel she's strangely insecure. She gives you the shivers about Europe.[35]

Pozzi's ambivalent view of marriage, *mariage par lassitude*, meant her radar would have seen through Annemarie's own diffidence on the subject.

Klaus and Annemarie continued their charm offensive on key figures in the publishing world. Annemarie introduced Klaus to Dominique Schlumberger, whose uncle Jean Schlumberger had co-founded the *Nouvelle Revue française* with André Gide and Gaston Gallimard. Klaus was worried about his father sitting on the political fence and that the Mann name on *Die Sammlung* would compromise neutrality. By September 1933, when the first issue appeared, Thomas Mann was indeed horrified to see his name under the masthead – it disappeared from subsequent issues. Annemarie too struggled with her elders. Her father discouraged her from becoming involved with no-good exiles and instead urged her to help build the new Germany. In late June, Klaus and Annemarie dined at the Dôme, joined Joseph Roth at the Deux Magots, and Klaus later took 'a long taxi ride with Annemarie to a doctor in Montmartre. Pharmacists. Took (lovely morphine). Entertainment.'[36]

Die Sammlung's French backers never materialized, though Fritz Landshoff in Amsterdam, embarking on developing a new German list at Dutch publishers Querido, liked the sound of Klaus's project and agreed to publish. With financial backing from Annemarie to the tune of 600 Swiss francs monthly, guaranteed publication for three issues from Querido, *Die Sammlung* was in business.[37]

History has proved Klaus, Annemarie and the group of exiled German writers correct: Hitler did indeed turn out as bad, indeed worse, than he portended. Dolfuss's opposition in Austria led to his assassination a year later. Concentration camps, opened initially for political prisoners, soon became sites of genocide. Burned books became burned bodies. Many German writers regarded the exiles as cowardly, 'tactless, noisy and hysterical'.[38] One such writer who clashed with Klaus was Gottfried Benn, who had the good grace to recant after the war: 'This 27-year-old had judged the situation correctly, he foresaw exactly the way things were developing, he saw things more clearly than I.'[39] But in 1933, Benn's appeasement was the order of the day:

> Aghast and horrified, we watched the international diplomats and intelligentsia being duped by blatant lies and transparent devices. What a nauseous, alarming spectacle! The Nazi regime wallowed in blood and filth: but the British Ambassador was smitten with the sanguine personality of Field Marshal Hermann Goring and with the sophisticated charm of Dr. Paul Joseph Gobbles. The Teutonic hooligans burned the masterpieces of world literature on public squares.[40]

*

Thomas Mann wrote in his diary for 11 October 1933: 'Anne Marie Schwarzenbach to dinner. Heading off to Persia in the morning.'[41] Over the course of the ensuing two years, she visited Persia and the Middle East a total of three times, her first *tour d'horizon* lasting seven months. From these journeys emerged a travel diary, a collection of short stories, a novel-travelogue, countless pieces of journalism and a husband. Clearly, travel corresponded to a need and produced a varied and colourful body of reportage and semi-autobiographical fiction. What drew this wealthy, well-connected Swiss traveller to these impoverished and exploited countries with their rich and ancient cultures? How deep was her engagement? How did she view these parts of the world carved out by competing colonial powers in the twilight of their dominion?

Annemarie's interest in archaeology was both academic and romantic. Like other travellers, she orientalized, framed a picture of local people on the basis of scant contact, and in doing so, often peddled a prelapsarian east for an audience back home. Rich-girl antics played a part too in opening doors; the cover of *Zürcher Illustrierte* for 27 October 1933 featured a full-page photo of her pensive attractiveness, as much a confection of her looks and courage as an account of the regions she visited. She liked glamping in caravanserais with horses provided, peasants, local colour and a good hot bath afterwards in a colonial hotel. While observing political change, which invariably meant westernization, conditions for women, religious orthodoxy and pastoral cultures becoming urbanized, her own cultural baggage was often in the back of a swanky car passing through at speed.

Perhaps Erika was right to disparage the dubious schtick of Annemarie's motives but the romance of travel was in her blood. She configured her journey east as a return to source at a time of 'decline in the West', parroting Spengler, as though by hightailing off on the Orient Express she was cocking a snook at Hitler. It may simply have been a desire for adventure, a gap year tricked out with high purpose. Like all such grandly conceived tours, it promised a good deal of communing with nature and old stones, her first exposure to non-European cultures, punctuated by hotels, guides and transport.

Claude Bourdet saw Annemarie off on the Orient Express from Geneva, observing that she was already gone in spirit and that his romantic pursuit of her was fruitless.[42] With grand explorer aplomb, she settled into the first-class carriage, her friend from Zurich University, Fred Pasternek, accompanying her. 'When I was a child I was enraptured by the sight of the Orient Express', she wrote, 'making its way through the Valais and up to the Simplon Pass: all you had to do was climb aboard and, unhindered, wake up one morning on the Bosphorus, on the shore of Asia.'[43] The drama of departure and arrival always appealed to her. Her writing and photography are littered with ports and stevedores, cars lifted into and out of the holds of steamers, letters written on-board ship on exotic notepaper, hotel rooms and colonial outposts. She wrote to Claude Bourdet from the Hotel Bellevue Palace in Ankara, from the Baron Hotel in Aleppo, from the Hotel Metropole in Beirut, the letterheads adorned with minarets, onion domes and palm trees. At Simplon she bought a loaf of black rye bread, a talisman of the Alps, like any backpacker leaving home.[44]

Her first stop was Istanbul and the Pera Palace Hotel perched on the Asian side. As always, Annemarie landed on her feet. She read in the German Institute library and explored the city astraddle the Bosphorus, snapping mosques, children and beggars with her new Rolleiflex. Her feelings were mixed and melancholic, her eye observant, her sense of smell acute:

> The smells were so penetrating I almost felt sick. There were fish on woven platters, big blue iridescent ones; a thousand spices; hanks of meat, oils, a display of cheese and dairy products, melons, sacs of pepper, beer, fermented grape juice; innumerable hole-in-the-wall taverns from which emerged a heady stink of mutton fat.[45]

Bourdet had arranged for her to meet his uncle, Jean Pozzi, permanent counsellor and former ambassador to the French embassy in Istanbul. Pozzi – 'very taken up with his ladies and his antiques'[46] – had been attached to the French diplomatic mission since 1907 and was a collector of Byzantine and Islamic antiquities, many now in the Louvre and the Sèvres Museum. He was in a long line of consular plunderer-dealers stretching back to Napoleon. Istanbul was undergoing a building boom and canny collectors often had to be one step behind the construction companies. Another contact was Clemens Holzmeister, whom she already knew from Berlin film and stage circles, a Viennese architect constructing the new capital of Ankara and the new presidential palace – his 'Schönbrunn' – for Mustafa Kemal Ataturk. With Holzmeister, she travelled to Ankara at the end of October for the tenth anniversary celebrations of the proclamation of the Turkish republic. Such men in positions of colonial and archaeological power opened doors for her but also framed her views.

In Ankara, she stayed at the Hotel Bellevue Palace, the venue for official balls and receptions, and compared the hotel favourably to the Bristol in Vienna and the Adlon in Berlin. 'From experience I know that the Ritz, Plaza and Palace hotels are similar the world over. Same bathroom dimensions, the cool Dry Martini in the lobby bar has the same taste, same price too, from Singapore to Barcelona.'[47] Despite her disparagement, she was a frequent guest. The picture of Annemarie roughing it on the Asian steppe needs framing by the hotels, embassies, well-placed connections, trains, steamships and automobiles that brought her imagined wilderness into focus. In Ankara, there were three days of fireworks, the diplomatic corps was out in force, and she had an opportunity to observe Ataturk up close: *'Many things have left their mark on that face.'*[48]

She compared Ataturk's nation-building to Bolshevik efforts. 'This constant shouting, bearing down, insisting, proclaiming – indoctrination by means of posters, speeches, cinema, radio, *parades*, music and newspapers.'[49] 'El Ghazi' was busy revising Turkish history, romanizing and simplifying the language, and giving a similar dressage to education, nomenclature and customs. Across the post-colonial world, flags were redesigned, national dress westernized, betel juice banned, bare feet exchanged for brogues, fingers for cutlery and absolute monarchies for a veneer of democracy. *The first duty of a ruler is to rectify names*:

Children in Turkey, 1933–34. Photo by Annemarie Schwarzenbach
Courtesy of Swiss Literary Archives and Wikimedia Commons

Constantinople was officially renamed Istanbul in 1930. Siam became Thailand. New national anthems were cranked out and obscure folk dances dusted off and given fresh lustre. It was her first brush with post-colonial nation-building – Iraq and Iran were in similar throes – much of which the new countries had learnt from European states themselves. Ironically, she had fled such top-down reorganization in Germany. Hitler's loss was Ataturk's gain, as El Ghazi brought over 1,200 Jewish scholars, linguists and archaeologists, denied work in Germany, to bolster his regeneration programme in Turkey.

Travelling through Syria, Lebanon, Palestine and Persia, Annemarie relied on embassies, foreign expeditions and their imperial backers. On 6 December her group of archaeologists pitched up at the Baron Hotel in Aleppo, dowager of the old-world hotels for nineteenth-century pilgrims heading south to Jerusalem. King Faisal had declared Syria's independence from its balcony in 1918. Lawrence of Arabia slept in Room 202 and left his bar tab unpaid. Agatha Christie began *Murder on the Orient Express* in Room 203. Annemarie sipped her mint tea from the same Royal Doulton china as Freya Stark.[50] In a melancholic mood, Annemarie wrote to Klaus, commiserating with him on the death in November of his childhood friend Frank Feiss from a morphine overdose. Klaus had in some respects supplanted Erika as a sounding board in Annemarie's correspondence and she adopted with him an easy, gossipy manner about drink, boys and Turkish baths: 'I won't be able to incorporate experiences in the Turkish baths into my "diary", but the Arab boys are pretty.'[51] This might imply that she had passed herself off as male in the segregated baths and that she was already thinking in terms of a published account of her travels. The androgyny of Arab boys struck her: 'A good few of these young Arabs could easily pass for girls: they are exceptionally beautiful, long curls peeping out from under an oxblood fez, and the sixteen to twenty-year-olds retain the soft features of women.'[52] There is no extant account of her thoughts among the girls and women at the baths.

After several days in Aleppo, her group of archaeologists repaired to the village of Reyhanli, joining the Syrian Expedition of the University of Chicago, on the Turkish border an hour east of the ancient site of Antioch. Reyhanli was to be Annemarie's base of operations for the next three weeks. It was a well-appointed house, with an attempt at a lawn around it. It rained a good deal, which interrupted the dig, and the end of year holidays gave the archaeologists an excuse to drive into Aleppo. Whiskey seems to have been the drink of choice, together with bottles of Mount Carmel wine and raki. Aleppo had always been a garrison town and Hussein, their driver, was familiar with the soldiers' bars under the citadel where 'Negroes, Algerians in bright turbans, Arabs and French listened to the melancholy songs of singers from Istanbul and Cairo.'[53] Annemarie's letter to Claude Bourdet describes a visit to the joy division – *les filles de joie* – in the shadow of the Sarrasin fortress. Annemarie was in her element, a woman passing among men watching the women ply their trade:

> The boys were sitting under the red light – Jacques, game for anything, with his puce head lying on a prostitute's knees, and Fred absolutely impeccable. The girl was called Valentine, twenty, and she remarked that I was '*plus petit*' than she was. And she had plenty of sweetness to offer![54]

This experience in an Aleppo whorehouse, long a staple of colonialist life and the grand tour, undoubtedly gave the tomboy in Annemarie a *frisson*, a sense of the East as a playground for foreigners. She wrote with more frankness to Erika about her escapades in Aleppo and Damascus – the letter has pointedly not survived. Annemarie returned to this night-town atmosphere in her story '*Adieux*' where the Algerian protagonist visits a whore with a heart of gold called Valentine under the shadow of the citadel in Aleppo. A piece published in *Die Weltwoche* in February 1934 confines itself to evoking history, the lively atmosphere of the surrounding streets, and the great mosque of Aleppo where:

> … an African watchman under a bright turban sits motionless with his back to us, observing the city. We greet him, and he turns and invites us in Arabic to climb up, pointing over the roofs towards the setting sun: 'The sea', he says, and with a grand sweeping gesture: 'Europe … Africa.'[55]

In this way the published journalism gives a tidy exotic picture while letters suggest a lascivious underworld that the short stories transcribe into heterosexual norms. Strategies of concealment operated in Annemarie's writing, reflecting her half-closeted life as a lesbian and her ability often to pass as a man among men.

The amount of actual digging she did is questionable; she observed the site, learned about the findings, and did some classifying in the laboratory. Her reports sent to Swiss newspapers had for the most part found favour and she turned them out with facility. The figure of the archaeologist in *The Happy Valley* personifies her regret at a parting of the ways but also shows what attracted her to the field. 'What opportunities did I renounce when I left Reyhanli? ... I could have dug deep through the sediment of centuries, from baked clay to bedrock, through ruins, collapsed houses, temples brought low, tombs turned to dust, gone down through the dross of ceremony, long-extinct religions, celebrated and forgotten victories, fire, earthquake, rebuilding – down to the deepest source.'[56] Her digging was all in the head; at Reyhanli and other excavations, her compassionate eye gets drawn towards the three hundred labourers who worked the site, together with wives and children who did the donkey work.

A three-week stay in Beirut sees her armed with introductions – to the French High Commissioner, to Henri Seyric, General Director of Antiquities in Syria and Lebanon and other functionaries of the French mandate, as well as the archaeologist Harald Ingholt. Fred Pasternek, occluded from her writings thus far, returned to Berlin. Annemarie, staying at the Hotel Metropole, was invited to the *Résidence*, and to ski at Bhamdoun on Mount Lebanon. She was glad to be among the French after three weeks rough-housing with the 'cold North Americans', whom she bad-mouthed despite availing of their hospitality.[57] Teaming up with archaeologist Daniel Schlumberger, they drove to Damascus to look at the whirling dervishes. An attractive woman travelling alone, she drew the attention of men in pith helmets keen to chaperone.

Beirut was a Mediterranean town of café terraces, umbrella pines and fragrant orange groves. Snow turned the mountains into the Switzerland of the Levant. She saw the old Roman bridge over the Dog River, fierce moustachioed men in the souks, the Maronite church in the rue des Martyrs, stalls of pomegranates and artichokes piled high, pyramids of condensed milk, barbers working in the street, scarlet cummerbunds, the Roxy cinema, signs in French everywhere. She took up with Mahmoud, a twenty-year-old 'shoeshine boy, a character, dancing attendance, and before long my friend. Handsome.'[58] Paying a visit to his home, she had tea and sugared almonds while he changed into his white pants embroidered down the seams and they went off to explore the coast road. Her letters to Klaus Mann are more colourful, detailed and unbuttoned than those to Claude Bourdet; occasionally a gay knowing slips between the lines. 'Tuna' came back on the menu in Beirut – her and Klaus's code-word for morphine – and this added to the louche cosmopolitan attraction of the city. Staying in Beirut with Admiral Joubert, Annemarie secured some morphine from his wife, and over the course of six weeks in Baghdad her consumption of morphine was one or two ampoules a day.[59]

By 23 January she was ready to move on to Jerusalem and Biblical sites further south: 'Now that I'm on the point of leaving Beirut, the city seems to take on a pivotal role. Life here is easy-going and I can take the measure of some outstanding characters.'[60] Accompanied by Paul, one of the Americans from Reyhanli, they drove along the coast road and stopped at Haifa where she photographed Jewish refugees arriving by ship from Trieste, the first of many over the coming decade, and a reminder of German politics. They tried the King David Tower Hotel, packed with 'the inevitable tribe of American and English pilgrims',[61] so Annemarie settled for a room in the guesthouse of the German Hospice not far away on Lloyd George Street, run by the Sisters of Charity.

She attended a concert by the Polish-Jewish violinist Bronislaw Hubermann, playing Brahms' Violin Concerto, during which the musician declared he would no longer play in the 'Third Reich' – as it was now termed. In the hotel, she 'met five young girls from a private academy in Boston, chaperoned by two teachers, ladies of a certain age. The girls were between eighteen and twenty, not yet engaged, were on their summer vacation and out to discover the world … When I met up with them after the concert, Paul had just ordered a bottle of Mount Carmel red wine and was letting it breathe.'[62]

The flight from Damascus to Baghdad took her over the Syrian desert with its herds of gazelles and dried-up watercourses; the pilot invited her into the cockpit; the Euphrates River gleamed tantalizingly; nomad tents with their wattle defences stood out against the wilderness. This second leg of her journey lasted a month, and took in a number of important sites: Babylon, Ur, Uruk-Warka, Hayy, Ctesiphon and Tell Asmar, for the most part along the Tigris and Euphrates basins and within striking distance of Baghdad.

After two months under the French mandate, she had entered the British sphere of influence. Settling into the Maud Hotel, her group of archaeology enthusiasts were driven the following day on the rough roads to the holy city of Karbala, site of the tomb of the Prophet's grandson, Hussein, a major Shiite place of pilgrimage. Cars and flatbed trucks ferried the precarious dead, blessed by burial in the holy city.

The extraordinary life of English traveller and diplomat Gertrude Bell (1868–1926) bears a number of points of comparison with Annemarie's. Bell hailed from a wealthy industrial background – steel – and was the first woman to graduate in history from Oxford; she was 'an accomplished young lady, of good family and brilliant intellectual gifts'.[63] Bell committed suicide in her Baghdad home eight years before Annemarie arrived, and memories of the Arabist and stateswoman were still fresh. Among diplomats in Baghdad and later in Tehran, Annemarie must have heard about Bell, and in exploring the Ukhaidir Fortress in the desert south-west of Karbala, Annemarie makes reference to Bell's pioneering excavations and photography of the Abbasid site.[64] She proposed to Klaus a piece she had written on Bell for *Die Sammlung*, but this never appeared and the manuscript is now lost.

In Baghdad Annemarie contacted the German embassy and visited the Archaeological Museum which held many of Bell's finds – plundered (including a statue of Bell) in 2003 when Baghdad fell to the Americans.[65] The German archaeologist Julius Jordan, in charge of the site at Uruk, was to hand. Travel was difficult and weather changeable; sandstorms gusted in off the desert and rain made the roads treacherous; the Euphrates and Tigris meandered, necessitating ferries and men to load their car. At the Ur excavations, the discoverer of the royal tombs, Leonard Woolley, showed her around. The great Babylonian staircase of the ziggurat, he explained, was only the upgrade of a much more ancient staircase buried underneath, a metaphor for many of the sites her group visited:

> Woolley testified to the presence of a stratum dating from the time of the great flood. He speaks of these things with great affection, as though they had taken place only yesterday. And one forgets the aeons gone by since and begins to see the humanity behind the remains unearthed here.[66]

Woolley had been a colleague and good friend to Gertrude Bell who used to make regular visits for what she called the 'division' – the division of spoils, with half going to the Iraqi government, of which Bell was the representative, and half to Woolley's backers, the British Museum and the University of Pennsylvania. When they couldn't agree, Bell would toss a coin.[67] At Uruk-Warka the young archaeologists impressed Annemarie with their knowledge and work ethic; the Americans at Reyhanli seemed 'like boy-scouts' in comparison.[68] Their arrival at Kut on a u-bend in the river was more dramatic, escorted by police, late for the ferry crossing the Tigris onto which their car had to be lifted. Annemarie spent the night in a government rest house on bare concrete with no facilities, and in the morning they made their way to Ctesiphon, a royal city under the Persians for eight hundred years, of which only the arch of the palace remained. Annemarie and her group wandered around the ruins in a cloud of dust observed by flocks of sheep and their bemused shepherds.

Between excursions up and down river, across dusty plains and saltbeds, she took note of life in Baghdad, its souks, its attempts at modernization, the royal and diplomatic comings and goings. She picked up copies of the Swiss newspapers and read her own articles. Somewhere in Baghdad's streets, Annemarie seems to have scored some morphine and in the Maud Hotel, while a diplomatic reception took place downstairs, she shot up.[69] Allaying Klaus's concern in her letter, she mentioned the early starts at 5 a.m., her lack of time to indulge, and the punishing after-effects of the drug which both of them knew well by this stage.

Snow on the passes left them kicking their heels for a week before crossing the Zagros mountains into Persia. She whiled away the time jackal-hunting to hounds at the British aerodrome at Hinaidi, the hunt cut short by dust storms. From her room she observed the yellow Euphrates, the far bank obscured, the city swimming in a peasouper punctuated by the red glow of the streetside braziers. The pass cleared and they hired a driver for the three-day crossing to Tehran.

Annemarie entered the final leg of her journey aware that all along she had been chasing Eden: the Persian empire which once had stretched from Anatolia to Mogul India. Crossing the border, her party entered Kurd territory, unspooling the route Darius had taken to expand his empire into the Mesopotamian plain. At Kermanshah the fields of poppies prompted a verse from Virgil; Haroun al-Rachid had given opium as a gift to Charlemagne; mothers put a bit on their fingernail to soothe teething children. At Tagh-e Bostan, the Gate of Asia, she

A horse-drawn tram in Iraq. Photo by Annemarie Schwarzenbach
Courtesy of Swiss Literary Archives and Wikimedia Commons

climbed for an hour to view the magnificent fourth-century BCE rock inscriptions in Babylonian, Alemite and Old Persian. Crossing the Asadabad pass, they came down into Hamadan and spent the night in the Hotel de France. It was early March with fresh snow underfoot but signs of spring lower down. Tea and Russian vodka were served and Annemarie sat and wrote. The following day there were camels in the caravanserais at the roadside. In the distance sacred Mount Damavand rose over Tehran.

Modernization and state-building were underway in Iran as in Turkey and Iraq. Annemarie preferred the mysteries of history to the bricks and mortar of constructing nations, and the desert wasteland to either. 'In these new towns, built along the lines of America or the Soviet Union, there is no room left for the Thousand and One Nights or the vine-draped pergolas of the poet.'[70] Much of this development was ascribed to Reza Shah. Rising through the ranks of the army and staging a coup, in 1925 he acceded to the throne of a 2,500-year-old monarchy and built the apparatus of modern Iran: westernizing education; opening up roles for women; rectifying names. His son and heir attended Le Rosey Institute in Switzerland, as had earlier princelings of the Qajar monarchy Reza Shah had deposed. A Western-educated Iranian elite steered development projects and kept the private international schools of Switzerland in clover. The writer Freya Stark, travelling in Iran's Luristan valley in 1931, noted the push towards dress reform: 'The aim of the Persian government is to have them all dressed à la Ferangi in a year's time, with peaked képis and the Shah's portrait stamped on the lining.'[71] In 1935 Reza Shah changed the name of the country from Persia (region of the Pars) to Iran (land of the Aryans), the term long used by Iranians themselves.

On this first visit Annemarie stayed at the German residence where ambassador Wipert von Blücher, and his wife Gudrun, no doubt apprised her of the sabre-rattling in Dolfuss's Austria and in Paris. Blücher was an old-school diplomat who shortly after Annemarie's visit was transferred to Finland where he attempted to resist Nazi policies towards the Jewish population. Annemarie got on well with his wife.

Her objective all along had been to join the archaeological dig at Rhages (Ray, Sahr-e Ray), thirty miles south-east of Tehran, led by Professor Erich Schmidt. She reported there almost immediately and by April knew she would be returning for a second voluntary working visit from September to November. The site, dating back to 6,000 BCE, is mentioned in the Apocrypha. 'Twice the city was destroyed, by earthquake and by Parthian invaders, twice to rise up afresh under new names.'[72] Annemarie must have impressed Field Director Schmidt with her acumen and enthusiasm, but also with her diplomatic connections. He had studied at Columbia under anthropologist Franz Boas and had been digging in Iran and Iraq since 1931. The University of Pennsylvania and the Museum of Fine Arts in Boston jointly undertook to back his current expedition with spoils accruing. He was a keen photographer.[73] A photograph taken by Annemarie at 6 o'clock in the morning near the citadel shows two archaeologists in hats – Schmidt wearing a tie and George Miles a dicky-bow. Annemarie's caption reads 'A Persian soldier watched us while we were fixing with white rope the first 10m² spot ... – and had some bottles of champagne!'[74]

She stayed in a house built against the adobe city wall, near a road on which camel caravans passed, within earshot of their bells clamouring all night long. With Klaus's 1929 novel *Alexander* in mind, she noted Rhages in connection with Alexander's 330 BCE pursuit of Darius III, king of Persia, and in a later article traced Alexander's route and his romancing in some detail.[75] Writing for a more specialist audience in the ethnographic magazine *Atlantis*, she displays a firm grasp of source material and archaeological knowledge without mentioning that she had visited most of the sites mentioned. Her romantic view of history comes to the fore: facts, for Annemarie, don't always speak louder, they merely underline an inadequacy. Gertrude Bell also mused at Rhages 'that it was wildly possible Alexander's eyes might have rested on this even brickwork'.[76] For Annemarie, the expansionist exploits of Alexander were 'drawn by necessity' and in terms of a clash of 'cultural forces' – the Hellenistic overcoming Babylonian civilization of which the Persian was a clapped-out last hurrah. This implies a destiny in the affairs of men with Alexander as 'the carrier and embodiment of one of the most generative ideas in the history of the world'.[77] What this idea was, we can only guess: democracy perhaps.

She wrote in a more popular vein for *Zürcher Illustrierte* about Schmidt's excavations, his financial backing, the motivations of archaeologists and museums, and payment for locals.

The tomb of Tutankhamun, the royal tombs of Ur and the palace of Persepolis have all whetted the public appetite for archaeology, almost as much as football or trans-oceanic flights. Now captains of industry and trust fund widows[78] generously finance and lend their names to scientific institutes and flagship expeditions. They hire private planes and come on a visit.[79]

Colonialism and Western soft power underwrote archaeology: in one of her photos, the repurposed oil cans used for hauling water have the BP logo – British Petroleum, much embroiled in Iranian politics then and since.

The digs were protected by night watchmen against tomb raiders. When a digger finds an object his name is noted and he receives a recompense in the form of 'bakshish' – this prevents diggers from selling whatever finds they make in the local bazaar. The water carrier delivers water to the diggers in an old petrol can.[80]

Writing to Klaus, Annemarie facetiously wanted to debunk the Nazi Ayrian fallacy. 'At Rhages, I will be mostly taken up by measuring skulls and if with these Iranian specimens I can refute the absurdity of those German racist idiots, it will be worth it.'[81] Nomad tribes, she claimed, were 'of older lineage than the Ayrians, who did not make their appearance in Iran until the second century AD'.[82] On her return to Zurich in May 1934, she took an anthropology course at the university in the field of cephalometry: 'I'm learning to measure skulls: narrow and short ones, aryan skulls, the skulls of young negroes from southern Africa.'[83] This field provided a pseudo-scientific foundation for Samuel Morton's race theories in America, in turn underpinned the slave trade, and in Britain bolstered Francis Galton's eugenics, to which the Nazis and many others gave credence. In writing of minorities – Jewish, Armenian, Chaldean – sprinkled among the majority Islamic population, Annemarie rejected the 'Blood and Soil' definition of race and nation then being propagated by Nazi pseudo-science: 'Hereditary and territorial prerequisites aren't the only markers of ethnicity.'[84]

Her investigations at Rhages confirmed Annemarie's view of the futility of history, its endless tessellation of human endeavour. Gertrude Bell responded similarly to the cultural ruins she encountered. In a letter from April 1905, Bell described 'race after race, one on top of the other, the whole land strewn with the mighty relics of them. We in Europe are accustomed to think that civilization is an advancing flood that has gone steadily forward since the beginning of time. I believe we are wrong. It is a tide that ebbs and flows, reaches a high water mark and turns back again.' Bell's view, nonetheless, is optimistic. Leaving the Tower of Silence, the necropole of the Zoroastrians where the dead are exposed to vultures, she felt that 'Life seized us and inspired us with a mad sense of revelry.'[85] Annemarie too saw the friable futility of it all. She described 'an eternal wall of dust, thickly clouding the earth':

The omni-present quintessential colour of the country, the colour of dust and camel hair, of plain mud, of earthenware, of soldiers. … One might be tempted to see the living town, built over the necropolis which it replaced, as glaring testimony of life's invincible energy ... but such a view is arrant fallacy – it's clear that not one potter in the new town is capable of creating a vase to match the freshness and harmony of colour of the simplest vase left to us from ancient times.[86]

Whereas Gertrude Bell saw the rise and fall of epochs but chose 'youth and the joy of living', for Annemarie time's arrow descended into the rough.

From Tehran she ascended by car east to the mountain village of Damavand, sacked by Genghis Khan, and then by hired donkey and mule they climbed by the old caravan route to the shrine of Imamzadeh Hashem on the pass leading into the Mazandaran, an upland valley running east–west along the southern shore of the Caspian Sea.[87]

> The name has a wonderful ring to it – Mazandaran, a tropical region on the Caspian Sea. Jungle takes over there – rainforest, humidity, malaria. In Gilan, the neighbouring western province, the rice fields have been drained and the Chinese teach malarial farmers the ancient art of tea cultivation. The small coastal towns are home to Russian caviar fishermen.[88]

Leaving Tehran by train on 14 April for the ferry at Pahlavi (now Bandar Anzali) on the Caspian Sea, she had the Middle East at her back as it tipped over into the Caucasus. Running into an acquaintance called Shanghai Willy, a Danish engineer building a bridge, she drank half a bottle of whiskey with him and watched the lagoon. With men Annemarie sometimes kept up a hard-drinking, hard-smoking swashbuckling style. She liked hanging out with gay men, where the camaraderie was untinged with desire, where she could be one of the boys, passing among them in mufti.

Six months on the Middle Eastern roads had turned her into a traveller, a travel writer and a photo-journalist. Some forty articles for publication written en route show her feet on the ground. Her style sharpened with the exigencies of writing on the hoof; her observant eye caught detail and she was able to bang it out on the typewriter and send it off. The Rolleiflex focused on children, ruins, landscapes, project development, horses – every now and again an image arrests, captures a time and place long gone. Her photography empathizes with ordinary people. It wasn't part of her writing style to quote but to describe in long, loopy, accreting sentences that create an atmosphere, sometimes ending in a car crash of abstractions and verbs in the German manner. An English-language editor would have reached for the red pen. She didn't interview or let the many archaeologists she encountered speak for themselves, never mind the views of the locally employed indentured labour and representatives from regional museums.

Annemarie's style, nonetheless, attempted to be 'sharp, clear and objective'[89] in the Hemingway manner. Notes in the journal made their way into newspaper articles, reworked for publication in hybrid texts. These travelogues and short stories come from a more spiritual questing cast of mind. The vast spaces she crossed acted as panacea; what the French term, in reference to the Sahara, *le baptême de la solitude*, the Portuguese characterize as *saudade*, a heart-stopping, unattainable longing, and the Peruvians 'the Pacific sadness, a loneliness in the midst of well-being'.[90] She liked to commune with place, searching for echoes and affinities, sitting cross-legged under the night sky as the camels grow refractory. There are passages of great beauty in this vein, relying on her old friends, cadence and rhythm. Sunrise or sunset over the ruins wears thin, however, and the lyrical prose strains towards the ineffable.

Her style of travel in the grand manner lay somewhere between exploration and quest but was, in fact, embedded with the earthly powers of the day – the so-called 'Great Game'. Archaeology, as Hubert Butler describes it, had become 'one of the whore sciences whose poxy favours can be bought by any government prepared to pay for them'.[91] Behind the soft power was the hard power of oil. The British government in 1914 purchased half the shares of the Anglo-Persian Oil Company – British Petroleum (BP), as it became – with 16 per cent of the company's profits accruing to Iran. Numerous wars, coups and takeovers owe their origin to this wresting of control of oil over the course of the twentieth century. Annemarie availed of the German embassy, French and British mandates, and American university funding for a range of archaeology expeditions, a network of shabby-chic hotels, drivers, cars and guides. There was always lashings of hot water back at the hotel, or the residence, and whiskey in the bar and perhaps a friendly pharmacist.[92] The idea that she was unearthing the mysterious East, communing with eternity in the ruins of history has a half-baked and over-egged flavour that doesn't quite stand up to too much scrutiny; her sorties into the desert or the mountains rarely lasted more than a few days. Erika's disparagement of Annemarie's 'explorer's puffed-up pride' is begrudging; the twenty-five-year-old could be justifiably proud of her achievements, the breadth and energy of her journalism, the verve of her journey.

> During the first months, I travelled with new friends and became familiar with everything – Persepolis and Isfahan, the garden of Shiraz, the dervish hermitages in the bare rock face, the great mosque gates, the endless streets, the endless plains. I drove through passes and rode along the bridle paths in the Elburz Mountains. I saw the shores of the Caspian Sea, jungles and paddy fields, zebus standing on sand-swept beaches, straw roofs in the heavy rain.[93]

In an Instagram world, pictures of Annemarie under a pith helmet, in dusty boots and colonial shorts in the august ruins, make for good copy. Her photographs helped create an image of the lonely traveller encountering an existential wilderness, whereas she was rarely alone. Did she see herself joining the explorers, those maverick English travellers? She certainly encountered Gertrude Bell's example and writings. Vita Sackville-West, staying with Bell in her house in Baghdad, and slowly making her way to her diplomat husband in Tehran, sounds disdainful in *Passenger to Tehran* (1926):

> What were Arabs to me or I to them, as we thus briefly crossed one another? They in their robes, noble and squalid, of impenetrable life; and I a traveller, making for the station? They had all the desert behind them, and I all Asia before me, Bagdad just a point of focus, a last shout of civilization.[94]

A third British traveller, Freya Stark, published her account of western Persia, *The Valleys of the Assassins*, in 1934. Her writing is more finished, less self-involved than Annemarie's musings, and wears its learning lighter. Like Annemarie and Sackville-West, Stark found herself married to a homosexual diplomat with an interest in archaeology.

Annemarie returned to a world changed and polarized by National Socialism. Between her first and second journeys to Persia she managed to write two books, both concerned with travel, exile and the Middle East. In the heat of August, she left Zurich with Klaus for the first Soviet Congress of Writers in Moscow. In September she was back in Persia. By November she was engaged to be married.

6

Lavender Marriages

She looked like a boy: she could do, and did do, a boy's work, and did it well: she had
been used to pass as a boy; and she preferred it: that way lay her taste and inclination.
Frederick Rolfe, *The Desire and Pursuit of the Whole*

A few days after returning to Bocken, Annemarie motored down to Bern for a performance of Erika's Peppermill cabaret, attended also by Thomas and Katia Mann. There was champagne afterwards in Erika's room at the Bellevue Hotel, where Thomas read fresh passages from *Joseph and his Brothers*, which he had sought to shepherd through the minefield of publication in Nazi Germany. For this reason he had repudiated *Die Sammlung*, his son's anti-Nazi magazine.[1] Erika had sneaked a section of her father's handwritten manuscript out of the family home in Munich, hidden among the tools under her car seat. Thomas Mann carefully played his cards from exile. Brother Heinrich's books had been on the previous year's bonfire; Thomas's for now had escaped the flames. Heinrich had been stripped of his German citizenship; Thomas still retained his passport.

At Bocken, marriage was in the air. Annemarie's brother Freddy had married Itala Bianchi, daughter of a Milanese silk merchant, on 18 January 1934, the ceremony conducted by pastor Ernst Merz. Claude Bourdet, stationed at Grenoble for his military service, proposed meeting Annemarie for a day in Geneva where he had bid her farewell seven months earlier. Notwithstanding driving to Bern to see Erika and to Amsterdam to see Klaus, Annemarie thought the drive down to Geneva too long and the proposed assignation too brief. This was disingenuous: almost in the same breath she suggested he might pick her up in Persia at the end of the year. She ends her letter with a rhetorical question: 'What am I going to do with my friend Claude??'[2] He had fallen for her in 1933 when she kissed him – once – in the front seat of her Mercedes Mannheim: 'That day, and since then, I was hers forever, although I never kissed her again, and never even said – though I wrote it – *Ich liebe dich.*[3] Besides, she had received and batted aside a 'high-handed marriage proposal' from Persia. Klaus Mann, another possible candidate for marriage, like his uncle Heinrich, had become stateless, in urgent need of a passport. Marriage, the right documents, allowed freedom of movement.[4] 'Passports were the only escape', writes Martha Gellhorn. 'None of the people I knew and cared for had passports, or anywhere to run. I saw them all as waiting for a sure death sentence, unsure of the date of execution.'[5]

Arguments at home about Annemarie's association with the Manns and Erika's Peppermill cabaret weren't long in surfacing. Emmy Krüger noted in her diary: 'Terrible scenes between Renée and Annemarie because of Giehse and Co. Devilish – Bocken's a madhouse as long as Annemarie is here!'[6] Conflict came to a head in June when Annemarie spent the night with Erika in Küsnacht, precipitating another mother–daughter row. Therese Giehse, brought in to mediate, arranged to meet Renée at her parents' house in Meilen and made clear that there was absolutely no question of a lesbian relationship between Erika and Annemarie. Furthermore, the Peppermill cabaret was just a vehicle for artistic expression, albeit with an edge. Renée had only good words to say, on this occasion, about German migrants.[7] Thomas Mann, himself living on Zurich's Gold Coast, mentioned in his diary for 24 June 'the rich, pathologically stupid Schwarzenbach family'.[8]

In June Annemarie travelled to Amsterdam to see Klaus and on the return leg stopped off in Berlin for a couple of days to visit the 'beautiful angel-headed'[9] Maud Thyssen. She was the second wife of industrialist and art collector Baron Heinrich von Thyssen, thirty-four years her senior. At this time, they were estranged, shortly to divorce. As a Hungarian-born Jew, Maud illustrates the fracture in many German families: her brother-in-law was an early Nazi supporter whose enormous Thyssen-Krupp business would profit so much from the coming war. On that same June occasion in Berlin, Annemarie called on Elizabeth von Schmidt-Pauli in Charlottenburg in the course of which Elizabeth's husband idly referred to Klaus Mann as a 'dirty bastard'.[10] Mann had been sneery about him in the December issue of *Die Sammlung*: it was a writers' tit for tat. Annemarie, while not revealing her financial backing for the magazine, invoked her friendship with Klaus. Schmidt-Pauli showed her the door and reported the incident.[11] Subsequently, the

Gestapo arrested and interrogated Maud Thyssen for having supposedly harboured a Swiss spy in the pay of Erika Mann. Thyssen was released on the word of a National Socialist friend of Hanna Kiel.[12] This brush with the Gestapo brought home to Annemarie the new reality of life under the Nazis and the vulnerability of her Jewish friends.

Schmidt-Pauli had supported the National Socialists since the failed Munich beer hall putsch of 1923. A member of the Reich Association of German Writers, he was one of the devil's scriveners. Following his denouncement of Annemarie, a message passed from Berlin to the German embassy in Bern. The Gestapo and the diplomatic mission became aware of Annemarie's association with *Die Sammlung*, as well as her friendship with the Mann siblings. The Consul-General in Zurich cautioned against a formal *persona non grata* move, citing members of the Schwarzenbach family's known sympathy for Germany. He also proved well informed about the mother–daughter conflict at Bocken and was aware of Annemarie's seven-month visit to the Middle East. However, he appears not to have known that she had co-conceived and was part-financing the magazine.

When the Consul-General enquired about the rows at home, Renée replied: 'Amsterdam, Querido Publishers, Klaus Mann',[13] and thereby enters the record as having shopped her daughter, with Klaus Mann and Querido as collateral damage. The upshot of this diplomatic exchange was an interview between Annemarie and the Consul-General, in the course of which she stated that she had only written two book reviews for *Die Sammlung* and that no further publications there were forthcoming. Furthermore, she had vacated her Berlin flat and was planning a long trip to Persia. Writing to her brother Hasi, Annemarie described Schmidt-Pauli as 'a greasy turd' and saw this family row in the context of Nazi score-settling: 'the system is gradually becoming so morally bankrupt that I don't really give a shit about being on some Nazi blacklist'.[14] There ended the matter, though Annemarie was now on the Gestapo's and Germany's diplomatic radar.[15]

The knives were out. Thomas Mann viewed Annemarie's Berlin incident as a 'symptom of the panicky tension in Germany'.[16] The Röhm Putsch, so-called Night of the Long Knives, took place between 30 June and 2 July 1934, at the time of Annemarie's diplomatic grilling. Hitler had shown his hand. Röhm's homosexuality and the depravity of his circle provided a convenient pretext to strike. Connected to the Manns and her gay friends, Annemarie could easily have been shaken down and made to talk. Writing to Klaus from Graubunden on 4 July, she used the phrase 'under the fig-leaf of morality' to describe Hitler's cynical machinations.[17] Thomas Mann mentions that she had been banned from Germany because of a 'single contribution to *Die Sammlung*'.[18] The incident with the German Consul gave a foretaste of difficulty to come.

*

Rows at home about the insalubrious Manns and the bloody Germans led Annemarie to decamp to the lakeside Villa Favorita in Castagnola outside Lugano, formerly owned by Leopold of Prussia and now by the cream of German manufacturing. She was there at the invitation of Baroness Maud. Like Rilke, Annemarie was rarely short of a feather bed in château or Schloss. It was a large estate bought to house the growing art collection of Baron Thyssen-Bornemisza and it was here that Annemarie wrote up her travel journal, which became *Winter in Vorderasien* (1934) (*Winter in the Near East*), a first draft completed in a matter of weeks on 21 May. After considering Orell-Füssli in Zurich and Niehaus in Basel, she came to an agreement quickly with Rascher-Verlag, a Zurich-based publisher with roots in the pacifist movement and a reputable list of authors that included Carl Jung, Somerset Maugham, Catherine Mansfield and Elias Canetti. Annemarie agreed to part-fund the publication herself, with a print run of 2,000, and the book came out in November 1934. Between publication and 1940, only 350 copies were sold and so Rascher was reluctant to take on a follow-up book of short stories, *Die Falkenkrafig* (*A Cage of Falcons*), covering similar territory and written shortly afterwards. A number of the stories concern emigration to Palestine by German-Jewish refugees. Rascher had garnered a reputation as a 'Jewish publisher' when a book by Stefan Zweig they had brought out had been impounded in the Reich. Swiss publishers, keen for German readers across the border, were risk-averse. It was not just the diplomats who were falling into line.[19]

Written in the same period as *Winter in the Near East*, Annemarie's suite of short stories stakes out similar territory but digs at a different level. Displaced European characters – colonials, mappers, archaeologists, female explorers – confront the landscape and cultures in and around the expedition house in Reyhanli, in Haifa, Jerusalem and the desert. 'I'm busy as a bee, and worried because they write themselves so easily: short stories, linked by character and set in the expedition house, coming together loosely almost like a novel.'[20] By early July she was feeling the draw of the East again.

> The well-made bed here still seems to me to float, an unreal state – and then I
> come down to earth again. Life here seems so superficial, no longer grounded
> – and back there is sunshine and shadow, dust, loneliness, reflection.[21]

The 'well-made bed' in the villa had nothing unreal about it. Baroness Maud's bed was equally comfortable. Her fifty-seven-year-old husband was busy at this time amassing an art collection, some of it of dubious provenance. The steel trade, already ramping up in 1934 under Hitler, would exploit industrial slave labour, contributing to the German war effort. 'Maud never went with us when we went dancing in our naughty bars, in the Friedrichgracht or the Eldorado', writes Ruth Landshoff. 'She was careful in one way.'[22] Annemarie described her to Claude Bourdet as 'a young ravishing woman, totally charming'[23] and as 'beautiful angel-headed'[24] to Klaus.

With Maud, in early July Annemarie decamped to the Hotel Astoria in Bad Gastein in Austria. There the relationship seems to have come to a crisis or an impasse. By mid-July the halo had fallen from the Boticelli angel and she was now 'the little lady Maud' and had returned to her husband, his art collection and the villa on the lake. Annemarie took stock of three recent fiascos: her ill-advised flying visit to Berlin; the deterioration of her relationship with her family; and Maud's lack of interest: 'I kept working hard at the writing but as soon as I put pen down, life was dull as dishwater. Things didn't pick up with Maud because I'm not entertaining enough, I'm not some boy with a speedboat and a pilot's licence. You'll laugh, but that's the way it is.'[25]

In July an agent in St. Moritz wrote to Annemarie about a stone house (seven rooms and an outhouse) available for rent on the lakeshore at Sils in the Engadine. She had been on the lookout for a place in the area for at least a year: a house to write in and welcome her friends but also an attempt to break from the controlling atmosphere at Bocken. 'If my papa gets behind the project',[26] she thought, it would be an ideal retreat in a part of Switzerland she had grown to know well. Eventually, she rented Haus Jaeger from the Godly family in Sils-Maria, and hired Martha Cadisch as housekeeper.

*

Her decision in the summer of 1934 to attend the first Congress of Soviet Writers in Moscow with Klaus must have been taken on the spur of the moment. They left Zurich on 12 August via Vienna and Warsaw to Moscow, indulging in morphine on the train. Writers had been invited to attend the congress from all over the Soviet Union, together with forty sympathizers from other countries. Annemarie blew hot and cold about the Soviet experiment. While expressing solidarity with the workers she harboured 'brooding scepticism' – wrongthink – about artistic conformity. Serious reading seemed widespread in the Soviet Union, in contrast to the shallows of the West where 'the writer, instead of being honoured, has to be content with an editor who pays a pittance'.[27] She was wary of the Soviet experiment as a land of milk and honey. In comparing Soviet collectivism to the American business ethic, her thinking has a Spenglerian cast:

> … the Russians, on the other hand, like the Americans, share a primal awe of the machine, speed and technical progress. This go-hung approach, however, accords with the needs of a large country that has been backward until quite recently.[28]

In Moscow she pursued an interest in documentary film already sparked in Berlin. She saw *Misery in the Borinage* (1933) twice, a silent film by Henri Storck and Joris Ivens about the 1932 strike in the Belgian coal-mining region. It included scenes of police firing on striking miners in Ambridge, Pennsylvania in 1933, anticipating her visit as a journalist there in 1936. While sometimes champagne socialist in behaviour, and rarely linking her own family's lucrative exploitation to labour misery, she showed a genuine empathy for social division and workers' conditions a number of years before she turned it to account in America's industrial heartland and the Jim Crow South. Unlike Joris Ivens' later denunciation of Dutch colonialism,[29] her empathy did not extend to challenging colonialism as such. Like Klaus, Annemarie saw the Soviet

Union as a bulwark against fascism in Europe while the anti-colonial struggle had to wait, a silent subaltern in the wings. 'I am convinced that we now need to side with the USSR if we are to make anything of our future. Despite this positive side to things, we – Klaus and I – didn't feel very happy here for other reasons. Klaus and I are in full agreement on that.'[30] It was a couple of years before Andre Gide's *Return from the USSR* (1937) turned the intellectual tide against the Soviet dystopia.

At the beginning of September Annemarie boarded the train south across Russia to Tbilisi[31] in Georgia, and from there to Baku. She had agreed to supply Otto Kleiber at Basel's *National-Zeitung* with fifteen articles based on her second visit to Persia. Writing on the train, she described the approach to Tbilisi, the rain, that peculiarly European habit of being in a hurry under an umbrella whereas the Arabs and Persians nonchalantly knew how to take their time. Young men disappeared into the sulphur baths. There were Armenian, Georgian and Jewish shopkeepers. It was East meets West again, a topography she was beginning to make her own.[32]

Archaeologist Friedrich Krefter picked her up in his car and they spent the night in 'the jungle of Rasht', no doubt sampling the caviar and the Georgian wines, and the next day drove through the rain down to Tehran. She gave a wide berth to the comforts of the German legation where the ambassador had been apprised of her connection to *Die Sammlung* and the fracas in Switzerland. Giving Claude Bourdet a forwarding address at the American embassy – she was never short of a diplomatic connection – one wonders what the reception there might have been for a young woman arriving alone from the Soviet Writers Congress. Compartmentalization was also a trait she would make her own.

Erich Schmidt was in charge of the Joint Expedition to Persia at Tepe Hissar and at Rhages. Annemarie describes him as 'our hyper-industrious little Director'[33] and 'a hard-working German' who drank little.[34]

In Moscow the French writer and later Gaullist minister of cultural affairs André Malraux had asked Annemarie what she was going to do in Rhages – a site he knew. Malraux too had started out as a romantic orientalist, involved in running artefacts out of Angkor Wat and passing plunder off as action-man adventure. In print at any rate, Annemarie doesn't provide an answer to Malraux's question, apart from mentioning the 'terrible sadness of Persia'.[35] In correspondence she was more prosaic: 'I'm learning how to live alone with my colleagues, days begin before sunrise at 5, consisting of fairly tiring work until nightfall. A short rest, and then another day. That's it. I find it strange, hard, and calming.'[36] She appears to have done mostly clerical work – typing catalogue cards – but also packing crates of ceramics for the museums in Boston and Philadelphia.[37] Schmidt may have thought she needed to learn archaeology from the ground up, like any intern.

Malraux's question and Schmidt the taskmaster may have prompted introspection; a crisis had been building which led her to consider marriage. Having recently completed two books set in the Middle East, the shine had gone off archaeology and she may have asked herself what she was doing cataloguing and packing. Morphine use is symptomatic – or the cause – of Annemarie's bewilderment at this stage. Her consumption continued at Rhages, as well as hashish with a Russian called Babinski. 'His servant filled our pipe – a chunk of yellowish, clay-coloured hashish powder, and over it a layer of tobacco … I choked and coughed. The servant Hassan, a fifteen-year-old boy, watched me and laughed.'[38] Perhaps, too, Maud Thyssens's rejection, compounding other failures, determined Annemarie to give marriage a twirl. Her brush with Nazi officialdom in the summer and her family's threat to cut her free might also have backed her into a corner. Marriage became a calculated move.

The solution to her dilemma came in the form of thirty-one-year-old French first secretary Achille-Claude Clarac who, of course, was the beneficiary of a diplomatic passport. Annemarie first mentioned Clarac in correspondence with Klaus on 4 November, a letter with a jaunty postscript: 'Now I could also marry a local Kurdish prince, he owns more than one village, but I'm too attached to you two.'[39] The 'also' here implies Annemarie was weighing her options: she wasn't the only one.

On 22 November she wrote to Bourdet of her engagement to Clarac, trying to soften the blow. Bourdet had first seen her in 1929 and had seriously pursued her since their kiss in 1933:

> She was living then in Berlin, in the vibrant, louche world before the Nazis, among its leftist writers, fabulously rich Jews, homosexuals and lesbians. Her mother, it was said, 'liked women' – maybe that was what took Annemarie in

Claude Clarac in Farmanieh, Persia, summer of 1935. Photo by Annemarie Schwarzenbach
Courtesy of Swiss Literary Archives and Wikimedia Commons

that direction, maybe her unfeminine traits could be seen under certain lights, maybe the influence of Erika Mann, the daughter of Thomas and the sister of Klaus – he too homosexual. It was rumoured, though I refused to take it in, and anyway was there truth to the whole story? She seemed to like me then.[40]

Bourdet's loss was diplomat Claude Clarac's gain. He took her to dinner, on night drives, and sometimes she had to sneak back into her cold room. Besides archaeology, the shine had gone off Persia too, and she was homesick; the dust and glare of the capital, the humdrum pettiness of expat life dulled her senses used to glitter and stimulation. She anticipated objections to her marriage from her family, since Clarac was French Catholic. Gertrude Bell had described Muslim wives looking 'like plants reared in a cellar'[41] and Swiss women of Annemarie's standing before the war were brought up as hothouse flowers. Outside Tehran there were horse-riding days and boozy nights with Countess Maud von Rosen, whom Annemarie described as 'a cross between Maria Daelen and Greta Garbo'.[42] The Swedish writer, traveller and equestrienne would later publish a travel book on Persia.[43] She becomes another of the face cards in Annemarie's colourful rather dog-eared pack of desert women, intrepid explorers and gender-benders.

Annemarie's surprising telegram announcing her engagement arrived at Bocken in the middle of ructions to do with Erika Mann's Peppermill cabaret in November 1934. The previous summer, both women had noticed a National Front in Switzerland agitating against German exiles and communists.[44] On 16 November further disturbances in the theatre spilled onto the street, with anti-semitic epithets heard and a police pistol going off. Over the following evenings, stink bombs and rabble-rousing continued. 'Motorized police formed a ring around the theatre every evening … Guns, strange knives, and brass knuckles were confiscated.'[45] The police arrested over a hundred National Front demonstrators on 26 November. 'Erika is certain', wrote Thomas Mann in his diary, 'that old Schwarzenbach's hysteria and hateful capitalist paranoia is behind all of this.' She had spotted family and friends of Renée's in the audience, stirring things up, including a nephew with a whistle. She also told the police that pictures of Hitler and Vice-Chancellor von Papen sat on Renée's writing desk.[46]

Investigations concluded that a personal feud between Renée and Erika was behind the rabble-rousing. Alexis Schwarzenbach, in his biography of Renée, quotes police interviews of the time.

… it is said that Annemarie Schwarzenbach is a lesbian. If relatives say so about her, we have to assume it is so. The same is said about Frau Mann. I myself confronted Frau Mann with these rumours. She simply explained that she has had no sexual relationship with Annemarie Schwarzenbach. It is further reported that the actress Therese Giehse, in the Peppermill cast, also has a similar sexual contact with Frau Mann, that both are 'in a relationship'.[47]

Death threats made against Erika, accusing her of being a 'traitor', were thought to stem from Germany or German agents. For the police, a family feud was the line of least resistance.

Returned from her travels on 16 December, Annemarie begged to differ. She laid the blame at the booted feet of the National Front, led by her old adversary Rolf Henne.[48] The Peppermill story had already become old news by the time Annemarie published her conclusion in the *Zürcher Post* (other newspapers weren't interested) on 27 December 1934.[49] It was a public salvo against some members of her family for stirring things up, but she did not finger Renée; Thomas Mann characterized the article as 'courageous'.[50]

Klaus, Erika and Annemarie reconvened in the Mann house in Küsnacht on 28 December. Klaus had been deprived of German citizenship in November: 'Congratulations', wrote Christopher Isherwood from Copenhagen, asking him to send his new novel *Flucht in den Norden* to Jonathan Cape.[51] Erika too expected her citizenship to be revoked and was thinking of asking Isherwood to marry her so she could acquire a British passport. Annemarie had become engaged to Claude three weeks before and nobody present was under any illusions as to her motives. She sent Claude a copy of Breslauer's photo (she always kept extra copies), writing on the reverse:

> Mother hates this picture because it makes me look a bit crazy? And Maud [Thyssen] tore it up, by the way, after having had it in her room for a long time. Now, at this painful time – (I have almost lost my nerve, darling) – this photo might take on a new meaning, maybe a likeness? Maybe you, my darling, can square up to it? Meaning – try to pin down the dark side ...![52]

This peculiar but revealing inscription alludes to Annemarie's half-shaded portrait. She had written to Bourdet ten days earlier: 'Claude, you're wrong. What do you know about my marriage, the reasons, the feelings? I'll explain to you one day.'[53] To her fiancé she was inclined to issue a challenge, – now you see me, now you don't! – while to Bourdet she mystified both reason and feeling but with the Manns she could be out. Where there is much ink there is much to hide, and here Annemarie seems to be playing peek-a-boo with family and friends.

It was clear by December 1934 that addiction had begun to exact a toll. Klaus remarked in his diary for 28 December: Annemarie 'is beautiful, thin and sweet. Very addicted to morphine. The three of us indulged together.'[54] She looked forward to the restorative power of her house in Sils, available in the new year, and hoped to bring her elective family together: Erika, Klaus and other friends. 'Tuna [morphine] eats away at me, tossing and turning on these sleepless nights, surrounded by such weak hamstrung people, so that I wonder what all of this is for – if the drug's not to hand.'[55] Annemarie was beginning to regret the 'strange intermittent period' of her time in Persia and to promise the stateless Klaus that she would see about getting him a French passport once she was married to Claude.[56]

Erika was crucial in convincing Annemarie on 3 January 1935 to book into Dr. Ernst Ruppaner's private clinic in Samedan in the Engadin for withdrawal treatment – the first of many. Annemarie's parents were worried by her drug habit though she appears to have been unaware that they knew. Writing to her mother, she called it a 'rest cure'. Her parents took exception to the tone of the letter and to Erika's chaperoning role; their view was that the Mann influence caused the problem. Alfred replied sternly:

> What I find so sad is that you have been shooting up and are still shooting up. When one is addicted to morphine and the like, I find it really concerning and appalling, and that's what sets me thinking, that your mother is perfectly correct and that you have gone even further down the wrong path than I had previously suspected … And I'm so sorry for you and even more so for your future husband, who deserved better than to marry a morphine addict.[57]

Renée wrote equally sternly a day after Alfred: 'I am done with years of sparring and fighting. You know quite well, in your more lucid moments, that I am the only person left out of account.'[58]

The Schwarzenbach parents were at wit's end and Annemarie felt rejected, both by them and by Erika. Clearly, the crux of the matter was lifestyle, unsavoury friendships as well as drug consumption – all areas where families are tested and many find compromise. On 14 January, Annemarie attempted suicide by taking an overdose of Veronal at the clinic. Renée visited and appeared to calm matters. Her father poured oil on troubled waters by attacking Annemarie's friends – Lisa von

Cramm among them – gathered by her bedside. Claude Bourdet, also in attendance, described her father as 'this old thick-headed Swissman'. Bourdet's photograph of Annemarie shows her bandaged wrists and pale, affectless demeanour, 'her beautiful inconsolable angelface'.[59]

She retreated to the house in Sils-Baselgia where Margot Lind, a Berlin friend, joined her. Like many of Annemarie's female friends, she drifts briefly into focus, ministering, providing a shoulder to cry on, and then withdrawing into the flux that was Germany in those years. Erich Maria Remarque visited and the two writers consoled each other. Despite a foot injury, Annemarie was soon keeping up her usual pace of writing and skiing.

Grandmother Clara and Annemarie's father might have given her the benefit of the doubt about her forthcoming marriage, but Renée was nobody's fool. She saw through the marriage as a sham. Ella Maillart later wrote that Annemarie thought that 'in marrying Francis [Claude] her main aim had been to free herself from her mother.'[60] Wedding arrangements kept changing. Initially, the bridal party was to travel by train to Trieste and then by steamer to Beirut where the ceremony was to take place at the Hotel St. George. Renée had agreed to accompany her, and was upset when Annemarie added Margot Lind to the passenger list, stealing Renée's unhindered access. The bride-to-be and Margot left for Paris together on 15 March, where Annemarie had a wedding dress made by the couturier Vera Borea. Annemarie's unthinking crassness surfaced when she suggested to Claude Bourdet that the two women could stay with him on the Avenue d'Iena while they shopped for her trousseau.[61] She was to reconnoitre with her father in Paris en route to America on business; it was to be a father–daughter moment on the eve of her marriage. However, she cancelled this arrangement in order to travel to Nantes to visit her future in-laws and continued to Rotterdam and Amsterdam to see the Manns. Erika was opening in the Hague on 1 April and Annemarie wanted 'to say goodbye' as she wrote to her father '... and for the three days before you arrive in Paris I have practically nothing to do'.[62] The family took umbrage at this slight against Alfred – presumably he was paying for the trousseau.

Then Annemarie wanted to add her cousin Gundalena Wille to the passenger list to Beirut, further enraging Renée who cancelled her reservation. Margot Lind too jumped ship, tired of being strung along by Annemarie's changing plans. Back in Bocken, the atmosphere was frosty but resigned. Renée wanted Marianne Breslauer, living in Zurich, to take

Annemarie en route to marriage, Trieste 17 April 1935. Photo by Renée Schwarzenbach-Wille
Courtesy of Zentralbibliothek Zürich

photos of Annemarie before she went off to Beirut. Marianne obliged, photographing Annemarie on the lawn in a long white silk evening gown – her Paris wedding dress – with an ultra-feminine grace and aristocratic hauteur so at odds from the earlier Berlin studio portraits – another Annemarie, the gilded heiress heading off to Persia to meet her prince.

Always more honest in her letters to Klaus, in early April she wrote about a frank conversation with her mother:

> … mother now knows that I just wanted to have somebody and picked a person I can get along with. To her that's clear and credible, and Claude is better than some total stranger, some real man that I might have used as a patsy, out of sheer convenience.[63]

The truth was out. On 16 April, Renée accompanied her daughter to the Trieste boat – the *Gerusalemme* of the Adriatic line – and from there

Annemarie in Trieste before boarding the boat to Beirut, 1935. Photo by Renée Schwarzenbach-Wille
Courtesy of Zentralbibliothek Zürich

she was on her own. Photographs Renée snapped on the quay show Annemarie pale and tense.[64] This was her third visit to Persia, it was to last three months and it would prove to be as eventful as the previous two. She intended to return to Sils in the summer.

*

Ships have a way of refocusing the land and the mind – *la melancolie des paquebots*, as Flaubert calls it – and Annemarie might have breathed a sigh of relief as the steamer puffed out of Trieste. The coast of Istria and the Kornati islands swam portside, which George Bernard Shaw thought God had created on the sixth day 'out of tears, stars and breath'. Shaw knew a thing or two about Pygmalion and wishful thinking. Last time Annemarie was in Tehran she had wanted marriage as a means of independence from her family. It looked as though she had pulled it off. Her frock was in her luggage. She had wanted a house in Sils, and now the Manns had agreed to chip in rent for the summer. In Beirut, a groom waited to make her a bride. Nonetheless, the way she shaped it for Ella Maillart four years later was far from relief. 'I felt that I was heading for a prison, I don't know why … but I was too weak-minded to free myself while it was still possible.'[65] When she was in one place she always wanted to be in the other place, and when she got what she wanted she was never happy.

The *Gerusalemme* docked in Beirut and Claude was there to meet her with a wedding present: a new Buick Packard sports model. They headed across the desert, each in a separate car, a symbol of how things stood. They planned to drive back to Tehran on the northern route through Mosul and Erbil in Iraq, across the mountains to Urmia in Azerbaijani Iran and from there south to the capital – a distance of over 2,200 kilometres, much of it on poor roads. Annemarie drove her new Buick and Claude his old Dodge.

Their first stop was the fabled caravan oasis of Palmyra 350 kilometres west of Beirut. The owner of the Hotel Zénobie, named after the famous queen of the desert, was Marga d'Andurain, a larger-than-life character who appealed to Annemarie's imagination. Since acquiring the hotel, d'Andurain had contracted an alliance with a local Bedouin in order to penetrate Mecca. Her new husband, however, died in suspicious circumstances in Jeddah. Following arrest, imprisonment and a stay in a harem, Marga returned to Palmyra and remarried her first husband who in turn was assassinated in December 1936 – nine months after Annemarie's stay. There were rumours that Marga was a spy. She takes on the sobriquet 'Queen Zenobia' in Annemarie's short story 'Beni Zainab' – an exoticized entitled Frenchwoman assuming power and a flickering half-life in the desert. Marga d'Andurain titled her biography *Le Mari Passport – The Passport Husband* – which says it all.[66]

*

On 21 May 1935 at 11.00 in the morning in the French legation in Tehran, Annemarie Minna Renée Schwarzenbach and Claude-Achille Clarac were pronounced man and wife by envoy extraordinary Jean Pozzi. The bride wore her white silk Vera Borea dress in the grand salon where the summer heat climbed under the revolving fans. She had lost the dark rings visible under her eyes six weeks before in Trieste and now bride and groom were somewhat sandblasted after their desert crossing. None of her family were present. None of his either. There were telegrams. A wedding breakfast of French champagne and Russian caviar must have been served by the hovering waiters behind the polite chatter of the *corps diplomatique*. He gave her a new Buick and she gave him cufflinks bought in Knize on the Champs-Elysées.[67] The couple made do with the invitations for the previously scheduled ceremony in Beirut.[68] No photographs have surfaced. The groom, chargé d'affaires Clarac, had made a good match and Annemarie was now entitled to a French diplomatic passport. She tactfully didn't mention her big day in letters to Claude Bourdet nor did she write anything to Klaus. Under the noonday sun the marriage got underway.

The *Flitterwochen* or *lune de miel* or honeymoon took place in Farmanieh, a garden retreat in the cooler foothills twenty kilometres north of Tehran, where 'the heat was so intense that it seemed to radiate from the walls like a brick oven'.[69] Farmanieh came with a country villa and dependencies, servants, a central water feature and romantic, lamp-lit gardens in the Persian style, somewhat reminiscent of the plantation houses of the American south. The villa had a wide, deep veranda supported by white pillars. Here the newly-married couple passed the summer months, entertaining, bathing, writing, escaping the rampant development and heat of the capital.

Farmanieh's owner, Prince Firouz-Mirza, was a descendant of the old Qajar dynasty and so would have regarded the Pahlavis as military upstarts – indeed, he spent three months in prison following the coup which brought Colonel Reza Shah Pahlavi to power. Attending the Lycée Janson de Sailly in Paris, Institut le Rosey in Switzerland, the American University in Beirut and the Sorbonne, the prince exemplified the Persian elite's respect for a certain idea of French culture as well as courtly tradition and habits of deference. In prison he translated Oscar Wilde's *De Profundis* into Persian. At the time of Annemarie's and Claude's acquaintance with him, his well-thumbed copy of *De Profundis* had been put aside and he was finance minister under Reza Shah. His tenure was brief. The Shah had him arrested in 1936 and the prince was strangled in his cell shortly thereafter.

Claude and Annemarie visited the prince at one of his tented properties high in the Elburz Mountains, travelling with camp beds, bedding, morphine, books, mosquito nets, first by car, then by mule and on horseback. Annemarie always appreciated a spot of glamping, the trappings of the explorer, the flapping of tents, a jaunty colonial attire. At the prince's camp, hunting dogs lolled on each other's necks and servants brought lamps. Under a reception tent they sampled a late supper of 'partridge and trout, all sorts of Persian dishes, pistachios, buttermilk, finely cut bread, a honeycomb, cloudy yellow Shiraz wine'. The prince chatted fondly late into the night about old Persia, and the new Iran which his children would inherit: 'petrol politics, English influence, the example of the Soviet Union and its vassal states'.[70] The prince didn't live to see the new Iran, nor did Annemarie, though both drank deep of an old aristocratic dispensation, the playing at nomadism that was almost an affectation on the part of Persian nobility as much as for rich Swiss girls. Gertrude Bell, made of tougher stuff, had seen through this hunting-and-fishing country-house style, not too different from her own background in England:

> The grandees bring their women with them; white canvas walls enclose the tents of wives and daughters whom captivity holds even in these free solitudes, and their negro attendants are familiar figures by the river sallows, where their shrouded forms hover sadly. They understand camp life, these Persian noblemen … But you are only playing at nomads, after all.[71]

The new Iran of Reza Shah had been installed with British backing. Vita Sackville-West described his coronation in 1925:

> The European women curtsied to the ground; the men inclined themselves low on his passage; the mullahs shambled forward in a rapacious, proprietary wave; the little prince, frightened, possessed himself of a corner of his father's cloak.[72]

By 1935 this royal pomp had been rejigged for a new Pahlavi dynasty, the little prince was attending Institute le Rosey with the sons of his father's courtiers, and Tehran had become a building site, a rapidly modernizing city of 300,000. On Firdosi Street, cars jostled with horse and carriage. Bauhaus-style administrative buildings contrasted with the more ornate arches and domes of traditional Persian architecture. The shah advanced women's rights: he had banned the veil or chador and promoted mixed primary schools. By 1936 there were over seventy female students enrolled at Tehran University, despite opposition from the clerical establishment and the *bazaris*.

The young attractive wife of the French chargé d'affaires, driving around in her Buick from Farmanieh to Chizar to Tajrish Square, from pharmacy to Turkish residence to French legation, did not pass unnoticed. The expatriate community was by and large a man's world where wives came out east as their husbands' decorative dependents. It was her first experience of Tehran's muggy summer and she suffered from malarial fever. Morphine was readily available. She alluded to being tortured by

Annemarie Schwarzenbach in Persia, 1935. Photo likely by Barbara Hamilton-Wright
Courtesy of Swiss Literary Archives and Wikimedia Commons

hypersensitivity, 'which Claude doesn't suspect'. In correspondence with Klaus, she wasn't long in holding forth on her marriage. Claude needed to apply for leave and had already used his annual quota. Annemarie was free to roam and planned her own independent move. 'For my part, if I can put up with the summer and autumn here, I would definitely return and spend the winter partly in Sils, partly close to Erika, and meet up again with Claude when he has leave.'[73] By 12 June, not yet a month after her marriage, she was finding diplomatic life a trial: 'it's just too absurd that I should faff around all winter here as the runt of the diplomatic litter'.[74] Henri Seyrig and his wife visited – director general of antiquities under the French mandate; his wife, Hermine de Saussure, was Swiss and a childhood friend of the traveller Ella Maillart. While planning an autumn visit by Klaus and Erika, Annemarie thought she might get her father to help financially with Sils. Claude's equanimity had become blithe naivety by August – 'such a school boy, as loving and loved as ever'.

She sent off her new collection of short stories to Friedrich Landshoff at Querido, the publishers of *Die Sammlung*. While Claude took a well-earned siesta, she practised piano at the empty German legation and went horse riding. Writing to Carl Burckhardt she is more off-hand and disingenuous, aware Burckhardt might relay news to Bocken:

> Here, among archaeologists and diplomats, I have led a rather 'adventurous' life – confident that circumstances will settle. Everything is topsy-turvy: marrying a young Frenchman, a man unknown to my family, marrying in Beirut or Tehran, especially since I had always been loud against marriage.[75]

'Human nature does not undergo a complete change east of Suez'[76] as Gertrude Bell well knew, and sometime in July 1935 Annemarie's eye began to rove again. The Turkish embassy garden adjoined the German embassy and the daughter of the Turkish ambassador became her friend.

> The girl's name was Jalé. Her mother was Circassian, and her father was an old man, one of those orthodox and respectable Turks who is loath to accept the changes taking place in his homeland.[77]

Suffering from tuberculosis, Jalé met a feverish Annemarie on a number of occasions.

When Jalé and I saw one another for the first time, I was running a fever. My room was darkened by the old trees and thick bushes in the garden. It was five o'clock in the evening, a hot day in July. I was lying on my bed, shaking from the chills and waiting for the fever. Jalé was pale; the blue powder on her eyelids made her eyes seem even bigger, her forehead even whiter. Artificial rouge lay like a sickness on her prominent cheekbones.[78]

The biographer, writes Terry Castle, 'must bring to life, not only the so-called dark side but also the distinctive pleasure-world of his or her subject'.[79] Pleasure-world is a useful phrase: one thinks of Persian miniatures, Rumi's poetry and the many descriptions of gardens going right back to Eden, whose Hebrew etymology means 'pleasure'. The word 'paradise' itself derives from old Iranian, meaning a walled garden or orchard. What was Annemarie's particular pleasure-world, how was it revealed in her brief contact with Jalé, and how trustworthy is Annemarie's account of this doomed affair?

A photograph taken by Annemarie shows all five of Enis Akaygen's children in the embassy garden – four attractive girls from two marriages, a handsome son in tennis whites – together with eighteen-year-old Princess Shams Pahlavi, daughter of Reza Shah. Jalé appears spirited, attractive, aiming a direct somewhat gaunt look at Annemarie's camera. The men have been swimming, but not the women; their hair is perfectly coiffed. Annemarie mentions 'calls from the tennis court', pillows in the garden and 'iced water in fogged glasses'[80] – an idyllic atmosphere in which to begin a romance in this select company.

Annemarie makes much of Jalé's 'Circassian and Arab blood' as she does of her sister's 'Nubian head ... like the heads of Akhenaten's utterly graceful daughters' in a way that strikes the reader as racial profiling. Jalé and Annemarie are attentive to each other's illnesses, setting them apart from the tennis-playing 'young people, who were guests in the Turk's garden'. Later, at a diplomatic reception, the two meet again:

As if through a narrow alley, Jalé came towards me, surrounded by other young girls. The alley was a path between dark bushes, the small lamps throwing their dim light on Jalé's very pale, heavily made-up face.[81]

Jalé (rear, third left) and her siblings at the Turkish Embassy in Tehran. Photo by
Annemarie Schwarzenbach
Courtesy of Swiss Literary Archives and Wikimedia Commons

Returning to Tehran from the Lar Valley for treatment of an infected
foot, Annemarie was a poorly-compliant patient for eight days. Her
doctor, according to her account, knew the Turkish family: 'Those Turkish
girls are very used to doing what they're told. She'll be destroyed by that
stubborn father of hers.'[82] Jalé's father intervened, forbade contact with
Annemarie, and sent his daughter back to Istanbul where, according to
Annemarie's account, she died soon after. Alexis Schwarzenbach reports
that Jalé committed suicide in Vienna in 1936.[83] There is no doubt that

the wife of the French chargé d'affaires had caused a scandal in Tehran diplomatic circles by consorting with this daughter of a strict family. Annemarie's orientalist pleasure gardens are hedged around with patriarchal watchfulness; illness makes this romantic attachment cloyingly ethereal, not really leading anywhere, and its bitter fruit is death. Her short contact with Jalé, blurring the lines between real and imaginary, glows feverishly like a Persian miniature in her work.

The Lar valley, now a national park, lies seventy kilometres from Tehran, extending eastwards towards the base of Mount Damavand, the holy mountain of the Zoroastrians, whose snow-covered slopes overlook the city. At the beginning of August, the Claracs and a couple from the British embassy travelled up into the valley, a circuitous journey of eight hours. A flotilla of tents provided by the British had already been pegged at an altitude of 2,500 metres in advance of their arrival. Climbing towards this encampment on muleback, the muleteers sang, the dry slopes were rocky, the riverbed rucked between them. While the shah's horses grazed in the August sun, there was fresh-caught trout for dinner; the bearers caught it, the diplomats ate it.

> The tents stand in a row on the grass slope close by the riverbank. ... a small, shaded portico in front of each tent where one sits in the morning with books and writing materials while the river at one's feet glides swiftly and peacefully down the valley. Below, the steadfast, gleaming pyramid of Mount Damavand.[84]

Photos tend to present an idyll but her writing shows that Annamarie was highly strung. *Death in Persia*, begun in the Lar valley and finished in Switzerland, has a fragmented quality, imbuing the landscape with the author's nightmares, her own fraught presence in it. The old 'Persian magic' seems to have escaped her. 'No, you think, suddenly in desperation – this can't go on, not for a quarter of an hour longer, you have to find something, find a remedy.'[85] Did she have morphine in her pack? Was she thinking of Jalé at this point? Was Jalé merely a divertissement and the real subject herself? Recounting this crisis in the Lar valley to Ella Maillart four years later, Annemarie had already mythologized it, turning it to account. Her communing with landscape and with her own angst are indistinguishable. 'There the silence whispered to her anguished pride that all was still not lost.'[86]

Back in the heat of Farmanieh, Annemarie looked forward to Klaus's visit but he cancelled under Erika's influence. She advised him against travel for reasons of malaria in Tehran, the possibility of war and Annemarie's drug-taking. Klaus and Erika were aware of the diplomatic scandal Annemarie had caused.[87] Klaus had been injecting himself daily: 'The craving for drugs is scarcely to be separated from the desire for death', he wrote in his diary for 22 October: the last thing he might have wanted was a holiday in Persia with his fellow addict. News of Klaus's decision to stay put came at a time when Annemarie had a new relationship underway, and was getting itchy feet.

In Ella Maillart's *The Cruel Way* (1947), her account of a journey to Afghanistan with 'Christina'/Annemarie, marriage is the subject of conversation over *gelato* on the quay at Trieste:

> Christina lived solely for her writing. While Francis had learned to compromise between his private life and his life as a diplomat, Christina could never attempt such a tour-de-force: she knew that legations are but the glass-cases of life, pleasant only for a moment. Francis, therefore, had assured her that she needn't change her ways at all.[88]

*

A new visitor to Farmanieh at the end of August took Annemarie's mind off the diplomatic scandal and her disappointment with Klaus for pulling out of their travel arrangements. Barbara Hamilton Wright arrived in Tehran at Claude's invitation, perhaps to distract his wife. Claude had courted Barbara in 1931 when he was junior officer at the French embassy in Washington under ambassador Paul Claudel, and had gone so far as to present her to his parents: 'I think she was to have married my Claude', wrote Annemarie, 'but what he had to offer was probably not enough for her.'[89] Clarac's parents might have deemed Wright unsuitable – as an American Episcopalian – or perhaps the Washburn-Wrights on her side thought the junior diplomat insufficiently pecunious. There was an air of fishing about this courtship between Barbara and Claude which, like his eventual marriage to Annemarie, didn't preclude genuine friendship.

From a prominent Washington family 'of distinguished Colonial lineage', as the papers of the day put it, this grand-daughter of Minnesota senator William Drew Washburn was privately educated in

Barbara Hamilton Wright, Annemarie, Claude Clarac, at the Scharis-Danek hunting camp, Persia, 1935
Courtesy of Swiss Literary Archives and Wikimedia Commons

Geneva and France and had travelled with her parents to Europe and China. Both parents were 'world leaders in national and international narcotics control'. In 1935 Washington's *Evening Star* reported in its society pages her departure for the 'Mediterranean and the Near East ...

she will visit M. and Mme Clarac at the French Legation in Teheran. She will return to Europe by way of Russia.'[90] The newspaper remarked on Barbara's fashion sense, her 'closely-fitted double-breasted long coats with puffed sleeves and high-crowned hats that are the vogue today'.[91] In photographs Barbara is boyish, loose-limbed, beautiful and feisty, hair cropped under a beret, in pants, game for adventure; one can see what Claude might have liked in her and certainly what attracted Annemarie. Both women came from similar conservative backgrounds of wealth and privilege, both had a sense of adventure at odds with their patrician families, and in Tehran quickly began a friendship that blossomed into plans for the future. This affair between two photographers led to a sojourn in Finland, several tours of the United States and some of the sharpest, most insightful photographs of Annemarie's career. The irony of Barbara, or Baa as she was known, pooling her interests and resources with a morphine addict was perhaps not lost on this daughter of narcotics legislators. There is no evidence of drug-taking on Barbara's part.

Baa took in the sights of Persia, both high and low. Annemarie's description of a local drinking den near Persepolis has a gritty realism:

Gathered here were what might be called the scum of Persia. ... They were smoking opium. They sat apart from the regular drinkers in a corner close to a clay oven where an enormous samovar stood. If a European asked what was going on back there, he was told: 'Those men are ill.' But most of the time they were hungry and numbed by the sweet-smelling smoke, squatting on their carpets like animals, growling at strangers.[92]

Besides Persepolis, they travelled into the Elburz Mountains and to Isfahan. By the time Baa returned to the United States, the two women had formed a bond and Annemarie was planning her next move. She had been married for an eventful four months.

'Barbara!' I shouted. She was sitting high up, almost in the shadow of the rocks. 'What makes you come all the way out here?' she asked. Couldn't you sleep without me? It's a decent time for going to bed!'

The moonlight lay on her feet like water lapping at the sand in waves and trickling back. I didn't say anything, I was just so happy to have found

Barbara. I sat, my head resting on her bent knees, watching as the little waves rose to her feet.[93]

In England, the lavender marriages got underway. Erika had initially approached Christopher Isherwood but he demurred and suggested his chum, the poet W.H. Auden – earning Isherwood Thomas Mann's moniker 'the family pimp'.[94] On 15 June 1935, a few weeks after Annemarie's marriage in Tehran, Erika married Auden in a Ledbury registry office, on the same day that her German citizenship was revoked. Just as Annemarie acquired French citizenship by marriage, so Erika could now claim a British passport. Afterwards, Auden drove the bride back to her room in the Abbey Hotel in Malvern and she packed her

Erika Mann, W.H. Auden by Alec Bangham, 1935
© National Portrait Gallery, London

bags and returned to Switzerland. The groom taught his afternoon classes at the Downs School. She was 'nine-tenths a man', a friend of Auden's described Erika at the time. The writer John Hampson celebrated his marriage to Therese Giehse in Birmingham a couple of months later. Hampson too was a paid-up member of the homintern. Giehse's English didn't stretch to answering the all-important question in the course of the ceremony and Auden, ever the schoolmaster, prodded her along. The party, including Auden, Louis MacNeice and journalist Walter Allen, repaired to the Burlington restaurant in Solihull where Thomas Mann, apparently, footed the bill.[95]

In November, Renée gave her daughter Suzanne in Sweden an account of Annemarie's marriage in the same breath as the news of Erika's marriage to Auden:

> Erika Mann by the way … has married an Englishman… and Mr. Clarac is not the kind of man to put up a fight, on the contrary, he's probably in on it – I have my suspicions – Annemarie will soon go down to her house and settle in and after New Year she will be off on a longer trip – so the show goes on.[96]

The knowing tone of Renée's comments implies a good grasp of how such lavender marriages worked. Claude, indeed, did not put up a fight. Annemarie weighed up dispassionately the give and take that any marriage entails and came to the following reckoning:

> … he is content to live with me – as regards the rest, his life hasn't in the least changed – do you know how much it pains me to rub shoulders with this stupid socialite lifestyle, to play a 'role' *that is completely false, and which I do out of loyalty to Claude?*[97]

Clearly fed up with playing diplomatic geisha, Annemarie left Tehran in October. Although she had put off telling him until late in the summer, it was not a complete break. He had done his best to entertain his wife by providing a Buick, gardens, tents, the best that Tehran had to offer. His commitment to their marriage in hindsight seems greater than hers, which had never been more than provisional. She considered taking the Buick Packard with her but this made travel arrangements too complicated. Claude and Annemarie met again in the summer of 1937, and after that not until 1942. Claude, at least in writing, held onto his initial romantic impulse:

> It proved impossible to follow her into the emotional world, imbued with literature, in which she took refuge, torn as she was between her needs for attachment and escape. I am sure she felt for me all the love she was capable of feeling for a man; and, on my part, I can only state the truth that I was in love with her. The idea of marrying was completely ridiculous.[98]

Annemarie's three visits to the Middle East had been fruitful: a travel journal, a book of short stories titled *The Cage of Falcons*, some fifty pieces of journalism and a new work taking shape – *Death in Persia*. Besides colonial hangers-on and refugees, her short stories also dramatize the lives of intrepid, rebellious women defying gender constraints – figures such as Gertrude Bell, Stella Benson, Maud von Rosen and Marga d'Andurain become avatars of Annemarie herself. She had begun by digging for history, searching for the spiritual in the ruins of Eastern civilizations and among nomads, but ended up back at the embassy with the canapés. Like these fellow travelling women – and the beatniks, hippies and wellness gurus after her – Annemarie was busy fashioning a fantasy of the Orient from her own reading, her psychological needs, her drug derangement, against a background of Europe drifting towards fascism.

*

On Annemarie's return from Persia her consumption of morphine was five to eight doses a day. The pharmacists of Tehran had been willing. She could function and appear in control but the scattershot of her letters to Klaus and the fragmentation of *Death in Persia*, jumping about all over the place in search of a centre, indicate that the drugs were talking. She was aware of her addiction: 'were it not for Barbara's arrival – only just – and her bringing me back from the brink, I wouldn't have made it, nor made the decision to leave.'[99]

Klaus, Thomas Mann and Renée all noticed the change in Annemarie's appearance.[100] She had lost weight, she was dependent; malarial fever masked the deeper problem of addiction. During the month of November there were a number of wild parties at the Mann house once the parents had retired for the evening.[101] Thomas Mann was well aware of her dependency, as his diary entry for 22 November 1935 indicates: 'she doesn't get the slightest enjoyment from the drug, but only feels impossibly bad if she does *not* take it'.[102] This would imply they had spoken of the matter. The Schwarzenbach family doctor advised detoxification treatment under Dr. Oscar Forel at his sanatorium, Les Rives de Prangins, on Lake Geneva. Renée drove Annemarie down to the clinic which had welcomed Zelda Fitzgerald and Lucia Joyce. Fees were well in excess of a thousand dollars a week. Dr. Forel managed to withdraw Annemarie from her morphine habit but was fairly pessimistic about her psychological state.

Annemarie confronted her contentious relationship with her mother in a frank account drafted for Dr. Forel. His diagnosis is framed by the cultural preconceptions of the day:

> Frau Clarac wants to but doesn't succeed in playing the male role in life, in work, in sexuality. And while or because she has a more or less pessimistic view of this failure, she demonstratively and inevitably gets locked into a cycle of failure in her life. ... The deeper, unconscious origins of the patient's assumption of the male role in the family context date back to childhood.[103]

He concluded that she was suffering from a 'schizoid personality' disorder without 'schizothymia' – perhaps what today might be termed 'on the autistic spectrum'.[104] Insight into her psychic makeup became mixed with the desire to 'normalize' her sexuality. Forel had wanted to treat and cure the 'inability to achieve a normal and erotic sexual relationship'.[105] He had used electroshock 'therapy' before and his beliefs about sexuality were forerunner to such homosexual aversion treatment meted out today in obscure camps and psych facilities across the Bible Belt. Forel's analysis was familiar to the patient, since she had contributed to it, and Annemarie saw no reason to continue treatment beyond her morphine addiction. '*Seelen Komplexe*' – a crisis of the soul, as Annemarie termed it in a letter to Klaus – was intimately tied up with her writing and the pretensions of the psychiatrists, *Seelenarzten*, knew no bounds. She had for a decade been relatively 'out' as a lesbian and was wary of the psychobabble of the day. Forel, moreover, found her a disruptive patient in an institution designed for calm:

... tired, sad eyes, limp, disordered attitude at meals; constantly restless and pursues insignificant acquaintances for her entertainment, immediately identifying herself as the grand-daughter of General Wille and from the Schwarzenbach family at Bocken, cleverly namedropping and insinuating her acquaintance with famous people, especially from the literary world, but doesn't brag about her own work. After a few days, all of the inmates know her story, her problems with addiction, and her lesbian preferences are remarked on.[106]

In his report he indicated that she could not be trusted to tell the truth, a mendacity that Renée had long known.

At the beginning of December Annemarie left the clinic against Dr. Forel's advice and headed to Basel to spend two weeks with Erika, who was performing at the Gambrinus Theater. Klaus found Annemarie seemingly in 'better condition but still shaky'.[107]

At Christmas 1935, at the end of a tempestuous peripatetic year, she played the piano at Bocken in a melancholy mood. In January she travelled to her rented house in Sils Maria. The travel writer, Gertrude Bell had observed, is just moving through and then moving on. 'Like packmen, we unfasten our wares, open our little bundle of experiences, spread them out and finger them over: the ship touches at the port, and silks and tinsel are gathered up and strapped upon our backs and carried – God knows where!'[108]

7

Two Women, a Ford and a Rolleiflex

... blues from everywhere and nowhere, the wild and steadfast song of the downtrodden, both jungle cry and feverish hymn, played with a perceptible undertow of seduction and protest.
Annemarie Schwarzenbach, 'Dark End of the Street in Washington'

The Schwarzenbach name had for decades been associated with silk in the mill towns of Pennsylvania and the factories of Hoboken. Labour at the looms was mostly female and non-unionized. The Depression had tightened silk belts and brought home the fragile balancing act between capital and manpower. By the time Annemarie visited the United States in the late summer of 1936, her writing had begun to focus on the social conditions of workers, on exploitation in factories, mines and lumber mills. For a boss's daughter, she pulled few punches:

> Success went hand in glove with ruthlessness, and the Puritan mind saw to it that this was pleasing to the Almighty. To become rich therefore took on a moral dimension – a cruel irony if we recall the origins of some of America's greatest fortunes. Despite everything, the survival of the fittest held sway.[1]

She left for the United States from Le Havre on 26 August. Klaus and Erika weren't far behind, on board the *Statendam* from Rotterdam. Klaus had corresponded with American publishers Knopf about a possible deal for his novel *Pathetic Symphony*, and hoped publication of *Mephisto* would follow suit. Unlike Annemarie, the Manns could rely on name recognition and fitted into the American cult of literary celebrity. Annemarie was an unknown – her books hadn't made much of an impression beyond Switzerland, her journalism had limited appeal, and her Middle Eastern travel writing hadn't sold. She was determined, however, to establish herself on a more professional footing as a journalist, and had arrangements with a string of Swiss papers. Her approach to photography professionalized apace: in New York she made contact with the Black Star photo agency in order to distribute her work.

In *Death in Persia*, a character called Barbara holds her own against a right-thinking young archaeologist called Heynes:

> They were having an intense debate about Roosevelt and the National Recovery Administration. Heynes was barely able to counter Barbara's wonderfully concise arguments. He was trying to play the sceptic but she was protesting in her deep, strident voice. ...
>
> 'What's the point?' asked Heynes, leaning his head on the back of the chair. 'What's the use of knowing that you can't solve the Black issue? That America is a pile of problems our best men fail to solve.'[2]

America's 'pile of problems' became a focus of Annemarie's writing and photography over the course of three trans-Atlantic visits during the next five years.

LIFE magazine launched in November 1936 with a cover photo showing Fort Peck Dam in Montana taken by Margaret Bourke-White, one of six female photographers on the staff.[3] It was a New Deal project, all concrete and pylons, and that the photographer was a woman can't have been lost on Annemarie. In the new year she planned to report with Baa on the miners' strike in Pittsburgh. In the meantime, President Roosevelt was coming up for re-election in November, facing Republican hopeful Alf Landon, and Annemarie covered it for the *National-Zeitung* in Basel.

During the President's first term, his New Deal had attempted to lift the country out of the worst of the Depression, shoring up ordinary Americans against the predations of 'business and financial monopoly, speculation, reckless banking'.[4] Roosevelt understood that when times are tough, employers double down and empathy is in short supply. Eight million Americans, however, were still without jobs and labour unrest had led to strikes. Roosevelt had supported the Wagner Act of 1935, guaranteeing the right to unions and collective bargaining, and the Social Security Act which provided relief for the unemployed. America was voting along its perennial fault line: democratic solidarity confronting Republican individualism, mild socialism versus laissez-faire capitalism.

Besides economic intervention, Washington was chronicling the effects of the Depression on the culture of the South, where a way of

**Annemarie Schwarzenbach with her Rolleiflex Standard 621 camera, 1938. Photo by
Anita Forrer**
Courtesy of Swiss Literary Archives

life that had endured since the Civil War was passing into history. In 1936 the Library of Congress started recording negro spirituals, work songs and field chants while the novel *Gone with the Wind* (1936), the musical *Porgy and Bess* (1935), Gershwin and jazz all appropriated and commercialized forms of Black and Southern culture. Annemarie's articles over the coming year anatomized the interaction of class and race on which the old south was predicated, and the north's ready exploitation of less organized and cheaper southern labour as industry expanded. She knew that cant phrases and twinkle-eyed founding myths rang hollow, that the American Dream was spun sugar on a very thin slice of pie.

In Washington, Annemarie stayed at Barbara's mother's house on Waterside Drive. Elizabeth Washburn Wright was the widow of Dr. Hamilton Wright, a government-appointed anti-drug crusader against Chinese opium. He died in 1917 when Barbara was still a child. His wife, well connected in Washington circles, carried on his delegate work. Barbara appears to have been one of thirty photographers under Roy Stryker, in charge of documentary photography at the Resettlement Administration, later renamed the Farm Security Administration (FSA).[5] This gave Annemarie access to the FSA archive. Her first reports in October 1936 for *Zürcher Illustrierte* made use of photos by Walker Evans, Dorothea Lange and Arthur Rothstein. Evans had worked with writer James Agee for *Fortune* magazine in summer 1936, and Annemarie made use of Agee's October 1933 and May 1935 articles in *Fortune* as background material for her reports. Her own photos began to take on the imagery and grittiness we associate with these pioneering photographers, capturing 'the unemployed, street children, the homeless and others left behind by American society'.[6] Perhaps too she was aware of the German photojournalist Hansel Mieth, employed by *LIFE* magazine, who recorded the effects of the Depression for posterity.[7]

In Washington, Annemarie wrote about the availability of cocaine out by the airport and black panhandlers by the port:

> Skinny young black guys wander around the port precinct, picking up cigarette butts, dancing barefoot or tap-dancing in tattered boots. They accompany their movements with a low-whistled ditty, waiting on a nickel or a dime tossed from the deck of the port restaurant. Then the pack mutely throws itself on this booty and in a split second it's a free-for-all.[8]

This keen observation, typical of her reports, pitches the have-nots against the haves and highlights 'the stark differences between rich and poor, white and black, while fundamentally casting doubt on the viability of the "American Dream"'.[9]

In September she travelled north to Maine where early voting was slated, and noted the Russian source of timber for the Hearst newspaper empire – an early instance of globalism coming into conflict with home production:

Hearst, the press baron, procured paper for his newspapers and magazines in a rival establishment that bought its timber from Russia instead of from Maine. Nonetheless, in the shop windows of the Republican end of town, posters trumpeted in black and white the great benefits the same Mr. Hearst had bestowed on local businesses … 'That's just bluff', explained the young Canadian.[10]

The Republicans won by a slim majority in Maine.

The Manns, meanwhile, had arrived at the Bedford Hotel on East 40th Street, which exiled German and Jewish intellectuals used as a base in New York. On arrival, the news wasn't good about Annemarie's health. An infected needle had led to septicaemia in her leg – perhaps a recurrence of a similar problem with her leg in Persia. Erika travelled to Washington to minister help, conscious that again she was playing nurse. Annemarie's messenger boy was Michael Logan, a friend of Baa's, and Klaus was smitten: 'Dancer, really nice; smart as well. … *Michael reste la nuit chez moi. Tendresse*', reads Klaus's diary,[11] and intermittently during his stay in America Michael danced attendance. The Bedford would become Klaus's home from home over the next four years as his family moved to Princeton and California and he himself criss-crossed the country on lecture tours. Erika had friends with benefits: Martin Gumpert, also resident at the Bedford, was a writer and doctor who supplied morphine and with whom Erika became involved; she also took up with New York banker and financier Maurice Wertheim who professed an interest in supporting her Peppermill cabaret, due to open on 5 January 1937 at the Chanin auditorium on Lexington Avenue.[12] There was an air of make-or-break about the operation.

Throughout the autumn, worries continued about Annemarie's health. She too based herself at the Bedford, and helped Klaus translate his articles into English. She was also on the cocktail circuit. On 3 November, election night, she was guest of a Republican women's club, 'in a quiet, well-to-do neighbourhood'. From there she went to an up-and-coming fashion designer's atelier where 'a group of young "radicals" – socialists, Communists, painters, journalists and writers – crowded around a small radio and heatedly discussed Roosevelt's re-election' for a second term:

Around one o'clock in the morning the defeated candidate Alfred Landon sent a congratulatory telegram to Roosevelt, clarifying his intention to go duck hunting. The radio announced that the President's famous laugh was audible from the balcony of his Hyde Park house.[13] In Times Square an incalculable crowd gathered.[14]

By early November Annemarie had settled in New York. The exiles celebrated Thanksgiving at their hotel with Erika and the crew and ended the evening with Annemarie, Magnus Henning (cabaret pianist) and Lotte Goslar (dancer) at the Apollo Vaudeville Theater. Annemarie wasn't, therefore, invited to celebrate Thanksgiving at the Hamilton-Wright home in Washington: or chose not to. The same group of friends dined again on the 28th, and in a Mexican restaurant on the 30th. In the midst of this social whirlwind, Klaus learned that his father had been deprived of German citizenship.[15] Now the whole Mann family was adrift. Klaus celebrated Christmas in Erika's room at the Bedford, a sad-sweet little fest with tree, presents, roast chicken from the deli, champagne and gramophone music. Annemarie and members of the cabaret joined them: no Christmas dinner with Baa and her mother in Washington. The New Year brought Klaus a proposal for a lecture tour of the United States in the autumn. Travelling on temporary Dutch papers, his three-month visa had run its course. He returned to Europe with hope of better success in the autumn: money was tight.[16]

'Somehow it didn't quite click'[17] wrote Klaus diplomatically about the fortunes of his sister's cabaret in the new world. The difference in cultures was as wide as the Atlantic: the American audience wanted cabaret with frou-frou shaking a leg – instead they got ironic, politically engaged German humour delivered with an accent. Barbara and Annemarie were at the première at the Chanin Auditorium, after which singer Spivey Le Voe regaled them at Tony's nightclub on West 52nd Street, where they waited for the early papers with their not-very-good theatre notices. Despite moving to a better venue, the New School for Social Research, the show that had been a success in a dozen European countries, died a death in New York. The re-jigged performance was sparsely attended by an audience of sixty – thirty of them press and only sixteen paying. The critics praised Therese Giehse but panned the show. On 6 January, Klaus ate with Annemarie at the oyster bar in Grand Central and already the première had become a 'fiasco'. On the 9th she saw him safely on board the steamer – the *Lafayette* – back to Europe.

The failure of Erika's cabaret venture brought grit to the mill and cracks surfaced in the relationships among this group of friends. Erika had travelled first class across the Atlantic on the *Statendam* and had been living it up with her investment banker Maurice Wertheim at the Bedford while the cast had travelled steerage in a cement freighter and been paid a pittance. Recriminations flew now that fortunes were not to be made.[18] Erika was bossy and not egalitarian at heart.[19] Annemarie, all fired up by her visit to the striking miners in Pennsylvania, sided with the cast. 'Annemarie was high on stirring things up, going from room to room, spreading malicious gossip in her puerile manner like a girl at boarding school',[20] wrote Erika to Klaus. Comrade Annemarie had got a dose of communism and reproached Erika for consorting with 'dirty capitalists' – meaning Wertheim; a bit rich coming from the grand-daughter of the king of silk. On a Sunday visit to Long Island, she went behind her old friend's back and told Wertheim – who had financially bailed out the show – of bad blood between cast members and Erika, suggesting he pay the performers their dues directly.[21] 'New York was a real nightmare in the end', Annemarie wrote to Klaus, suggesting that she, Therese Giehse and Magnus Henning hightail it off to Hollywood to seek their fortunes and leave Erika in peace.[22] 'We closed temporarily, leaving a sizeable deficit and a situation that had all the makings of a financial disaster',[23] wrote Erika to her mother. Annemarie always liked a bit of high drama, Erika had a propensity to boss people around, and Wertheim, playing the field between marriages, knew how to roll with the losses.

The elephant that stalked the rooms of the Bedford was morphine addiction, hiding in plain sight. Both Annemarie and Klaus were strung out, with Erika occasionally indulging. On the *Lafayette*, Klaus couldn't sleep and had recourse to Pantopon, an opium derivative supplied by the ship's doctor. Annemarie fared no better, on morphine supplied by Gumpert and in the jazz bars of Greenwich Village.

*

'Nobody in his right mind goes to Pittsburgh without being sent, certainly not for pleasure', began Annemarie's account of her visit with

Baa in the bitterly cold January of 1937. The General Motors strike in Flint was on and John L. Lewis, leader of the United Mine Workers of America, the most powerful union in the States, was all over the news. The two women were determined to see the effects of the Depression and mining conditions for themselves. In Mount Pleasant, a borough of Westmoreland County, a seam excavated by the Frick Mines darkened the landscape, settled by Dutch and German immigrants from the Rhine Palatinate 200 years earlier. 'The hotel is a fleapit', wrote Annemarie, 'water trickles from a tap, the one movie theatre screens an old Hollywood standard and is packed. In the bar, two Scotsmen whine about the "hunkies" – Hungarians and Slovakians who have recently pitched up on the labour market and undercut wages.'[24] They met the project manager of the Westmoreland housing and re-employment initiative:

> He is in charge of some fifteen hundred men and the job is not easy. Americans, Slovakians, Scottish – many illiterate, few understanding English, all unemployed miners with years of dark misery ingrained on their faces. Given a house, a small garden, they are signed up for work schemes either on the cooperative's farm or on new construction sites. Some drive tractors, others raise chickens, still others become fine agricultural workers.[25]

In Pittsburgh, 'the main struggle in America today plays out contentiously: the struggle between big business and labour'. She noted the wide gap between rich and poor, black and white, attributing wealth in the iron towns to exploitation of cheap labour, the old squeeze of capitalism.

> On an early evening in January, under mizzling rain, we drove along Fifth Avenue where all the wealth of the city is concentrated: the Carnegie Museum, the Greek temple-style Mellon Library, all Parian marble and hewn stone. The soulless décor of the Webster Hall Hotel … Negroes manned the bar, heaving with commercial travellers, rich sons of good family, students, women in showy evening dress, accessorized with artificial nosegays and costume jewellery.[26]

They ran the gauntlet of letters of introduction and private security guards – revolvers, truncheons – in order to visit Jones and Laughlin steel works at Aliquippa near Pittsburgh, the fourth largest in the US, employing 11,000 blue collar workers. Met with suspicion, these were the first female visitors in two years. 'What's a foreigner looking for in Pittsburgh? What might interest a young woman in the Iron City?'[27] American capitalists only wanted a public-relations story told; they preferred journalists on message and employed lawyers and public relations people to keep it that way. Four hours later, burnished from the furnaces, the two women paid a call on the Committee for the Organization of Steelworkers where a former student apprised them of union membership. In a handful of articles about the strike and the iron towns, Annemarie showed labour and capital at loggerheads in a perspective that few tackled in American journalism.

> Up to now America has had no sense of social responsibility nor legislation other than that which is pro-business – a state of affairs which today can only have dire consequences when it comes to conflict, since there is no legal basis for accepting *human rights*, nor the needs of a forty-million strong blue-collar labour force. Legally they don't have a leg to stand on.[28]

In Pittsburgh she met labour leader John L. Lewis, former miner and man of the hour, who arranged letters of introduction to United Mine Worker representatives. Everywhere in the mining towns Annemarie noticed the ramshackle precariousness of employment and housing. '"In America everybody feels free to shape his own destiny and well-being as long as he has two strong arms and an ounce of courage." This tired old rallying cry of the right-wingers justifies an absence of social legislation and social security.'[29] At Scotts Run, a ghost town, site of a mine that had opened quickly and boomed in wartime, the Quakers were dispensing soup to 'the unemployed, young and old, black and white, leaning against the front of the drugstore in the sunshine, hunkered down waiting on – what?'[30]

Writing to Klaus, Annemarie seemed bowled over by the solidarity among workers, thinking it a shame that he has 'neither seen nor experienced all of this'.[31] The articles and photos resulting from her foray into Pittsburgh labour politics and mining towns appeared in a swathe of mostly left-leaning Swiss publications. Her contact with bosses and miners, on the one hand suspicious and entitled, on the other welcoming and downtrodden, galvanized Annemarie's sense of justice. She saw that American society needed 'to put into practice the principle that human rights should take precedence over property rights'[32] – a moral hierarchy that still needs realignment.

She noted the paranoid fear bosses felt towards collective action. She had few illusions about the cant terms – freedom, American Dream, individualism – employed to paper over the lack of real social protection and provision in American life: healthcare, sanitary housing, minimum wage, the right to unionize, a legal framework for employment that sided with workers: the old chestnuts still with us. She saw all that capitalist blagging for what it was and witnessed the United States move from what V.S. Pritchett calls the 'swaggering, self-righteous and hectoring mood of the twenties, into the humiliation and revolution of the thirties'.[33]

Besides the Protestant ethic and the spirit of capitalism, what struck Annemarie was the degradation of the environment that this entailed. Fresh from Pittsburgh's coal fields, the highway strip malls and temporary housing of factory towns, she saw that capitalism exploited and moved on, leaving an exhausted environment and people in its wake:

> The First World War ushered in speculation on the price of wheat, resulting in enormous prairies being converted to wheat fields, left fallow when the price of grain again fell. Wind skimmed off the thin exposed topsoil. In crisis years, devastating dust storms raged for the first time, threatening to transform large swathes of the Midwest into desert, if they hadn't already done so. As far as the Canadian border in the north, timber companies bought up the forests and carelessly felled them – exposing the terrain to rampant erosion. And more and more small farmers and ruined sharecroppers join the army of 'migrant workers' on the great American highway, turning up in Florida to pick raspberries, in Texas for the cotton harvest, migrants against whom rich California in 1936 closed its borders.[34]

At the beginning of February 1937, after five months in the United States, Annemarie and 'the matronly, gregarious, thespian'[35] Therese Giehse boarded the steamer bound for Le Havre. Giehse felt somewhat battered by the American failure of the cabaret but also by Erika's defections from the distaff side – Erika remained in New York and had broken up with Maurice Wertheim.[36] Christopher Isherwood described Giehse at this time as an 'unforgettable actress', singling out a scene 'in which she nursed the globe of the world on her lap like a sick child and crooned weirdly over it',[37] anticipating Chaplin's handling of the globe in *The Great Dictator* (1940).

They descended the gangway at Le Havre to a Europe on tenterhooks. At the back of Annemarie's mind was the precarious state of her father's health. Alfred was in Arosa, recuperating from a third cancer operation. On the way to Sils, she visited her mother and Emmy at Alp Blüemlisberg, the Schwarzenbach mountain chalet in the Canton of Schwyz, where photos show the mannish older women (Emmy in cardie and dicky-bow) affectionate with each other, Annemarie thinner and sporting round dark glasses.[38] It was Valentine's Day and there was snow on the mountains. New York had been 'a nerve-racking nightmare' – Annemarie never really took to the city – and she outlined to Klaus her changed financial circumstances as well as what he owed her for his earlier stay in the house in Sils. Winter season in the Engadine was drawing to an end. She and Therese Giehse were welcomed back to Sils by the American cabaret singer Spivy Le Voe, who appears to have been house-sitting in their absence. Klaus had met Spivy at Tony's nightclub in New York in December. Born Bertha Levine in Brooklyn, a lesbian entertainer, nightclub owner and character actress, she was sometimes described as 'The Female Noël Coward'. Annemarie must have extended an invitation since Klaus expressed surprise that Spivy was *in situ*:[39]

> She is a lovely person but neither of us knows what to talk about, except how to introduce and set her up with the Palace beau monde, the owners, the maitre d', the jazz band. She has managed to create an impression. Of course she was really pleased, but seems curiously helpless. And so she is here in Sils with Mr Doctor the dog, Therese and me, and our little family has caused a stir.[40]

Spivy's song 'The Tarantella' gives a flavour of her character: 'She dressed up like a fella in a suit of real bright yellow just to give the audience a thrill,/ She would prance in her dance with the chance that her pants wouldn't stand the strain.' Quite what sedate Sils made of Spivy is left to the reader's imagination but she was not invited to Bocken. Ten days later, Spivy had gone to Zurich and a firmer note entered Annemarie's correspondence with Klaus: 'It is sweet of you to take on the wickedly funny and somehow particularly nice Spivy – but of course she should head off to Paris and London, that has to be made clear to her.' Perhaps Spivy had overstayed her welcome. In Zurich, Klaus picked her up at her hotel and they had dinner followed by '*genommen*' – Klaus's code word for drugs.[41]

*

In late September, Annemarie and Baa boarded the *Dampfer* again, third class on the *S.S. Berengaria*, bound for New York. A remarkable sequence of photographs survives, of fellow passengers on deck, young refugees in ill-fitting suits and greasy hats, the tired and poor, huddled against the cold Atlantic wind, heading for a new life in America. Klaus and Tomski had preceded the two women by a week, Klaus in love and struggling with his addiction and the twenty-two-year-old Tomski returning home to mother after an adventurous three years in Europe. Erika met her brother and his new boyfriend off the steamer. They were greeted by a pack of photographers and journalists, one of whom asked Klaus about his love life. He alluded to a romance with a Swiss girl, Tomski standing po-faced beside him, yet another tableau from the closeted life.[42] Klaus had a lecture tour in the offing, as had Erika, and their manager had sent the press to the pier.[43]

Annemarie and Baa had no such reception. They planned a three-week road-trip of the American South, focusing on the plight of sharecroppers, on industrial exploitation and race – the dark underbelly of the Cotton Belt – but also visiting colleges and New Deal flagship projects. Swiss editors had assured Annemarie that her articles were in demand and she had spent the eight intervening months touring Germany, the Baltic States, the Soviet Union and Sweden, observing fascism on the move in Europe.

Klaus went on the road, giving talks in bookstores and libraries in Detroit, Chicago, Rochester, New York and Richmond, Virginia. There were chatty lunches and dinners with organizers, reading in the Pullman car, meetings with professors and students, enthusiastic women's clubs, that vast metropolitan and provincial America, eager for culture. His speech, 'A Family Against Dictatorship', was delivered each time as though new-minted. In Richmond an audience of three hundred women

Barbara Hamilton-Wright, 1936–38. Photo by Annemarie Schwarzenbach
Courtesy of Swiss Literary Archives and Wikimedia Commons

lapped it up, at Boston's Ford Hall Forum there were twelve hundred. He was on the American road, earning a buck.

Annemarie wrote about refugees. One of her most charged pieces of writing at this time concerns a German political exile called Max Meister, perhaps a pseudonym. The Workers Defense League had suggested she meet 'a typical case, representative of the particular historical moment we are going through'.[44] Meister, an unemployed metalworker, member of the Workers Socialist Party, was unassuming: 'there's nothing special about my case, there are hundreds like me you could interview, who were in concentration camps for political prisoners and who escaped … A few days after the Reichstag fire, the first arrests began, and a few weeks later, they nabbed me. I had just finished handing out my leaflets.'

169

Meister's tale of concentration camp, and staying one step ahead of German officialdom, distils the feeling of being stateless, between worlds. Shuttled from country to country, pitching up in Spanish North Africa, prey to people smugglers, seeking safe haven, Meister had stowed away on a Norwegian boat heading to the United States and was seeking asylum. His tale resembles countless stories of refugees in our own time:

> Now it's 7 July 1937. The American press rushed to Ellis Island where Meister was held in quarantine. He was going to be returned on the same boat, back to Germany. ... An hour before he was due to board ship the Workers' Defense League intervened – in the nick of time, like in a movie.[45]

'Driving a Ford 8, equipped with two Rolleiflex cameras, three weeks before us, we went in search of the South – the real South of present-day America.'[46] Annemarie and Baa were also equipped with contacts and letters of introduction. As they motored south, Annemarie noticed the land:

> Mile after mile of highway goes by. Scorched and parched after the summer drought, the land is exhausted by poverty that has endured seventy years. Along the wide Tennessee River Valley, fall leaves brighten the hills, matching the exposed cracks in the red earth, their flanks scoured by wind and flood.[47]

First stop was Knoxville where the Tennessee River Valley Authority had its offices. The newly completed Norris Dam was thirty miles upstream while 'whole districts have neither electricity nor running water'. Annemarie immediately noticed the poverty by the river, under the enormous neon sign of the Andrew Johnson Hotel.[48] Knoxville's movie theatre was showing *Damaged Lives* and down on Waterfront Street they were in evidence:

> Today it's the poorest part of town. Pasty children play under the pylons of the bridge, climbing its iron struts, growing up in its shade. Furtive black kids, shivering in flimsy clothes, lean against the sides of sheds or slip with ease through the scrublands at the edge of the river, holding a cigarette between skinny fingers.[49]

Officialdom and polite society bracketed their movements, eager to project a positive picture: 'A policeman emerges from the shade of the bridge and asks me if he can escort me "home". He makes sure to follow me until I reach the bright neon-lit streets of the upper town.'[50]

The two women headed to Chattanooga and Monteagle. Filling up with gas, they got a flavour of the fault lines of the South:

> While a black man wearing torn blue overalls cleans the windscreen of my Ford and the tank slowly fills up, a limousine pulls into the forecourt of the gas station with a squeal of brakes, and rear ends my bumper. ...
>
> 'Hey, nigger!' (They can see from the licence plate that my automobile's from Washington.) 'Come over here, boy, and fill 'er up instead of that Yankee tourist. We're in a hurry.'[51]

They're from the American Legion and heading to the Highlander Folk School to stir trouble. Annemarie and Baa had a letter of introduction to the school's director, a young Miles Horton, from the American Civil Liberties Union. Horton and his school's Communist reputation had riled the rednecks. 'The legionnaires are usually drunk and looking for trouble', the gas station owner tells the two women. When the two reporters eventually arrived at the school, they found a collection of activists:

> Ruby, a young sociologist and teacher at one of the best US women's colleges, is reading a workers' newspaper. ... She's here for a six-week course on the American Labor Movement ... Spright, a boy whose real identity is kept from me and who is here neither as teacher nor student but as refugee. He had been locked up for daring to get involved in the mobilization of workers in Memphis. The CIO bailed him out, but he had to flee the state.[52]

Founded in 1932, the Highlander Folk School – still there as the Highlander Research and Education Center – was Horton's attempt to put into practice social and political views that influenced a generation of Civil Rights activists. Horton's connections with the CIO, the school's anti-segregation stance and the founder's radical philosophy all raised the reactionary south's hackles. Annemarie's photos show a bespectacled Horton in homespun clothes, a man with the common touch – 'one of their own, a farm boy who speaks their language, smokes the same tobacco'. Horton facilitated contact with labour and union activists in the area, as well as opening up the intricacies of square dancing and the effects of the Depression on ordinary farmers, lumberjacks and miners. 'Besides teaching, Myles is also a union organizer. While we're driving along in his beat-up Chevy on the bumpy forest tracks, visiting mines, lumber camps, work camps, it's clear that he's the most popular man around.'[53]

Through Horton, Annemarie met Aline Bryant:

> Aline is twenty-four and has been working for seven years in a variety of textile factories. She has been a doffer and a carder, a spinner, sewn pockets, trousers, overalls on the sewing machine. ... The shift was from 6.20 in the morning until 15.30, with a break of twenty minutes for lunch. Saturday and Sunday were off.[54]

Aline was sacked when she joined the TWOC union. She'd been hitched to the infamous Bedaux system with its hiked-up 'performance targets' linked to 'production targets' – standard employers' pincers movement: how to get more from the workers for less. 'Younger factory girls took up the slack: girls from the hills, from the back of beyond, who don't know what they're letting themselves in for.'[55] Aline organized a strike, 'Be wise – organize!' ran the slogan of the day, while police hand in glove with factory owners landed her in prison. Aline's case, like Max Meister's, was indicative of what happens when workers buck the system.

With Myles, they headed into the Cumberland Mountains around Palmer, where a miners' strike was ongoing. Myles was keeping his head down. 'The mining and timber company bosses tell their workers that the CIO labour leaders are Reds, outsiders from the North. "If you sign up to the CIO, your dues get sent to Russia and Spain where Commies are setting fire to churches."'[56]

In Grundy County, Tennessee, as in Pittsburgh mining towns earlier in the year, Annemarie observed a ravaged community: timber barons and mining companies exploited people and landscape, then moved on, leaving landscape scarred, tree cover removed, inhabitants and their only resource despoiled.

Monteagle was a haven for the two roving reporters. They spent a week at the school, saving on hotel bills, served porridge, bacon and watery coffee for breakfast, and made sorties into the backwoods, met activists, labour organizers – 'made of different stuff here than in New York' – and ordinary mountain folk. Annemarie drafted a series of articles about the Tennessee Valley Authority, Knoxville, and the American South – appearing in *National-Zeitung*, *ABC* and *Die Weltwoche* before the year was out or soon after her return.

By 11 November they were on the road to Birmingham, Alabama, where clouds of pollution ringed the city, 'like unseasonable thunderheads'. They took a room at the Hilton – 'big, bleak, unbelievably filthy', with gum-chewing shady-looking men in the lobby. Their contact was Mrs. Clara Martin, a handler of the CIO and TWOC,[57] who had switched allegiance from the Works Progress Administration to more direct action. Visiting Smithfield Court, a New Deal public housing project for the black community, she comments: 'If the negroes are down in the hole, some white folks have to stay with them.' The 1937 US Housing Act facilitated finance for low-rent housing. Annemarie's writing on Birmingham shows an understanding of how race and exploitation went fist in glove:

> When Roosevelt launched his New Deal, Birmingham was one of the cities most in need of government support. Diseases such as syphilis were widespread.[58] A housing development called Smithfield Court is one of few such government projects in a black neighbourhood. … [T]housands of negroes still live in miserable shacks without water or electricity. The number of unemployed and needy is high; prospective wages for those seeking employment are extremely low.[59]

Mrs. Martin accompanied them to Siluria, a mill-town south of Birmingham, where the mill was on a three-day week and company housing lacked running water – the whole place 'like a prison camp'.[60]

Montgomery proved more refined: its old houses with pillared porches, the Capitol buildings, its negro market selling sugarcane, cotton, fruit. Annemarie and Baa drank cocktails in the Drum Room bar of the Jefferson Davis Hotel – segregated, of course, right into the sixties. The next day they took photos of a gang of road workers – all of them black – with their picks and shovels in front of the State Capitol.

En route to Columbus they stopped off at Tuskegee:

Road labourers in Montgomery, Alabama. Photo by Annemarie Schwarzenbach
Courtesy of Swiss Literary Archives and Wikimedia Commons

We are now deep in the black belt – and most impressive is Tuskegee – where Booker T. Washington founded his negro school. He was a liberal struck by the tragedy of his race. The goal of his college was not education and emancipation – but resignation: the negroes were obliged to stick to their 'station' and learn a trade![61]

Traditional southern hospitality welcomed them to Columbus, Georgia, where the plantation class hosted the two women warily. 'Invited for cocktails, dinners of roast turkey, stuffed oysters, tender artichokes and avocado salad', their hosts' antebellum spiel about the South proved equally embellished and self-serving. Among activists and New Dealers, Annemarie and Baa came across as fighting for the cause but these business-minded, plantation-raised Southerners, two generations on from slavery and eighty years before Trump, kept suspect journalists at bay behind Southern charm. 'They sent us flowers, mentioned us in their newspapers, made sure we sampled their strong corn whiskey, and never let up for one minute the suspicion they had of us – less so towards me, a foreigner, than towards my American colleague from the North, and therefore a Yankee.'[62] The *Columbus Ledger* for 11 November 1937 focused exclusively on the genteel side of these visitors, their family backgrounds and social cachet. Annemarie had developed a 'hard nose for the unadorned grim reality of the struggle playing out here between the plantation system and industrialization, racism and cheap wages, fascist methods and the working-class future.'[63] Had her hosts in Columbus read this account they would have called the police and run her out of town. She saw through the Southern hospitality schtick, its gentility and paternalism.

> She was President of the Daughters of the American Revolution and of the local chapter of a charity society, together with the Georgia Patriots and the National Society of the Colonial Dames of America. Her husband was a district judge, her brother Chief of Police, her brother-in-law on the Roads Department and Board of Health, her uncle had been a Senator and in his hale seventies took on the mantle of patriarch, in the shoes of their blessed father who had held the rank of captain in the Civil War. Over the previous three days I'd managed to learn this saga by heart.[64]

By now, Annemarie has got a handle on the true winners of the Civil War: white Northern industrialists, investors and conglomerates who took advantage of cheap labour and favourable conditions in the South. 'Money and enterprise drifted south, where the "slavocracy" remained dormant and justified a multitude of sins.'[65] The abolition of slavery had been a noble-sounding fig-leaf; once slaves got their freedom they were indentured anew: Black Codes under Johnsonian recon-struction; vagrancy laws; white suprematism; the Jim Crow South and its abrogation of rights.

Annemarie's gatekeepers presented a united and curated front. William Clark Bradley, a mill owner in Columbus, Georgia, parroted 'performance enhancement', competition and efficiency. Annemarie brought up the plight of the workers while her hostess-chaperone upbraided her for being so bold: 'People should be happy that they're earning anything at all these days. But they're ruined by these government hand-outs.' At the entrance to the mill, seated between a lawyer and a grotesque chaperone, security guards 'with guns and truncheons checked our visitor passes, then let the car through'.[66]

> I observed a girl changing bobbins in a spinning room. Her arms and hands flew back and forth speedily and rhythmically. But the fixed, haunted look in her eyes in a lean, prematurely-aged face, covered in sweat, belonged to an automaton. She worked an eleven-hour shift. ... A shaft of sunlight fell obliquely into the room through frosted glass. My chaperone bunched up a towel against her mouth and nose to guard against the cotton fibers and tried to shout feebly over the din of the looms. 'See how sunny the room is', she said. 'It must be so lovely to work here surrounded by all these colours and fabrics.'[67]

Security was tight, too, at the penitentiary in Harris County, Georgia, which she visited with the state medical officer. 'A white guard, a giant of a man, prevented me from taking photos of the inmates – mostly blacks, sitting in the prison yard, their ankles heavily shackled. A few days after my visit, black inmates enticed a prison guard into a cell and lynched him before the police were able to put down the riot with tear gas.' She annotated what photos she could take: 'The penal system of the southern states is extremely backward. Black people in particular take the brunt. For petty theft, disobedience to plantation overseers etc. they are sentenced to hard labour as chain-gang convicts ... Even inside prison, there's segregation: white convicts have separate cells and eat at separate tables.'[68]

The two roving reporters turned their Ford north, homeward through the Carolinas. In Charleston, Annemarie snapped the gravestones of the French Huguenot cemetery before moving on to the DuPont Belle chemical plant – 'Ammonia Department' – spewing pollution into a leaden sky, with dirty snow in the shunting yards where coal and chemical-laden freight trains waited. Her interest in documenting industrial landscape – 'the downside of technological progress' – stemmed

Children in Charleston, South Carolina. Photo by Annemarie Schwarzenbach
Courtesy of Swiss Literary Archives and Wikimedia Commons

from Joris Ivens' *New Earth* (1933) screened at the Soviet Writers Conference. She 'observed and reported on enormous modernization, industrialization, urban development and infrastructure projects in the Soviet Union, Turkey and Iran.'[69] Now American industrialization joined this list.

In Charlottesville, home to the University of Virginia, founded by Thomas Jefferson, with James Madison and James Monroe on its board of governors – presidents, statesmen, plantation owners and slavers all – the two reporters were back under the Palladian pillars. Slaves built the university, served its august masters, and their descendants weren't admitted until the 1960s. Annemarie's flying visits to Tuskegee, Wesleyan College, the University of Virginia and Princeton, as well as her observations about child labour in field and factory, gave her a clear picture of how private white education operated in the American body politic. Industrial and racial exploitation was the grubby fertilizer under the groves of academe, a truth found less palatable to a generation of students a century later.

A strike was underway at the Mansfield Mills in Lumberton, North Carolina, and factories on a three-day week. When they asked for directions to East Lumberton, the policeman was immediately suspicious: 'What are these two more or less smartly-dressed classy women doing in this workingman's town? ... Conditions among cotton workers resembled those described by Dickens',[70] wrote Annemarie.

> Mrs. Jacobs, mother of eight, working in Lumberton since the age of twenty, still earns five and a half dollars a week, is in debt to the factory, hasn't received cash wages in over a year, and is living with her husband and children in a two-room shack. ... There was no running water, toilets were outside, the company switched electric power on and off at will.[71]

The Depression meant orders were down. A large unemployed labour force – black and 'white trash' (a term frequently heard on her travels) – in company towns, logging towns, mining towns, presented a recipe for trouble. 'If their manpower was no longer needed, then any excuse would do to get rid of them.'[72] Annemarie – fresh from Moscow – understood this class struggle as a consequence of the American belief in laissez faire with competitive carelessness as the bedrock of capitalism.

She could also see the planter class was isolationist, defensive, racist, often ignorant and religiously fundamentalist. The poor whites underneath them weren't much better. Sentimentality about the South – *Gone with the Wind* and all that – was a way for the United States to face its headwinds. 'American memory was seduced by juleps, hoop skirts, Uncle Remus and fear', as writer Marilynne Robinson decades later described it.[73] Annemarie could see that the underclass of American prosperity was uneducated, often illiterate, stuck in corners of the South where exploitation of natural resources – wood, coal, cotton, slaves – was the only raison d'être for mining and logging towns, those boom and bust company outposts:

> In Alabama 26% of blacks are illiterate, in Mississippi 23%, in South Carolina 27%. In Alabama two fifths of the population are black, in Mississippi it's over 50%, in South Carolina almost 50%. The more blacks there are, the more widespread illiteracy, illness and crime. More blacks means more lynching, more Ku Klux Klan wielding force, a group whose terrorists methods keep the blacks subjugated in fear.[74]

Their return to Washington after a three-week swing across the Dixie Line coincided with debate in Congress about lynching. The endless filibusters of segregationists and racists, blocking black voting rights and access to justice, were in rhetorical force once more – and not for the last time: similar blocking techniques came into play with Johnson's Voting Rights Act of 1965. Time and again in her travels, the sore subject was race, which Annemarie tackled head on in one of the last of her reports, 'For the Honour of the South':

> There are good reasons these days to remind ourselves of the Scottsboro Boys. Seven years ago, on 6 April 1931, the first court case opened against nine black men and boys, aged between thirteen and twenty, who were arrested on 25 March of the same year and accused of raping two young white women, Victoria Price and Ruby Bates. The accused were dragged through trial after trial and finally sentenced to the electric chair.[75]

She pointed to Southern intransigence and injustice as the culprits:

> In January 1938, draft anti-lynching legislation was discussed in Washington in front of Congress – and not for the first time, Southern Senators and representatives boycotted and succeeded in holding up parliamentary proceedings to the point where the motion was postponed and eventually shelved.[76]

She had no illusions about the historical roots of the problem. 'For generations, the dominant class of whites has been preoccupied by its political suppression of and supremacy over the blacks.' She had few easy solutions either: unionization, social policy, housing, education, better distribution of wealth. Her picture of the black areas in America's northern cities was high on local colour without holding out much in the way of optimism. Vaudeville and jazz performed for a white audience while the performers entered and left by the kitchen door:

> New York's black precinct, the infamous Harlem, is merely an entertainment district with nightclubs, restaurants, shows and more or less louche bars. The black district of Washington, Second Street below the river, is a world unto itself, its denizens poor people, shoeshine boys, taxi drivers, newspaper sellers, labourers, barefoot street urchins, fishwives and maids, doormen, whistling corner boys – a people apart and a vibrant part of the American scene.[77]

She returned to New York with a visual record to match her fighting words. The hundreds of photos of Knoxville, Tuskegee, Charleston and elsewhere in the South capture careworn black faces, unemployed men gone to seed, women wary of a well-dressed white photographer, while children play in a grimy, impoverished wasteland. Street kids sport a thirties fashion for leather aviation caps with ear flaps, chin strap and goggles. Stevedores in the old river port of Savannah are waiting on ships to offload, and in Charleston's port they're grappling with large blocks of ice. Few of their expressions welcome her white woman's gaze for posterity, many turn away in embarrassment or shame. Annemarie and Baa explored the 'Old Porgy' world of DuBose Heyward, the germ for the opera *Porgy and Bess* (1935), set in Catfish Row in Charleston's port precinct; 'a white man's vision of Negro life', according to James Baldwin, its fraught cultural appropriation salient again. She snapped the imposing Palladian architecture, its pretensions to classicism, the quaintness of an elegant courtyard behind St. Philips Episcopal Church (pillars again) and the commodification already gaining ground – an antiques store called 'Porgy's Shop', an area designated 'Porgy's Courtyard'. Snaps of urchins in rags posing for a nickel tell a truer story. Contrasting these pictures of an underclass are snaps of American pop culture of the thirties: movie posters, photo booths, storefront ads, mannequins – consumer kitsch peddling its wares in the South. In Athens, Tennessee, an auto-graveyard caught her eye: wrecks, detritus, abandoned chassis. Annemarie saw herself as a reporter, not an art photographer, and enough of these snaps endure to form a genuine record of how things were.

They returned to the world of the Bedford Hotel's washed-up exiles and their rich urbanity. With Erika, Klaus and Klaus's boyfriend Tomski they drank whiskey until three in the morning. By 22 December, Erika and Annemarie had retreated to Boonton, New Jersey, to write. It was here that Annemarie situated the beginning of a fresh crisis in her relationship with Erika – implying the limitation of her working agreement with Baa. 'The crisis began in Boonton – due to overwork, lack of sleep, poor nutrition, whatever.'[78] Annemarie was nervy, clingy, working up to one of her scenes, wanting a closer relationship:

> … nine years ago Giehse was there, and I was young and stupid and like a well-behaved child, then came the conflicts with my mom, and Hitler, and a clean break from home: and Erika, supportive and loving, became a mentor of sorts.[79]

This reckoning (leaving Baa out of account) did not produce its desired result: Erika still wasn't really interested but let Annemarie down gently once again. 'Somewhat worried about Princess Miro', she wrote to Klaus, 'who all of a sudden, after eight years, is back at her old emotional entanglements.'[80] Erika had talks to prepare and had begun *School for Barbarians* (1938), a book about the Nazi education system which sold 40,000 copies in the US in the first three months after publication. She went on to become one of the most successful and highly paid female speakers in the country.[81]

Klaus, too, was in demand. His talk 'Germany and the World' alternated with 'A Family Against Dictatorship' in college towns across the nation. Returning from a Quaker school in Westtown, Pennsylvania, he read *Of Mice and Men* (1937) in the Pullman car. After a Quaker dinner washed down with milk or water, he was glad to break into the whiskey with old friends back at the Bedford.[82] Following lunch in the Rainbow Room atop the Rockefeller Center, Klaus was off again, this time to Hollywood – with a stopover at Duke University in North Carolina, the University of Virginia, and Chicago with Tomski. Fêted in timeworn manner on ivy-clad campuses, seminars with student and faculty literati, a talk in the hall, then back on the Pullman: his life threw up glamour and tedium in equal measure. *UND SO WEITER*, his diary reads, in block capitals, at year's end: and so on.

Annemarie prepared a fresh assault on Erika. She drove the 450 miles to Cincinnati, Ohio, where Erika was giving a series of talks in mid-January. The roads were icy, the city provided some of her best photos of unemployed men and industrial landscapes. She met the Cincinnati-based photographer Paul Briol, with whom she plied the steamers on the foggy river. But Erika wasn't interested in putting their relationship on a different footing. Annemarie's neediness was often a sticking point with women; there were crises, her psychological weather ran to stormy, and her woe-is-me entitlement did not endear. Her relationship with Baa, as with earlier romances, seems to have frittered away. Erika was strong-willed, independent, practical, and no longer wanted to play nurse to an emotional addict. Any intensification of the relationship with Annemarie would be a provocation to Renée, and all three of them had been there before.

Annemarie had always taken her measure from Erika and Klaus, now busy establishing a life for themselves in the United States, jockeying on the name-recognition of their father. It was at this point that she resumed her drug consumption after three months in the South.[83] At the end of January 1938, Annemarie wanted to visit the Schwarzenbach-Huber silk mills in Altoona, Pennsylvania, in order to investigate conditions for employees and to give a talk on behalf of the Committee for Industrial Organization (CIO). In Harrisburg and Columbia, Pennsylvania, Schwarzenbach mill workers had joined the strikes in August of the previous year.[84] Understandably, Annemarie's brother Hasi, based in New York, was less than pleased at this biting the hand that fed her. Ernest Glaesel, director of Schwarzenbach American operations, kiboshed her visit. It would have been a propaganda coup for the CIO to have the daughter of the owner agitating on their behalf, not to speak of articles in the Swiss press. Clearly, Annemarie was stirring the pot. Schwarzenbach wealth, like many a family fortune, was invested in the industrial North and, since the end of the First World War, had taken advantage of favourable labour conditions in the cheap South; in 1920 the Schwarzenbach-Huber Co. established a silk mill in Albany, in 'the negro state' of Alabama.[85] Two approaches to capital had come to blows in the same family. In the event, icy January roads prevented the visit. Hasi, visiting the factory some time later, took delivery of a package that had arrived for her; it contained morphine ampoules, which he disposed of.[86] This implies foresight on Annemarie's part and the seriousness of her addiction. 'No addict *ever* tells the truth when it comes to his addiction', wrote Klaus knowingly in his diary.[87]

In her professional life she had undergone a change, reflected in the style of the thirty or so articles she had published in the course of the previous year and the twenty articles in the year following. America's New Deal had given her a sense of purpose, and focused her writing almost exclusively on labour and social problems. Her style had become less discursive, honed by contact with the harsh realities of the South. Arnold Kübler, editor at *Zürcher Illustrierte*, proposed that Annemarie travel to China to report on the war there, an offer she declined:

> I have interviewed what seems like half the city, from factory owners to commercial judges, trade unionists, city engineers, unemployment office directors, journalists and far too many ladies' committees, and now I know EVERYTHING. The electric lights are on in broad daylight and the fog-bound Ohio River impervious to photos.[88]

Fresh from yet another ladies' committee in Washington, she characterized herself to Kübler as 'something of a "labour writer"'.[89] Sensing the Mann family drift westwards to California, and smelling the wind from Europe, Annemarie at this time was weighing a career in the United States. A number of her photos and articles are stamped with the logo of the Black Star agency in New York, which supplied magazines such as *Life*, *Colliers* and *The Saturday Evening Post*. A photo essay about the mountaineer Lorenz Saladin appeared in the February 1938 edition of *Asia* magazine, published in New York.[90] To Kübler she explained why she worked abroad. 'It seemed better to establish myself, to learn something, to make a name for myself first – all of this abroad, because Switzerland is a small country.' Conflict with her family came into the equation: 'I fit ill with my family. I am somewhat of a troublemaker.'[91]

Not everybody championed her hard-won style. Otto Kleiber, editor at *National-Zeitung*, had reservations about her focus on industry and labour. She defended her writing over the preceding year:

> Since my first stay in America ... I have tried to move away from the amateurish jotting down of travel impressions and to become a professional,

useful journalist. It is, of course, particularly galling if this leads me to write worse rather than better.[92]

This comment on the jobbing journalist – neither hack nor dilettante – is astute. Thomas Mann, for one, appreciated her new style.[93] A year later she reflected on what drove her:

> … the focus of my current writing is almost exclusively on economic and social problems in America, rather than extolling the more idyllic America of boundless opportunity. Everywhere there is light and shade but one writes about what moves one.[94]

Cross-Atlantic third class was not an experience she wanted to repeat – 'even in third class I'd have to scrimp and save. Firstly, I can't save more than I already do – *sandwiches and no drinks* – and secondly, I don't really want to travel third class again.'[95] On 12 February 1938 Annemarie and Klaus steamed out of New York, tourist class on the *Ile de France*. Her photos show the majestic Manhattan skyline wreathed in fog, rising from an ice-flecked bay. They had a spacious cabin on the art deco liner, and *Heidi*, starring 'ghastly little Shirley Temple', was screened in the shipboard cinema. It was a kitsch new world. They met Waverly Root, Paris-based correspondent for the *Chicago Tribune* and the *Washington Post*, and skipped over to first class for a gala evening with captain Roger Raulin and a one-act play by Musset. War hogged the horizon – the ship's paper reported ominous news from Austria: Chancellor Kurt Schuschnigg had been cosying up to Hitler in Berchtesgaden. Klaus and Annemarie talked about morphine – Klaus had stayed clear for five months while on his lecture tour and Annemarie was using again and needy. She held fast until the last day of their crossing, and then shot up two ampoules. On arrival in Le Havre, they caught the Paris train and Klaus met his German émigré friends in their old Latin Quarter haunts – *chez* Michaud on rue Jacob, the Select in Montparnasse with 'Toni' Altmann and Joseph Roth. In Sybille Bedford's flat they listened to most of Hitler's three-hour address to the Reichstag commemorating the fifth anniversary of Nazi rule. The Führer was in fine fettle, Austria in his sights. On the day of Annemarie's departure for Switzerland, Thea 'Stoisy' Sternheim (mother of the more infamous Mopsa) left in her diary a glimpse of Annemarie for posterity: 'The manifestly drugged Schwarzenbach looks like death warmed up. This callow youth thinks she's a thorn in the [Nazi] side but doesn't have what it takes to inflict a serious blow on the enemy.'[96] After popping into Mopsa's flat, Klaus accompanied Annemarie to the Zurich train at the Gare de l'Est, despite his annoyance with her usual wheelie-dealie about money and drugs.[97] All her ready cash – $30 – had been stolen on the boat and he must have been keeping her afloat since. Klaus had been clean for five months and Annemarie had quite likely stocked up for Sils. His friend safely on the train, Klaus went back to Mopsa's and they made a night of it – *une nuit blanche* – until half past four in the morning.[98]

8

Enemies of Promise

But for women, I thought, looking at the empty shelves, these difficulties were infinitely more formidable.

Virginia Woolf, *A Room of One's Own*

Between two visits to the United States, Annemarie spent eight months of 1937 in Europe as National Socialism began to spill over into Germany's backyard – the Baltic States, Poland, the Rhineland and Austria under the Anschluss. Restlessly on the move, she was motivated by assignments; it was in this period that she burnished her credentials as a journalist at large. Stays in expensive Swiss clinics alternated with spells of recovery, often in Sils, followed by hasty decisions to get back on the road again, not so much confronting her demons as running away from them. Erika or Klaus were rarely far off. Girlfriends came and went. The times when Annemarie was 'clean' grew shorter. Domestic life in Sils could be quiet but often wasn't: Annemarie tended to write a good deal about communing with nature, as she did about poverty, but she sustained stillness and lack of money more in the breach.

Her addiction to morphine caused increasing concern to those around her. Like Klaus, Annemarie wanted to quit but seems to have relapsed into her old habit by January 1936. Neither seemed to get much fun from morphine but of the two it was Annemarie who developed a reputation for being miserabilist and causing scenes. An incident in June 1936 at Hotel Camp de Mar in Majorca boded ill. Annemarie had a breakdown in the hotel dining room, passed out with her hair in the spinach, vomited, was stroppy and needed to be assisted from the table. Klaus too had morphine-induced weeping fits over the course of the spring when 'his addiction to heroin, morphine, and Eukodal had reached a frightening level'.[1] An alumnus of Zurich University commented on Annemarie's appearance at this time: 'her life of adventure has left its mark on her sad face, which nonetheless has retained some part of its former charm … such great promise had not been fulfilled'.[2]

Returning to Sils a year later in the spring of 1937, following assignments in Maine, New York, Washington and the mining towns of Pittsburgh, Annemarie caught the end of the ski season and Barbara Hamilton-Wright joined her in Sils. The two women motored up to Bocken to meet the family. 'She looked like a young man, but seems to me a decent sort', remarked grandmother Clara, though both women turning up in pants seemed 'a bit grotesque'.[3] Thomas Mann, a couple of years earlier, also remarked in his diary that Annemarie had stayed for dinner wearing pants.[4] Clara Wille had always been better disposed towards her grand-daughter's circle of friends than Renée. Despite Renée's disapproval of aspects of her daughter's lifestyle, the mother nonetheless remained welcoming to whomever Annemarie chose to invite – with the notable exception of the Manns.

Marriage was again the topic of conversation. Annemarie had been mulling over divorcing Claude Clarac, and in spring 1937 she discussed this with her family. Alfred Schwarzenbach's health had been cause for concern and Claude's enquiry received a blunt reply from Renée: 'she could not bring herself to show any respect for Annemarie's marriage and hence her husband, given that Annemarie's absence from Tehran for months had rendered it null and void on both sides'.[5] Clarac was put in his place and Renée had become an unlikely champion of uxorious propriety. Ever the diplomat, Clarac took it on the chin. Behind this jockeying about marriage, the question of inheritance, given Alfred's precarious health and considerable wealth, must have played a part. Perhaps the sudden death of Claude's father in August deferred Annemarie's decision. She had always shown understanding of what was needed to put her life in order but little willpower to follow through.

One by one her peers were making good matches. In March 1937, Gundalena Wille, Annemarie's cousin, married the physicist Carl Friedrich von Weizsäcker, son of the German ambassador to Switzerland. Ernst von Weizsäcker was 'an easy-going southern German', as Grandmother Clara put it, who rose to the position of State Secretary under the Nazis, second only to Joachim von Ribbentrop. Weizsäcker's last

Alfred Schwarzenbach in the train at Arosa, 1936. Photo by Renée Schwarzenbach
Courtesy of Zentralbibliothek Zürich

posting in 1943 was to the Vatican, where he took refuge at war's end with the German-leaning pope. Slippery, careerist, compromised (the deportation of Italian Jews took place under his watch), Weizsäcker's role before and during the war was staunchly defended at the *Wilhelmstraßenprozess* of 1947–49, which put on trial careerist Nazi foreign ministry officials. Weizsäcker was indicted for having signed deportation orders for French Jews in his function as Staatssekretär in the Foreign Office from 1938 to 1943. He was pardoned after only eighteen months in prison. Richard von Weizsäcker, the accused's son and later President of Germany, himself challenged the prevailing exculpatory blind eye of German functionaries in wartime: 'Anybody with a modicum of curiosity, eyes open and ears to the ground, inevitably knew the deportation trains were rolling.'[6]

It was not just the diplomats who could smell the wind – academia too got a whiff of it. Gundalena Wille-von Weizsäcker spent much of the war as a faculty wife outside Strasburg, where her physicist husband had been appointed professor. Their next-door neighbour was August Hirt, a Swiss-German heading Himmler's SS Institute for Anthropological Research, conducting experiments – mustard gas on live specimens – and collecting skeletons of political prisoners, homosexuals, Sinti and Roma from the nearby Natzweiler-Struthof concentration camp. The specimens 'were to be treated with great care, photographed, measured and all relevant facts recorded, before the heads were expertly severed by a Wehrmacht physician and sent in cans of preserving spirits to Strasburg'.[7] Gundalena was obliged to play hostess to such people.[8]

Annemarie was a moth between two flames, her political convictions and her family married into the highest echelons of Nazi Germany: 'To live astraddle two milieus seems, from tough experience, to be my lot',[9] she wrote to her psychiatrist, Dr. Binswanger.

*

By May 1937, the Nazis had tightened control over Germany by means of laws, bureaucracy, overt anti-semitism and an expanding network of concentration camps. Annemarie set out on a mass observation mission, of a piece with her interest in documentary film and the social-realist photographs she had seen in Washington: 'chance encounters, in the train, on a farm, in a Berlin suburban café, at the newspaper stand'.[10] She observed street life in a Rhineland town replete with marching Hitler Youth singing the Horst Wessel Song. She forgot to give the ubiquitous salute and a passing woman upbraided her: 'Lift your arm immediately or we will inform the police.'[11] Membership of Nazi cliques helped job promotion. Behind their obedience, however, ordinary Germans recognized the thuggish incompetence of the Nazi type:

> These jumped-up Party functionaries with their overblown ranking titles, they're all good-for-nothing. They failed in life, in their jobs, failed at school – dregs who never amounted to much, and now they're chancing their arm in the Party.[12]

From small-town Germany she moved north to Danzig, enjoying its last autonomous years before Germany's invasion of Poland in 1939. A Baltic seaport given special status under the Treaty of Versailles, with access to the Silesian coalfields, Danzig was a strategic symbol for the Nazis. Together with the Rhineland, Czechoslovakia, Austria and Poland, it was a piece of the grand jigsaw of *Lebensraum*. The Nazis dominated public and propaganda space: avenues of linden trees festooned with gonfalons, swastika bunting zig-zagging across Adolf-Hitler Strasse. Even the gantry-cranes in the docks seemed to be giving the Hitler salute. In a patisserie-café Annemarie's neighbour asks: 'You're not Jewish, are you?' The woman's husband is second in command in the SA, her children in the Hitler Youth and her eldest, seventeen-year-old Horst, in the SA marine corps. The whole family is a Nazi caricature – pigtails, swastikas and lederhosen. 'The young belong to our Leader', the woman parrots, and blames Poles and Jews for rigging the exchange rate.[13]

Annemarie met Carl Burckhardt, recently appointed League of Nations High Commissioner in Danzig while still vice-president of the Red Cross. Hitler was to tell him as early as August 1939 that he would attack the Soviet Union: 'if the West is too stupid and blind to grasp this, then I will have to reach an agreement with the Russians and then, after defeating [the West] to turn with all the forces I can muster against the Soviet Union.'[14] Burckhardt was not a figure Annemarie could trust at this point and she described their meeting as stiff and cautious. Wary of her politics, Burckhardt himself trod a fine line with the Nazis dominating the city senate. Annemarie suggested an interview with his wife for the *National-Zeitung*, which might appeal to a Swiss female readership, but even this could be seen as a partisan political act in a city walking on eggs.[15] Disappointed, Annemarie didn't quite know which leg to stand on, conscious in her correspondence that other eyes might be watching.[16] Minister for Propaganda Joseph Goebbels, fresh from staging the Berlin Olympics in 1936 and gearing up for the degenerate art exhibition there in July 1937, was due to arrive on 6 May. The Nazi circus had come to town.

In Riga, Annemarie stayed at the Hotel de Rome, the city's swankiest, and attended a choral concert seated between French and Czech foreign ministers in all their finery. Her French diplomatic passport provided an entrée to embassy life that had bored her in Tehran; she used it for what it was worth. She described the Russian-inflected Baltic states as a 'Janus-headed mix of military socialism and socialist fascism ... Jew-baiting was common.'[17] A similarly incendiary mix of xenophobia and nationalism was rife among students in Estonia – pro-German, anti-Russian, anti-semitic. One young person said to her: 'You can't just bundle the Germans in with inferior beings like Russians and Jews. Germany, because of its undeniable superior intelligence and character, is entitled to govern these countries.'[18]

A photograph spotted in a Zurich agency in March 1937 sparked Annemarie's 'natural journalistic curiosity'[19] and led to her best-selling book, a biography of the Swiss climber Lorenz Saladin (1896–1936). A member of the Communist Party, as well as a photographer, in September of the previous year the forty-year-old Saladin had died while descending with his team from the summit of Khan Tengri in Kyrgyzstan. Saladin was an intrepid figure in Switzerland and had points in common with his would-be biographer: 'He ran ahead to escape his fate and his existence became a sequence of pitfalls.'[20] Annemarie might as well have been describing herself. Saladin's communism chimed with his deprived childhood. Climber and biographer came from opposite poles of Swiss society. Saladin was from Nuglar, a village in the Canton of Solothurn, and had been hired out as a farm labourer at the age of nine, when his parents divorced. He was a *Verdingkind*, one of thousands of children from poor or morally marginalized backgrounds who were separated from parents and exploited as cheap agricultural labour under a semi-official policy of the Swiss government.[21] A string of petty trades, work as a border guard, Alpine climbing and travels in South America and the United States, led to Saladin discovering his passion for adventure.[22]

In Moscow, in a 'tiny student room' with a piano, two survivors of the climb apprised Annemarie of Saladin's final hours: '"We all had frozen hands and feet – my brother Evgeni is a cripple. But Saladin must have poisoned himself.[23] He died suddenly, on horseback, September 14th. The same evening we met a rescue expedition … We buried Saladin in the delta of Sari Djas." … Then the boys showed me the negatives of about 1,200 photos Saladin had taken.'[24] Saladin's fatal last climb corresponded to Annemarie's sense of heroic adventure in the face of adversity. In short order she wrote the climber's biography – *Lorenz Saladin: A Mountain Life*, published by Hallwag in 1938. It became her best-selling book.

Her brother-in-law crossed the Baltic Sea to meet her in Helsinki and after a sailing regatta and a boozy night on the town, they flew to Stockholm. Sweden's social democracy proved welcome relief after her swing through German and Baltic fascism on the one hand and Soviet communism on the other. Suzanne Öhman-Schwarzenbach was the thirty-one-year-old mother of five children (a sixth was born in 1940). Her marriage at age nineteen to a man fifteen years her senior was happy, and their move to Sweden had established a comfortable distance from Renée's overbearing presence. Annemarie had always liked the mild landscape and cooperative ethos of her sister's adopted country. A photograph taken by Annemarie of her six-year-old nephew Peter standing by a barn brings out his humour and small-town country life.[25] Young people photographed in Uppsala and at Schloss Gripsholm radiate a similar calm. Such photos of an almost folksy idyll contrast with the trumped-up 'völkisch' posturing of Nazi youth in the lands she has just visited.

*

Annemarie was back in residence in Sils in March 1938, following her trip through the southern United States. Increasingly dependent on morphine, she answered a recriminatory letter from Klaus with a long self-involved missive of her own, piling up the failures of her life and loves. More dependent on Erika than ever, she attributed somewhat disingenuously her own instability and increased morphine consumption to Erika's refusal of a closer relationship.[26] Klaus and Annemarie seem to have had a temporary falling out about who had used who in Paris. Perhaps Klaus blamed Annemarie for renewing contact with Mopsa when he had been drug-free for three months.

Her return to Sils coincided with Hitler's annexation of Austria next door. He crossed the border at Brunau and received a rapturous welcome at his birthplace near Linz. Cardinal Innitzer ordered all the bells of Austria to be rung in celebration. Annemarie observed first-hand the country's transformation barely eight days after the 12 March Anschluss. Following a brief detox in the Ruppaner Clinic in Samedan, she drove down the Inn valley to Salzburg (where Dolfuss Platz had already been renamed Adolf Hitler Platz), motoring onwards to Linz and Vienna. Klaus wondered if she could be trusted on a humanitarian mission, given her drug use. 'Rest assured I am healthy, well-behaved, ready and willing to cross the Austrian border; so put your mind at ease.'[27] She intended to help Germans who had taken refuge in Austria since 1933 and Austrian anti-fascists, both groups now in a precarious situation. Klaus noted the danger to Magnus Henning, musician with the Peppermill cabaret, exiled in the Tyrol.[28] Hitler's annexation had many watching their backs and others offering a way out. Anthony Heilbut had described the Anschluss as 'no national rape but a marriage in which the groom found

Erika Mann in Sils, 1936. Photo by Annemarie Schwarzenbach
Courtesy of Swiss Literary Archives and Wikimedia Commons

himself overwhelmed by his bride's enthusiasm'.[29] Annemarie's precise
movements to save this or that figure ensnared in the German and
Austrian marriage are elusive. She wrote about the Anschluss in a series
of fifteen articles for Basel's *National-Zeitung* and other hard-hitting
pieces in the *Luzerner Tagblatt*. 'A Pair of Shoes Falls into the Inn River'
described the desperation of Hungarian and Polish refugees attempting
to cross the whitewater river into Switzerland in the dead of winter:

> Things have changed at the border. These days two enormous flags sporting
> the swastika flutter across the frontier with Austria at Martinsbruck. Strapping

German SS have replaced the old Austrian customs officers and border patrols.
Now refugees join the stateless people turning up at the Swiss border crossing.[30]

Here and in 'Max Meister, Refugee' she advocated for those caught
in the crossfire of larger forces at border crossings. It was a plight that
would become all too common in the years ahead and one the diplomat's wife never much had to suffer. The official Swiss response to these
Flüchtlinge was sometimes helpless, at times heartless, often providing
practical aid. At Landegg, the inn she usually stayed at admitted military
personnel only; trucks, tanks and artillery rumbled over the Arlberg Pass
as disgruntled ne'er-do-wells strutted in new uniforms. At Salzburg's arty
Café Bazar, the waiters were already sporting swastika pins in their lapels
and anti-semitism was openly expressed. Brownshirts ransacked Jewish
shops in Vienna and forced Jews to clean the streets and barrack toilets.
The Anschluss reopened long suppurating class wounds:

> The Viennese middle classes are uncomfortable with their old imperial capital
> being turned into a German garrison town, a playground (to say the least) for
> young Nazis from the provinces. These days, the better class of people keep to
> themselves at home. Working-class areas are to be avoided.[31]

In Vienna she checked on her old friend from Berlin and Ankara,
architect and Director of the Austrian Academy of Fine Arts, Clemens
Holzmeister, but he was safely in Turkey. In his absence, the Nazis
stripped him of titles and honours and denied visas to his wife and
children. Annemarie left her car and went on foot to the working-class
district of Ottakring to reconnoitre with endangered socialists. In a bar
window, besides the ubiquitous Hitler portraits and swastikas, a notice
informed customers it was a '*guaranteed German, Aryan house. Aryan
service only*'. In conversation with two suspicious barmaids, Annemarie
gleaned that 'all the best and most important jobs go to the Germans'.
The Nazis had already arrested one of her contacts, the other opted to
stay put with his wife, and keep his head down. The word 'comrade' stuck
in their throats; 'worker' had been replaced by 'folk'; the communist
struggle had not bettered their lives.[32] The Irish essayist Hubert Butler,
also helping refugees in Vienna at this time, captured the base violence
of the Prater Strasse:

The street must have had a great many Jewish shopkeepers in it, because all the way down there were broken windows in front of looted shops with VERHOLUNG NACH DACHAU ('Gone for a rest-cure to Dachau') scrawled over the surviving panes.[33]

The Nazis dressed up Austria's annexation as a liberation and the proliferation of uniforms betrayed how ordinary Austrians fell into step. 'They're all Nazis. All except a small group of intellectuals', reported a highly-placed Catholic who dared to speak out and was arrested.[34]

In Austria the Nazis aren't just the clique in power. They're also a *populist* party which has more or less lost touch with reality. Perhaps one day they will reconnect with their Austrian conscience.

For the moment, a totalitarian regime is in place, and we Swiss can only wait and see. All resistance is futile, for now, since the crowd is drunk with enthusiasm.[35]

Everywhere she went she photographed the jackbooted Nazi theatre joined at the hip to the local oompa music; the imperialists liked a good triumphant march, especially now that the pretender to the throne, Otto von Hapsburg, was in exile in London. In Vienna, young men sorted through swastika bunting, and schoolboys had the afternoon off to trot in the Schillerplatz. Annemarie returned to Switzerland with a verbal and visual record of how easily the annexation of Austria had come about. The Swiss wondered if they were next.

More dependent on morphine than ever ('I let myself go – eyes wide open and fully aware of what I was doing'[36]), shortly after her return she began another session with Dr. Ruppaner. Over the course of 1938 and into 1939, Annemarie spent six months in a total of five clinics, each stay that bit longer than the last, assurances and resolutions made and broken. While recognizing the seriousness of her condition and the need to take it in hand, she tended to conflate her addiction with 'the havoc-making fascism of our time'. She had a new girlfriend, Anita Forrer, who rented an apartment in Schloss Bethmar in Malans, a couple of hours' drive north over the mountains. Writing to Klaus from the clinic in Samedan, Annemarie placed hope in the relationship: 'Our mutual love has been expressed and stirs in me great confidence for the future.'

Forrer was eight years older than Annemarie, with bookish tastes, and eventually became her literary executor.

Renée rallied round, given the seriousness of her daughter's condition. She hoped a stay in Bocken, under doctor's supervision, would wean Annemarie off the drug. Ruppaner's treatment consisted of insulin and a gradual reduction to two Eukodal injections a day; the patient's weight of 50 kilos made the full cold turkey precarious. Three years previously, Renée had concurred with Dr. Forel that Annemarie's addiction was a symptom of a deeper malaise, existential and schizophrenic, for which Renée herself partly accepted responsibility. And so with a new girlfriend, mother on hand, and several expensive doctors treating her case, Annemarie received the attention she needed.[37]

Annemarie was always wary of institutionalized psychologizing, the psycho-babble of her day, and preferred to trust her own instinct. She outlined a plan to her mother: 'Sils, work, closeness to Frau Forrer, Bocken and attachment to you, divorce from Claude.'[38] Shortly after, on 1 June, behind her mother's back, Annemarie met Erika who had driven down to Landquart in an attempt to persuade the patient to stay the course. But the addict was not for turning.[39] She left Dr. Ruppaner for Anita Forrer in Malans, where under supervision from a Doctor Salis and a nurse from Davos, she managed to bring her morphine consumption down to zero over four days. Back in Sils, she fared less well and relapsed within the month, quickly realizing she required supervision. With Renée's intervention, they decided on the Bellevue clinic in Kreuzlingen, overlooking Lake Constance, a Swiss institution which had been in the Binswanger family for four generations. Annemarie was admitted on 11 July and Dr. Binswanger thought she would need at least a three-month stay; her doctor got her to sign that she wouldn't leave without her mother's consent. Severe withdrawal symptoms followed: 'The patient paces the room like a panther, upsets a lamp and threatens with her fists so that the room is cleared. The mother, to the amazement of all, absolutely calm – this was clearly nothing new to her.'[40]

Days later, Annemarie was able to work on her biography of Lorenz Saladin, which she finished on 24 July, and to play the hospital piano. There ensued the usual battle of wits to check out now that the worst was apparently over. The doctor stuck to his guns. Renée suggested early

August. Annemarie had a hissy-fit – five nurses and two male attendants had to hold her down.[41] As in the Prangins clinic under Dr. Forel, Annemarie was a disruptive patient who always thought herself better than her doctors.

Binswanger confirmed Forel's earlier diagnosis of schizophrenia. Klaus Mann, too, independently mentions schizophrenia in his diary entry for 22 July. 'Her suffering in that closed institution, in Kreuzlingen. *Pauvre enfant*. Her pronounced moral sense doing battle with the self-destructive tendencies of her psyche – and body. Schizophrenia.'[42] This lay analysis indicates that Annemarie's personality disorder, however attenuated, had become evident to her friends. Professional opinion concurred: all three doctors – Forel, Ruppaner, Binswanger – agreed that she needed at least a month-long recuperation under supervision, and that there was more to her case than drug addiction. Nonetheless, Annemarie checked out of Bellevue clinic on 2 August and made her way via Malans to Sils. Once the initial detoxification had passed, Annemarie always reasoned her way out of arrangements made at wit's end, against the better judgement of three doctors and ignoring family trepidation.

Following the Binswanger cold turkey, Annemarie was estranged from her parents once more, and took up with her '*Ersatz*' or elective family holidaying at the nearby Hotel Margna, while Erika and Klaus stayed at the house in Sils. Renée viewed the Manns as exiled, unpatriotic German *Mischlinge*. The Manns saw the Schwarzenbach-Wille clan as stupid fascists, tainted by wealth. They understood Annemarie's break with her parents as a consequence of Renée's intransigence: Klaus notes 'the diabolical role of the mother'[43] while Thomas's diary entries chart Annemarie's struggle with morphine over the course of summer 1938. On 14 August, he remarked on her having 'escaped' from Binswanger.[44] However, by 9 September, the 'desolate angel' was back at his dinner table in Kusnacht, and back on the morphine.[45]

In September, emboldened by the success of the Anschluss, Hitler annexed the Sudetenland, the German-settled areas of Czechoslovakia which had always been in his sights. This became a refugee crisis as much as a political one and on 19 September Annemarie took off from Dubendorf Airfield outside Zurich to join 'the elite of international journalists' in Prague, anticipating developments but under a media embargo. Listening to Hitler's speech, she found him 'narrow-minded, short-sighted and dim'. In correspondence with Anita Forrer, she describes the 'phoney, uneasy peace – and we can no longer pretend to avoid a looming conflict between Hitler, fascism, pseudo-socialism.'[46]

She made her way to the underground Communist newspaper, *Rote Fahne* (Red Flag), banned in Germany since 1933. The German editorial team were busy sifting truth from lies, and a youth from the border village of Schwaderbach told her only thirty people remained from a population of three thousand – the rest had fled.[47] They had joined a wave of refugees numbering a hundred thousand – Czech and German – who had escaped the border regions for the relative safety of Prague's Masaryk Stadium. Meanwhile, in the august surroundings of Berchtesgaden, Hitler played Chamberlain and the Western powers, resulting in the Munich agreement at the end of September. War had been averted for now. Annemarie's thoughts turned to the precarious position of Switzerland where one 'could no longer ignore the fact that we are an island only incidentally spared, by no means safe, defenceless.'[48] While abhorring Hitler and all he stood for, she also thought responsibility for the crisis lay with the policy of appeasement pursued by communists, social democrats and conservatives alike.[49]

In mid-October she entered her longest period of hospitalization, four months in the Bellevue Clinic on Lake Neuchatel. A difficult settling-in period followed the pattern: withdrawal, an attempt at escape, condescension – 'a terrible place' – and cutting short her treatment on the insistence that she was 'cured'. This time, romance entered the mix and Annemarie fell in love with thirty-nine-year-old Dr. Gustava – 'Gucia' – Favez, of Polish-Jewish origins and married with a son. 'I have latched onto my lady doctor in the most perilous way',[50] she informed Klaus. In October her biography of Lorenz Saladin sold well, her first book on the shelves since 1934's *Winter in the Near East*. This encouraged her to rework the unpublished *Death in Persia*. While excited to be writing fiction again, Annemarie's January 1939 letter to Klaus suggests her manic princessy manner, the hospital like a royal court:

> I've pulled the curtains, plugged my ears with cotton wool, and complain when a kind nurse disturbs me. Naturally, the clinic can't believe such a patient. I weigh only 49 kilos, don't sleep very well, don't observe any house rules.[51]

With war on the horizon, her friends were searching for an exit. Ruth Landshoff, concerned for Annemarie's health, was in New York. Vollmoeller in Basel was considering moving to the United States.[52] The Mann family had decamped to Princeton and New York. In January 1939, Christopher Isherwood and W.H. Auden docked in New York City aboard the *Champlain*, and were met by Klaus and Erika. 'They were full of liveliness and gossip. And, at once, the Giantess stopped threatening, the towers no longer appalled. Christopher felt himself among friends, cared for, safe.'[53] On the penultimate crossing of the *Champlain* in 1940, the Nabokov family fled revolution for the third time; on its final trans-Atlantic voyage a U-boat torpedoed the liner. Across Europe, refugees from Berlin, Munich, Vienna, Prague and countless shtetl under Nazi menace were haggling for Nansen passports, manoeuvring towards the ports, settling into steerage.

The Nazis unleashed their state-abetted *Kristallnacht* pogrom on the night of 9–10 November. We can gauge the extent of Renée's anti-semitism from her reaction to *Kristallnacht* in a 3 March 1939 letter to Suzanne. While disliking the violence, her sympathy doesn't stretch far: 'a Jew is still a Jew, with very few exceptions ... you know I don't get along with most of them anymore – but still, I don't like the Jews.' She attributes rumours of war to 'the Jewish press'. Renée found Hitler's methods crude but the man admirable: 'Hitler's a genius, without question.'[54] For her, Germany's advance was payback for its treatment at Versailles. It would show the English who was boss. When Hitler invaded Poland, Renée thought that world dominance was in the balance: 'What has Poland got to do with England?' She justifiably saw the English as having throughout history their own smash and grab policy. Renée viewed the outbreak of war later in 1939 as a continuation of the struggle of the First World War, a vindication of German might and a war to end all wars.[55] Hitler's pact with the Soviet Union, however, Renée and Clara saw as a betrayal of principles – they were the kind of entitled women who knew on which side their bread was buttered. Clara, while deploring Hitler's goons, admired the genius in the man; the Soviet pact opened her eyes.

*

Annemarie first met the internationally renowned traveller Ella Maillart at the Bauer Hotel in Zurich in the summer of 1938. Kini, as she was known, described the younger Swiss writer as 'hatless, smart in a grey suit, so thin that she was almost ethereal, she sat most of the time drooping and silent. ... One thing was certain: she believed in suffering.'[56] After this unpropitious encounter, Kini visited the patient in Bellevue on New Year's Eve. Annemarie had likely heard of her from Hermine de Saussure, a mutual friend and wife of Henri Seyrig, both encountered in Tehran in 1935. Kini too heard a not quite reassuring assessment of Annemarie from the same source: the scandal of her affair with the daughter of the Turkish ambassador in Tehran, her drug-taking, her impetuous marriage.

A Geneva-born ethnologist, traveller and writer with a sporty, adventurous streak, Kini had already made a name for herself: 'captain of the Swiss women's hockey team, she was also an international skier ... She had done a good deal of journalism and had written two travel books, of which the second had been a considerable hit in Paris.'[57]

Annemarie recognized 'a similarity of mind and motive ... I was reassured and overjoyed'[58] and suggested Kini might visit Sils to write.[59]

Kini's account of their journey, *The Cruel Way: Switzerland to Afghanistan in a Ford, 1939* begins with Annemarie's return from Prague, 'convalescing after months of an exhausting cure'. They have been skiing, and Annemarie makes a remark about her father possibly getting her a new car. She wanted the latest Ford model and if she couldn't get it in Zurich she was prepared to travel to Stockholm and pick the car up there.[60] Maillart's mind 'was already in Persia'.[61] Both were strong-willed adventurers, unmoored from female convention, sharing a love of the road. The older woman urged Annemarie to fatten up:

> 'Unless you put on twenty pounds of flesh you cannot possibly tackle such hardships. Besides, who would finance us? And anyway war will soon break out ...' I didn't mention my main objection: provided she were soon normal ... Her thin hand held a cigarette, the yellow knuckles sharp under a skin as thin as tissue-paper.[62]

Misgivings on Kini's side and personality differences boded ill. Annemarie 'did not know how to be at rest' whereas Kini sought spiritual enlightenment in India. Kini was impervious to discomfort, plucky, full of stamina as opposed to Annemarie's rich-girl proclivities, whose well-worn plea for escape from her oppressed life had been sounded once

Ella Maillart packing the car, British Consulate, Meshed, Iran, 1939. Photo by Annemarie Schwarzenbach
Courtesy of Swiss Literary Archives and Wikimedia Commons

too often. Kini offered dependency and trust that mirrored Annemarie's relationship to her mother; an older woman who would play nurse and pay attention.

They left Kini's home town of Geneva on 6 June 1939, Annemarie at the wheel. The press posed the two women on the bumper of their car in front of the International Labour Organization, Kini in polka-dot blouse, skirt and sensible shoes, a skinny Annemarie in blouse and pants, one hand in pocket, the other on Kini's knee, eyes raised to high heaven in that odd fetching way that has over time characterized her. They were nobody's calendar girls. A caption on the back of a snap, taken at the Simplon Pass as they crossed the Alps, reads in the driver's handwriting: 'Why do we leave this loveliest country in the world? What urges us to go east on desert roads?'[63] This retrospective rhetorical flourish – one of Annemarie's favourite devices – remained unanswered but sounds a note for the journey ahead. Kini already knew her driver was not 'sparkling with *joie de vivre*' after the best part of a year in and out of detox clinics and dangerously close to suicide. Annemarie wanted to try on her travelling boots once more.[64] She was not the first to imagine horizons widening out east. In the same month the second Baroness Blixen motored from Stockholm to China, also in a Ford; in 1941 Rebecca West headed east; joined after the war by Nicolas Bouvier, Dervla Murphy and countless trippers on the hippy trail.[65] A vogue for intrepid travellers in search of spirituality was in the making.

At Trieste, breaking their journey for *gelato* in the port, Annemarie recalled the *Gerusalemme* on which she had steamed to Beirut and marriage in April 1935. How honest was she in the fashioning of her story? Kini was not the marrying kind and 'could guess how difficult it must have been for these two to become a couple. As long as one is single it does not matter if one is extremely self-centred.' Claude was still in the French diplomatic service at the time of Kini's writing and the mother of the bride exercised oversight of the narrative. We might take Annemarie's and Kini's layered account with a pinch of backward thrown salt and a grain of truth:

> Mother foretold disaster if I married. And it was happening. There was no way out, for Francis' people were strict Catholics. It was very foolish of me to be always acting against mother – the person who knows me better than anyone else. I had no hope of freeing myself from her, no hope of ever being simply myself.[66]

They intended to travel south through the Balkans, ferry-hopping east along the Black Sea shore to Trebizond, skirting the southern Caucasus to Tehran and from there over the Hindu Kush to Kabul, arriving in the heat of August. By then the boil of the thirties had been lanced and war had broken out. Germany was on everybody's lips: in the Slovenian rump of the Austro-Hungarian empire; among Swabian settlers in

Serbia; in the Prussian strutting of Yugoslav garrison towns. They didn't linger. 'Along the road, people often greeted us with the Nazi salute. A schoolmaster raised his arm with great determination staunchly followed by his gaggle of kids. Were we taken for Germans?'[67]

The car was a two-seater, 18-horsepower with reinforced suspension, customized radiator and two spare tyres. Annemarie saw it as a symbol of Western civilization, know-how and industrial exploitation, all that Ford stood for in the American psyche and in Huxley's *Brave New World* (1932). Behind the driving seat they rigged up a shelf of forty reference works also representing the human spirit: Marco Polo, Maritain, Jung, a life of Alexander the Great, a compendium of seeker-travellers. They slept rough, under canvas and summer stars, brewing coffee on a primus. Both writers noticed the gradual change from west to east, at times lamenting 'cinemas, newspapers, railings, pavements, electric wires'[68] – at others regarding westernization with ethnographic dispassion. In Tabriz, north-west Iran, Kini finds an outdoor cinema in the ruins of the Mosque Ali Shah, 'the fire-proof cabin of a cinema projector, new god, and bestower of oblivion to our mass civilization.'[69] The Shah, like Ataturk, was modernizing, while the Anglo-Iranian Oil Company reaped rewards. Both writers tended to see development as a mixed blessing.

Reaching Sofia on 14 June, Annemarie took to her hotel bed while Kini went in search of a garage to repair the car. Later she found 'the brittle glass of an ampoule' on the bathroom floor and knew that her charge had relapsed. In Istanbul, the stand-off came into the open when Kini surprised Annemarie phoning a doctor friend who had been at dinner the night before. They had dined in Therapia, a diplomatic enclave north of Istanbul on the Bosphorus, with Clemens Holzmeister, Annemarie's architect friend who had built Ankara for Kemal Ataturk. Therapia occasioned one of Annemarie's characteristic meditations on east meets west, in which she conflated the optimism of her travels five years earlier with present circumstances. Her oriental quest had become a search for cure – therapy:

I heard the surging noise of the cramped metropolis and ate the fried fish and sugared fruits I had tasted once before. Everything had been once before! Everything was mirrored as in a glittering scabbard, the white bridges milling with people, the gently rocking steamships, the gulls.[70]

Kini noted her driver's self-centredness and lack of humour: 'the business of living is so urgent that there is no leisure for the palliative of humour'.[71] When she confronted Annemarie's duplicity in the Grand Hôtel de Londres in Istanbul, ready capitulation and empty promises came in return:

> I give you complete power over me, day and night. Don't leave me alone. If it happens again, I leave the car with you and go back. Let's go away quickly. I have to be far from towns. Then I know I can't get it and I live more easily. ... It does not even give pleasure; it is more like a pause in nothingness ... the only relaxation that I know.[72]

She had said the same thing to Thomas Mann: pleasure wasn't in it; it was all about oblivion. Annemarie herself knew that she was not to be trusted. Writing to Erika, she complained about the Balkan roads, the hard ground under her sleeping bag, the tough travel regime. Tired and sick, with a 5 a.m. start ahead of her, Annemarie made no mention of the showdown with Kini.[73] Kini wrote: 'After the Sofia incident, I chose to appear hard and determined not to forgive another relapse.'[74]

Their car was winched ashore at the white town of Trebizond on the Black Sea coast, a strategic trading post connecting Persia, the Caucasus and Constantinople, conferring a distinct mixed identity. Annemarie, like Gertrude Bell before her, associated Trebizond with Xenophon 'when he and his Ten Thousand saw it lying at their feet with the blue sea beyond, and knew that an end was set at last to their weary march.'[75] Crossing the Pontic Alps to central Asia, for the two travellers it was just the beginning:

> We are following his path in the opposite direction. And already we've climbed to more than 2,000 metres, to the top of Zigana Pass; it's cold, but not dark yet. We see a magnificent panorama, range upon range, a sea of brown and barren mountains, Asiatic landscape, Asiatic grandeur.[76]

At Erzurum, in eastern Anatolia, the principal of the Seljuk-era Cifte madrassa invited them to an assembly, where the students knew some French: 'lamps are brought in and glasses of tea, while more than fifty great boys surround us, each with a question on his lips. We spend a splendid hour surrounded by their eagerness.'[77] At Bayazit

(Dogubeyazit), the last city before Iran, they climbed to the fortress and Kini noted the 'pungent smell of burning dung' and the faded grandeur of the architecture. As they rose to go, their guide remarked to Kini that her son seemed very tired. It was one of the many times on their journey that Annemarie was mistaken for a boy, which always pleased her.

Beyond Bayazit they crossed the border with a wrangle over visas. They were two peas in a Ford roadster deluxe rattling along the roads of northern Iran, one seeking 'fullness in joy', the other a bit of a misery guts. Rubbing shoulders, swerving around potholes, smoking like a trooper, weighing not much over 50 kilos, Annemarie opened up about her ill-starred love-life:

> Kini, what is wrong with me? Those I loved most, X, Y, Z, Mother even (I would have given my life to 'find' them again) – how is it that I could not settle the practical side of our relationship? Though at first they are devoted to me, I soon scare them, torture them with my love, with my impetuous demands … They tell me I destroy their lives … and after some time they even hand me over to strangers or to doctors.[78]

Approaching Tehran, backdrop to her marriage during the summer of 1935, Annemarie's sense of personal failure must have been acute. Ghosts of her past rose up; not just the disappointment of her marriage but the death of Jalé, the beginning of her affair with Baa, and the temptation of morphine. Tehran's torrid heat meant they stayed in the diplomatic enclave of Shemiran on the cooler slopes of the Elburz Mountains. Neither of these adventurous travellers was averse to a cocktail or two beside a swimming pool, with local-hire attendants bowing and scraping in the noonday heat: golden marmalade in the morning and 'tall glasses of pale whiskey before and after dinner' in the British legation; 'small glasses of brown vermouth' and fine champagne with the Italians; 'frothy beer drunk at all hours of the day and night', no doubt accompanied by clicking of heels, at the German legation, where 'all the servants, gate-keeper, gardener, and seamstress included, made the Hitler salute whenever we passed'.[79] Kini and Annemarie relinquished the hardships of the road for the well-polished corridors of diplomacy.

They spent three weeks in Tehran, acquiring visas and permissions for the next leg. Cholera in the eastern border region and vaccinations delayed them further. Kini kept close watch: 'Had she not been inexplicably upset when the chemist recognized her and presented an old bill? I was continually uneasy: did she want to go to town alone? Was she planning it?'[80] Annemarie drafted notes and articles and played the legation piano. They decided to take the northern route into the Mazandaran: 'Fertile, melancholy land – familiar from early life, from dreams and the memories of recent years – where the Shah had cotton mills built, model plantations and tobacco sheds.'[81] She contrasted the trappings of nomadism ('colourful saddlebags, rugs, tent bands') and development: 'No schools or hospitals without factories, no factories without workers, no workers without exploitation, no exploitation without class struggle. And on the roads laid down in the name of progress the tanks of war will roll. A nightmare?'[82]

Gains and losses attendant on Westernization litter her writing, and occasionally she sounds like a backpacker lamenting tourism, seeking elusive purity. Her style sometimes relies on exotic cliché: 'blessed India … land of Gandhi, jewel in the British crown', 'the turquoise and lapis-lazuli courtyards' above which the moon always seems to be winched up, and 'the immeasurable expanses of Asia' – deployed to signal the ineffable. Kini's observations on development are equally pessimistic: 'whenever crops were exploited and manufactured, boys and girls were good at their work until they were about eighteen. Then the boys took to opium and the girls to marriage and child-bearing.'[83] Everywhere they encountered Western engineers, builders and hydrologists. 'As elsewhere, we saw the poor deprived of rights and exploited by their rich overlords.'[84] The cotton-mills of Pol-i-Khumri were in competition with those of the southern United States, which Annemarie had witnessed with her own eyes: one country's development caused the decline of the other:

> … there is a cry for quinine, schools, hospitals, roads and soldiers. To pay for these there must be factories, docile subjects and tax-paying workers. So, little by little, we come to the sort of development that characterizes Europe … more machines and more specialized workers.[85]

They were Western travellers in search of the authentic, seeking enlightenment in the east, on the heels of engineers, missionaries and investors.

Fatalistic about development, they saw it as the questionable march of progress.

Bedding down for the night in an Armenian doss-house, 'swarms of invisible sandflies' began to wear on Annemarie's nerves and she had a meltdown: 'why were people so silly, so dirty, houses so badly built, why was it impossible to wash oneself?'[86] They decided to cover the 320 miles to Mashhad in one cross-country spurt, attracted by the prospect of a bath on arrival. There they stayed at the elegant British Consulate with its porticoed balconies and swimming pool, and spent three days in the company of two French cyclists, Raymond and Nicole Leininger, also heading to Kabul. 'They had cycled all the way from Paris, their intention being to reach Indo-China. Splashing at each other in the swimming pool of the Consulate, dawdling together through the lanes of the bazaar.'[87] It was three days of souks, mosques and cholera injections in Iran's second-largest city, observing pilgrims at the shrine of Imam Reza.

In Afghanistan they were *khanums*, unaccompanied women, and so objects of suspicion and perhaps lascivious speculation, but also worthy of protection if not independence. The young bloods in town after town stared at them, rarely having seen uncovered women. Kini persuaded Annemarie to buy a skirt so she could have access to the Afghan harems.[88]

> Here, no more high-heeled sluts in short frocks: you've come to the country where women are not seen, where men are capped with snowy muslin and walk with heavy shoes like gondolas. You've come to a country that has never been subjugated – neither by Alexander the Great nor by Timur the Lame, neither by Nadir nor by John Bull. It is the Switzerland of Asia.[89]

While lamenting unbridled modernization on the one hand, Annemarie had mixed feelings about traditional female subjugation on the other. Attempting freedom from patriarchy herself, she knew traditional cultures often survived by keeping their womenfolk and slaves under the male thumb. However, nowhere in her writing does she address the vexed question of female suffrage in Switzerland, nor lend her shoulder to the wheel of feminist politics agitating for greater freedom in the West.[90] This paradox glimmers faintly behind the two pieces she wrote on the subject, 'The Chador' and 'The Women of Kabul':

I've encountered other European women who have married here and wear the burqa. At first I sought them out, curious to know their stories, what their lives were like – lives to me so discrete and retiring, behind their adobe walls, their garden gates, their veils. But I never learned anything, even when they began to open up, to complain, to confide. Nonetheless, they spend whole afternoons, half their lives, idly gossiping with their friends and sisters-in-law. They all live under a constant, fearful mummery.[91]

She proposed to the *National-Zeitung* a series of articles on the 'unbelievably oppressed' lives of women in Afghanistan.[92] 'The stifling confinement of women today in towns and villages is unworthy of such a proud culture, so marked by intelligence and vitality.'[93] She was presciently aware of what would come to be known as 'the Western gaze'. Looking works both ways, however, and one woman, a mayor's wife, observed that Annemarie was too skinny to bear children. In Kabul, both women visited a girls' school, established in defiance of the mullahs. The students 'showed the same keenness, the same defiant attitude, as if to say: "It is daring of us to be here. But we are proud to be the new Afghanistan."'[94] The mullahs were of the view that 'modern education causes mischief in feminine heads' and the confrontation between government forward-thinking and religious backwardness was to play out over the following century to no peaceful end.

They took the more difficult northern route out of Herat along the border with Turkestan and proceeded in stages south across the Hindu Kush. Bamiyan was the apogee of their journey, where giant Buddha statues, one fifty-three metres tall, the other thirty-five, carved into the sandstone cliff in the sixth century, testify to its strategic position on the Silk Road travelled by Chinese merchants. The Taliban blew both statues up in March 2001, a final act of long-running desecration; faces and hands had already been hacked off by previous zealots. 'Some years ago the Afghan government issued a stamp reproducing the Buddha of Bamiyan but it was withdrawn', reports Kini, 'for too many Muslims were shocked at a representation of the human form.'[95] Like education for girls, the statues represented intolerable values and beliefs.

At Bagram, eighty kilometres north of Kabul, Joseph and Ria Hackin and their team of archaeologists were packing treasures. Joseph Hackin was the best-known Frenchman in Afghanistan, close to the king, with

The standing Buddhas in Bamiyan, Afghanistan. Photo by Annemarie
Schwarzenbach
Courtesy of Swiss Literary Archives and Wikimedia Commons

a deep knowledge of the region and its archaeology. Ria had been an
auditrice at the École du Louvre when she met the director of the Musée
Guimet. She was pretty, nineteen years her husband's junior, a gutsy
horsewoman. Annemarie arrived in Bagram sick with fever and the
attractive, grey-eyed thirty-four-year-old Ria took on the role of nurse,
always a way to win the patient's heart – which is exactly what ensued.
They returned to Kabul at the end of August, Annemarie suffering from
bronchitis and put to bed for ten days and ordered off the cigarettes. As
usual, she was a poorly compliant invalid:

> … though still coughing, Annemarie would not obey the doctor's orders. She
> looked tired and bored except when we called on the Hackins. No longer
> sustained, as she had been all these months, by the need to realize our plan,
> she began to show wantonness. She had no faith in the doctor's potion, she

did not want to see him again and she forced me to get a syrup of codeine from the chemist in town. I did not know then what codeine contains.[96]

Writing to Anita Forrer from Kabul, Annemarie is clearly feeling the need once more:

... since Tehran, at least since Meshed, we have not passed through any place where there was a pharmacy ... I live on my nerves, at wit's end – you know what it's like with this poison: sleep, exhaustion.[97]

On 1 September 1939 war broke out in Europe, changing everybody's plans. Kini could no longer leave Kabul to travel in Kafiristan. Their cycling friends, the Leiningers, last seen by the pool of the British Consulate in Meshed, curtailed their journey and the husband was mobilized at Pondicherry and sent to Saigon, where he donned the uniform of the colonial army. Annemarie felt her place was in Europe. Over the course of the previous decade, she and the Manns had been weathervanes for war and now it had come to pass. Sleepless in Kabul when war broke out, she records the moment in her diary: 'It's five o'clock in the morning. The roosters of Kabul are crowing.' On 2 September she notes 'vomiting, once again I've given in, I wanted to fight this horrible depression'.[98]

After twelve weeks on the road and a month cooped up together in Kabul, relations between the two travellers had grown fractious. Staying with Dr. Gabriel Monod-Herzen, professor of combined sciences and great-grandson of the Russian socialist, Alexander Herzen, Kini shared his interest in Buddhism and host and guest were inclined to rise above Annemarie's preoccupation with politics – 'both seeking happiness in dispassion, goodness, a detachment from all earthly things'.[99] Availing of her diplomatic connection, Annemarie moved to the French legation, where the Hackins were billeted and where 'between sheets, in a real bed, the rich food will do her good, she will have the peace and rest she needs'. Annemarie presented this interlude with the Hackins and the two cyclists as a time of 'writing our travel journals, afternoons stretched out in the garden under the mild autumn sun, carpeted evenings with the gramophone – Mozart operas, Bach suites – excursions'.[100] Yet, privately she realized the moral support Kini had given. The record suggests mounting addiction and self-regard: 'I don't want to be relieved of my suffering.'[101] Wallowing in self-pity, Annemarie was unable to separate her own suffering (embassy bed, French cuisine) from the objective context of war. She longed for a shoulder to cry on.

Kini was glad of a respite:

> Yes, I was tired of Annemarie, I had been centred on her for the last six months and I could not sustain the effort. I was now absorbed in my immediate future.
>
> We sorted our belongings. From the box containing our mountain boots, to my surprise she produced a hypodermic needle which she gave me, saying:
>
> 'This journey has freed me from the drug.'
>
> I decided to believe her.[102]

Annemarie noted this split somewhat differently in her diary: 'I had broken our "pact", trust had also broken down, her role and duty towards me had come to an end.'[103] On the one hand, a dubious success, on the other a failure. Kini kept in touch since Annemarie's health continued to be concerning. She had found a ready supply of morphine ampoules in Kabul, probably from the British and German legation doctors who had been treating her, and from a compatriot businessman.[104]

Kini arranged with archaeologist Jacques Meunié for Annemarie to be accompanied three hundred kilometres north to Kunduz on the Afghan–Turkestan border, to join the Hackins at a dig. It would remove her from the city. Annemarie travelled – 'without syringe, without even one ampoule'[105] – on a journey of two days to Kunduz and the desert village of Tashqurghan (present day Kholm), thirty kilometres from the Soviet border on the Oxus river. It was winter, a freezing desert wind blew, snow and dust storms were forecast. With war declared, the 'Russian army could be here in a few hours' to occupy the buffer zone. Annemarie had a kind of baptism of solitude or a rude session of detoxification in this isolated, extreme environment – 'a village that seemed to lose itself in ruins and strange clay cliffs, as in the labyrinth of a Dantesque entrance to Hell'. She had been reading Dante.[106] In the published record of this moment she omits any direct mention of her struggle with addiction by conflating several visits and orientalizing: 'the police chief who had been alarmed escorted my car to the gate of a fairy-tale palace that lay white in the moonlight at the end of a gently and endlessly upsloping garden'.[107] The reader might be inclined to think the police chief's suspicions justified: a woman in trousers in a Swiss car with a French diplomatic passport wandering around the desert near the Soviet Union at the outset of war.

> I set out to the north, always to the north, driven by a strange perversity; I could just as well walk in a circle, or to the east, or the west, leaving it to chance. Some distance behind a soldier follows, to guard and watch me. … here and there is waste and vastness, steppe, desert, hardness and want, endlessness: the heart of Asia.[108]

The stint at Kunduz lasted two weeks. The convoy of archaeologists returned to Kabul, where she felt 'reasonably healthy'. Many of Annemarie's journalistic pieces bear dates in November and December 1939, coinciding with a frenzied period of work in the capital, writing in the museum. Many never saw publication in her lifetime, written as they are in a visionary style, heavy on local colour, not quite journalism, not quite fiction. Her editors in Switzerland must have had more concrete affairs to contend with. Nonetheless, the trip to Kunduz and her work ethic had done the trick: she had broken the back of her addiction.

The war began to impinge on petrol supplies, the price of Peshawar whiskey rose, the 'modest colony of Europeans' leaned into the French legation radio. December days dawned, cold and sober; she went horse riding, as she had done in the Tiergarten in 1933 when Hitler came to power. 'I had few modest wishes: that Mister Gai would send me a new typewriter ribbon from Peshawar, that the little shop next to the Kabul bridge, at the entrance to the bazaar, wouldn't run out of American cigarettes.'[109] She wrote to Kini in India, determined to contribute to the war effort and to sort out their respective book projects:

> I hope to find something to do, in Switzerland or in France. Maybe I could work as a newspaper correspondent in Scandinavia. Anything at all seems better than what I'm doing here and now.[110]

On 21 December she left Kabul with ethnologist Jacques Meunié, crossed the Khyber Pass to Peshawar, and down to Delhi along the

A seated boy in Mandu, India. Photo by Annemarie Schwarzenbach
Courtesy of Swiss Literary Archives and Wikimedia Commons

asphalt imperial roads. Before setting out from Switzerland she had made her will, suspecting she would not live long.[111] Virgil's Carthaginian phrase had increasingly become Annemarie's motto: tears dried to salt in the wind and thoughts of mortality.[112] Meeting up with Kini on 28 December at Indore, they spent a couple of companionable days. Annemarie had been clean since mid-November but it was too early to tell; thin but healthy, she was 'not unlike the young Bhils we played with on these reedy shores where they fish with bow and arrow, their nakedness showing long slim thighs, ribbed chests and a mop of hair falling over the brow.'[113] Kini proposed a wellness year in Mandu – ashram, yoghurt, horses – but Annemarie was determined to return to Europe.

The *Conte Biancamano* left Bombay on 7 January 1940, behind schedule. Annemarie spent the return voyage writing an article a day about Afghanistan for Swiss outlets, watching Aden and the Red Sea, Port Saïd, Haifa and Naples go by. Shipping was disrupted – the British were keeping a controlling eye on the strategic Suez canal: between a stronghold and a stranglehold was a matter of a syllable, and the *Conte Biancamano*, as an Axis vessel, must have been one of the last to navigate the canal during the war.

> … the old, true Aden, the city of Hindus, Arabs, half-breeds and negro boys, a filthy, wretched place, an ancient one laden with secrets, rich in ivory and sandalwood, shimmering with alabaster in bright nights.[114]

On the final leg of the journey from Naples to Genoa, they rerouted full steam ahead to come to the assistance of the *Orazio*, a trans-Atlantic steamer carrying 645 crew and passengers, many of them Jewish refugees fleeing to South America. The *Orazio* had caught fire off Toulon and 106 passengers were lost when the ship went down in freezing weather with the mistral blowing. It was a foretaste of the war to come. Annemarie's account of the fire and rescue published in Basel's *National-Zeitung* five days later shows compassion and solidarity:

> Then we saw little bundles lying at the bottom of the boat, here and there a tousled head peering up – they were children, nothing but children, and the rowers, their legs spreadeagled between the hull and the seats, lifted them up and handed them over the side to our gangway where helping arms grabbed hold of them and took them onto the boat.[115]

The *Conte Biancamano* docked five days late and Annemarie joined other passengers and refugees in a hotel. 'It was a mild Italian winter's day, driving towards the Gotthard. I needed to acclimatize to war in Europe, to these same green meadows and ripening fields I had traversed in peacetime and had looked back on from far-off Asia.'[116] Diplomatic passport in hand, Annemarie was one of the lucky travellers 'not under the jurisdiction of this place'[117] – and while her sympathies with refugees were genuine, her staying power tended to be short-lived.

When she arrived in Bocken on 25 January, her family were apprehensive about her physical and mental health, keen to know if she was truly drug-free. For Renée this was once again a mixed blessing: there had been too many promises of no drugs and three expensive attempts at cure during the previous year. Both mother and grandmother warily took Annemarie's assurances at face value; Renée had too much experience with her daughter's deviousness to commit and, besides, Alfred's health needed attention.

Hindsight and the war give Annemarie's movements a trajectory, as though she knew what she was doing, but it is a trajectory with a harum-scarum quality. There were harbingers of war in June 1939 when they left Europe: had she wished to put her shoulder to the wheel she could have stayed. When war was declared, Kini stuck to her original plan while Annemarie's response was at once more political though vague and idealistic. Unlike her friends the Hackims, who had pledged allegiance to de Gaulle's resistance and had a plan of action, Annemarie had no definite role in mind and even considered travelling to the United States with Anita Forrer. As an accredited Swiss journalist on a French diplomatic passport, Annemarie's options were facilitated rather than hampered by nationality.

Judicious details and the photographic record create a story of gutsy women on a voyage of discovery east of Eden. Kini sat out the war in an ashram in India and Annemarie returned to an uneasy Europe, strung out, restless still, only to make a disastrous final visit to the United States. Their Afghan journey has all the makings of a road movie: war, drugs, local colour, legations, female adventurers pitted against the elements. War and hindsight confer nostalgia on this costume drama of pith helmets, turbans and women in cinched pants lounging by vintage cars, the standing buddhas of Bamiyan magically restored from the desert dust and Annemarie in her element. She had a tendency to see Afghanistan as a paradise, a Swiss-like federation of tribes holding out between the mighty Soviet Union and the British in India.[118] While tempering this exotic tendency in her journalism, she could not altogether abandon it – to do so would threaten the long-cherished poeticization in her writing: if there was no poetry then she was just a jobbing journo after all. Nonetheless, the scales had fallen from her orientalist eyes. Closer attention to the record reveals her distracted state of mind, aware that she is romanticizing a harsher reality. The belief in travel as an ineffable end in itself, or indeed travel as therapeutic, had failed her. She had come to the end of a certain kind of love affair with the east.[119]

9

Running on Empty

All her life she had played with death, desperately trying to learn how to die.

Ruth Landshoff Yorck, 'Annemarie'

Between Afghanistan and her final trip to the United States, Annemarie spent three months in Switzerland, weighing her options. Mother and daughter were at loggerheads. Renée's allegiance to Germany was common knowledge among staff and neighbours. A former worker at Bocken remembered 'not long after the war began, swastika graffiti appeared overnight on all the gateposts'.[1] The decline of the family firm, exacerbated by the conflict, put its future in question, and impressed upon Annemarie the need to find, at age thirty-two, a regular income. At the end of January 1940, her grandmother trumpeted in her diary that Annemarie was drug-free, though Renée reserved judgement.[2]

She took time to organize and caption the photos she and Ella had taken on their road trip and to prepare articles in German and French for a range of Swiss publications. Among the photographers, it was a crowded field. German language outlets for Annemarie's writing and photographs were confined to Switzerland, where magazines enjoyed a renaissance due to censorship across the border in Germany. *ABC* and *Du* published her work, as well as the photographs of Werner Bischof, Walter Bosshard and Paul Senn, photographers who brought the outside world into Swiss living rooms. Bosshard had traversed China and India since the early 1930s. Senn had chronicled social and political crises since labour protests in Geneva in 1932. France's capitulation in June 1940 found Senn at Le Chauffour in Switzerland's Jura Mountains, where 40,000 French troops were welcomed by the Jurassiens. The Swiss-born

American photographer Robert Frank, whose portraits of Americans in the 1950s waited in the wings, descended from these pre-war socially minded photographers.[3] There was no shortage of assignments Annemarie could have picked up on the home front, but instead she chose to escape once more.

Despite her success, Annemarie tended to think of reporting as provisional. Ella Maillart regarded Annemarie as at heart a poet, albeit a writer of poetic prose. The enemies of Annemarie's promise – journalism, drugs and travel – seemed to have conspired against the longer, more sustained imagination required for fiction. She was only thirty-two, and might have looked back on a decade of increasingly fragmented and unsuccessful writings somewhat in a minor key. Like countless others on the boat to the United States, she might also have looked forward to a new start in the English-speaking world.

Having come full circle, she framed her Afghanistan journey to Klaus as 'a need to end once and for all with a large part of my past',[4] a phrase sufficiently vague as to be meaningless. She hoped to work as a correspondent, perhaps in Scandinavia. There were plans for Anita Forrer and Annemarie to travel to America together. As it turned out, Anita travelled there alone and joined the Red Cross.[5]

Instead of following through on any of these plans, Annemarie took up with Baroness von Opel, whom she had known since 1935. 'Annemarie was in Sils Maria. I was in St. Moritz. We couldn't really avoid each other.'[6] In March 1940 the intensity of her relationship with the Baroness changed and she found herself once again, as she had with Ria Hackin in Afghanistan in November and Dr. Favez in the Bellevue Clinic, the third person in someone else's marriage. Baron Fritz Adam Hermann von Opel – 'Rocket Fritz', as he was known in the press – hailed from a German industrialist family that began developing cars at the turn of the twentieth century. In March 1929 General Motors bought Germany's largest car manufacturer, and Fritz, an only child, inherited a fortune. Passionate about rocket propulsion, he spent his youth experimenting with speed – cars, gliders, motorcycles and boats. He married the actress and aviatrix Margot Löwenstein, née Sellnik, in 1929 and since 1933 they had lived mostly in Switzerland and had acquired Liechtenstein passports. Margot's Jewish origin doubtless explains their expatriation but Fritz was also antipathetic to Hitler. The phoney war – *Krieg ohne*

Krieg – was coming to an end by spring 1940 and they were considering moving to the United States.

Married for ten childless years, the couple wintered in St. Moritz in a fast, wealthy milieu. Margot was no stranger to the Zurich police who suspected her of being a spy; her movements were followed and her phone tapped. Annemarie turns up in police records sharing Margot's room in Zurich's exclusive Dolder Hotel, sporting cropped hair, both women wearing trousers.[7] In April 1940 police questioned Annemarie about her connection to the couple, perhaps a deciding factor in her precipitate departure for America. She hoped to sell her Afghanistan photos and to visit the Mann family settled in Princeton – they hadn't met in a year.

Renée was aware of Annemarie's affair but kept a wary distance, miffed that her daughter had drawn the attention of the police once again: 'Of course, the diplomatic passport opens all doors.' In a letter to Suzanne in Sweden she showed her disapproval of Jewish actresses masquerading as Baronesses: 'Currently Annemarie is staying at the Dolder. … She has a new girlfriend, a very wealthy but coarse woman – and Annemarie has been living in St. Moritz for some time. I had the "lady" here for tea on Sunday and so have done my duty by her. Any day now they're heading off to St. Moritz and I hope soon to America.'[8]

On 4 May Annemarie and Margot boarded the American liner, the *SS Manhattan*, docked in Genoa and bound for New York, travelling first class. Fritz mysteriously must have travelled earlier than the two women. He was taken off the Italian liner *Conte di Savoia* by British authorities at Gibraltar on 25 April 1940 and interrogated.[9] Maybe Zurich police had alerted MI6 to the presence of a German rocket scientist holding a Liechtenstein passport. Maybe it was the wife in trousers they were after. He was detained at Gibraltar for sixteen days and allowed to proceed to the United States. FBI files note he arrived in 'New York City on the steamship *Rex* on May 9 from Gibraltar'.[10] Once America entered the war, the von Opels were arrested by FBI agents in February 1942, and held in enemy alien internment camps. Fritz's considerable American assets were seized.

On board ship Annemarie continued to write about Iran, Afghanistan and Turkistan, locales now rendered somewhat peripheral by the war. Dated 9 May 1940, her short article 'Nach Westen' ('Westward Ho!')

gives us a glimpse of her restless state of mind following three months in Switzerland. 'Even if you have managed to sidestep war zones and battlefields and slept through the night crossing the Swiss border. ... coming or going amounts to much the same thing in hindsight.' The writer drifts aimlessly between east and west, a homing pigeon not quite knowing where to settle:

> I woke once more in Genoa, on the ship's bridge, in sight of the sea, the old Mediterranean, with the coast slipping away, its olive-green slopes and foam-flecked rocks, our unruffled wake. The sight of this coast on returning from India barely three months before had me almost in tears. Now I'm steaming west, as though merely continuing the same journey.[11]

*

Germany invaded Denmark and Norway in April 1940. Hitler began his march into Belgium, Holland and Luxembourg on 10 May, while Annemarie was mid-Atlantic on the *Manhattan*. On 10 June Mussolini brought Italy into the war, on 14 June Paris fell to the Germans and three days later the French government under Pétain was seeking an armistice. The Nazi advance seemed unstoppable. Many Swiss believed they would be next. There was much discussion about how Switzerland would react in the event of a German invasion – whether to defend the homeland or, as other small nations had done, to accept the inevitable and capitulate. Swiss public opinion was resolutely against German expansionism.

Annemarie's was a strange ménage conducted in luxury hotels on both sides of the Atlantic – Zurich's Dolder Grand, Badrutt's Palace in St. Moritz, the Plaza and the Pierre in New York. Margot and Fritz were footing the bill but very quickly Margot found Annemarie's intensity and drug use overwhelming. Shuttling between the lavish world of the von Opels at the Plaza and the Pierre and the raffish Manns at the Bedford, Annemarie was astride industrial wealth and high bohemia – milieux she had negotiated all her adult life. The Manns, like the British and the Swiss, were suspicious of the von Opels' non-declared politics, wary of spies in their midst. Sybille Bedford, who had left from Genoa shortly after Annemarie, was also booked into the hotel and, with the help of the Manns and their servants, drove to California that summer in their 'large, luxurious Lincoln'.[12] Refugees of one stripe or another were on the move, on the make, navigating the new world. The von Opels had invested wealth in the United States which, for now, kept them afloat between a house on Nantucket, another in Palm Springs, Florida and the luxury hotels of New York City.

In the first of her articles written from the United States in June, Annemarie ostensibly reported on the World's Fair taking place in New York but it was a veiled note of warning about the complacency of business as usual. She contrasted the naive innocence of a group of Swiss girls, safe in their neutrality, crossing on the *Manhattan* to staff the Swiss pavilion, with international events unfolding at blitzkrieg speed:

> The news on the radio didn't really dampen the spirits of these pretty, cheerful girls, even less so the Americans on board, most of whom were businessmen. I hardly remember how I came by the news that the Nazis had invaded Holland. I thought immediately of my German emigrant friends in Amsterdam.[13]

At Flushing Meadows, where the World's Fair was held, flags and pennants drooped, as though aware of their countries' disgrace; it had been so-named by New York's original Dutch settlers and now Holland itself was overrun, not by water, but by German troops. The writer Joseph Roth had committed suicide in Paris the previous year – 'it's as well he didn't fall into the hands of the Nazis' – and Annemarie wanted to underline his prescience:

> The European mind is capitulating. It is capitulating out of weakness, out of sloth, out of apathy, out of lack of imagination (it will be the task of some future generation to establish the reason for this disgraceful capitulation).[14]

Writing from the relative comfort of the Vesper Country Club in Lowell, Massachusetts, in June 1940, she lamented the fate of German literature now that its greatest exponents were exiled:

> Already many German emigrants who had taken refuge in Holland and France have pitched up in New York in the five weeks since the Battle of the Netherlands and my own arrival. For a bond of forty dollars a month, they can travel to San Domingo. Maybe with enough English you could keep on writing.[15]

She was considering whether to continue writing in German or, like a number of writers evacuated from Europe at the time – Nabokov, a salient example – to adapt to English. Annemarie mulled over her dilemma from the Plaza Hotel: 'I'm holding off from deciding because the language I write is German, and when I use English it comes out shallow and ephemeral. My grasp of English is inadequate and I feel isolated.'[16]

'Communazis' was the term used by J. Edgar Hoover and his boys at the FBI for German exiles whose allegiance to American capitalism was questionable. The Bedford was under surveillance, its phones wiretapped and its guests followed. The von Opels and their movements were being tracked from the Vesper Country Club in Lowell to the Plaza in New York and Siasconset, Nantucket, where mail was opened and the postmaster acted as informant. Annemarie appears in the von Opel FBI records on numerous occasions, in the Back Bay Railroad Station in Boston, for example, she was picked up by the von Opels in their car. She wore 'a tailored suit, had a boyish bob' and all three arrived at the Vesper Country Club at one in the morning.[17]

Hollywood extended so-called 'Lifesaver' contracts to German and Austrian refugee writers, many of whom were Jewish. There was a steady westward drift to 'Weimar on the Pacific' where life was sunnier but shallower. Refugees soon became suspect, 'enemy aliens', in their newfound paradise. Thomas Mann, for one, was astutely aware of the conformist requirements for an American passport. As for Klaus, 'a well known sexual pervert', his overnight guests and visitors were noted and trailed.[18]

The Mann family base of operations was Princeton University, where Thomas held a sinecure. On 22 May 1940, shortly after her arrival, Annemarie was there for lunch with Erika and Klaus and again for the old maestro's 65th birthday celebrations on 6 June.[19] They were preoccupied by the refugee crisis, particularly anxious about Heinrich Mann and his wife Nelly, as well as Golo, all three stuck in France. Erika attended a hastily assembled funding luncheon at the Commodore Hotel on 25 June, together with Dorothy Thompson. Klaus was attempting to turn himself into an English writer by using translators and hustling for work with the *Reader's Digest*.[20] He mulled over starting another magazine, along the lines of *Die Sammlung* of 1933, but in English and editorially based in the United States. This would become *Decision*, running from January 1941 to February 1942.

Annemarie, for her part, wrote about refugees and empathized with their plight, but held off from becoming involved in the Emergency Rescue Committee and its ladies' committees set up to help exiled children. 'It's not my way of working, this mix of nattering, female rivalry and social cachet, the stuff of committee projects – it's so dilettante it makes me sick.'[21] During these first three weeks she was busy interviewing, attempting to place her photos with the Black Star agency and also meeting her father who was in town on what would prove to be his last business trip. Given Italy's entry to the war on 10 June, trans-Atlantic crossings were suspended and Alfred had to kick his heels in the city. Annemarie suggested accompanying him home but Alfred and Freddy thought it prudent for all that she stay away from the European battlefield – and at a remove from Renée.[22] Alfred was eventually able to fly back to Milan via Rome on a Pan American Airways clipper and wrote about his flight experience for the *NZZ*.[23]

By the time of the 6 June dinner in Princeton, Annemarie had tired of the city. She wrote to Ella Maillart: 'in a little over four weeks I have seen enough of New York, its busy life, committees, social contacts etc., etc., to feel deeply discouraged.'[24] While Klaus and Erika had created a niche for themselves, picking up work and book contracts, Annemarie was more impatient. She had contacted American magazines and the *Washington Post*, as well as elicited interest from the Intercontinental News Service, but she kept wrong-footing her own plans. There was something spur of the moment about her being in the United States in the first place. Now she wanted to get away – again. Writing to Klaus in July, she described herself as 'unhappy because I have not yet settled down and because no environment seems sufficiently interesting to me to adopt as my own'.[25] Late-night parties, alcohol and Benzedrine didn't help matters.[26] Her self-involvement and tendency to cause scenes, at a time when the world was going to hell in a handbasket, taxed the patience of her friends. At the Plaza Hotel, a drunk and drugged Annemarie and Margot were involved in a loud, late-night argument, with objects thrown, which disturbed the other hotel guests.[27] The tiara had fallen.

*

New York City in the summer of 1940 suffered a heatwave, lowering the murder rate, as thousands fled to Coney Island and sheltered under the hot boardwalk. Kids jumped off the piers into the Harlem River and boys uncapped fire hydrants and started block parties. City-dwellers dragged mattresses onto fire escapes and tried to get a night's sleep. By early September, temperatures had cooled and the Battle of Britain had begun.

For twenty-three-year-old writer Carson McCullers, meeting Annemarie Schwarzenbach in June 1940 was a bolt of lightning. Three years married to her husband Reeves, the young southerners were in New York for the launch of Carson's first novel, *The Heart is a Lonely Hunter*, a Book of the Month Club selection. The *New Yorker* acclaimed it 'a first novel that reads like a fifth' and the *New York*

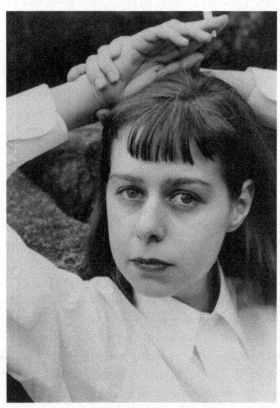

Carson McCullers, c. 1940
Bridgeman Images

Times simultaneously lauded its astonishing maturity.[28] The couple had travelled from Fayetteville, North Carolina, the week before, with uncertain prospects, and were staying in Greenwich Village. 'When we arrived here, my husband and I, all my money was stolen from my bag. But the publishers gave me enough to live on, and my husband will be able to find a job soon', she told Annemarie.[29] McCullers was not new to the city; night classes at Columbia University and creative writing classes at New York University as well as publication had widened the gap between her and her aspiring-writer husband who had nothing much to show for his efforts. She was being promoted by Houghton Mifflin as something of a wunderkind and her success prompted Annemarie to profile her for the *National-Zeitung* under the headline 'A Young American'.

McCullers' editor, Robert Linscott, was instrumental in bringing the two writers together. He agreed to meet Carson for the first time in the Bedford Hotel on 5 June, after weeks of correspondence about editorial matters, to discuss the novel's promotion. She was excited about her first book and its reception. Literary editor of *Harper's Bazaar*, George Davis, had opted to serialize her second novel, retitled *Reflections in a Golden Eye*, starting in August. A third work underway, an early draft of the novella *The Ballad of the Sad Café*, was serialized in *Harper's Bazaar* in 1943. McCullers wanted to verify the authenticity of her depiction of the German and Jewish immigrant experience in her work in progress, and had arranged to meet Erika Mann in the Bedford for this purpose, although adulation might also have played a part. McCullers was good at veiling her motivations behind eccentricity. Reeves, her husband, had gone sailing in Nantucket for a week. Earlier she had tried Greta Garbo for the same purpose – a mix of research and admiration – but the star 'made it clear that she was not interested in a developing friendship' with the coy young author of the moment.[30]

Klaus noted in his diary for 12 June that he had met Carson the previous week '… just arrived from the south. Strangely unsophisticated, naive morbid creature, maybe very talented. Wrote something about an emigrant and a negro.'[31] He had spotted the aura of illness about her and, like many others, her peculiar gamine awkwardness. This encounter between the worldly-wise Manns from old Europe, trailing literary and historical baggage, and the twenty-three-year-old Southerner from a modest background, has about it the meeting of old and new cultures. When Annemarie entered the room, McCullers didn't know where to look:

> She had a face that I knew would haunt me to the end of my life, beautiful, blonde, with straight short hair. There was a look of suffering on her face that I could not define. As she was bodily resplendent I could only think of Myshkin's meeting with Nastasya Filippovna in *The Idiot*, in which he experienced 'terror, pity and love'. She was introduced by Erika as Madame Clarac.[32]

In her unfinished autobiography, written decades later, McCullers presents a string of unlikely assertions about Annemarie and their meetings. Hyperbole and uncertainty about facts reveal the younger writer's leanings towards Southern grotesque.[33] McCullers liked oddballs and in Annemarie she had met her match. The two got together again the following day and Annemarie apparently baldly admitted her addiction: 'I've been taking morphine since I'm eighteen years old.' Not getting the reaction she expected (McCullers was innocent about drugs), Annemarie tried regaling the twenty-three-year old with her traveller's tales: 'She skipped abruptly to her wanderings in Afghanistan, Egypt, Syria and all the Far East.' Then it was the turn of the wicked mother: 'She had left home because her mother had beat her regularly.' 'At home she lived in a castle with her mother and an idiot brother, who could barely speak.' This unburdening to a recent acquaintance seems unlikely but there is enough truth in these assertions, however much they have been worked up and coloured later by McCullers, to show that Annemarie confided in her. The two got on well and went out on the town. When Carson returned in the early hours, Reeves slapped her 'quick and powerful as a panther', suspecting an affair with 'Madame Schwarzenbach'.[34]

Annemarie, for her part, was taken by Carson's 'mix of precocious resignation and innocence'[35] and had already decided she would write a review of this new novel and its winsome author. More threadbare in matters of the heart, Annemarie could likely see through the younger writer's infatuation and europhilia. It neatly reversed the terms of her own adulation of Erika ten years earlier. Annemarie's correspondence with Robert Linscott shows tact and a desire not to wound Carson's innocence: 'I feel so bad being unable to do anything for Carson, I'm deeply fond of her, & I wish the world would be different, easier for her to face.'[36] Linscott was keen to promote his writer, and in Annemarie's mind was the need to establish herself as a journalist in the American market.

The two writers met the following day in the bar of the Bedford and for lunch in a diner:

> 'I felt very strongly yesterday', she said to me, 'when I met you and your friends, that none of you liked me. You come from Europe, most of you are refugees, emigrants, Jews. You hold it against me that I'm American and you think I can't understand you. But I came here today especially to let you know that I understand you …'
>
> 'But you're wrong', I said. 'Nobody here holds it against you for being American, and besides, I'm Swiss – nobody's got it in for me. Switzerland is still above the fray.'[37]

Carson is eager to find common cause and Annemarie to put her right. There is something comical in the notion of the Mann siblings and this scion of Swiss democracy and wealth as somehow oppressed or rootless, rooming in the Bedford Hotel while Carson is in a fifth-floor walk-up in the meatpacking district. Annemarie's dispassionate description of Carson tells us she was not erotically interested in her. The Southern writer's childlike presentation – the looks and manner of a sixteen-year-old – much remarked on by others at this time, was not to Annemarie's taste, which ran to older more maternal women:

> I had a coffee and she had a glass of milk and a slice of buttered bread, which she left untouched. While she wrote down her address, I noticed her hands trembling and that her handwriting was barely legible. When I spoke, she stretched forward her pallid child's face and fixed big grey eyes on my lips, as though she were hard of hearing.[38]

Annemarie honed in on the social and racial fault lines of Carson's novel, territory which the Swiss writer felt she knew from her swing through the South in 1938 and from her few days in Columbus, Georgia, Carson's home town. Its ante-bellum plantation class had co-opted the Swiss reporter and she had 'endured three days of "Southern hospitality" before I dared to express the wish to visit a local cotton mill.'[39] Carson, on the other hand, knew the South intuitively; her character Jake Blount 'was driven to the point of near madness by the inequalities of the working conditions of the masses' and Dr. Copeland 'a black physician, was repudiated by the people of his own race, as well as by the whites'.[40] Despite her youth and airy-fairy manner, Carson had taken into her imagination the sprains and poverty of the American South. Privately underwhelmed by *The Heart is a Lonely Hunter*,[41] Annemarie reviewed this first novel as a true reflection of the current state of the South as she and its author had experienced it:

> It has no truck with the romanticism of *Gone with the Wind*, or with the heroic, rose-tinted treatment of Lincoln and George Washington in plays and novels, nor does it have the moving drama of *The Grapes of Wrath*. A young Negro is so mistreated on a chain gang that he returns home with both feet amputated. His father, a black doctor who has idealistically struggled all his life for the freedom of his brothers, conceives a deep fanatical rage against whites, leading him and his family to ruin.[42]

Besides music, the American South and sartorial eccentricity, both writers had in common marriage to ambivalent men: Claude Clarac was homosexual and Reeves bisexual. Carson's husband was the first person to kiss her when she was nineteen and her sole comment on the physical side of marriage is at once literary and side-stepping: 'The sexual experience was not like D.H. Lawrence. No grand explosions or coloured lights, but it gave me a chance to know Reeves better, and really learn to love him. We treated ourselves to pink champagne and tomatoes out of season.'[43] On their wedding night they shared a box of candy but Carson noted that Reeves scoffed the lot on his own later: he was not to be trusted.[44] At the time of meeting Annemarie, the McCullers' marriage was in difficulties and Carson had begun to notice that Reeves was stealing from her.

Not long after Thomas Mann's birthday celebrations and the meetings with Carson at the Bedford, Annemarie decamped with Margot to the Vesper Country Club on the Merrimack River in Lowell, a move which nipped in the bud any furthering of the relationship with Carson for the duration of the long hot summer. Much as she had always enjoyed New

York, Annemarie never took to its furious pace. In her country club room she wrote with the help of 'so much alcohol that I decided to give it up last night'. Switzerland's isolated neutrality was on her mind, but also her own writing prospects; perhaps Carson's precocious success brought into focus Annemarie's own relative failure. Klaus and Erika were soon off on a speaking tour and Erika was to travel to London in August to work for the British Information Service. The rest of the Mann family decamped to California. Rows with Margot added to Annemarie's depression and she felt at a loose end. On 14 June, Paris capitulated and by the end of the month northern France was in Nazi hands. Annemarie knew that reactions at home in Meilen and Bocken would be jubilant – the Treaty of Versailles had been avenged. At Europe's darkest hour, knocking back the country club liquor on Margot's tab, Annemarie again felt she was in the wrong place at the wrong time, a rebel without a cause.[45]

In the middle of this fug of politics, writing and cocktails, Carson wrote to Annemarie about her new apartment and her difficult husband:

> Getting up this morning, I thought of Brahms' sonata in D minor for violin and piano, and since then I've felt strangely happy. As soon as we move in, I'll get down to work . . . and the result will be very different and purer than what I've written up to now. What I'm looking for, in a general sense, is a new poetic form, a poetic style which requires imagination and finding the right tone.[46]

At Carson's urging, Linscott arranged for the Swiss writer to be invited to the Bread Loaf Writers Conference in Vermont at the same time as Carson in August. But Annemarie had no intention of turning up and called to say she couldn't make it. Carson pleaded with her to meet in Boston instead, where she had an appointment with her editor at Houghton Mifflin. In the meantime, Margot and Annemarie had planned to move to Siasconset on Nantucket for the remainder of the season. She wrote to Klaus from Nantucket on 23 July when Carson's infatuation was at its height:

> It will probably be very difficult for you to understand that it is young Carson McCullers who has sparked such a violent crisis; she is seriously ill and lives in an imaginary world so bizarre, so remote from reality that it is absolutely

impossible to get her to listen to reason. I thought I had acted with all due caution and had treated her gently, but she is waiting for me to arrive from one day to the next, convinced that I am her destiny. And now her husband has left her because of it.[47]

Summer on Nantucket brought her relationship with Margot to a head. As with earlier affairs, Annemarie's neediness and alcohol intake taxed her girlfriends. Photos show her emaciated, blue under the eyes, wearing a natty blazer at the wheel of a Massachusetts-registered Ford coupé fronting 'wild briar roses, growing in profusion over picket fences,

Annemarie at Dubendorf Airfield, September 1939
Courtesy of Swiss Literary Archives and Wikimedia Commons

climbing on the roofs of sea captains' houses, on barns, farmhouses'.[48] Siasconset, on the eastern tip of the island, was about as far away as you could get from New York, and from the war. Nonetheless, the FBI placed a 'sixty day cover on Siasconset Massachusetts Post Office on the mail' of Margot, Fritz and Annemarie, 'all Box 66'.[49] They went horse riding. Margot remembered the summer months as a gin-fuelled torment[50] while a year later, from the tropical heat of the Belgian Congo, Annemarie waxed lyrical:

> I still feel how profoundly invigorating the air was, filling the heart with hope, and one returned home under moonlight across grassy clearings between the white-painted houses with tumbling roses, and prolonged the evening by the fireside.[51]

Annemarie shut herself up in her room and tried to write. She sent articles laboriously drafted in English to *The Nation*, where editor Freda Kirchwey was encouraging, and to the *Washington Post*. She drafted a long unpublished essay about Switzerland's place in the German hegemony.

Zürcher Illustrierte was interested in commissioning a series of articles about either Alaska or China but by 23 July Annemarie expressed doubt about the project. 'The nomads, you see, really don't have anything to teach us, we can't learn from their primitive goodness, any more than we can get rid of original sin. Nor will the Indian sages or Chinese wise men save us.'[52] Her tone here is self-deprecating, and that curious persistence of religious concepts recalls the poet Stefan George. She thought war would solve – purge – the West's decline and bring regeneration in its wake. In point of fact, travelling to Alaska would void her United States visa and make re-entry difficult. Entangled with Annemarie's decision not to hightail off to the ends of the earth was her fraught relationship with Margot. 'Of course, it would be completely remiss to put in writing what Margot and I talk about half the day and half the night, so intensely and no holds barred on both sides.' Margot had made Annemarie understand that she was unreasonable to live with and impossible in love, a home truth others had relayed over the years.[53]

In New York on a flying visit on 5 July, she sent to her Zurich publishers the final version of the Persian travel book, which she had been working on since April. She asked Busy Bodmer to inform Morgarten Verlag that two major American publishers were interested but she wanted to see it come out in German first. 'The Forty Pillars of Memory' eventually formed the basis, together with her newspaper articles, for *All the Roads Are Open*, edited by Roger Perret, and published posthumously.[54] It must have been on this occasion that she wrote:

> It's July 1940, in the dead heat of New York City, and I'm staying at the Plaza and waiting on the European papers three times daily. I need to work out whether it's possible for a young European, pitched up here by accident, to live in America. Why wouldn't you make a go of it here, in this forward-looking, rich country?[55]

The comings and goings of Erika had often steered Annemarie's movements. Back in New York in mid-August, she bid goodbye and safe crossing to her oldest friend, who had flown in en route to London for her reporting job with the British Ministry of Information. Marriage to Auden had provided a British passport and her German made her useful for BMI/BBC propaganda purposes. At the same time, Golo, Heinrich Mann and his wife were attempting to escape from France and to cross the Atlantic in the opposite direction. In this context, Annemarie summering on Nantucket, the von Opels footing the bills, seems far from a hardship post. She stayed on in New York to meet with the Emergency Rescue Committee – but also took the opportunity to investigate her own immigration prospects. The city was sweltering. While the Manns seemed to land on their feet, Annemarie felt acutely that she was drifting between continents and unrealized assignments. 'They have settled in well', she wrote to an old girlfriend, Florianna Madelung, in Basel, 'and I can foresee a certain form of European cultural heritage being carried on here.'[56]

By mid-September, Nantucket's seasonal visitors had left, shops were shut and Annemarie collected her milk and butter directly from the local farm in timeworn Swiss fashion. Horses returned to mainland stables for the winter and fog descended on the island. Wartime visa restrictions prevented Annemarie crossing Canada to Alaska. She wrote a long personal letter to Otto Kleiber, her editor at *National-Zeitung*, who had agreed to part-fund the trip, explaining that she no longer needed 'to recapture in Asia the virtues lost to Europe, in a bleak, simple, prelapsarian paradise ...'[57] This was her old travel hobby-horse: a bedraggled quest for redemption in the East. She knew she could be accused of 'retreating to safety' in America – Auden, Isherwood and Britten were being arraigned in the British press for similar dereliction of patriotic duty. Fossicking around the 'flora and fauna of the Arctic', Annemarie thought, was a waste of time and reputation better spent reporting the war at home.

In her September 1940 letter she mulled again over Switzerland's balancing act and was at pains to trace her opposition to the Nazis back to university days. Now she had decided to return to Switzerland, or at least consecrate herself to the Allied struggle, but the long-winded exalted letter to Kleiber prefigures her decline a month hence. Her mind was coming apart at the seams. The *Thurgauer Zeitung*, which had also proposed part-funding her trip to Alaska, had turned down some of her pieces as being too subjective.[58] She had probably also realized that a journalistic career in America was not going to be made overnight, and she was impatient. An ambitious search for glory appears as a watermark in her writing, and in her letter to Kleiber a grandiose, missionary sense of self that is slightly unhinged.

*

When Klaus checked back into the Bedford Hotel after a summer spent drumming up contributors and funds for his new magazine *Decision*, the phoney war was long over and the torrid heatwave in abeyance. Margot and Annemarie closed up the house on Nantucket and returned to New York, Margot staying at the John Paul Getty-owned Pierre while Annemarie took a room at the Bedford. The Greenwich Village drink of choice was stingers – crème de menthe and brandy – though Annemarie preferred gin. Over the course of dinner on 26 September she regaled Klaus at length about her difficulties with Margot, who had already alerted Klaus on the telephone to the deterioration of their affair and Annemarie's fractious state of mind. Klaus was hearing the saga from both ends.[59] Carson too was back in town, fresh from the Bread Loaf Writers Conference – her tipple was 'sonnie boy', a mix of tea and sherry, what her mother called 'a little toddy for the body'. Carson was about to move into a house in Brooklyn Heights, at the instigation of George Davis, former fiction editor at *Harper's Bazaar* and a friend of W.H. Auden.[60] Reeves helped her pack her things.

The infamous February House at 7 Middagh Street has gone down in literary history for the calibre of its residents and for their rackety lifestyles in the shadow of war. Besides W.H. Auden presiding high-handedly at the dinner table, composer Benjamin Britten, the burlesque stripper Gypsy Rose Lee, writers Jane and Paul Bowles, Carson McCullers and Golo Mann were at one time or another contributing to the kitty. The atmosphere was bohemian and gay, a mix of high-table and hijinks, but work-oriented as well. By day the shipfitters, welders and longshoremen thronged the luncheonettes and diners of nearby Sand Street, between Brooklyn Bridge and the Navy Yard, and at night the heaving sailors' bars added to the attraction for men and women alike. 'At three o'clock in the morning, when the rest of the city is silent and dark', Carson wrote, 'you can come suddenly on a little area as vivacious as a country fair. … where sailors spend their evenings when they come here to port.'[61] Auden kept this arty homintern on its toes with his best 'Uncle Wiz' housemaster manner. Middagh Street's mostly homosexual renegades were experimenting with communal living but also with a type of elective family that the Manns and Annemarie had toyed with a decade earlier. She was an occasional visitor to the Brooklyn house in September and October. Klaus, there in October, found Carson still wittering on about Annemarie. He thought the whole menagerie would make a great novel.

Annemarie arranged to meet Dorothy Thompson with the intention of writing a profile and prepared a review of Richard Wright's *Native Son*. Wright had praised McCullers' 'astonishing humanity that enables a white writer, for the first time in Southern fiction, to handle Negro characters'.[62] Thompson, an old German hand of the Weimar years, was in favour of women's suffrage and had gone over to the Democrats ahead of the upcoming election. Annemarie also reviewed Charlie Chaplin's *The Great Dictator* which had its world premiere in New York on 15 October 1940. The singular absence of any sense of humour in her own work didn't prevent Annemarie from enjoying within limits this master-piece of political satire. Both she and Klaus (also wanting in the humour department) found the 'sentimental and farcical' treatment of Nazis and pogroms disturbing, and she noted how different its reception would be in the blithely free United States and in Nazi-conquered Europe, where it was of course banned for the duration of the war.[63]

In September 1940, the prognosis for Alfred Schwarzenbach's stomach cancer was not good. Renée contacted Hasi in New York and dissuaded Annemarie from coming home. Suzanne in Sweden was able to make a last visit in July with Alfred's first grandson, fourteen-year-old Lars. One weekend at about this time Annemarie and Carson, Klaus and Erika visited the Mann family home in Princeton; Annemarie played the piano, and Carson responded with her childhood party piece, Liszt's Second Hungarian Rhapsody.[64] They had had sporadic contact since the long hot summer days and Carson was coming round to Annemarie's indifference.

Klaus and Erika grew weary of Annemarie's constant self-involvement, her navel-gazing. Her physical and mental health deteriorated during October and November. Klaus's sister Monika had lost her husband in September when their trans-Atlantic steamer, *City of Benares*, was sunk by a German U-boat. In the same month Erika had worked through the London Blitz. Seventy-year-old Heinrich Mann, together with his wife, Klaus's brother Golo, Franz Werfel and Alma Mahler Werfel finally arrived in the United States in mid-October, after being 'compelled to cross the French border, secretly and by night, like a criminal'. Golo had been in a string of French internment camps.[65] Annemarie's personal crisis seemed minor in comparison to such tragedies. Klaus and Margot talked her out of returning to Europe, as did her family; they concurred that Annemarie was more hindrance than help. Following a scene at the Pierre, when she was drunk and disorderly, Klaus, Margot and Martin Gumpert managed to persuade a 'defiant and swaying' Annemarie to go to bed. Gumpert, a medical doctor, thought she was beginning to have a breakdown.[66] Later there was a scene at the Mann house in Princeton where she had gone to see Erika who had returned from London on 1 November. Celebrating Erika's thirty-fifth birthday on 9 November, with Gumpert, her boyfriend, Klaus makes no mention of Annemarie being present. Erika had plans to return to Europe to carry out refugee work. She and Klaus, habituated to Annemarie's scenes at this point, had come to the end of their tether in dealing with her.

The residents at 7 Middagh Street decided to throw a party on Thanksgiving Day[67] as a housewarming but also to celebrate Roosevelt's re-election which portended America's entering the war. A third reason to celebrate was Benjamin Brittan's twenty-seventh birthday occurring just as he moved into the house. Annemarie was one of the invitees to dinner, along with Klaus, Erika, Golo, Reeves, Chester Kallmann and his father, as well as the poet Louis MacNeice. Carson served up turkey with all the trimmings and there was a case of champagne. Dinner was followed by a party that went on till dawn when the sound of bells alerted Carson to a fire nearby, which gave her the ah-ha moment for the novel she was writing, *The Member of the Wedding*.[68] Klaus in his diary never had a good word to say about Carson, characterizing her as morbid, consumptive, with a hacking cough. The party was a success, one of the high points of the experimental gay commune on Middagh Street. It seems strange that Annemarie chose to attend since her father had died four days earlier.

Alfred Schwarzenbach died at home in Bocken on 17 November 1940, aged sixty-four. Her grief compounded Annemarie's already serious alcohol and drug dependency and her condition deteriorated rapidly. A further more violent scene took place at the Pierre on 23 November when Annemarie tried to strangle Margot in her bed. Guests alerted house security. Back in the Bedford, she attempted suicide and Margot contacted Annemarie's brother, Freddy, who wrote to Hasi at home in Bocken:

> During the night Annemarie had constantly been telephoning her to let her know that she was going to commit suicide,[69] and so of course the friend was horrified and called the emergency services who contacted me to tell me that Annemarie had in the meantime regained consciousness and was acting crazy and they wanted my permission to take her immediately by ambulance to the hospital. ... I learned by the way that this was not her first such ruckus in the hotel, the Opel woman and Annemarie keep fighting and making up. Only this time she didn't just stop at a dose of amphetamines and play Schumann's symphonies, but took to the whiskey and the sleeping pills.[70]

Restrained and taken to Doctors Hospital at 170 East End Avenue, a treatment centre for the well-to-do on the Upper East Side, she was transferred some days later to Blythewood Sanitarium near Greenwich, Connecticut. This was an upscale, enlightened facility comprising 'twenty-two buildings on eighty acres of Stanwich property'[71] situated in rolling lawns and woods, with Greenwich Creek running through the grounds. Blythewood catered mostly to New York and Long Island alcoholics. 'One source described it as a dumping ground for the black sheep of wealthy families ... holed-up in a fancy Connecticut retreat in the midst of the Great Depression.'[72] In the wooded grounds a 'violent house' contained a padded cell. At Blythewood, Annemarie smashed the windows with her feet and had to be restrained in a straitjacket.

By 16 December she was calm enough to write home to Renée, imagining a mournful Christmas around the tree in Bocken and antici-pating release from the sanatorium in a couple of weeks. She thought she might visit the Manns in Princeton. Her brother Freddy came to see her, and Margot as well, before travelling to California in the company of their mutual friend, photographer and documentary filmmaker Erika Anderson. Annemarie urged her mother to write back and close the distance that had widened between them: 'I haven't had it easy in life, Mama.' Annemarie's letter, typed flawlessly, shows her remarkable ability to bounce back from psychotic episodes, to *present as normal*, to consider work, a lost diamond ring that Claude had given her, her dog Dokterli, the horses at home: this self gives the impression that nothing much was wrong with her.[73]

Despite this contrite tone, she made her escape from the clinic at Christmastime:

> The night nurse had come on together with the night guard. ... and while the nurse put my cell in order, I knew quite suddenly that the guard had left his key in the front door. I had known that before. ... It was dark and cold and I let myself fall under the bushes ... When I heard them talking in the distance, I bolted over the fence. I knew all the time they wouldn't take *me* alive.[74]

She convinced people in a house nearby to cash a cheque for her and flagged down a car to New York. The following morning she called her brother, retrieved her suitcase from the hotel and took a taxi to the studio of Alfred (Freddy) Wolkenberg at 44 West 56th Street.[75] He shared the studio with a friend so space was tight – nonetheless he rigged up a dividing sheet to provide Annemarie with privacy. In the fortnight she spent there her condition deteriorated and her mood waxed desperate.

Annemarie's brother arranged for a day-and-night nurse who vetoed telephone calls and Annemarie tried to strangle her.[76] Wolkenberg wired Carson, who immediately took the train from Columbus to New York. 'I'd been home only a day or so when a wire came. It was not the wire I had been dreading about Reeves, but an almost equally upsetting one. "Have escaped from Blithe View. Staying at Freddy's." What shall I do now?'[77] Annemarie telephoned a number of friends, some of whom hung up when they recognized her voice. During this period, she also met Ruth Landshoff-York and showed her a poem which Annemarie thought highly of but which her old writer friend from Berlin found incomprehensible. The Mann family, whose embrace Annemarie had been anticipating, cold-shouldered her suggestion that she join them for the festive season in Princeton. Margot in California refused to take the call and in a fit of anger Annemarie flung the phone out the window and locked herself in the bathroom where she slit her wrists. Wolkenberg and his flat-mate tried to stanch the blood while Carson, in her own account, fetched a doctor. The doctor stitched up the superficial cuts and the police were persuaded to leave. By law, a suicide attempt required follow-up at New York's Bellevue Clinic, and several days later, in early January 1941, while Freddy was out, Annemarie was removed from the apartment and taken under restraint to Bellevue.[78]

Carson's therapy transcripts dating from 1958, as relayed in Jenn Shapland's account of what happened at Freddy Wolkenberg's studio, give the gist while eschewing quotation:

> When Carson arrived at the apartment, Annemarie was playing Mozart endlessly on the gramophone. She was delirious and desperate for morphine, and at first she didn't even recognize Carson. Instead she started asking her for Dr. February, a woman Annemarie claimed gave her insulin shock treatments and then 'made love' to her while she was institutionalized. … Carson was, naively but earnestly, expecting a warmer, more heartfelt welcome. Annemarie began asking Carson to get her some dope, so Carson took matters into her own hands and walked down the street to a bar. Carrying a martini in each hand several blocks back to Annemarie, she thought, *Here goes the night.*[79]

In this account it was Annemarie who sent the telegram and not Freddy. Perhaps Dr. February is a mis-transcription of Dr. Gustava Favez with whom Annemarie had become romantically involved at another Bellevue clinic – in Yverdon on Lake Neuchatel. According to Carson's psych transcripts, a botched seduction took place in the studio where three people were living (not including the nurse), with all the hallmarks – imperious orders, mood swings, whim, suicide attempt, cry for help – of another psychotic incident:

> Annemarie told Carson she was too skinny, she wanted Gypsy Rose Lee, Carson's housemate, instead. According to Annemarie, people had seen Carson and Gypsy together at night clubs, and she knew that they had stayed together over weekends. She demanded that Carson fetch Gypsy for her, and offered to let her watch while they fucked. Carson fled the room naked.[80]

It was a cold January for standing in a stairwell naked. Back in Columbus in January 1941 and writing to her editor Robert Linscott, Carson admits to not being present in the studio when Annemarie was restrained in a straitjacket and taken to Bellevue:

> But there is nothing I can do. Her illness is mostly mental – they think just now that it is schezophrenia [*sic*]. She escaped from the hospital where she was before, hid all night in the woods up in Conn, and finally got a taxi driver to take her to N.Y. She stayed with two friends of mine who have a room together, and I went back to N.Y. when I heard she was there. But the exposure had made her physically ill, also. It is too dreadful to write about. They took her finally to Bellevue (the doctor and all the policemen came when I was not there) and for some time she was there in just the ordinary ward, which is too much to think about.[81]

As Carlos L. Dews, editor of McCullers' letters, has noted, Carson 'at times was more concerned with making a story more interesting than in recording a story accurately.'[82]

Bellevue is the United States' oldest public hospital, comprising an 'unimaginably gruesome warren of cells and wards',[83] as Annemarie described it. Kept in the dark for nine hours a day, without hot tea, without cigarettes – the need for 'a cigarette became as indispensable as a phial [of morphine] had been in years gone by'.[84] Strenuous efforts on the part of Freddy Schwarzenbach led to Annemarie being transferred from Bellevue some time in early January for treatment at the New York Hospital, Westchester Division, in White Plains.[85] Her letters from there to Ella Maillart and others show lucidity, stubbornness and self-justification in equal measure. Ella was still in British India and Annemarie wrote in English now that war restrictions were in force. Annemarie upbraided Klaus for his desertion of her in her hour of need and remarked that nobody had got in touch in the three weeks she had been in White Plains. 'What are the boundaries of friendship?' she asked, when someone is in such trouble. Should they be left to perish?[86] The note of recrimination is unmistakable, if not strictly justified: Freddy Wolkenberg had sent flowers and her brother had visited and was footing the bill.[87] Klaus was busy with *Decision*, the first number of which he launched at a party on 7 January, attended by 150 guests. He summarized her plight in his diary: 'straitjacket, slitting her wrists, ambulance, padded cell, escape, raving, more confinement: and so ends this frail tragedy in these heartless times.'[88] Margot, for her part, felt unfairly blamed by Annemarie, who had become astute by this stage in framing herself as misunderstood victim:

> This is the way it looks – and it will always look like this – as if I had let her down when she most needed me – and that I consigned her to 'doctors, straitjackets and the madhouse' – as she put it in her recent letter from Lisbon – and all because I refused to be tender once and to comfort her.[89]

Writing to Freddy Wolkenberg, Annemarie was at pains to declare herself 'normal' while admitting she had been 'half-crazy for months' and had lost friends as a result.[90] As with previous hospital stays, she saw doctors ganging up to restrain her and the tone of exalted delusion is unmistakable. In the Westchester hospital she heard 'the crazy people shouting day and night: from the typical "What have they done to me" to the usual: "Let me out!"' It was important for Annemarie's self-esteem not to be seen as one of them:

> ... the madhouse in full swing. I love many of the patients, and the Headnurse tells me that everyone loves me, but sometimes the noise, the raging shouts and cries become too much for me – and *I get NERVOUS!*[91] – At night I sleep

in a bright, guarded cell next to the tub-room, where the raving patients are all the time being taken.[92]

Responsibility and blame get apportioned more neatly in retrospect than in the heat of crisis: four psychiatric clinics, two suicide attempts, and a writer falling apart because a love affair slips out of her grasp; it can't have been easy for all concerned. Mental illness compounded by alcohol and drugs – sleeping pills, Benzedrine but not, apparently, morphine – were the culprits. Annemarie's poor compliance had always made her a difficult patient – socially needy, wilful, inclined to self-right-eousness and the princess manner. There was a war on, it was Christmas, and her father had died. By all accounts she was not allayed by a fireside chat and a turkey sandwich. Margot had retreated, licking her wounds, to sunny California. Annemarie's brothers did what they could – she acknowledged Freddy's efforts to get her out of Bellevue.[93] Three private clinics and a berth negotiated on the boat home through U-boat-infested waters; it is too convenient to cast the brothers as inept: they too had lost a father, had stockings to fill, babies to lull to sleep. 'It's always women trouble with her', wrote Freddy to Hasi, 'and you should see the types of women, disgusting.'[94] When it came to the crunch, however, the women and the gay Manns made themselves scarce, and it was left to the brothers to pick up the pieces.

Deep snow blanketed the east coast in January 1941. It looked more and more likely that America would enter the war as Roosevelt had signalled in his fireside chats. The Pittsburgh steelworkers that Annemarie had written about four years earlier were now smelting like there was no tomorrow.[95] The Mann family were guests of the Roosevelts at the White House on 26 January. Soon they would relocate to Pacific Palisades in California. Annemarie wrote to Klaus that her only way to get out of the clinic was to be deported from the United States with no possibility of return: a plea-bargain of sorts. 'I am not allowed to know the date – but if you get in touch with Freddy Wolkenberg he will be able to give you details, day, ship etc.'[96] Carson had returned to Georgia and late in February had the first of her series of debilitating strokes and her own health to worry about. Annemarie summed up her situation in a draft note to editor Otto Kleiber: 'I can't shake off the feeling of being a deserter here and tend to think that one should leave America to the Americans.'[97]

Freddy Schwarzenbach's telegram to his mother read: 'After colossal efforts Annemarie sails tomorrow 1 February on the *SS Siboney* to Lisbon.'[98] An Anglo-French blockade of shipping made any crossing fraught.[99] Freddy provided a nurse to accompany his sister on the treacherous return voyage after what had been a disastrous few months for all concerned.

On 14 February 1941 – Valentine's Day – *Reflections in a Golden Eye*, Carson's second novel, was published with a dedication to Annemarie. That the author fell for the Swiss writer, and fell deeply, over the course of the previous summer is not in question. Annemarie, however, was not really sexually or romantically interested in Carson, tried to put her off, worked behind the scenes with Linscott in order to soften the blow and altogether showed an understanding of the twenty-three-year-old's emotional weather without allowing it to deflect her own troubled life. Annemarie does not mention her at all in her mid-January letter to Freddy Wolkenberg from the White Plains clinic. Later, Annemarie acknowledged the difficult beginnings of their relationship, coming close to a *mea culpa*: 'I have the burden of a painful knowledge: you have suffered from me, & I meant to give you tenderness and help.'[100] Much has been made of this romantic encounter in part because their correspondence in a Texas archive falls into the Anglosphere, and because McCullers went on to become a writer of distinction and an emotional oddball in her own right. Her creative juices got going by building castles in the air: veracity and the biographical record are another thing. Between these two *modus operandi* falls the shadow. In the letters she sent Carson from Lisbon, the Congo and Tetouan, once an ocean separated them, Annemarie tended to play up the fevered also-ran of their relationship in ethereal terms. Carson did her own exaggerating. It was touch and go.

In June 1942 Carson looked back on their momentous encounter:

> Let us try to believe in the world after this war. I feel so close to you. It is true that in the past I asked of you more than you were able to give. But all that is over, thank God. Remember only that I do love you.[101]

Margot got to experience her own spell of confinement and spent the war years in an internment camp in Seagoville, Texas, from where she wrote to Klaus on 15 November 1942 in English, her writing paper stamped 'DETAINED ALIEN ENEMY MAIL EXAMINED'.

> The fact to be locked in with Nazis, surrounded by that godforsaken spirit from morning to night, persecuted from these Nazis as an 'outsider'… Do you know that Annemarie is ill – this time seriously ill, again.[102]

In the first couple of months of 1941 – perhaps on the *SS Siboney* sailing back to Europe – Annemarie wrote 'White Plains', a short text about her car running out of gas:

> Around eight o'clock in the evening I noticed my Ford running on empty. Deep night beyond the windscreen. At this time of year, the sun sets early in New England and the hard winter throws up unrelenting blizzards and nor'easters, punctured by patches of mild damp air.[103]

The title alludes to her stay in the White Plains clinic but also to her escape from Blythewood when she spent a night under the stars. The tone of finality is strong; she had come to the end of the road and a way of living. Mentioning the damage of American prosperity, she seems to prefigure its prison-industrial complex:

> Of late I had observed in America a good few prisons and institutions for the sick or those on welfare. I heard desperate prisoners riot, shouts soon muffled by the powers that be, prisoners caught up in a cycle of reprisal, punishment and fresh torment. I had seen miserable men, women and even children stripped of all dignity and sense of responsibility, lose humanity and trust.[104]

In the course of her final visit to the United States, Annemarie never really domiciled anywhere; provisional was her element. The rose-tumbled house on Nantucket was the nearest she got to home. Once the argumentative summer of her affair with Margot was over, Annemarie shuttled around New York, from hotel room to clinic, padded cell to ward. Manic depression morphed into bipolar disorder in those bright palmetto dayrooms. Annemarie's nine-month stay in America laid bare the underside of the country's wealth and mental health, just as her earlier stays had done for labour and race. She was a fellow traveller in the drink and drugs culture of the generation that had followed the dollar in the twenties, crashed in the thirties and was now gearing up for war. Gatsby's yellow cocktail music, dopplered over Long Island Sound, is not far off. F. Scott Fitzgerald had died in December 1940, age forty-four, burnt out and alcoholic at about the time Annemarie was banging her head against the walls of Blythewood. One by one the green lights were going out on the docks of all those moneyed dormitory towns soaked in alcohol.

10

Heart of Darkness

I don't know when this continual urge to escape becomes a real sickness and at what exact moment schizophrenia, base of all artistic action, is to be judged insanity.[1]

Portugal, like Switzerland, was neutral when war was declared and Salazar, Portugal's dictator, now looked rather benign in comparison to his peers. He took care to maintain his country's neutrality as ever more refugees spilled south following the Nazi rout of France during the summer of 1940. Lisbon was one of the few European ports where trans-Atlantic ships could dock, becoming not just a refugee 'waiting room', as Annemarie put it, but a clearing house for goods offloaded for distribution across the continent. Refugees, like freight, encountered a bureaucratic bottleneck and the city was rife with spies, consular personnel and representatives of relief organizations. The *S.S. Siboney*, on which Annemarie steamed from the Jersey docks, was chartered on the return voyage to assist Americans fleeing the war in Europe.

Putting into port on 10 February, Annemarie hadn't intended to stay long but the newly-appointed Swiss *chargé d'affaires* in Lisbon was Henri Martin, an old friend from her time in Ankara a decade earlier. He introduced her to Red Cross delegates, leading to two articles in the *NZZ*, written at the behest of Martin and checked by Portuguese censors. Abandoning the by-line Clark, which she had used in the United States, henceforth she wrote under the name Clarac-Schwarzenbach. She remained in the city for three weeks, no doubt recuperating and enjoying the southern sun after the rigours of the East Coast winter.[2] Her ability to pick up the pieces and write, to go about the world as normal after immense trauma, is both remarkable and dubious. Was she completely drug-free at this time? Apart from sleeping pills, quite likely. The nurse-minder had kept her on the straight and narrow on the voyage out. Was she off the booze? Harder to determine. She had been dissatisfied with her writing over the past year in the United States and habitually used alcohol to get going.[3]

Once again she had landed on her feet, armed with a wealth of connections and a readiness to lend her pen to the work in hand. She met the seventy-one-year-old writer Annette Kolb – they had first met in 1933 in Berlin. Perhaps it was Kolb, now stateless and without valid passport, Annemarie refers to in one of her articles: 'Soon I'll have to beg.'[4] A week after making landfall, Annemarie wrote to her old mentor Carl Burckhardt in Geneva, offering her services to the Red Cross: 'it would give me the right backing – I would like to travel to Egypt, Marseilles, or the Middle East in some capacity. But I was going to stay in Switzerland for the time being'. Anxious about being perceived as having 'deserted' the war, she saw herself as 'the prodigal son returned'.[5] Burckhardt and Annemarie met later in Geneva but the outcome of her offer remained inconclusive.

She conceived a project to travel to French Equatorial Africa where supporters of de Gaulle in Brazzaville provided troops and finance to the Free French movement. Annemarie planned to follow the war from the apparent backwater of Brazzaville and booked passage on the SS *Colonial*. Her well-meaning desire to be in Europe, just like her return from India a year earlier, had become side-tracked by a journey with tangential connection to the war. It did not occur to her that the wife of a Vichy diplomat in this theatre of competing forces might incur suspicion.

Meanwhile, she went home to Switzerland, an island of tranquillity in turbulent Europe. Switzerland, too, was concerned with maintaining its neutrality, effectively pursuing accommodation dressed up as resistance.[6] The Swiss had 'become specialists in the art of non-cooperation with tyranny',[7] which often segued into its opposite. Official neutrality could be overzealous, a display of correctness. In 1938 the Swiss requested German passports be stamped with the letter J, for Jewish, facilitating *triage*. By spring of 1941, a working relationship with the Nazis was in place in the border cantons. Exports from Basel's chemical-pharmaceutical industry to Germany increased from 13.8 per cent at the beginning of the war to 30.8 per cent by war's end. Geigy, for example, produced the polar red dye for the swastika flag while at the same time assuring its Nazi customers that its workforce was Jew-free.[8] Since 1933 other Swiss pharmaceutical companies – Ciba, Sandoz – had fallen into step with Germany's anti-semitic employment regulations. During the war both Roche and Geigy used forced labour – civilians from the occupied territories as well as prisoners of war – at their chemical plants at Grenzach near Basel.[9] Only in recent years has historiography begun to win out over self-serving contemporary accounts.[10]

Alfred's influence had often acted as a brake on Renée's Medusa-like tug-of-war with Annemarie. With Alfred dead, his widow's exhausted nerves could no longer handle her daughter's volatility, her addictions, not to speak of her political sympathies. Rows about Annemarie's supposed drug use began not long after her arrival at Bocken on 13 March. The three clinics and one insane asylum in New York spoke for themselves, as did the bills, despite Annemarie's assurances to her mother and others that she was no longer taking morphine. Who to believe? The mother's accusation had behind it a decade of failed treatment while Annemarie's protestations had been aired before. Hasi undertook to finance Annemarie's trip to Africa while no longer paying the rent on her house in Sils from family funds – 200 Swiss francs a month.[11] 'They put me very much under pressure',[12] she wrote in English to Ella. The frosty reception at Bocken, as well as the money, must have given added impetus: push and pull factors were in the balance.[13] 'I don't really see what to do, except to go ahead with the African project which came up in Lisbon.'[14] She stayed three days at Bocken and drove to Sils.

Given the dangers to Atlantic shipping, a search for glory glimmers behind Annemarie's motivation to head to French Equatorial Africa.[15] Careerism drove her towards 'the brilliant war job as I hoped when I left the US a year ago'.[16] Erika's stint with the BBC in London and the Hackins' ill-fated role in the French Resistance further fuelled Annemarie's ambition. Before she left Switzerland, a copy of Carson's *Reflections in a Golden Eye* arrived in the post, the dedication *for Annemarie Schwarzenbach* on the flyleaf. Though delighted to be its recipient, she considered her time in New York 'a terrific, a painfully hurting defeat'.[17] The African project gave her an opportunity to start afresh. Writing to Ella in the abstracted euphoric style that Annemarie had adopted since her hospitalization, she sees 'clearly the prospect of a happier, steadier, more contented life'.[18] On 10 April 1941, Clara Wille noted that Annemarie had been to lunch and was heading to Zurich in the afternoon to catch the train across a divided France.[19]

Annemarie had until now enjoyed unhindered passage, often first class on trans-Atlantic steamers, thanks to Swiss neutrality, her French diplomatic passport and the von Opels' and her family's largesse. Equipped with pith helmet, khaki shorts and mosquito repellent, she tackled the long, slow, fits-and-starts rail journey across France, through the *zone libre*, a journey she had often undertaken in her green Dodge Victory Brougham and Mercedes Mannheim. Now the local trains smelled of 'Gitanes and newsprint, sometimes wine and goat cheese'. In a station buffet she ordered a hardboiled egg and bread, but *sans* ration card, the bread was taken from her. She traded Swiss chocolate for ration coupons with a couple of skiers. A four-hour stopover in Lyon allowed her to expedite letters and packages on behalf of the Red Cross, held up by the convoluted bureaucracy of France at war:

> I was asleep when we pulled into Nîmes. Just in time, I heard the tannoy announce the name of the stop, grabbed my bags, and a young stranger helped me lug my cases onto the connecting train. A minute later, we pulled out in the direction of Narbonne.[20]

At Narbonne, changing trains again, she trundled south along the Vermillion Coast to Port Bou on the Spanish border, where countless escaping Jewish refugees had crossed the *garrigue* over the course of the previous year, and where Walter Benjamin had committed suicide six months earlier.

Back in Lisbon, waiting on visas, she spent the time in her room in the Lis Hotel writing articles. She had become adept at a kind of elegant hustling for assignments as testified by her correspondence over the years. Drumming up articles, she feared her career as a journalist had eclipsed the fiction writer. The month of April 1941 was typical of her prolific output: some ten features, with accompanying photographs, appeared in Swiss papers and magazines, on topics as diverse as Chaplin's *Great Dictator*, the American army's need for nurses, oil in Iraq, the Red Cross and the refugee crisis, as well as travel pieces about the United States and France.

Just before departure she learned of the fates of Ria and Joseph Hackin, her archaeologist friends encountered in Afghanistan.[21] Steaming from

Liverpool to India on a mission for de Gaulle, the Hackins were killed when their ship was torpedoed south-west of the Faroe Islands on 24 February 1941. On hearing the news, another archaeologist friend from Afghanistan, Jean Carl Meunié, committed suicide in London. Travel writer Robert Byron was also a casualty on the *SS Jonathan Holt*. 'The fact that they are likely no longer alive has an almost petrifying knock-on effect on the prospect of my own, perhaps imminent death, and yet unignorable.'[22]

*

On 17 May 1941, she boarded the Portuguese *SS Colonial*, flying a neutral flag and chock full of refugees: Belgian and Dutch mothers with children resettling to the ends of the earth, some to the Congo, some navigating the Cape of Good Hope to South Africa, to new lives even further afield. While German women were being ushered towards *Kinder, Küche und Fabrik*, these refugees had lost everything – house, husband, homeland. This was Annemarie's fourth shipboard voyage in a year: Bombay to Genoa in the teeth of war with her car in the hold, two trans-Atlantic crossings paid for by others and now, drifting along the Barbary Coast, her thoughts plumbed the whither and the wherefore, as they tended to do on deck. Her shipboard musings, part cabin fever, part war reports, show her knack of assembling a thousand words of observation, often riffing on orientalism and the exotic. At thirty-three, she was an old salt. When the *Colonial* dropped anchor at Funchal on Madeira, she was taken by the island's tropical landscape, and produced in short order three articles on the first leg of her journey for two different papers. Barbary gave way to the Gold and Ivory Coasts, the magic names a swag-bag of colonial plunder. On her birthday, the *Colonial* crossed the Tropic of Cancer; flying fish and the Southern Cross hove into view.

Aptly named, the ship also carried Portuguese passengers returning to their colonies: São Tomé, Angola and Mozambique. Passengers were for the most part white, a Belgian priest saying mass and bearded Portuguese missionaries taking service. Eugenics and notions of racial purity, standard Nazi belief, underpinned colonialism as well. The French bedtime story about its colonies was *la mission civilisatrice*. The Belgian Congo had been an unapologetic slavocracy for King Leopold II. German South West Africa (present day Namibia) was a land grab of territory held by the Herero and Nama peoples, subsequently confined to reservations and exterminated.[23] The Portuguese empire had been the longest running of the lot, founded in the age of exploration, running to slavery, sugar and cocoa trades, the colonization of Brazil under the Jesuits, the scramble for Africa and forced labour.

Shipboard life on the SS *Colonial*, for the fortnight it plied the West African coast, lived up to its name. Madame de Vleeschauwer, wife of the Belgian Minister for the Colonies, held a homework club for children in the ship's small salon, where Annemarie retired to write in the morning. The son of Belgian investment banker Félicien Cattier was also on board, heading roundabout to America to take up citizenship. His father was chairman of the Mining Union of Katanga, controlling 70 per cent of the Congolese economy, and had been advisor to two kings – Albert I of Belgium and King Chulalongkorn of Siam: not a man to side with the unions. His son, Jean Cattier, thought 'war and the Belgian defeat would not even temporarily interrupt industry and trade – it would naturally seek new outlets and means'. In such pukka company, Annemarie was unlikely to encounter anti-colonial sentiment.[24] In São Tomé, she failed to mention the island's long history as an entrepôt for the Portuguese slave trade to Brazil, noting the cocoa bean trade but not the slave and child labour that provisioned the Belgian, Dutch and Swiss chocolate industries.[25] Her prime concern was combating fascism in Europe by reporting on the Free French in the colonies. The war effort prevented her from questioning colonialism itself. Free French forces in Africa, Syria and London, according to Annemarie, were the rightful heirs and 'guarantee of the moral renewal and future of the French nation'.[26] Whatever reservations she might have had about colonialism were kept in check by the war and by a knowledge that her letters were censored.

Landing at Pointe-Noire, the principal seaport of French Equatorial Africa under the control of de Gaulle's Free French troops, she felt 'so close to events, so positively involved in the forthcoming tragical battle'.[27] Pointe-Noire was a dock, a few cranes, wooden huts and a military barracks, a 'larva-like town, which has scarcely emerged from underground', as André Gide had found it sixteen years earlier.[28] To an extent she was following in Gide's footsteps. His *Journey to the Congo* (1927) had criticized exploitative practices without undermining colonialism itself. Gide in turn had dedicated his account to the memory of

Joseph Conrad and his *Heart of Darkness* (1899). Always well researched in her travels, Annemarie's lack of reference to these seminal accounts is striking – a couple of passing allusions to Conrad is all she manages. 'It is estimated that around half a million lives were lost every year to transport 80,000 to 90,000 black people to the coast', is Annemarie's only reference to the slave trade.[29]

Honorary Swiss Consul Adrien Orlandi and his wife Marguérite invited her to stay at the residence in Léopoldville. She had a letter of introduction to the Belgian Governor-General Pierre Ryckmans who had

Annemarie and Madame Orlandi, wife of the Swiss Consul, and dog Folette, Thysville, Belgian Congo, 1942
Courtesy of Swiss Literary Archives and Wikimedia Commons

rallied to his government in exile in London. Once again she had landed on her feet in diplomatic geisha-land. 'I found myself one morning in Free French Africa, at a breakfast table in the officers' quarters, dressed up in khaki, and ready to get started for Brazzaville.'[30] From 'Léo' she crossed the river by motorboat to the studio of the radio station established the previous year by Pierre Bernard as a Free French mouthpiece, disseminating the speeches of de Gaulle to the world, as well as providing news in English, Spanish and Portuguese.[31] Lieutenant Desjardins was interested in Annemarie broadcasting and, as she wrote to Erika, 'we might start German emissions from the RADIO BRAZZAVILLE, – you know from your work you did last year in London how important this weapon might become.'[32] Keen for Erika to see her as useful after the disastrous American visit, Annemarie admitted that 'matters in this part of the world are less romantic than what I had thought'.[33] After a few days Bernard reneged on his offer of radio work; his superiors had intervened.[34]

What exactly she was up to evinced suspicion. Who was this crop-haired German-speaking journalist travelling solo on a French diplomatic passport, tricked out in khaki uniform? She wanted to travel via military outposts north-east through Chad from where it was possible to reach Egypt and the fighting front. Men, supplies and ordnance were conveyed upriver and overland along this route to Fort Archambault in Chad, where Colonel Leclerc was busy establishing a rearguard base of operations.[35] Annemarie, wife of a Vichy diplomat, constituted a security breach; the supply route did not require publicity in Swiss newspapers; and the rumour mill among colonials turned against her vainglorious project. Journalists and spies employ a similar set of skills; Henry Morton Stanley had, after all, been a war correspondent like Annemarie, fond of derring-do and a by-line. She liked to walk solo at night out to the edge of town and her freewheeling manner might have rubbed the colonial wives up the wrong way.[36] Swanning around Léopoldville in khaki mightn't have helped. She disparaged the artificial mediocrity of 'Léo society', condescending to it as a writer in tune with 'higher things'[37] – an attitude that no doubt some people saw through. She was suspected of spying. Claude was French Consul in Spanish Morocco and didn't declare for the forces of General de Gaulle until December 1942 in Algiers: technically this constituted a reason for refusing her request to

Annemarie in her pith helmet on the Jturi (Aruwimi) river. Photographer unknown
Courtesy of Swiss Literary Archives and Wikimedia Commons

work with the Free French forces in any capacity.[38] This refusal stymied her stay in the Congo and dampened her spirits. For this decade-long anti-fascist to be suspected of being a Nazi agent must have stuck in the throat.

In the first days of July 1941, she headed upriver on the steamboat *Colonel Chaltin* with the intention of reaching a Swiss-run plantation at Molanda that she had heard about on the ship. The steamboat captain was Flemish, her fellow passengers were a Scottish missionary couple, two French officers heading to Sudan and two Belgians. 'The negroes lived on the rear deck' and the riverboat consisted of 'three small cabins with beds for six, a bathroom, cabins for the officers and a room with two tables and some wicker chairs.'[39] The 1200-kilometre boat journey from Léopoldville to Lisala took seven days in oppressive July heat. 'I saw nothing but the settlements of the Blacks lit by flickering lights in tiny clearings, and all we heard were their tom-tom drums, or the cry of a monkey or a parrot.'[40] The endless wall of jungle frightened her and, as on the ship from Lisbon, she found scant time alone to sort her thoughts and write.

In Lisala she lodged in the spare room belonging to an old planter, Kommandant Roos, veteran of the First World War, whose wife and son had run off to Brussels. 'Old colonials remember the last war', Annemarie wrote to Erika. 'They know what a German occupation means.'[41] Every morning the boy brought her coffee, a fried egg and bananas. The telegram announcing her arrival was still sitting in the town post office; her destination was a further 250 kilometres into the jungle and the post was picked up by bicycle every fortnight. The plane from Léopoldville to Stanleyville touched down once a week, and twice a month the steamboat plied the river. For twelve days Annemarie kicked her heels among Lisala's forty or so whites – government officials on three-year postings, traders in palm fruit, peanuts, cotton and rice, missionaries of commerce and faith. The presence of an attractive Swiss journalist in shorts must have been something of an event. The Cathédrale Saint-Hermès and its mission buildings were the most imposing brick structures in town. There was a leprosarium, a barracks and a prison.

After a fortnight, a truck negotiating the 250 kilometres through the jungle to Molanda agreed to take her. Picking up peanuts and copal, they stopped off at Catholic missions, at Portuguese shops, slip-sliding on the muddy track when it rained. The 'indigènes' loaded the truck onto three pirogues lashed together in order to cross a river. Everywhere there was the oppressive wall of green, squalor, a struggle for survival. 'Men doze on rattan platforms, women hunkered at fires carry their babies swathed in front of their low-hanging breasts; wild bat-faced dogs blindly throw themselves under our wheels – we killed many in our wake.'[42]

Ami Paul Vivien and his fifty-one-year-old wife Hedwig were a childless Swiss couple who had laboured at their coffee and palm oil plantation at Molanda since 1925. Her husband's poor health left strong-willed Hedwig to manage one of the largest, most successful plantations in the Congo, extending over 1,250 hectares. Crown Prince Leopold III had visited in the mid-1920s on a 'study trip', riding around on his motorcycle. Two cars, a large cool farmhouse, goats, chickens, the jungle cleared for agriculture, made the place seem like an island of Swiss efficiency – a *Swiss Family Robinson* overseeing some four to five hundred labourers. On arrival Annemarie had a welcome hot shower, sat down to roast kid, corn, fried eggs and a glass of red wine, and was given a straw-roofed house in the grounds to herself. Laid up sick for two days, she appreciated Hedwig's maternal attention. The six-part series of articles Annemarie began to write presents the Vivien couple's hard-working benevolence. In the morning the boy brought Annemarie a thermos of coffee from the main house, she donned her pith helmet, and a car drove her around the palm groves where the Blacks were working. Once more, in this improbable idyll, with somebody to care for her and a refuge to write in, the old trope of paradise on earth popped into her mind – at least paradise for Annemarie – working to good effect on her spirits. 'The Blacks don't readily take to work, they all the time have to be watched, and on a plantation of 1,200 hectares it's not easy.'[43]

It was a white paradise with a dark underside, like the Belgian Congo itself. 'The less intelligent the white man is', wrote Gide, 'the more stupid he thinks the black'.[44] While decrying the exploitation of labour on the plantations of the American South, Annemarie is silent about similar treatment in the Congo. At the beginning of the war there were trade unions for whites, for example, but not for blacks. Labour unrest in late 1941 among black miners led to strikes with fatal consequences.[45] Annemarie did not connect Nazi beliefs and practices to European colonialism, as Aimé Césaire did: 'People supported and abetted, absolved and closed their eyes to Nazism, thereby legitimizing it, because up to then it had only been brought to bear on non-European populations.'[46]

Annemarie sat down on 29 July to write to Carson McCullers:

> I arrived, Swiss too, wearing trousers too, looking to them like a boy and pretending too to be a woman … Of course they don't understand us, nor should we pretend to understand them … They stretch out in the humid and fievrish [sic] night air, naked, and they never eat enough, and they never react. They have no god, no ambition, no love.[47]

Madame Hedwig Vivien, Belgian Congo. Photo by Annemarie Schwarzenbach
Courtesy of Swiss Literary Archives and Wikimedia Commons

This echoes the standard colonial view of feckless natives and enterprising Westerners, gussied up by Oswald Spengler into an over-arching philosophy in *The Decline of the West*. André Gide's understanding of race stereotyping is much more sympathetic. 'The black races are described as being indolent, lazy, without needs, and without desires. But I am inclined to believe that the state of slavery and wretched poverty in which they are sunk, only too often explains their apathy.'[48]

Looked after by Hedwig Vivien and surrounded by a modicum of Swiss comfort, Annemarie began to recover her spirits and to reflect on the year gone by. She intended to resume propaganda work in Brazzaville and reiterated her intention to be of service to the Free French cause in a letter to Ella: '*I thought it was my duty to offer my services and share the burden of the war. In Brazzaville and Léopoldville I was thwarted.*'[49] The ports of call since she had departed from India eighteen months earlier – Genoa, Switzerland, New York, Nantucket, Lisbon, Switzerland, Brazzaville – indicate more a rudderless wanderlust than a firm commitment. Her reports from Lisbon were serviceable to the Red Cross, as was her brief propaganda work in Brazzaville, but ambition drove her to the front line. Molanda, a jungle outpost in the middle of nowhere, where she enjoyed free bed and board, was essentially colonial life with all the trimmings; its connection to the war effort was tenuous.

Nonetheless, it was not towards Léopoldville that she travelled, but in the opposite direction – further upriver with Madame Vivien and then east and south to Kivu province bordering Rwanda. This journey into the interior took six weeks. Given a set of Chrysler wheels and a strong-willed driving companion, Annemarie always flourished. Annemarie photographed dancers with elaborate headdresses and shell ankle bracelets. She snapped pygmies and roadside children. The jungle's gold, copper and tin mines, its Christian missions, were the raison d'être for tracks and settlements. Shelters and way-stations at intervals provided whites with shade, food and petrol. Annemarie was well aware of the strategic importance of Congolese mining to the war effort; profits flowed from the territory and coercive labour recruitment practices were the norm. In their dismantling of organized unions, brutal repression of strikes and deployment of corvée labour, the regimes of Vichy, Nazi Germany, and colonial Congo were alike.[50] 'With the start of the Second World War, the legal maximum for forced labour in the Congo was increased to 120 days per man per year. More than 80 per cent of the uranium in the Hiroshima and Nagasaki bombs came from the heavily guarded Congo mine of Shinkolobwe.'[51] By the time of Annemarie's stay in the Belgian Congo, the major part of the Congo's uranium stockpile had been transferred to the United States as a precautionary measure.[52] As always with colonialism, economics lay behind the civilizing mission: who did the work, for how much, under what conditions and to whose profit. Annemarie's writing is unapologetic about plunder and takes colonial ownership of the produce for granted: 'it is a vital artery opening up the enormous heart of the country – now navigable and carrying our ivory, our palm oil, our coffee, our copal, our riches, our machines, our soldiers, and our precious timber.'[53] The 'our' here gives pause.

Jungle gave way to savannah and the lakes of central Africa promised a mini-Switzerland. At Beni, 200 kilometres south of Lake Albert, 100 kilometres north of Lake Edward and 400 klicks west of Lake Victoria, Annemarie was dwarfed by colonial nomenclature:

> The next morning, emerging from the round hut in which I had slept, I saw from a rise the plunging view of a plain dotted with hills rising gently to splendid mountains, criss-crossed by blueish undulations – mist, clouds, flickers of dawn. … A sense of happiness reigns over this land bathed in magnificent morning quiet as daylight dawns – the heart of Africa.[54]

In this quasi-Alpine landscape her 'sense of writing became clear again'.[55] Shortly afterwards, she descended the Congo river on the steamboat *General Baron Jacques*,[56] and was back in Léopoldville by the end of September 1941. Free French authorities still didn't take her at her word and she was refused a visa to travel to Egypt: 'How is it possible that a solo traveller like me could be rejected, accused, suspected by a group of people who can by mere whim put me in the dock?'[57]

In the middle of this high dudgeon about visas and spying, she began writing the novel *Das Wunder des Baums* (*The Miracle of the Tree*) in Léopoldville on 22 October 1941, the anniversary of her father's death. The germ of the novel grew from a tree she saw on a night walk 'and later in the silence of the bush and the pristine magnificence of the great mountains in Kivu – all my old life seemed to fall away'.[58] This wonderment in the face of trees had also struck André Gide in his Congo travels.[59] The male narrator, Marc, a young Swiss in Africa who has run afoul of the authorities, is her old gender-bending standby. He meets Louise, a war widow, but they agree to part. Marc identifies with his jungle-clearing forebears who spent 'a lifetime hunting ivory and prospecting for gold'. Marc's grandfather is an old planter, drawn from Annemarie's time in Molanda, who disappears into the mountainous district to the east, never to be seen again. Her colonial characters in search of spiritual meaning seem to do a fair bit of exploiting along the way.

Gossip and the heat drove Annemarie from Léopoldville to the relative coolness of Thysville, a hill town on the railway line linking the coast and the capital. Colonel Albert Thys was yet another no-nonsense imperialist who had interviewed the young Joseph Conrad in Brussels. Marlow in Conrad's *Heart of Darkness* observes the slave labour laying down the railway track as he travels inland: 'each had an iron collar on his neck and all were connected together with a chain whose bights swung between them, rhythmically clinking'.[60] One of the surveyors involved in charting the railway's course was a young Roger Casement.

Thysville as a writing retreat had been suggested by a friend, a diplomatic wife or widow who had sculpted Annemarie's head during the weeks she had spent in the capital and who visited her in the hill town on 12 January 1942. The identity of this sculptor remains unknown. 'We experienced such a spiritual connection that we didn't even need to speak', wrote Annemarie, 'and I was so grateful for her presence, for this friendship, this good will.'[61] The Thysville air was fresher and her writing routine uninterrupted: three hours in the morning, a couple of hours after lunch, punctuated by morning and evening swims, as well as walks. Already her mind was made up to return to Lisbon. '*My* only work is to overcome the lower self', she wrote to Ella Maillart. 'Just as I have to overcome disturbances, distraction, noise, pain, weakness, – in order to listen to what I must write.'[62] She conceived of her novel as a therapy project, in terms of seeking calm, transcendence, in a landscape of trees. For two weeks at the beginning of February she was hospitalized with malaria but nonetheless finished her manuscript of 375 pages on 20 February 1942.

Back in Léopoldville she found the same atmosphere of intrigue and back-biting that had made her leave in the first place. Investigation by the Belgian authorities found no particular evidence to support the accusation of spying. She was granted an exit visa to Lisbon, but the damage to her reputation had been done. Robert Parr, British Consul at Brazzaville, warned that suspicions were likely to dog her for the duration of the war, tarnishing her reputation, and proposed to check with London if there was any evidence against her. Annemarie declined the offer and felt that she was better served by rising above the fray. Stealing a march on her oppressors, she voluntarily submitted the manuscript of her novel to the scrutiny of Belgian censors. The night before her appointment at the governor's office at Kalina, a telegram from Renée informed Annemarie that her paternal grandmother had died.[63]

Chef de cabinet to Governor Ryckmans was Léo Pétillon, who had overseen censorship of her articles in the course of the previous ten months, a circumstance Annemarie had accepted under the exigencies of wartime. Pétillon would in turn become Governor-General of the Belgian Congo in the 1950s and briefly rise to the position of Minister of the Congo. His line of nervous censors and inquisitors in the colonial service had peddled a self-serving story in the face of journalistic and humanitarian enquiry for over half a century. The deep research and damning conclusions of the American journalist George Washington Williams, British journalist E.D. Morel and Sir Roger Casement, all of whom wrote truth to power about the horrors of Leopold's Congo, were as yet unacknowledged by the successor regime of which Pétillon was the gatekeeper.

Pétillon was consternated by her ingratitude, by the perceived slights in her manuscript, at the betrayed confidence he had placed in her. In the course of his two-hour convocation, he took exception to Annemarie's depiction of autonomous groups among the 40,000 black population of Léopoldville, although there is no evidence of her socializing with the so-called *évolués*, as the native elites were designated, never mind with the more radical anti-colonial movements. He was not happy about the way she depicted insufficiently fervent Belgian resistance in the colony, nor with the aura of tribulation in her novel.

> My interviewer informed me that the Governor was apprised of my fractious manuscript, that they were to discuss the matter in the afternoon, and that he had wanted to see me in person beforehand in order to exercise a personal judgement.[64]

Pétillon cited the following innocuous passage for approbation:

> At dusk, in the thickening gloom, the blacks could be seen hunkered or leaning against walls or dusty hedges at the edge of the street, and under their half-closed lids the whites of their eyes lit on passersby like the eyes of night creatures caught in the glare of day. ... hearing the tom-toms from the *quartier des Noirs*, the so-called 'Belga' or simply '*le Village*'. The Blacks

lived there in their thousands in miserable shanty towns, behind barbed wire, like prisoners. Nonetheless, they kept up their traditions: drums made from hollowed tree trunks, and drunk on palm wine, under a full moon, they gathered on the wide empty streets between their shacks, and the dull monotonous rhythm of their tom-toms worked its magic.[65]

Their tussle played itself out until lunchtime when, no more taxis being available, the *chef de cabinet* drove her back downtown. A couple of days later the tatty envelope containing the manuscript, stamped with a *laisser-passer*, was returned to her. She wrote to Ella: 'the complete copy is sealed by the Government, and safe at the Consulate of Switzerland.'[66] Thanks to Swiss Consul Adrien Orlandi she had the diplomatic bag at her disposal, a *deus ex machina* against censorship after all. She and her work were free to go.

There were mostly white women and children on board the *SS Quanza*, which had rounded the Horn of Africa from Portuguese Mozambique, dropped anchor at Luanda, capital of Portuguese Angola, before heading north to Lisbon. Mines, torpedoes and spotter planes were likely around Dakar, capital of French West Africa still in Vichy hands. Annemarie spent the fourteen-day voyage drafting articles. Some revisited the *nostalgie de paquebots* that was her trademark. One article for the *NZZ* focused on the war effort in the colonies, in particular on cooperation between the Belgians and the British. Her longest, most personal piece, more of a shipboard journal – *Beim Verlassen Afrikas* (*Leaving Africa*) – displayed a good deal of inflated victimhood now that her brush with the censors was behind her. She skewered the colonial mindset and its petty bourgeois pretensions: faux-nostalgia for the 'home country'; complaints about black servants; humdrum expat life. Nonetheless, her critique rarely strays far from the ex-pat veranda nor questions the fundamentals of Belgian and French colonialism while at times condescending to the little people trying to make a buck among the natives. Disparaging her fellow passengers for their misplaced faith in Europe as a paradise, she forgets that she herself had so often in the past employed a similar trope. 'I have come back from a strange paradise, my African exile', she wrote to Carson McCullers from Lisbon.[67]

Given her American journalism and the critique of Westernization in Turkey, Persia and Afghanistan, we might have expected Annemarie to write more freely and incisively about her ten months in the Congo. As Michel-Rolph Trouillot puts it: 'Something is always left out while something else is recorded.'[68] The Congo mattered to Annemarie as the site of her own aborted attempt at journalistic glory, 'the brilliant war job' that had eluded her. In January, Ella Maillart had accused her of going on and on about the war like a gramophone record played once too often. Before departing for the Congo, Annemarie had outlined her aims to Ella if the project to join the Free French failed: 'to discover a new part of the world and to learn to live alone'.[69] Annemarie had briefly achieved these two aims.

We can gauge the degree of Annemarie's detachment from Congolese experience by comparison with the propaganda mission of New York lyricist John Latouche. He had performed at Erika's ill-fated Peppermill première in New York, and travelled to the Congo in late October 1942 – six months after Annemarie's departure. Following a similar route to hers, he journeyed upriver with cineast and photographer André Cauvin. *Congo*, a photo book published in 1945, focuses on mining, schools, statistics, medicine and tribal life. Text and photos present a forward-looking positive face of colonialism in keeping with Allied war aims. All three writers and photographers operated within similar constraints, in a country historically suspicious of journalists, where truth-telling had been seen as whistleblowing right from its inception: 'some of your journalists, *m'sieu l'américan*, are hard to satisfy. Now that they cannot find lurid stories to exploit, they have other complaints.'[70] Wartime propaganda emphasized the three c's of European development: civilization, commerce and Christianity, whereas documentary film-maker Raoul Peck is free to pull no punches: 'the Congo adventure was pure looting. Leopold II running the numbers, plundering bodies, plundering resources. The draining of the whole continent a multi-billion-dollar heist.'[71]

Latouche was friends with Ruth Landshoff-Yorck, who leaves this intriguing glimpse of our legendary heroine:

In the hall of a lovely embassy in the Belgian Congo stands, modelled by the mistress of the house, the bust of a girl. She is recognized by many for she is a legend. A legend only three decades after her birth. And when the poet John Latouche came to Leopoldsville, he recognized the lovely stone head from stories about her and from the tenderness with which some of her friends had described her.

'That must be Annemarie', he said.[72]

*

Lisbon still seemed a good base of operations to Annemarie. On 22 May she had breakfast with five ministers from various Allied European countries, and dined with a German general. Renée had been in touch with the Swiss Consul, Henri Martin, who had given assurances about her daughter's health, and Hasi had sent 1,000 Swiss francs. In thanking him, she let him know that she had been free from 'moral and health crises for a long time now' – a way of saying she was drug-free and behaving herself.[73] Hasi acted as intermediary with Renée, who resumed communication with Annemarie shortly before her thirty-fourth birthday.

On 16 May she was at the docks covering the arrival of the trans-Atlantic steamer *SS Drottningholm* and its 1,200 VIP passengers, among whom was the *Frankfurter Zeitung* correspondent and traveller Margret Boveri, returning from the United States. She had been briefly interned as an enemy alien when America entered the war, and had managed to secure a place among the ship's passengers.

Boveri's fortuitous get-together with Annemarie, whose work she knew and who had previously been suggested to her as a travelling companion, led to a revealing correspondence over eight days in Lisbon. Both journalists and travellers were independent women operating in a male world at war. Boveri sent Annemarie roses for her birthday and identified the limitations of the thirty-four-year-old's writing talent:

> Read Annemarie Schwarzenbach's book *Das glückliche Tal* today at the dentist's and while waiting for the tram. … It's even worse as travel writing than [the new novel] – first-person musings. Nonetheless, some lively or well-imagined bits. I met her in Lisbon and liked her. We had managed to extricate ourselves from very similar circumstances: I from internment in America, she from a similar experience in the Congo; both of us quixotic, indifferent to the mundane, characteristically detached. But what I thought was singular about her experience – her altercation with the apparently finger-pointing world and the way she stood up for herself – is how clearly

deep-seated and chronic it is with her, and that is surely awful. To no longer be able to see the world because of oneself.[74]

This astute observation is all the more penetrating from a well-disposed fellow writer and traveller. Boveri read the first twenty or thirty pages of Annemarie's new novel and suggested publishing an extract in the *Frankfurter Zeitung* – nothing came of this. In two long letters to Boveri from Tetouan, Annemarie outlined her writing process:

> … writing … is like the conduct of a religious life, an absolute concentration that detaches one from the sensual and the material world. And as writing proceeds, unimagined forces stir, clairvoyance and sixth sense come into play, and one taps into the source of happiness and suffering, courage and fear.[75]

English doesn't handle the ineffable as well as German in full flight. Her turn to religiosity and therapy lent itself to an indulgent, subjective style. The critic Charly Clerc, who had taken her to task about the earlier *Lyric Novella*, suggested trimming the draft of the new novel by fifty or a hundred pages.[76] Anita Forrer read it several times and thought it was 'utterly bad, that is, with beautiful set pieces in places, but unmoored, insubstantial'.[77] At thirty-four, Annemarie needed to move beyond beautiful set pieces and poetic prose.

The day after her birthday, she escaped to Madrid with Marie-Louise ('Bunny') Lüscher, a childhood friend who had worked in the Swiss Consulate in New York and had come over on the steamer with Boveri. They went on to Seville, where Marie-Louise's father lived. He drove them out to his eucalyptus estate near Huelva where Annemarie, to the consternation of Lüscher 'approached many of the plantation trees, with their silvered trunks, caressing them, listening to the "song" of their bluish leaves'.[78] This tree-hugging left him fearful for Annemarie's sanity. Her letters to Ella and Carson over the previous six months had been full of animated nature, angels, God, persecution complexes and psycho-babble in two languages, making heavy weather of a dichotomy between 'outside reality' and 'her inner real self'.

From Spain she flew to meet her husband in Casablanca.

*

French North Africa – Morocco, Tunisia and Algeria – was still under the authority of Maréchal Pétain's Vichy government. Claude Clarac, consul in Tetouan, Spanish Morocco, despised the armistice and the German occupation of France. Diplomacy was of the hour and by late 1942 'many French people were willing to believe that the Germans had not won the war after all. The Resistance became a force in the land.' What Robert Paxton has called 'crusted layers of postwar perspectives' obscure the initial foot-dragging of French *grands hommes* and their diplomatic corps.[79] Germaine Krull, sent to Algiers to organize the photographic service, described this pivotal moment in the war as 'a basketful of crabs'.[80] By May 1943 de Gaulle was in Algiers, by October the Free French authorities had appointed Clarac as commercial representative to Salazar's Lisbon, and the balance of power had shifted in the Mediterranean.

Claude met Annemarie's plane and over the course of the month of June 1942 the couple toured the sights and archaeological ruins of Morocco. They hadn't lived together since the fiery summer of 1935 in Tehran. In the intervening six years they had met once. Clarac's professed feelings, and his loyalty, were still being retailed in interview at the conclusion of his long diplomatic life in the 1990s.[81] Annemarie's feelings for him are less easy to disentangle. Writing to Busy Bodmer, she mentioned leading 'exactly the kind of life which suits me – lots of work, long walks, the use of a library and some music in the evening. Claude has a photo enlarger and we have fun developing snaps.'[82] Reviewing Claude's position on this list, our guard ought to be up against the happy-ever-after trope of normalizing marriage. Writing to Florianna Madelung, Annemarie felt 'better here and can work more calmly than in Lisbon'. Claude is mentioned in passing.[83] Annemarie was capable of opportunism and there is every reason to think that Claude was exploring the delights of Morocco in time-worn fashion; it wasn't all mint tea and mimosa.[84]

Morocco was a new country for a writer always well disposed towards Islamic culture. They travelled to Rabat and the tessellated ruins of Chella. Annemarie visited schools, drank mint tea overlooking the sea, and wrote in a room with a view of the Rif mountains. Claude's status as consul in Spanish Morocco provided visas and connections, diplomatic car and driver, hotels and deference. She had swapped her pith helmet

Claude Clarac, Rabat, Morocco. Photo by Annemarie Schwarzenbach
Courtesy of Swiss Literary Archives and Wikimedia Commons

for white linen harem pants. As during their first months of marriage in Persia, Claude employed the romance of travel to counterbalance domesticity. 'I saw open up in front of me a long life of happiness by her side, a route freely chosen by both of us.'[85] Annemarie, for her part, saw a life shuttling between Lisbon, Madrid and North Africa, without too much pressure as a diplomat's wife. She left with a return ticket in her pocket and an all-important transit visa for France delivered by her husband. Divorce had been put off for now – it remained a marriage with benefits.

It had been a productive month for her writing. She returned to an old chestnut – deploring mass tourism, what she calls 'globe-trotters':

These tourists parcel out the world between the boring and the less boring bits, like an enormous playground, based on novelty value and rarity, without ever really seeing anything in between. And finally, they spare a thought for the coolies of Siam and indentured labour in Jamaica.[86]

In her Moroccan journalism, however, travel and life writing form a successful hybrid, and she deploys her famously long sentences clause by clause to cumulative effect. Fond of 'enchanted gardens', 'sultans' courts', 'Mongolian princes', 'shepherd boys with torn tunics', her palette of local colour and the sights often ends in a bejewelled dusk, the call to evening prayer, sunset over the bazaar or the ruins. What's missing from this picturesqueness is any hard-nosed analysis of French colonialism. Her exotica, the oriental rug underfoot, was already passé by 1942 – Albert Camus published *l'Étranger* in the same year. The descriptive pile-up of her writing recalls the varnished orientalism of the painters Jean-Léon Gérôme, Frederick Arthur Bridgman and Étienne Dinet; nothing much in its melancholy poetry and world-weariness rocks the casbah. A text titled 'Moonshine in Chella' retells the worry beads of her earlier travels – Persian samovars and caravans, Afghan carpets on oases, Rabat mint tea under moonlight and the tombs of the sultans:

A boy prepared the tea, a Roman oil lamp was lit, and we stretched out on cushions and gazed into the distance. It was as though our mesmerized eyes, caught off-guard, were attempting to follow the souls ascending in the moonlit darkness, above the rustling undergrowth of the valley, over the pale hills, far away to where the world became a shining ebbing sea.[87]

*

On the morning of Annemarie's return to Switzerland, Renée suffered a fall from her horse and was confined to bed for three weeks with a head wound. Annemarie went to see her in hospital and they buried the hatchet. Her paternal grandmother's will had left Annemarie with means to purchase her beloved house in Sils. Intending to consolidate her position as Lisbon correspondent for Swiss newspapers, she spent ten days in Zollikon with her amanuensis Busy Bodmer, sorting articles and photographs for publication. In the autumn she planned to rejoin Claude in France and to proceed to Tetouan. With a house in the Engadine, a husband in Spanish Morocco and a job in Lisbon, Annemarie could write and travel to her heart's content.

Readers of her new novel concurred that it needed revision and over the course of five weeks in Sils in August she did just that. Rather than dramatize and clarify in the new draft, however, Annemarie chose instead to internalize and poeticize. The resulting sixty-three-page prose poem, published as '*Marc*' (2012), is not any clearer than the original novel: this turn towards bedizened poetry indicates Annemarie's psychological malaise in the summer of 1942.

Among Annemarie's friends in Sils was the aviatrix Isabella Trümpy, one of few female Swiss pilots. On 6 September the two women set out by horse and trap with the intention of finalizing the purchase of Annemarie's house at the notary's office in St. Moritz. En route they overtook another friend travelling by bicycle, who suggested they swap places – Annemarie mounted the bike for the three-quarter-hour ride on the flat, along the valley of the Inn river. Five minutes later she fell, injuring her head, perhaps while attempting to ride without hands as she had done on the grounds of Bocken as a child. Her local doctor administered first aid but the patient remained unconscious for three days. He had been aware since 1938 of Annemarie's morphine addiction and of her attempts to kick the habit and so referred her to Dr. Forel at Rives de Prangins, who had examined her as far back as 1935. Renée, still recovering at the chalet from her own fall, delegated Hasi to travel to Sils. She might have initially thought it was another of Annemarie's relapses.[88]

Renée wasn't alone in thinking morphine might have played a part. Dr. Heinrich's initial diagnosis was tentative and he decided to wake the patient from her three-day coma. Her bewilderment led him to administer Pantopon, similar to the Eukodal she had been addicted to. At Prangins, X-rays revealed neither fractures nor neurological damage. Doctors induced a four-day coma to calm the patient (insulin coma therapy), from which she emerged initially subdued but confused. Increasingly aggressive behaviour over the following days led to treatment with insulin in combination with electroconvulsive therapy. To the relief of all concerned, Dr. Forel could find no symptoms of morphine withdrawal and turned to his earlier diagnosis of incipient schizophrenia, for which the above therapies were standard at the time. What should have been treatment for a head wound with possible concussion became an exercise in psychiatric assault.[89] A distressed Annemarie may have thought she was back in the clutches of the over-zealous psychiatry she had spent a lifetime attempting to escape.

Claude, on furlough in France, visited the clinic on 4 October but Forel prevented Annemarie's husband from seeing her, warning that she should avoid excitement. Nonetheless, the doctor assured Claude that their planned journey to Tetouan could proceed. Claude knew that Annemarie despised Forel and he found the doctor's statements inconsistent.[90] Forel likewise advised against Renée visiting but she persisted and made an appointment for 8 October. She managed to gain access to Annemarie and was shocked by her condition. Forel agreed to release her into the care of a nurse, and patient and mother returned to Bocken on 10 October. Doctors in the Burghölzli Clinic in Zurich took over Annemarie's treatment and proposed that she should enter the clinic for tests and observation – which Renée, mindful of previous experience with her eldest son in the same institution, vetoed. Dr. Manfred Bleuler, director of the clinic, was the son of Eugen Bleuler who had coined the term 'schizophrenia'.

Five days later Annemarie was able to draft a letter to Annigna Godly, who over the years had readied the Sils house for guests. 'Mama took me here out of that hell-hole in Prangins, where Dr. Favez was very kind and everybody else hellish. I'm feeling better here – looking better and more settled. Mama is still very nice, but we think I should head down to Sils *soon*.'[91] On 15 October, however, Busy Bodmer reported in her diary that Annemarie did not recognize her and 'crawled along the floor like an animal'.[92] On 18 October the patient returned to Sils by train, accompanied by a nurse. Five days later Renée visited. In the interim Annemarie's health had sharply declined, both morally and physically. While chatty and coherent, her attempts at writing had produced scribbles and nonsense.[93] She played over and over a recording of the Schumann concerto for violin. Renée had come round to the view of Forel and Annemarie's local doctors, that her condition was psychological rather than due to a bicycle accident.[94]

Renée returned to Sils where Annemarie no longer recognized her. Two nurses in attendance were under strict instructions to allow no visitors. Dr. Gut, a St. Moritz ski-injury specialist, prescribed Eukodal up to three injections per day – the very drug the patient had weaned herself off. On 5 November the doctor's observations seem optimistic if not outright euphemistic: 'given the patient's good will, affection and gratitude even at the best of times, never difficult or even aggressive, things are going very well in Sils'.[95] Gut's treatment of Annemarie during her last two weeks, in consultation with Renée, amounts to palliative care aided by sleeping pills and morphine. Given the diagnosis of schizophrenia and the patient's deterioration, it was decided to let her die.[96] While confusion about Annemarie's final illness and suggestions of mis-diagnosis lingered, Renée, as time went by, regarded Annemarie's accident as the final twist of fate in a saga of drugs and mental illness.[97]

On 15 November, Renée returned to Sils following notice of further deterioration in her daughter's condition. When she arrived that Sunday, Annemarie was already dead. She died with Dr. Gut in attendance on 15 November 1942 at 9.45 in the morning. The church bells in Sils rang the hours and the first snow lay on the mountains. Renée marked the solemn occasion by photographing her daughter on her deathbed, her jaw held in place by a bandage, the high prow of her nose, her fine profile laid to the side.[98]

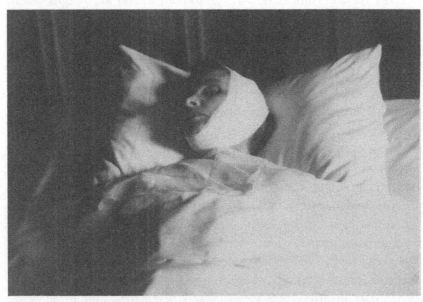

Annemarie Schwarzenbach on her deathbed, Sils Baselgia, 15 November 1942. Photo by Renée Schwarzenbach-Wille
Courtesy of Zentralbibliothek Zürich

Rather than being buried in Sils, as Annemarie had wanted, her remains were brought back to Bocken and cremated in Zurich on 18 November. The coffin was bedecked with white asters and a violinist played Schubert's Litany for the Procession of All Saints and part of a Bach cantata.[99] Minister Gerhard Spinner eulogized her as 'a candle in the wind, burning with a flickering flame',[100] comparing her to that stormy earlier inhabitant of Sils, Friedrich Nietzsche. Mourners were starkly divided between family and friends. 'In the front pew, the implacable cold mother, the one most likely responsible for the difficult fate of her child. Flanking her, the grieving family, for whom Annemarie had long been a lost sheep. And much further back the few people who were really close to her.'[101] As the funeral service proceeded, the bells of St. Lurench in Sils Baselgia, St. Michael's and the Church of Christ the King in Sils Maria tolled in the deceased's honour.

News of Annemarie's untimely death was reported widely in Swiss papers, for which she had written so assiduously over the course of the previous decade. Writer Carl Seelig singled out her early novels for their portrait of troubled youth and un-Swiss-like cosmopolitanism. Her world of 'cocktails and cigarettes, sleepers and sleek limousines' had already become remote in wartime.[102] Newspapers and magazines focused on her intrepid travels into the wilderness, the myth of a restless life already beginning to overshadow the work. Early death gave this portrait a tragic dimension and her eulogists had difficulty extricating writer, traveller and photographer from her elegant image, her androgynous presence. 'Everything about her was extraordinary, exceptional and noble. An object that she used, an item of clothing that she wore, whatever she touched became idiosyncratic', wrote Manuel Gasser in *Weltwoche*.[103]

The news reached her friends far and wide, exacerbated by wartime restrictions. They found it difficult to understand how a fall from a bicycle could prove fatal. The mythmakers began to turn Annemarie into a tragic victim of time and circumstance, of family controlling her spirit, more candles in the wind. Klaus was in New York and Erika in California. In the revised German version of his autobiography, completed in 1949 months before his own drug-induced death, Klaus recalls 'the inconsolable angel' and turns her into a spirit of the times: 'Absurd, death-marked martyr, brought low by some horrible authority with inscrutable design. As though there were not enough endless, cruel agonies on the battlefield, in the death camps and torture chambers.'[104] Carson was at Yaddo when a telegram arrived from Klaus. 'All I had ever felt was gathered together around this woman ... And this woman was something like an assembly line for my soul.'[105] By the time Carson came to dictate her memoirs in the 1960s, Annemarie had morphed into melodrama that mangled the facts. She 'worked with de Gaulle forces in the Congo where a statue of her was made by a native. John Latouche, who was a mutual friend, mentioned that statue and said he wished he could have taken it home to me, but the natives had worshipped it as a sort of tribal [deity]. ... Annemarie's bicycle had plunged over a ravine and she was knocked unconscious. She died in a hospital in Zurich without regaining consciousness.'[106] In Pondicherry in 1943, Ella Maillart learned of her old travelling companion's death in a telegram from Dr. Forel. Returning to Switzerland after the war, she sensed Annemarie's wandering spirit in Sils; Maillart's diary leaves us with an image of Annemarie walking slowly into the lake in her camel-hair coat.[107] Margot von Opel, in Seagoville, Texas, 'locked in with Nazis', had heard that Annemarie was ill and wrote to Klaus for news. 'We just got a wire from Switzerland. Did you hear anything? Is she in a clinic? I only hope that the family did not bring her in 'safety' to get rid of her. The thought of it frightens me to death.'[108]

Families, as Margot intimated, want to own the story and tidy the reputation. Renée burned most of the letters – letters from the Manns, Annette Kolb, Erich Maria Remarque and Carson McCullers.[109] Over the following months, mother and grandmother Clara read and then burned the diaries.[110] That the diaries lambasted Renée is acknowledged and downplayed in a letter from the ninety-two-year-old Clara to Annemarie's executor, Anita Forrer:

> I assume full responsibility. Someone who clearly loved to write as much as Annemarie, who moreover frequently said she would never malign her mother, cannot be held to account for such outpourings in the heat of the moment, which would only redound against the writer.[111]

Likewise, when Ella Maillart came to write about her journey with Annemarie to Afghanistan, *The Cruel Way* (1947), Renée employed editorial oversight and a measure of tact by imposing a pseudonym. Anita Forrer, Annemarie's literary executor, also destroyed letters and suppressed key phrases about Ria Hackin in Annemarie's account of the Afghan journey – the original drafts are not in the archives.[112] Tact, discretion and outright censorship work towards reinforcing sexual, familial and political norms.

In the battle between imagination, liberal politics and sexual freedom on the one hand, propriety, fascism and family values on the other, the latter seemed to have won by November 1942. There are battles and wars, however. Albrecht Haushofer, as a young man smitten by Annemarie's beauty and grace, had been implicated in a plot to assassinate Hitler, and ended the war in Moabit prison in Berlin. There, before being taken out and shot, he wrote a poem to her ghost: 'so young, intact, and weirdly close … you nodded, whispered. Are you on the mend?'[113] Yet it was an earlier Haushofer sonnet, 'Burnt Books', that was eerily prescient about freedom, literature and the fate of Annemarie's writing:

Across a vast empire
raged mayhem and murder, a wall of fire
smelling of burnt flesh and imperial blinkers.

The tyrant died in the twelfth year of his reign.
New books rose from the ashes of the pyre
and found their old burnished readers again.[114]

Afterword

Annemarie Schwarzenbach's (1908–1942) writings, travels and photographs began to be rediscovered in the 1980s. All her work is currently in print, published by Lenos Verlag in Basel. A major photographic retrospective took place at the Paul Klee Centre in Bern in 2021.

Claude Bourdet (1909–1996) was active in the French Resistance and a founding member of the journal *Combat*. Arrested by the Gestapo in 1944, he was interned in Neuengamme, Sachsenhausen and Buchenwald. In 1950 he founded *l'Observateur*, which in 1964 became France's seminal news magazine *Le Nouvel Observateur*.

Marianne Breslauer (1909–2001) gave up photography in 1937. With her husband, art dealer Walter Feilchenfeldt, she established an art gallery in Amsterdam and, from 1939, in Zurich. Her decade of work as a photographer between the wars is much prized.

Claude Achille Clarac (1903–1999) ended a long diplomatic career as ambassador in Bangkok. Under the pen name Saint Ours, he published a number of homosexual erotic tales and a poem 'Farmanieh', recalling his marriage to Annemarie. He adopted a son, Henri Pageau-Clarac.

Maria Daelen (1903–1993) Following Operation Valkyrie of 1944, the Gestapo searched her Berlin clinic and country house, suspecting involvement in the attempted assassination of Hitler. In 1953 she represented Germany at the World Health Organization. Late in life, she married Dr. Ludwig Strecker who with his brother controlled Schott Music, one of the world's leading music publishing firms, all the while maintaining her independence.

Anita Forrer (1901–1996) as a teenager corresponded with Rilke, published as *Lettres à une jeune poétesse*. In the last years of the war, she worked for the American Red Cross and for the OSS. She was Annemarie's literary executor as well as a founder of the *Biblioteca Engiadinaisa*, a cultural centre and library based in Sils.

Therese Giehse (1898–1975) went on to play the lead role in the premiere of Berthold Brecht's *Mother Courage* in Zurich in 1941, and to enjoy an illustrious postwar career as an actress.

Barbara Hamilton Wright (1913–1966) worked at the War Manpower Commission in Washington and with the American Occupation Forces in Seoul, Korea. In 1953 she married Anglo-Irish war hero Col. Alan George Ferguson-Warren. In 1966 Barbara died in his arms. 'It's been fun, Cocky', were her dying words.

Albrecht Haushofer (1903–1945) Following the July 1944 bomb plot against Hitler, Haushofer was interned in Moabit prison. Poems discovered in his coat pocket after his execution in April 1945 were published as the *Moabit Sonnets*, a record of resistance and survival in the teeth of death.

Karl Haushofer (1869–1946), geopolitician and friend to Rudolf Hess and Hitler, was found 'as guilty as the better-known war criminals' at Nuremberg. He committed suicide, together with his Jewish wife, by drinking arsenic beside the Ammersee in March 1946.

Ursula von Hohenlohe-Oehringen (1905–1988) as Ursula von Zedlitz was the German language translator of Mary McCarthy's *The Group* and future Nobel laureate V.S. Naipaul among others.

Miles Horton (1905–1990), founder of the Highlander Folk School, went on to become an influential figure and teacher in the Civil Rights movement, mentoring Martin Luther King and Rosa Parks among many others.

Hanna Kiel (1898–1988) was one of a handful of art historians who protected art critic Bernard Berenson during the Nazi occupation of Italy, translating his books into German. When Germany bombed

Florence, she made a public declaration never to return to the country of her birth.

Emmy Krüger (1886–1976) wrote to Hitler requesting his endorsement of her travel visa to Switzerland on health grounds in June 1942, to which Hitler gladly assented. Her long relationship with Renée Schwarzenbach fizzled out in acrimony and she did not attend her old patron's funeral.

Ruth Landshoff (1904–1966) settled in New York for the duration of the war, on Cornelia Street, where she worked as a writer and translator of Cocteau, Brecht, Celan and McCullers.

Ella Maillart (1903–1997) spent the war years in the south of India. She wrote about her journey to Afghanistan with Annemarie in *The Cruel Way*. After the war Ella lived in Geneva and the mountain village of Chandolin, where there is a tiny museum in her memory.

Erika Mann (1905–1969) attended the Nuremberg trials and was fierce in her denunciation of the Nazi defendants. In the face of the McCarthy communist witch hunt, she returned with her parents to Zurich, where she acted as her father's amanuensis.

Klaus Mann (1906–1949) joined the US Army and witnessed the liberation of Europe. He overdosed on sleeping pills in Cannes in May 1949. His novels, particularly *Mephisto*, and the autobiography *The Turning Point*, are a fine record of his time.

Carson McCullers (1917–1967) was on Nantucket with Tennessee Williams in the summer of 1946. Margot von Opel invited them to supper. The women reminisced about Annemarie and the war years, while Carson continued to embroider her brief infatuation in *Illumination and Night Glare*.

Margot von Opel (1898–1993) was interned as an enemy alien in Texas. Separated from husband Fritz in 1951, she was granted $60,000-a-year alimony.

Doris von Schönthan (1905–1961) was interned in France and joined the French Resistance. It was she who informed the Mann family of Klaus's death on 21 May 1949. After the war she spent two years in a mental institution in Germany, became homeless and destitute. She died of a stroke in Paris.

Renée Schwarzenbach (1883–1959) survived her daughter by sixteen years, never recanting her support for the Nazi regime. Her four-decade relationship with Emmy Krüger ended when the singer took up with someone else.

Dorothea 'Mopsa' Sternheim (1905–1954) joined the French Resistance in Paris and was deported to Ravensbrück in 1943. She survived and returned to Paris where she died of cancer aged 49.

Baroness Maud Thyssen (1909–?) was a passenger in Alexis Mdivani's blue Rolls Royce cabriolet in August 1935 when the car overturned in Catalonia, Spain. Mdivani died and Maud survived, though reported as having lost an eye and bitten her tongue off.

Hedwig Vivien (1889–1955) returned from the Congo to Switzerland in a wheelchair in 1946. The Viviens left their plantation to ETH, Zurich's prestigious technical university. Following Congolese independence, the plantation was bought by a crony of kleptocratic Mobutu. Annemarie's 'paradise' was lost.

Notes

Introduction

1 Charles Linsmayer, *Annemarie Schwarzenbach: Ein Kapitel tragische Schweizer Literaturgeschichte*, pp. 198–202.
2 Alicia P.q. Wittmeyer, 'Overlooked No More: Annemarie Schwarzenbach, Author, Photographer and "Ravaged Angel"', *New York Times*, 10 October 2018.
3 Klaus Mann, *The Turning Point*, p. 278.

1. Cocoon

1 Frank R. Mason, *The American Silk Industry and the Tariff* (American Economic Association Quarterly, Volume II, 1910).
2 D.H. Lawrence, *Twilight in Italy*, p. 124.
3 Alexis Schwarzenbach, *Die Geborene*, p. 239.
4 Ibid., pp. 13–16.
5 '*Frau Schwarzenbach ritt heute Herrensattel*', a phrase perhaps translatable as 'rode like a man', in AS '*Die Hut*'. SLA.
6 Renée Schwarzenbach-Wille's photographs are in the Graphics and Photo Archives. ZBZ.
7 Alexis Schwarzenbach, *Die Geborene*, p. 39.
8 Mantel is borrowing from the Jungian theories of Marian Woodman. 'The Princess Myth: Hilary Mantel on Diana', *The Guardian*, 26 August 2017.
9 Areti Georgiadou, *Das Leben zerfetzt sich mir*, p. 24.
10 Emmy Krüger, 8 September 1915, Tagebücher, Emmy Krüger Archive. MLM.
11 Alexis Schwarzenbach, *Auf der Schwelle des Fremden*, p. 18.
12 Alexis Schwarzenbach, *Die Geborene*, p. 219.
13 AS, 'Über meine Mutter zu schreiben, ist der Anfang aller Dinge', 24 November 1935, 190/8 Suzanne Öhman-Schwarzenbach Archive, Schwarzenbach Archives. ZBZ.
14 AS, '*Pariser Novelle*', p. 24. SLA.
15 Alexis Schwarzenbach, *Auf der Schwelle des Fremden*, p. 29. 'Annemarie mit ihrer Liebe: Fräulein Fischer', 9 April 1919, scr F RS VI 85, Renée Schwarzenbach-Wille Archives. ZBZ.
16 Alexis Schwarzenbach, *Die Geborene*, p. 220.
17 Cited by Areti Georgiadou, *Das Leben zerfetzt sich mir*, p. 29.

18 Alexis Schwarzenbach, *Auf der Schwelle des Fremden*, p. 29, scr F RS VI 34, Renée Schwarzenbach-Wille Archives. ZBZ.

19 Anecdote related in Areti Georgiadou, *Das Leben zerfetzt sich mir*, p. 18, and also in Dominique Laure Miermont, *Annemarie Schwarzenbach ou le mal d'Europe*, p. 43.

20 Ella K. Maillart, *The Cruel Way*, p. 4.

21 Suzanne Öhman, cited in *Das Leben zerfetzt sich mir*, p. 30.

22 Emmy Krüger, 27 December 1922, Tagebücher, Emmy Krüger Archive. MLM.

23 AS, '*Interview Ohne Reporter*', in *Auf der Schattenseite*, p. 11.

24 Friedrich Ratzel, *Der Lebensraum* (Tubingen: H. Laupp, 1901).

25 German consul in Zurich to the German Embassy in Bern, 4 July 1934, cited in Alexis Schwarzenbach, *Die Geborene*, p. 265.

26 Martin Huber, 'Hitlers Rede in Zürich', *Tages Anzeiger*, 23 October 2015 and also Harold Sander, *Hitler: The Itinerary* for 27 and 28 August 1923.

27 Alexis Schwarzenbach, *Die Geborene*, p. 173. Clara Wille-von Bismarck Tagebücher, Schwarzenbach Archives. ZBZ.

28 In her account of travels with Annemarie Schwarzenbach, *The Cruel Way: Switzerland to Afghanistan in a Ford, 1939*, Ella Maillart writes: 'It reminded Christina of another shouting scene in her home some fifteen years ago. Her grandfather came out of the room in which he had received a certain Adolf Hitler, complaining with his hands over his ears: "*Um Gottes Willen*, why must the man shout like that all the time?"' p. 66. Translation Ella Maillart.

29 Alexis Schwarzenbach, '*Hitler und wir*', *tachles* magazine, 10 December 2021.

30 Joseph Roth, 'The Myth of the German Soul', in *Report from a Parisian Paradise: Essays from France 1925–1939*, p. 235, translated by Michael Hofmann (New York: Norton, 2003).

31 Oskar Panizza, 'Bayreuth und die Homosexualität', *Die Gesellschaft*, 11, no. 1 (1895).

32 Interview with Dr. Kevin Clarke, curator Siegfried Wagner exhibition, Schwules Museum, Berlin. http://www.wagneropera.net/interviews/kevin-clarke-interview-siegfried-wagner.htm

33 Cited in an interview with Dr. Kevin Clarke, Ibid.

34 Áine Sheil, 'Performances of Victory in Wagner Reception', in *Performance in a Militarized Culture*, edited by Sara Brady and Lindsey Mantoan (Abingdon: Routledge, 2018), p. 106.

35 Interview with Dr. Kevin Clarke.

36 AS, *Lyric Novella*, translated by Lucy Renner Jones, pp. 14–15.

37 AS letter to Ernst Merz, 3 August 1925. Ernst Merz Archive. SLA.

38 Emmy Krüger, 29–30 July 1925, Tagebücher, Emmy Krüger Archive. MLM.

39 Letter from AS to Clara Wille-von Bismarck, 15 August 1925. 161.3. Schwarzenbach Archives. ZBZ.

40 AS letter to Dominique Schlumberger, 12 July 1927. SLA.

41 Alexis Schwarzenbach, *Die Geborene*, pp. 221–2.

42 AS letters to Ernst Merz, 11 and 19 October, 1925. Ernst Merz Archive. SLA.

43 AS letter to Jacqueline Nougarède, undated letter 1930? SLA.
44 Areti Georgiadou in conversation with Ella Maillart, cited in *Das Leben zerfetzt sich mir*, p. 36.
45 AS, 'Über meine Mutter zu schreiben, ist der Anfang aller Dinge', 24 November 1935. 190.8. Schwarzenbach Archives. ZBZ.
46 Ernst Merz Archive. SLA.
47 AS letter to Ernst Merz, 12 February 1926. Ernst Merz Archive. SLA.
48 Afterword by Roger Perret to AS, *Lyric Novella* in English translation (Calcutta: Seagull Books, 2011), p. 89.
49 Ernst Merz, *Meine Beziehungen zu Annemarie Schwarzenbach*, p. 3. SLA.
50 Peter Gay, *Weimar Culture: The Outsider as Insider*, p. 51.
51 AS, '*Zur Mädchenfrage*' in *Der Wandervogel*, issue 3–4, October 1925.
52 Ibid.
53 Annemarie took the same dim view of female achievement and staying power in a letter to Albrecht Haushofer, 21 December 1930. SLA.
54 AS, '*Pariser Novelle III*', p. 8. SLA.
55 AS, *Das Buch von der Schweiz, Süd und Ost*.
56 Ernst Merz, *Tradition und Einkehr* (Amsterdam: Castrum Peregrini, 1985), p. 85.
57 'Miro tells a funny gay story from her childhood; with a maths teacher. Would make a fine Colette-style novella.' Klaus Mann, 10 July 1937, *Tagebücher*.
58 AS correspondence with George Reinhart-Schwarzenbach, Georg Reinhart Archive, Stadtbibliothek Winterthur.
59 Areti Georgiadou, *Das Leben zerfetzt sich mir*, p. 34.
60 AS letter from Fetan to Suzanne Öhman-Schwarzenbach, 3 November 1927, 186.1. Schwarzenbach Archives. ZBZ.
61 scr F RS XXVII 88 and scr F RS XVII 89, Renée Schwarzenbach-Wille Archives. ZBZ. Alexis Schwarzenbach, *Die Geborene*, pp. 224–5.
62 AS, *Friends of Bernhard*, pp. 10–11.
63 AS letter to Dominique Schlumberger, 19 September 1927. SLA.
64 AS letter to Anita Forrer, 26 November 1938. SLA.
65 Ernst Merz, *Tradition und Einkehr*, p. 89.
66 AS letter to Ernst Merz, 6 August 1928, Ernst Merz Archive. SLA.

2. Women on the Left Bank

1 Gundalena v. Weizsäcker, AS's cousin and fellow student, cited in Areti Georgiadou, *Das Leben zerfetzt sich mir*, p. 67.
2 AS in an undated letter [1930?] to Jacqueline Nougarède. SLA.
3 Carl Burckhardt Archive. BUL. See '*Briefe von Annemarie Schwarzenbach an Carl Jacob Burckhardt: Einleitung, Edition und Kommentar von Andreas Tobler*' in *Annemarie Schwarzenbach: Analysen und Erstdrucke* (Eds. Fähnders & Rohlf), pp. 229–78.
4 AS letter to Erika Mann, 28 October 1930, *Wir werden es schon zuwege bringen, das Leben*, p. 26.

5 Haushofer and his wife committed suicide shortly after the end of the war. See Philippe Sands' *East West Street* (London: Weidenfeld & Nicolson, 2017), p. 298.

6 Sonnet XXXIX '*Schuld*', *Moabiter Sonette*, Albrecht Haushofer. My translation.

7 Clara Wille-von Bismarck Diary, 4 October 1929. 158.1. Schwarzenbach Archives. ZBZ.

8 Sonnet LXXIII '*Traumgesicht*', *Moabiter Sonette*, Albrecht Haushofer. My translation.

9 AS letter to Dominique Schlumberger, 15 January 1928. SLA.

10 Ibid., 30 July 1928. SLA.

11 Joseph Roth, *Report from a Parisian Paradise*, pp. 159–60, translated by Michael Hofmann.

12 AS, 'Paris III', p. 1 / p. 15. SLA.

13 Maren Richter, '*Aber ich habe mich nicht entmutigen lassen*', p. 45.

14 Ibid., p. 19.

15 Ibid., p. 38. Perhaps derived from Enzio (Heinz), King of Sardinia (c.1220–1272), the illegitimate son of Friedrich II, whose afterlife in 'Canzoni di re Enzio' (1909) by Italian poet Giovanni Pascoli gave the dead king the allure of romantic sadness.

16 AS letter to Jacqueline Nougarède, 3 October 1929. SLA.

17 Ibid., 29 December 1939. SLA.

18 Ibid., 31 October 1931[?]. SLA.

19 Dominique Schlumberger, '*Les divers procédés du film parlant.*' *La revue du cinéma*, 2, no. 9 (April 1930). AS review of *Emil und die Detektive* published in *NZZ*, 22 November 1929.

20 AS letter to Dominique Schlumberger, 17 and 31 August 1929. SLA.

21 See Ilse Kokula's interviews with survivors of the twenties.

22 AS letter to Ernst Merz, 23 December 1928. SLA.

23 AS, 'Paris III', p. 19. SLA.

24 AS, '*Pariser Novelle I*', p. 12. SLA.

25 See AS, '*Aus dem 30 jährigen Krieg*', a novella dated September–November 1928 and '*Das Märchen von der gefangenen Prinzessin*', dated January 1929, Paris. SLA.

26 AS, *Pariser Novelle I*, p. 15. SLA.

27 AS, *Pariser Novelle II*, p. 13. SLA.

28 AS letter to Jacqueline Nougarède, 11 September 1929. SLA.

29 AS, *Pariser Novelle II*, p. 5. SLA.

30 Ibid., p. 11.

31 Ibid., p. 6.

32 Ibid., p. 9.

33 Ibid., p. 8.

34 Ibid., p. 12.

35 AS, *Paris III*, p. 15. SLA.

36 Ibid., p. 23.

37 '*Dass der Junge kein Junge ist, begreife ich vollkommen*', AS in a letter to Erika Mann, 20 October 1930, *Wir werden es schon zuwege bringen, das Leben*, p. 23.

38 Virginia Woolf in a letter to her nephew Quentin Bell, 1 November 1928.

39 Shari Benstock, *Women of the Left Bank*, p. 115.

40 Neil Miller, *Out of the Past: Gay and Lesbian History from 1869 to the Present*, pp. 190–1.

41 See Alexis Schwarzenbach's Afterword to Annemarie Schwarzenbach, *Eine Frau zu Sehen*, pp. 75–6.

42 Klaus Mann, *Treffpunkt im Unendlichen*, p. 206.

43 AS letter to Ernst Merz, 9 June 1929. Ernst Merz Archive. SLA.

44 Renée Schwarzenbach letter to Dominique Schlumberger, 30 October 1929. Annemarie Schwarzenbach Archive. SLA.

45 Ibid.

46 AS letter to Jacqueline Nougarède, 11 September 1929. SLA.

47 Ruth Landshoff-Yorck, 'Autobiography', unpublished typescript, p. 192. Ruth Landshoff-Yorck Archive. HGARC.

48 Ibid., p. 114.

49 Ruth Landshoff-Yorck, 'Autobiography', p. 289. Ruth Landshoff-Yorck Archive. HGARC.

50 'The Life of a Dancer', p. 14. Ruth Landshoff-Yorck Archive. HGARC.

51 Klaus Mann, *Treffpunkt im Unendlichen*, p. 85.

52 Stefan Grossmann, '*Lenas Glück und Ende ...*' (1929), undated newspaper clipping in the German Dance Archive, Cologne. Cited in Walter Fähnders' Afterword to Ruth Landshoff-Yorck, *Roman einer Tänzerin*, p. 120.

53 AS, *Pariser Novelle II*. SLA. My translation.

3. Breaking the Threads

1 'Annemarie' included in *Klatsch, Rhum und klein Feuer*, Ruth Landshoff-Yorck Archive. HGARC.

2 Ibid.

3 Published in *NZZ*, 13 October 1929. SLA.

4 Published in *NZZ*, 22 November 1929. SLA.

5 AS to Dominique Schlumberger, 25 November 1929. SLA.

6 AS letter to Jacqueline Nougarède, 22 September 1929. SLA.

7 Claude Bourdet letter to his mother, Catherine Pozzi, 6 June 1930, cited in *Lettres à Claude Bourdet (1931–1938)*, p. 6.

8 Claude Bourdet papers, cited in Dominique Laure Miermont, *Annemarie Schwarzenbach ou le mal d'Europe*, pp. 56–7.

9 Emmy Krüger in her diary mentions Annemarie in connection with Vollmoeller as early as 28 June 1929, Emmy Krüger Archive. MLM.

10 AS letter to Dominique Schlumberger, 22 January 1930. SLA.

11 As she was in 1927, by the photographers Zander and Labisch, a photo which resurfaced to mark the centenary of the 1920s on the front page of *Die Zeit*, 23 January 2020.

12 'Autobiography', pp. 116 and 172. HGARC.
13 'Annemarie', pp. 1–2, text in English by Ruth Landshoff-Yorck, Ruth Landshoff-Yorck Archives. Included in *Klatsch, Ruhm und kleine Feuer*, p. 161. HGARC.
14 AS to Ernst Merz, 6 January 1929. Merz Archive. SLA.
15 Annemarie Schwarzenbach, *Eine Frau zu sehen* (Zurich: Kein & Aber, 2008), p. 1.
16 Ibid., p. 6.
17 'Annemarie', p. 4. Ruth Landshoff-Yorck Archive. HGARC.
18 'Autobiography', p. 201. HGARC.
19 Géza von Cziffra, *Kauf dir einen bunten Luftballon: Erinnerungen an Götter und Halbgötter* (Munich: Herbig, 1975), p. 89.
20 Ruth Landshoff Archive. DLA. See also Jan Burger, et al., *Im Schattenreich der wilden Zwanziger: Fotografien von Karl Vollmoeller aus dem Nachlass von Ruth Landshoff-Yorck* (Marbach am Neckar: Deutsche Schillergesellschaft, 2017).
21 Emmy Krüger diary, 27 September 1930. Emmy Krüger Archive. MLM.
22 AS letter to Erika Mann, [early October 1930], Erika Mann Archive. MLM.
23 Erika Mann deposition, 20 November 1934, Erika Mann file, Zurich City Police, V.E. c. 63, Folder 341, Zurich City Archives. Cited in Alexis Schwarzenbach, *Die Geborene*, p. 274.
24 *Ein Reisefilm unter der Führung von Erika Mann: Werbefilm für die Hapag-Lloyd 1928*, Austrian Film Museum, Vienna.
25 Cited in Frederic Spotts, *Cursed Legacy: The Tragic Life of Klaus Mann*, p. 258.
26 Elisabeth Tworek, *Literarisches München zur Zeit von Thomas Mann*, pp. 32–3.
27 AS letter to Erika Mann, [8 December 1930], Erika Mann Archive. MLM.
28 V.S. Pritchett, *At Home and Abroad*, p. 177.
29 AS letter to Erika Mann, 20 October 1930, Erika Mann Archive. MLM.
30 AS letter to Erika Mann, 15 October 1930, Erika Mann Archive. MLM.
31 AS letter to Erika Mann, [early October 1930], *Wir werden es schon zuwege bringen, das Leben*, p. 19.
32 Ibid., [September/October 1930], p. 17.
33 Ibid., 20 November 1930, p. 34.
34 Ibid., 20 October 1930, pp. 23–4.
35 Ibid., pp. 26–7. The princelings were Alfonso (b. 1907), Jaime (b. 1908) and little Gonzalo (b. 1914).
36 Ibid., 8 December 1930, pp. 38–9.
37 Ibid., [16 November 1930], pp. 29–30.
38 Ibid., 15 October 1930, *Wir werden es schon zuwege bringen, das Leben*, pp. 21–2.
39 Anthony Heilbut, *Thomas Mann: Eros and Literature*, p. 442.
40 Klaus Mann, *The Turning Point*, p. 86.
41 Peter Gay, *Weimar Culture: The Outsider as Insider*, p. xiii.
42 Prior to 1955, this could be achieved in seven semesters at Zurich University.
43 Erika Mann and Klaus Mann, *Das Buch von der Riviera*, published in 1931 and still in print.
44 AS, '*Brief von der Côte d'Azur*', 28 June 1931 in the *NZZ*. SLA.

45 Sybille Bedford, *As it Was: Pleasures, Landscapes and Justice* (London: Sinclair-Stevenson, 1990), p. 9.

46 Klaus Mann, *Treffpunkt im Unendlichen*, p. 18.

47 Ibid., p. 205.

48 Sybille Bedford's *A Compass Error* (London: Daunt Books, 2011), p. 44.

49 AS letter to Erika Mann, 25 January 1931, *Wir werden es schon zuwege bringen, das Leben*, p. 45.

50 Wilhelm Speyer, *Die Goldene Horde*, p. 105.

51 AS letter to Erika Mann, 18 August 1931, Erika Mann Archive. MLM.

52 AS letter to Erika Mann, [August 1931], *Wir werden es schon zuwege bringen, das Leben*, p. 56.

53 AS letter to Renée Schwarzenbach-Wille, [June 1931]. 190.8. Schwarzenbach Archives. ZBZ.

54 AS letter to Albrecht Haushofer, 30 November 1930. SLA.

55 AS letter to Erika Mann, 20 November 1930, *Wir werden es schon zuwege bringen, das Leben*, pp. 32–3.

56 AS, *Freunde um Bernhard*, p. 97.

57 Ibid., p. 170.

58 Ibid., p. 176.

59 AS letter to Erika Mann, May 1931, *Wir werden es schon zuwege bringen, das Leben*, p. 52.

60 'Annemarie', a text in English by Ruth Landshoff-Yorck, Ruth Landshoff-Yorck Archive. HGARC.

61 Areti Georgiadou, *Das Leben zerfetzt sich mir*, p. 52.

62 *'Seit ich von Berlin weg bin, schlafe ich täglich einige Stunden länger.'* AS letter to Hans Schwarzenbach, 7 May [1931]. 201.2. Schwarzenbach Archives. ZBZ.

4. Closet of Selves

1 Epigraph to chapter 4 reproduced with the generous permission of the Truman Capote Literary Trust.

2 Karola Gramann and Heidi Schlüpmann, interview with Hertha Thiele, in *Frauen und Film*, no. 28, 1981.

3 Like Annemarie herself, *Mädchen in Uniform* was resurrected from oblivion by German feminists in the 1970s.

4 Karola Gramann and Heidi Schlüpmann, interview with Hertha Thiele, in *Frauen und Film*, no. 28, 1981.

5 AS letter to Erika Mann, [September/October 1931], *Wir werden es schon zuwege bringen, das Leben*, p. 65.

6 Sybille Bedford, *Aldous Huxley: Volume 1, 1894–1939*, p. 255.

7 Klaus Mann, *The Turning Point*, p. 239.

8 Curt Moreck (pseudonym for the cultural critic Konrad Haemmerling), Führer durch das 'lasterhafte' Berlin (1931), cited at Brendan Nash's site, http://www.cabaret-berlin.com/?p=824, to which I am indebted.

9   Klaus Mann, 18 October 1931, *Tagebücher*.
10 Erich Kästner, lyrics of 'Fin de Siècle Rag'.
11 'Autobiography', unpublished typescript by Ruth Landshoff-Yorck, p. 260. HGARC.
12 Ibid., p. 194. HGARC.
13 Mel Gordon, *Voluptuous Panic: The Erotic World of Weimar Berlin*, p. 243.
14 Louise Brooks, 'On Making Pabst's Lulu' in *Women and the Cinema*, eds. Karyn Kay and Gerald Peary (New York: E.P. Dutton, 1977), p. 81.
15 AS letter to Erika Mann, [15 October 1931], *Wir werden es schon zuwege bringen, das Leben*, p. 65.
16 Ibid., [30 October 1931].
17 'Annemarie', p. 7, Ruth Landshoff Archive. HGARC.
18 AS letter to Erika Mann, [30 October 1931], *Wir werden es schon zuwege bringen, das Leben*, p. 66.
19 '*Meine 17jährigen Komplexe*', AS letter to Erika Mann, 9 November 1931, *Wir werden es schon zuwege bringen, das Leben*, p. 67.
20 '*Masslos verwöhnt sein*', AS letter to Erika Mann, 9 November 1931, *Wir werden es schon zuwege bringen, das Leben*, p. 67.
21 AS letter to Anita Forrer, 26 November 1938. SLA.
22 I have taken some liberties with the translation of '*Es ist hundekalt u. feucht in den hübschen Herbstwäldern hier*', AS letter to Erika Mann, 9 November 1931, *Wir werden es schon zuwege bringen, das Leben*, p. 68.
23 See Michelle Minden, '"*Die Welt ist mir vollständig unbegreiflich*": *Zum Verlorensein des Individuums in Leben und Werk der Schweizer Autorin Annemarie Schwarzenbach*', University of Luxemburg, April 2015.
24 AS letter to Charles Clerc, 15 June 1933, cited in Roger Perret's Afterword to *Lyric Novella*, p. 87.
25 AS, *Lyric Novella*, pp. 5–6.
26 See Roger Perret's excellent Afterword to the English translation, *Lyric Novella*, translated by Lucy Renner Jones / Nachwort zur *Lyrischen Novelle*. 'Ernst, Würde und Glück des Daseins' (Basel: Lenos Verlag, 2008).
27 Ibid., p. 38.
28 AS, *Lyric Novella*, p. 57.
29 Klaus Mann, 'Zwei kleiner Bücher', *Basler National-Zeitung*, 14 May 1933.
30 AS letter to Erika Mann, [December 1931], *Wir werden es schon zuwege bringen, das Leben*, p. 70.
31 Areti Georgiadou interview with Marianne Feilchenfeldt-Breslauer, Zurich 1992, cited in *Das Leben zerfetzt sich mich*, pp. 105–6.
32 Klaus Mann, *The Turning Point*, p. 187.
33 Turin's *Turksib* influenced the earliest video poem, also a documentary on the railways, *The Night Mail* (1936), with text by W.H. Auden and music by Benjamin Britten. See Henry K. Miller's introduction to both documentaries: https://vimeo.com/238965479.

34 AS letter to Erika Mann, [mid-January 1932], *Wir werden es schon zuwege bringen, das Leben*, p. 74.

35 AS, 'Besuch in den Ufa-Ateliers', *Insel Europa: Reportagen und Feuilletons 1930–1942*, p. 21.

36 AS, 'Filmregie und Filmmanuskript', *Insel Europa: Reportagen und Feuilletons 1930–1942*, p. 29.

37 AS letter to Erika Mann, 26 December 1931, *Wir werden es schon zuwege bringen, das Leben*, p. 71.

38 Ibid., 3 January 1932, p. 73.

39 Letter from Clara Wille to her daughter Isi, 26 July 1932. 158.2. Schwarzenbach Archives. ZBZ.

40 Klaus Mann, *The Turning Point*, p. 251.

41 Ibid., p. 257.

42 The new year began for Klaus with a pick-up on Lenbachplatz in the company of Babs, who played the lead in Klaus's adaptation of Cocteau's *Les enfants terribles*. The boy they picked up was called 'Narciss' and they took him back to Babs' place for a threesome. 'Quite funny and rough, but exciting.' Klaus Mann, 2 January 1932, *Tagebücher*.

43 Klaus Mann, *The Turning Point*, p. 187.

44 Ibid., p. 188.

45 AS letter to Erika Mann, [27 March 1932], 'Sonst lockt mich Berlin nicht sehr …', *Wir werden es schon zuwege bringen, das Leben*, p. 76.

46 AS letter to Claude Bourdet, 4 July 1932, *Lettres à Claude Bourdet 1931–1938*, p. 17.

47 AS letter to Erika Mann, [23 June 1932], *Wir werden es schon zuwege bringen, das Leben*, p. 78.

48 Matthias's wife left him and married the writer Kurt Tucholsky, whose short novel *Rheinsberg* plays a background role in Annemarie's *Lyric Novella*.

49 AS letter to Erika Mann, [23 June 1932], *Wir werden es schon zuwege bringen, das Leben*, p. 78.

50 AS letter to Erika, [5 November 1932], *Wir werden es schon zuwege bringen, das Leben*, p. 81.

51 Klaus Mann, 'Nördlicher Sommer', in *Die Neuen Eltern*, pp. 412–13.

52 Erika Mann, 'Fremdes Nordland', in *Blitze überm Ozean*, pp. 101–3.

53 Klaus Mann, 28 July 1932, *Tagebücher*.

54 Klaus Mann, *Flucht in den Norden*, p. 8.

55 His marriage to Swedish Countess Sigrid Eva Gabriella Oxenstierna lasted six years.

56 Klaus met his old love Aminoff again in New York at the beginning of the war, 'in a semi-gay little French restaurant on Third Avenue … accordion music, camp comic turns'. The air had gone out of it.

57 Ulrich Wille Jr. letter to Carl Jacob Burckhardt, 20 November 1931, Carl Burckhardt Archive. BUL.

58 Ella Maillart, *The Cruel Way*, p. 75.

59 'Annemarie', Ruth Landshoff Archive. HGARC.

60 AS letter to Erika Mann, 1 November 1932, *Wir werden es schon zuwege bringen, das Leben*, p. 80.

61 Dr. Oscar Forel to Dr. Theodor Hämmerli, 20 December 1935. 190.8. Schwarzenbach Archives. ZBZ.

62 'Annemarie', p. 6, Ruth Landshoff Archive. HGARC.

63 AS to Erika Mann, 6 January 1933, Erika Mann Archive. MLM.

64 Cited by Barbara Ulrich in her essay 'The Women of Weimar', extracted from *The Hot Girls of Weimar Berlin*, https://www.thefreelibrary.com/The+women+ of+Weimar.+(Essay).-a096223443

65 'Annemarie', p. 7, Ruth Landshoff Archive. HGARC. Landshoff herself appears not to have drunk alcohol.

66 AS letter to Erika Mann, [December 1931], *Wir werden es schon zuwege bringen, das Leben*, p. 70.

67 Ibid., [24 November 1932], p. 82.

68 Ibid., [December 1931], p. 70.

69 'Autobiography', unpublished typescript by Ruth Landshoff-Yorck, pp. 247–50. HGARC.

70 Ibid.

71 Marianne Feilchenfeldt-Breslauer, *Bilder meines Lebens* (Wadenswil, 2009), p. 136.

72 Interview with Breslauer cited in Dominique Laure Miermont, *Annemarie Schwarzenbach ou le mal d'Europe*, p. 9.

73 Clara Wille-von Bismarck diary, December 1932. 158.2. Schwarzenbach Archives. ZBZ.

74 Clara Wille in a letter to her sister Isi, 1 January 1933, cited in Alexis Schwarzenbach, *Die Geborene*, p. 264.

75 Kurt Wanner and Marianne Breslauer, *Wo ich mich leichter fühle als anderswo*, pp. 36–7.

76 Klaus Mann, 25 and 26 January 1933, *Tagebücher*.

77 AS, *Lettres à Claude Bourdet 1931–1938*, p. 23.

78 Roger Perret, Afterword to *Lyric Novella*, p. 128.

79 AS, *Romane (Lyrische Novelle, Flucht nach oben, Tod in Persien)*, pp. 100–1.

80 AS, *Flucht nach oben*, p. 42.

81 Perhaps based on Annemarie's friend Ruth von Morgen.

82 AS, *Flucht nach oben*, pp. 163–6.

83 Ibid., p. 54

84 Ibid., p. 163

85 Klaus Mann, 'Zwei kleiner Bücher', *Basler National-Zeitung*, 14 May 1933.

86 Klaus Mann, *The Turning Point*, pp. 236–7.

87 Klaus Mann, 30 January 1933, *Tagebücher*.

88 Roger Perret's Afterword to *Lyric Novella*, p. 138.

89 Twelve years later in 1944, her distant relative Gottfried Bismarck was one of the conspirators in the 20 July plot to assassinate Hitler. '… a Bismarck trying

to kill Hitler would not sound too good, even *they* realise that.' *The Berlin Diaries of Marie Vassiltchikov* (Munich: Deutscher Taschenbuch Verlag, 1988), p. 217.

90 Cited in Roger Perret's Afterword to *Lyric Novella*, p. 120.

91 AS, *Lyric Novella*, p. 84.

5. Pilgrim Soul

1 Erika Mann letter to Thomas Mann, 4 June 1933, Erika Mann, *Mein Vater, der Zauberer*, p. 79.

2 Alexis Schwarzenbach, *Die Geborene*, p. 268.

3 Alexis Schwarzenbach, 'Hitler und wir', *tachles* magazine, 10 December 2021.

4 'Über Moral und Politik', Clara Wille-von Bismarck. 158.2.a. Schwarzenbach Archives. ZBZ.

5 'Warten wir ab, was daraus wird...' Typoskript von Clara Wille betr. Machtübernahme von Adolf Hitler. 158.2.a. Schwarzenbach Archives. ZBZ.

6 Renée Schwarzenbach letter to her daughter Suzanne, 3 April 1933. 185.6. Schwarzenbach Archives. ZBZ.

7 Maren Richter, *'Aber ich habe mich nicht entmutigen lassen'*, p. 57.

8 Erika Mann letter to Eva Herrmann, 18 April 1933, *Briefe und Antworten*, p. 36.

9 Maren Richter, *'Aber ich habe mich nicht entmutigen lassen'*, p. 58.

10 AS letter to Erika Mann, 19 January 1933, *Wir werden es schon zuwege bringen, das Leben*, p. 84.

11 Marianne Feilchenfeldt-Breslauer, *Bilder meines Lebens*, p. 132.

12 Roger Perret, Afterword to AS, *Bei diesem Regen*, p. 225.

13 Christopher Isherwood to Klaus Mann, May 10 [1935], Klaus Mann Archive. MLM.

14 Klaus Mann, 6 May 1933, *Tagebücher*.

15 Thomas Mann diary, 15 March 1933, *Diaries 1918–1939*.

16 Ibid., 31 December 1933.

17 Erika Mann letter to Klaus Mann, 12 April 1933. Erika Mann Archive. MLM.

18 AS letter to Claude Bourdet, [16 April 1933], *Lettres à Claude Bourdet 1931–1938*, pp. 26–7.

19 Ibid., 4 May 1933, pp. 29–30.

20 Andreas Tobler, '"Beteiligt sind wir alle": Annemarie Schwarzenbach *und* Die Sammlung', *Wendepunkte – Tournants, Jahrbuch für Internationale Germanistik, Reihe A, Band 91*, 2008.

21 Klaus Mann, 3 May 1933, *Tagebücher*.

22 Sybille Bedford, *Aldous Huxley: Volume 1, 1894–1939*, p. 276.

23 Joseph Roth, 'The Auto-da-Fé of the Mind' in *What I Saw: Reports from Berlin 1920–1933*, translated by Michael Hofmann, p. 207.

24 Christopher Isherwood, *Christopher and his Kind* (New York: Farrar, Straus and Giroux, 1976), pp. 128–9.

25 Marianne Feilchenfeldt-Breslauer interview with Dominique Laure Miermont, 8 January 1989, cited in *Annemarie Schwarzenbach ou le mal d'Europe*, p. 121.

26 AS, 'Vom Mittelmeer zum Atlantischen Ozean', *Insel Europa: Reportagen und Feuilletons 1930–1942*, p. 45.

27 Ibid., p. 48. It is tempting to make a broader link between Schwarzenbach's lesbianism, her interest in gypsy culture and her nomadism. See Kirstie Blair, 'Gypsies and Lesbian Desire: Vita Sackville-West, Violet Trefusis, and Virginia Woolf', *Twentieth Century Literature*, 50, no. 2, Summer 2004.

28 Joseph Roth, *What I Saw: Reports from Berlin 1920–1933*, p. 19.

29 AS, 'Vom Mittelmeer zum Atlantischen Ozean', *Insel Europa: Reportagen und Feuilletons 1930–1942*, pp. 49–50.

30 AS, 'Kinder in der Pyrenäen', *Zürcher Illustrierte*, no. 40, 6 October 1933.

31 Nina Zimmer and Martin Waldmeier, *Annemarie Schwarzenbach als Fotografin*, p. 12.

32 See Walter Fähnders and Andreas Tobler, 'Briefe von Annemarie Schwarzenbach an Otto Kleiber aus den Jahren 1933–1942', in *Zeitschrift für Germanistik* 2/2006, and Otto Kleiber Archive. BUL.

33 Marianne Feilchenfeldt-Breslauer, *Bilder meines Lebens*, pp. 134–6. At the same time all public expressions of homosexuality were officially banned and punishable by law, enacted on 23 February 1933.

34 Marianne Feilchenfeldt-Breslauer interview with Carole Bonstein, *Une Suisse rebelle*. TSR/Arte, 2000.

35 Catherine Pozzi letter to her son, Claude Bourdet, 14 June 1933, cited in *Lettres à Claude Bourdet*, p. 34.

36 Klaus Mann, 23 June 1933, *Tagebücher*.

37 '*Garantie betreffend der Zeitschrift* Die Sammlung', 14 June 1933, Klaus Mann Archive. MLM.

38 Klaus Mann, *The Turning Point*, p. 269.

39 Gottfried Benn, *Doppelleben* (Wiesbaden: Limes Verlag, 1950).

40 Klaus Mann, *The Turning Point*, p. 268.

41 Thomas Mann, Wednesday 11 October 1933, *Tagebücher 1933–1934*. This dinner must have been on the evening of 10 October, as she was in Geneva with Claude Bourdet on 11 October.

42 See note 3 to Annemarie's letter to Claude Bourdet, 4 October 1933, *Lettres à Claude Bourdet*, p. 45. In 1935 Bourdet married Ida Adamoff.

43 AS, 'Neben dem Orient-Express', *National-Zeitung*, 18 July 1939, reprinted in *Orientreisen: Reportagen aus der Fremde*, p. 16.

44 Ibid., p. 17.

45 AS, *Hiver au Proche-Orient* (Paris: Payot, 2006), p. 26.

46 AS letter to Claude Bourdet, 1 November 1933, *Lettres à Claude Bourdet*, p. 45.

47 AS 'Plaza Hotel', *National-Zeitung*, 1 August 1940, reprinted in *Orientreisen: Reportagen aus der Fremde*, p. 9.

48 AS letter to Claude Bourdet, 1 November 1933, *Lettres à Claude Bourdet*, p. 46.

49 Ibid.

50 Flavia Amabile and Marco Tosatti, *Das Hotel von Aleppo; Die Geschichte eines Landes und einer Familie* (Munich: btb Verlag, 2018), p. 24.

51 AS letter to Klaus Mann, 6 December 1933, *Wir werden es schon zuwege bringen, das Leben*, pp. 104–5.

52 AS, 'Markt in Rihanie', *National-Zeitung*, 3 January 1934.

53 AS, 'Schrecken der orientalischen Landstrassen', *Orientreisen: Reportagen aus der Fremde*, p. 72.

54 AS letter to Claude Bourdet, 9 December 1933, *Lettres à Claude Bourdet*, p. 48.

55 AS, *An den äussersten Flüssen des Paradieses*, ed. Roger Perret, p. 53.

56 AS, *La Vallée heureuse/Das glückliche Tal*, chapter IV.

57 '…*nach dem kalten amerikanischen Norden*', AS letter to Klaus Mann, [January 1934], *Wir werden es schon zuwege bringen, das Leben*, p. 106. '*J'ai été déçue et triste chez les Américains a Rihanie qui, tout en étant charmants, ne sommes pas de notre coeur.*' AS letter to Claude Bourdet, [11 January 1934], *Lettres à Claude Bourdet*, p. 52.

58 AS letter to Klaus Mann, [January 1934], *Wir werden es schon zuwege bringen, das Leben*, p. 106.

59 'Während den 6 Wochen die sie allein in Baghdad verbrachte…' Typescript Dr. Forel, Prangins, to Dr. Hämmerli, 20 December 1935. 190.8. Schwarzenbach Archives. ZBZ.

60 AS, *Hiver au Proche-Orient*, p. 110.

61 Ibid., p. 115.

62 AS, 'Plaza Hotel', *National-Zeitung*, 1 August 1940, reprinted in *Orientreisen: Reportagen aus der Fremde*, p. 11.

63 Preface by A.J. Arberry to Gertrude Bell's *Persian Pictures*, p. viii.

64 Gertrude Bell, *Palace and Mosque at Ukhaidir: A Study in Early Mohammadan Architecture* (Oxford: Clarendon Press, 1914).

65 See Gertrude Bell, *A Woman in Arabia: The Writings of the Queen of the Desert*, selected and introduced by Georgian Howell, xix.

66 AS, *Hiver au Proche-Orient*, p. 139.

67 Gertrude Bell, *A Woman in Arabia: The Writings of the Queen of the Desert*, p. 54.

68 Although in an 8 February 1934 letter to Claude Bourdet she was somewhat mocking towards the German work ethic, now at the service of Hitler.

69 '… *ich habe mich ziemlich __vergiftet__ dies Mal…*', AS letter to Klaus Mann, 8 February 1934, *Wir werden es schon zuwege bringen, das Leben*, p. 108.

70 AS, 'Spuren des alten Persien', *National-Zeitung*, 2 January 1936.

71 Freya Stark, *The Valleys of the Assassins and Other Persian Travels* (New York: Random House, 2001), p. 13.

72 Gertrude Bell, *A Woman in Arabia: The Writings of the Queen of the Desert*, p. 91.

73 *Exploring Iran: The Photography of Erich F. Schmidt, 1930–40*, ed. Ayşe Gürsan-Salzmann (Penn Museum, 2007).

74 AS Archive. SLA.

75 AS, 'Alexanders Eroberung von Persien', *Atlantis*, October 1936.

76 Gertrude Bell, *Persian Pictures*, p. 15.

77 AS, 'Alexanders Eroberung von Persien', *Atlantis*, October 1936.

78 Allusion to the Foundation of Mrs. William Boyce Thompson, part-underwriting the expedition at Rhages.

79 AS, 'Gelernte und ungelernte Schatzgräber', *Zürcher Illustrierte*, 17 May 1935.

80 Ibid.

81 AS letter to Klaus Mann, 4 April 1934, *Wir werden es schon zuwege bringen, das Leben*, p. 111.

82 'Citizens, peasants and nomads of Iran'/'Citadins, paysans et nomads d'Iran', in AS, *La Quête du Réel*, p. 198, and in *National-Zeitung*, 10 December 1935.

83 AS letter to Claude Bourdet, 22 May 1934, *Lettres à Claude Bourdet*, p. 65.

84 AS, 'A Christian city in the heart of Persia'/'Une cité chrétienne au cœur de la perse', *Annemarie Schwarzenbach: de monde en monde*, p. 70, and in *National-Zeitung*, 14 November 1935.

85 Gertrude Bell, *Persian Pictures*, p. 18.

86 AS, 'Nachbarstädte', *National-Zeitung*, 22 November 1934.

87 AS, 'Imamzade Haschim', *National-Zeitung*, 12 April 1934.

88 AS, *Tod in Persien*, p. 24.

89 '*Je travaille, moi, à m'exprimer. À trouver la sûreté de style pour le "Tagebuch" et pour les articles. À être nette, claire, objective.*' AS letter to Claude Bourdet, 2 February 1934, *Lettres à Claude Bourdet*, p. 54.

90 V.S. Pritchett, *At Home and Abroad*, p. 18.

91 Hubert Butler, 'Lament for Archaeology', in *Escape from the Anthill* (Mullingar: The Lilliput Press, 1985), p. 244.

92 In contrast to Gertrude Bell, Annemarie was spartan. Bell carried 'Egyptian cigarettes, insect powder, a Wedgwood dinner service, silver candlesticks and hairbrushes, crystal glasses, linen and blankets, folding tables, and a comfortable chair'. Gertrude Bell, *A Woman in Arabia: The Writings of the Queen of the Desert*, p. 67.

93 AS, *Death in Persia*, p. 62.

94 Vita Sackville-West, *Passenger to Tehran* (New York: Tauris Parke, 2007), p. 62.

6. Lavender Marriages

1 Thomas Mann, 28 April 1934, *Tagebücher 1933–1934*.
2 AS letter to Claude Bourdet, 4 May 1934, *Lettres à Claude Bourdet*, pp. 63–4.
3 Claude Bourdet, '*Annemarie Schwarzenbach*', undated manuscript annexe to *Lettres à Claude Bourdet*, p. 118.
4 AS letter to Klaus Mann, [7 May 1934], *Wir werden es schon zuwege bringen, das Leben*, p. 112.
5 Martha Gellhorn, 'The Thirties', *Granta*, 30 June 1988.
6 Emmy Krüger, May ? 1934, Tagebücher, Emmy Krüger Archive. MLM.
7 Erika Mann deposition, 20 November 1934, Erika Mann file, Zurich City Police, V.E.c. 63, Folder 341, Zurich City Archives. Cited in Alexis Schwarzenbach, *Die Geborene*, p. 274.
8 Thomas Mann, 24 June 1934, *Tagebücher 1933–1934*.
9 AS letter to Klaus Mann, 8 February 1934, *Wir werden es schon zuwege bringen, das Leben*, p. 109.
10 '*Schweinehund*'.
11 Andreas Tobler, '*"Beteiligt sind wir alle": Annemarie Schwarzenbach und* Die Sammlung', *Wendepunkte – Tournants, Jahrbuch für Internationale Germanistik, Reihe A, Band 91*, 2008, p. 109. See also the report of the German Consulate-General Zurich for 14 August 1934, Bern Embassy file, Volume 1937, in the Political Archive of the Ministry of Foreign Affairs, Berlin.
12 Erika Mann letter to Klaus Mann, [June 1934], Klaus Mann archive. MLM.
13 Andreas Tobler, '*"Beteiligt sind wir alle": Annemarie Schwarzenbach und* Die Sammlung', *Wendepunkte – Tournants, Jahrbuch für Internationale Germanistik, Reihe A, Band 91*, 2008, p. 111. See also the 4 July 1934 exchange between the German Consulate-General Zurich and the German Embassy in Bern, Volume 1937, in the Political Archive of the Ministry of Foreign Affairs, Berlin.
14 '*... der letzte Dreck von einem schmierigen Kerl ist...*' AS letter to Hans Schwarzenbach [early August 1934]. 201.2. Schwarzenbach Archives. ZBZ.
15 Alexis Schwarzenbach, *Die Geborene*, pp. 275–6, based on documents in the Political Archive of the Ministry of Foreign Affairs, Berlin.
16 Thomas Mann, Wednesday 20 June 1934, *Tagebücher 1933–1934*.
17 '*das moralisch Getarnte, immer schon Hitler-Art.*' AS letter to Klaus Mann, 4 July 1934, *Wir werden es schon zuwege bringen, das Leben*, p. 116.
18 Thomas Mann, Thursday 3 August 1934, *Tagebücher 1933–1934*.
19 Figures cited by Roger Perret in his Afterword to AS, *Bei diesem Regen*, p. 219.
20 AS letter to Klaus Mann, 4 July 1934, *Wir werden es schon zuwege bringen, das Leben*, p. 117.
21 Ibid.
22 'Autobiography', unpublished typescript by Ruth Landshoff-Yorck, pp. 247–50. HGARC.

23 AS letter to Claude Bourdet, 22 May 1934, *Lettres à Claude Bourdet*, p. 65.

24 AS letter to Klaus Mann, 8 February 1934, *Wir werden es schon zuwege bringen, das Leben*, p. 109.

25 AS letter to Klaus Mann, 14 July 1934, *Wir werden es schon zuwege bringen, das Leben*, p. 119.

26 Ibid., 5 July 1934.

27 AS letter to Claude Bourdet, 19 August 1934, *Lettres à Claude Bourdet*, p. 72.

28 AS, 'Notizen zum Schriftstellerkongress in Moskau', 19 August 1934, in *Auf der Schattenseite*, p. 39.

29 For reactions to Joris Ivens' documentary film *Indonesia Calling* (1946), see Paul M.M. Doolan, *Collective Memory and the Dutch East Indies: Unremembering Decolonization* (Amsterdam: Amsterdam University Press, 2021), pp. 37–43.

30 AS, 'Notizen zum Schriftstellerkongress in Moskau', 31 August 1934, in *Auf der Schattenseite*, p. 31.

31 '*...im Oktober 1934 fuhr sie nach Tiflis wo ein Arzt ihr gegen die Schmerzen ... zwei Ampullen Dicodid oder Pantopon verschreib.*' Typescript Dr. Forel, Prangins, to Dr. Hämmerli, 20 December 1935. 190.8. Schwarzenbach Archives. ZBZ.

32 AS, 'Regen in Tiflis', *National-Zeitung*, 10 October 1934 and in *Auf der Schattenseite*, p. 63.

33 AS letter to Klaus Mann, 4 November 1934, *Wir werden es schon zuwege bringen, das Leben*, p. 120.

34 AS, *Death in Persia*, p. 57.

35 Ibid., p. 27.

36 AS letter to Claude Bourdet, 24 September 1934, *Lettres à Claude Bourdet*, p. 77.

37 AS, *Death in Persia*, p. 64.

38 Ibid., p. 58.

39 AS letter to Klaus Mann, 4 November 1934, *Wir werden es schon zuwege bringen, das Leben*, p. 121.

40 Dominique Laure Miermont, *Annemarie Schwarzenbach ou le mal d'Europe*, p. 118.

41 Gertrude Bell, *A Woman in Arabia: The Writings of the Queen of the Desert*, p. 24.

42 AS letter to Klaus Mann, 4 November 1934, *Wir werden es schon zuwege bringen, das Leben*, p. 120.

43 Countess Maud von Rosen, *Persian Pilgrimage* (London: Robert Hale, 1937).

44 The fear of being 'overrun by foreigners' (*Überfremdungsangst*) ran high at this time.

45 Erika Mann, Swiss television interview, 1969, cited in Andrea Weiss, *In the Shadow of the Magic Mountain*, p. 108.

46 Alexis Schwarzenbach, *Die Geborene*, pp. 281–2.

47 Zurich municipal police report for 7 January 1935 cited in Alexis Schwarzenbach, *Die Geborene*, p. 285.

48 AS, 'Bericht über den Fall Pfeffermühle', 20 December 1934. SLA.

49 Ibid.

50 Thomas Mann, 27 December 1934, *Tagebücher 1933–1934*.

51 Christopher Isherwood letter to Klaus Mann, 8 November 1934, Klaus Mann archive. MLM. *Flucht in den Norden* was published as *Journey into Freedom*, trans. by Rita Reil (London: Victor Gollancz, 1936).

52 The original inscription mixes German, French and English. Photo in the Musée de l'Elysée, Lausanne. Cited in Alexis Schwarzenbach, *Auf der Schwelle des Fremden: das Leben der Annemarie Schwarzenbach*, p. 214.

53 AS letter to Claude Bourdet, 16 December 1934, *Lettres à Claude Bourdet*, p. 80.

54 Klaus Mann, 28 December 1934, *Tagebücher*.

55 AS letter to Klaus Mann, 21 December 1934, *Wir werden es schon zuwege bringen, das Leben*, p. 122.

56 Ibid., p. 123.

57 Alfred Schwarzenbach to AS, 8 January 1935. 190.8. Schwarzenbach Archives. ZBZ.

58 Renée Schwarzenbach to AS, 9 January 1935. 190.8. Schwarzenbach Archives. ZBZ.

59 Claude Bourdet, 'Annemarie Schwarzenbach', undated manuscript annexe to *Lettres à Claude Bourdet*, p. 119.

60 Ella Maillart, *The Cruel Way: Switzerland to Afghanistan in a Ford, 1939*, p. 14.

61 AS letter to Claude Bourdet, 9 March 1935, *Lettres à Claude Bourdet*, p. 86.

62 AS letter to Alfred Schwarzenbach, 21 March 1935. 190.8. Schwarzenbach Archives. ZBZ.

63 AS letter to Klaus Mann, 6 April 1935, *Wir werden es schon zuwege bringen, das Leben*, p. 127.

64 Renée Schwarzenbach-Wille photographs, Graphics and Photo Archives, Schwarzenbach Archives. ZBZ.

65 Ella Maillart, *The Cruel Way*, p. 13.

66 Annemarie was never one to waste a story, and wrote about d'Andurain in journalistic form in 'Eine moderne Zenobia', *Zürcher Illustrierte*, 20 November 1936.

67 See note 3 to AS letter to Claude Bourdet, 28 March 1935, *Lettres à Claude Bourdet*, p. 89.

68 'Auszug aus dem Zivilstandsregister der "Légation de France à Téhéran"'. 190.1. Schwarzenbach Archives. ZBZ.

69 AS, *Death in Persia*, p. 13.

70 AS, 'Spuren des alten Persien', *National-Zeitung*, 2 January 1936.

71 Gertrude Bell, *Persian Pictures*, p. 62.

72 Vita Sackville-West, *Passenger to Teheran*.

73 AS Letter to Klaus Mann, 19 May 1935, *Wir werden es schon zuwege bringen, das Leben*, p. 129.

74 '… *als Diplomaten-Nesthäkchen durchtaumeln soll.*' AS Letter to Klaus Mann, 12 June 1935, *Wir werden es schon zuwege bringen, das Leben*, p. 132.

75 AS letter to Carl Burckhardt, 2 July 1935, Fähnders and Rohlf, *Annemarie Schrwarzenbach: Analysen und Erstdrucke*.

76 Gertrude Bell, *A Woman in Arabia: The Writings of the Queen of the Desert*, p. 95.

77 AS, *Death in Persia*, p. 73.

78 Ibid., p. 76.

79 Terry Castle, *The Apparitional Lesbian* (New York: Columbia University Press, 1993), p. 197.

80 AS, *Death in Persia*, pp. 11–12.

81 Ibid., p. 87.

82 Ibid., p. 95.

83 Alexis Schwarzenbach, *Auf der Schwelle des Fremden: das Leben der Annemarie Schwarzenbach*, p. 271.

84 AS, *Death in Persia*, p. 17.

85 Ibid., p. 34.

86 Ella Maillart, *The Cruel Way*, p. 15.

87 Klaus Mann, 'Sie hat einen Skandal in Teheran.' 3 September 1935, also 19 and 20 September 1935, *Tagebücher*.

88 Ella Maillart, *The Cruel Way*, p. 13.

89 AS Letter to Klaus Mann, 9 August 1935, *Wir werden es schon zuwege bringen, das Leben*, p. 135.

90 *Evening Star* (Washington, DC), 7 August 1935, p. B-2.

91 *Evening Star* (Washington, DC), 14 October 1936.

92 AS, *Death in Persia*, pp. 50–1.

93 Ibid., p. 53.

94 Christopher Isherwood, *Christopher and his Kind,* pp. 206–8.

95 Walter Allen, *As I Walked Down New Grub Street* (London: Heinemann, 1981), pp. 56–58.

96 Renée Schwarzenbach-Wille to her daughter Suzanne, 3 November 1935. 185.6. Schwarzenbach Archives. ZBZ.

97 AS letter to Claude Bourdet, 27 July 1935, *Lettres à Claude Bourdet*, pp. 93–4.

98 Claude Clarac interview with Dominique Laure Miermont, 23 July 1989, cited in *Annemarie Schwarzenbach ou le mal d'Europe*, p. 184.

99 AS Letter to Klaus Mann, 27 September 1935, *Wir werden es schon zuwege bringen, das Leben*, p. 140.

100 Klaus Mann, 'sehr schmal, sehr süchtig, aber lieb', 5 November 1935, *Tagebücher*.

101 Ibid., 9 November 1935.

102 Thomas Mann, 22 November 1935, *Tagebücher 1935–1936*.

103 Dr. Forel to Dr. Hämmerli, 20 December 1935. 190.8. Schwarzenbach Archives. ZBZ.

104 Alexis Schwarzenbach, *Die Geborene*, pp. 315–16.

105 Dr. Forel to Dr. Hämmerli, 20 December 1935. 190.8. Schwarzenbach Archives. ZBZ

106 Ibid.

107 Klaus Mann, 'In etwas besserem Zustand; immer noch sehr durchsichtig', 13 December 1935, *Tagebücher*.

108 Gertrude Bell, *Persian Pictures*, p. 188.

7. Two Women, a Ford and a Rolleiflex

1 AS, 'Democracy Viewed from the New America', Zurich radio transcript, 29 April 1937. SLA.

2 AS, *Death in Persia*, p. 48.

3 In August 2019 the photographers were celebrated in a joint retrospective, *LIFE: Six Women Photographers*, at the New York Historical Society Museum.

4 President Franklin D. Roosevelt, Madison Square Garden speech, 31 October 1936.

5 AS letter to Arnold Kübler, 7 August [1936], *Jenseits von New York*, p. 243.

6 Nina Zimmer and Martin Waldmeier, eds., *Aufbruch ohne Ziel: Annemarie Schwarzenbach als Fotografin*, p. 22.

7 Thank you to Roger Perret for alerting me to this interesting photographer.

8 AS, 'Dark End of the Street in Washington' / 'Unbekanntes Washington', *National-Zeitung*, 11 November 1936.

9 Zimmer and Waldmeier, eds., *Aufbruch ohne Ziel*, p. 22.

10 AS, 'Paper Mills and Smallholdings in Maine' / 'Papiermühlen und kleine Farmen in Maine', *National-Zeitung*, 7 October 1936.

11 Klaus Mann, 27 November 1936, *Tagebücher*.

12 Frederic Spotts, *Cursed Legacy: The Tragic Life of Klaus Mann*, p. 123.

13 Top Cottage in Hyde Park near Poughkeepsie, NY, Roosevelt's retreat, designed during his second term with wheelchair access.

14 AS, 'Wahlnacht in New York' / 'Election Night in New York, 1936', typescript. SLA.

15 'Zauberer ist ausgebürgert', Klaus Mann, 3 December 1936, *Tagebücher*.

16 'Meine *sehr* heftigen GELDSORGEN', Klaus Mann, 7 January 1937, *Tagebücher*.

17 Klaus Mann, *The Turning Point*, p. 300.

18 Dominique Laure Miermont, *Annemarie Schwarzenbach ou le mal d'Europe*, pp. 213–14.

19 Igor Pahlen, cited in *In the Shadow of the Magic Mountain: The Erika and Klaus Mann Story*, pp. 107–8.

20 Erika Mann letter to Klaus Mann, 1 February 1937. Erika Mann Archive. MLM.
21 Dominique Laure Miermont, *Annemarie Schwarzenbach ou le mal d'Europe*, p. 215.
22 AS letter to Klaus Mann, 31 January 1937, *Wir werden es schon zuwege bringen, das Leben*, p. 148.
23 Erika Mann letter to Katia Mann, 1 February 1937, *Briefe und Antworten*, p. 109.
24 AS, 'Journey to Pittsburgh', *National-Zeitung*, 7–8 April 1937.
25 Ibid.
26 Ibid.
27 Ibid.
28 Ibid.
29 AS, 'Meeting the Union of American Miners', 13 May 1937, *ABC*.
30 Ibid.
31 AS letter to Klaus Mann, 31 January 1937, *Wir werden es schon zuwege bringen, das Leben*, p. 148.
32 AS, 'Meeting the Union of American Miners', 13 May 1937, *ABC*.
33 V.S. Pritchett, *At Home and Abroad*, pp. 213 and 206.
34 AS, 'Democracy Viewed from the New America', Zurich radio transcript, 29 April 1937. SLA.
35 Andrea Weiss, *In the Shadow of the Magic Mountain*, p. 74.
36 Klaus Mann, 9 February 1937, *Tagebücher*.
37 Christopher Isherwood, *Christopher and his Kind*, p. 206.
38 Renée Schwarzenbach-Wille photographs, '*Besuch von Annemarie*', scr F RS XL 7, Graphics and Photo Archives, Schwarzenbach Archives. ZBZ.
39 'Spiphy (!) – in Sils, bei Annemarie wohnend. (!)', Klaus Mann, 26 February 1937, *Tagebücher*.
40 AS letter to Klaus Mann, 25 February 1937, *Wir werden es schon zuwege bringen, das Leben*, p. 149.
41 Klaus Mann, 5 March 1937, *Tagebücher*.
42 Andrea Weiss, *In the Shadow of the Magic Mountain*, p. 149.
43 Klaus Mann, 24 September 1938, *Tagebücher*.
44 AS, 'Max Meister, Refugee', *ABC*, 4 November 1937.
45 Ibid.
46 AS, 'In the American South' / 'Im amerikanischen Südosten', *ABC*, 23 December 1937.
47 AS, 'Dark End of the Street in Knoxville' / 'Auf der Schattenseite von Knoxville', *National-Zeitung*, 16 December 1937. *Jenseits von New York*, p. 152.
48 The Andrew Johnson Hotel was Knoxville's premier hotel until 1973. Its guests included Amelia Earhart in 1936, pianist Sergei Rachmaninoff in 1943 and writer Jean-Paul Sartre in 1945. The country singer Hank Williams spent the last night of his life in the hotel, 31 December 1952.
49 AS, 'Dark End of the Street in Knoxville', *Jenseits von New York*, p. 156.
50 Ibid., p. 157.

51 AS, 'Lumberjacks, Miners and Farmers in the Tennessee Mountains' / 'Holzfäller, Bergarbeiter, Bauern – und ein Farmhaus in den Bergen von Tennessee', *ABC*, 9 December 1937. *Jenseits von New York*, p. 158.

52 Ibid., p. 162.

53 Ibid., p. 168.

54 AS, 'Miss Bryant's Struggle' / 'Wie lebt Aline Bryant, Textilarbeiterin?', *ABC*, 25 March 1938. *Jenseits von New York*, p. 171.

55 Ibid., p. 172.

56 AS, 'In the Cumberland Mountains' / 'In den Cumberland-Bergen', *National-Zeitung*, 30 December 1937. *Jenseits von New York*, p. 175.

57 Committee for Industrial Organization and Textile Workers Organizing Committee.

58 Begun in 1932, the 'Tuskegee Study of Untreated Syphilis in the Negro Male' was conducted without benefit of patients' informed consent. In 1974, a $10 million out-of-court reparations settlement was reached.

59 AS, 'Birmingham: City of Perpetual Promise' / 'Die Stadt des unaufhörlichen Versprechen', *National-Zeitung*, 17 January 1938. *Jenseits von New York*, p. 188.

60 AS, 'Chattanooga, Birmingham, Siluria, Montgomery, Tuskegee, Columbus Notizen', *Jenseits von New York*, pp. 182–3.

61 Ibid., p. 184.

62 AS, 'The Cotton Crisis in Alabama' / 'Baumwollkrise in Alabama', *National-Zeitung*, 25 January 1938. *Jenseits von New York*, p. 193.

63 AS letter to Klaus Mann, 10 November 1937, *Wir werden es schon zuwege bringen, das Leben*, p.161.

64 AS, 'The Fine People of Georgia' / 'Fabrikschlote und feine Leute in Georgia', *A-Z Arbeiter Zeitung [Basler Arbeiter Zeitung]*, 19–20 April 1938. *Jenseits von New York*, p. 201.

65 Ibid., p. 199.

66 Ibid., p. 203.

67 Ibid., pp. 203–4.

68 AS, 'Das Drama im amerikanischen Plantagen-Gürtel', *Zürcher Illustrierte*, 10 June 1938. SLA.

69 Zimmer and Waldmeier, eds., *Aufbruch ohne Ziel*, p. 15.

70 AS, 'Strike in Lumberton' / 'Streik in Lumberton', *ABC*, 17 February 1938. *Jenseits von New York*, p. 218.

71 Ibid., p. 222.

72 Ibid., p. 223.

73 Marilynne Robinson, 'America, disjointed', *Financial Times*, 7–8 November 2020.

74 AS, 'The Cotton Crisis in Alabama' / 'Baumwollkrise in Alabama', *National-Zeitung*, 25 January 1938. *Jenseits von New York*, p. 195.

75 AS, 'For the Honour of the South' / '... um die Ehre der amerikanischen Südstaaten', *Die Weltwoche*, 15 April 1938. *Jenseits von New York*, p. 231.

76 Ibid., pp. 232–3.
77 AS, 'Amerikanisches Tagebuch II, Von New York nach Washington', 17 June 1940. SLA.
78 AS letter to Klaus Mann, 18 March 1938, *Wir werden es schon zuwege bringen, das Leben*, p. 163.
79 Ibid., p. 164.
80 Erika Mann letter to Klaus Mann, 26 December 1937. Erika Mann Archive. MLM.
81 Andrea Weiss, *In the Shadow of the Magic Mountain*, p. 161.
82 Klaus Mann, 11 December 1937, *Tagebücher*.
83 'In New York, im Januar, begann ich, ein wenig zu nehmen.' AS letter to Klaus Mann, 18 March 1938, *Wir werden es schon zuwege bringen, das Leben*, p. 165.
84 *The Evening News*, Harrisburg, PA, 24 August 1937. *Intelligencer Journal*, Lancaster, PA, 17 August 1937.
85 Alexis Schwarzenbach, *Auf der Schwelle des Fremden*, p. 153.
86 Alexis Schwarzenbach, *Die Geborene*, pp. 327–8.
87 Klaus Mann, 28 April 1938, *Tagebücher*.
88 AS letter to Arnold Kübler, 29 January 1938, *Jenseits von New York*, p. 249.
89 Ibid., p. 251.
90 AS, 'His Last Mountain' with photos by Lorenz Saladin, *Asia*, February 1938.
91 AS letter to Arnold Kübler, 4 February 1938, *Jenseits von New York*, p. 253.
92 AS letter to Otto Kleiber, 10 March 1938, Walter Fähnders and Andreas Tobler, '*Briefe von Annemarie Schwarzenbach an Otto Kleiber aus den Jahren 1933–1942*' in *Zeitschrift für Germanistik* 2/2006. Otto Kleiber Archive. BUL.
93 Thomas Mann letter to Ferdinand Lion, 25 August 1938, referencing *Das Drama der amerikanischen Südstaaten*. Thomas Mann, *Briefe*, Volume 2: *1937–1947*, ed. Erika Mann, pp. 55–6. Thomas Mann was instrumental in having Annemarie's article reprinted in *Mass und Wert*, March 1939.
94 AS, 'Why did you become a writer?' / 'Interview ohne Reporter', *Annabelle*, March 1939.
95 AS letter to Klaus Mann, 10 November 1937, *Wir werden es schon zuwege bringen, das Leben*, p.161.
96 Thea Sternheim, Paris 20 February 1938, *Tagebücher 1903–1971*, Volume 3: *1936–1951*, p. 64.
97 '… hinter allerlei kleine tricks und schwindeleien – Mops und Thun betreffend –, die mich ziemlich ärgern.' Klaus Mann, 20 February 1938, *Tagebücher*.
98 Klaus Mann, 13–19 February 1938, *Tagebücher*.

8. Enemies of Promise

1 Frederic Spotts, *Cursed Legacy: The Tragic Life of Klaus Mann*, p. 121.
2 Letter from Eduard Fueter to Carl Jacob Burckhardt, 10 May 1936, Carl Burckhardt Archive. BUL.
3 Clara Wille-von Bismarck, Tagebuch 1940. 160.1. Schwarzenbach Archives. ZBZ.

4 Thomas Mann, 9 November 1935, *Tagebücher*. Annemarie was chez Mann for tea *and* dinner.

5 Renée Schwarzenbach letter to Claude Clarac, 2 April 1936. 190.8. Schwarzenbach Archives. ZBZ.

6 Speech by Richard von Weizsäcker, President of Germany (1984–1994), 8 May 1985.

7 Hubert Butler, 'Lament for Archaeology', in *Escape from the Anthill*, p. 243.

8 Kirsten Esch, *Science and Crime* (2018), a documentary film.

9 AS to Dr. Binswanger, 22 August 1938, Medical history 5563, 11 July–4 August 1938, Tubingen University Archives 44/5563, file Annemarie Clarac-Schwarzenbach. Cited in Alexis Schwarzenbach, *Die Geborene*, p. 336.

10 AS, 'Kleine Begegnungen in Deutschland', *Insel Europa: Reportagen und Feuilletons 1930–1942*, p. 107.

11 Ibid., p. 114.

12 Ibid., pp. 118–19. Rebecca West, travelling in Austria at the time, confirms the view. '[T]he Nazis had put a director into his company who knew nothing and was simply a Party man in line for a job.' *Black Lamb and Grey Falcon* (Edinburgh: Canongate Books, 2006), p. 31.

13 Ibid., p.124.

14 Carl Burckhardt, *Mein Danziger Mission 1937–1939*, cited in *The Berlin Diaries of Marie Vassiltchikov*, p. 48.

15 AS letter to Florianna Storrer-Madelung, 7 June 1937. Storrer Archive. SLA.

16 Carl Burckhardt's compromising relationship with the Nazis in Danzig is explored in the documentary *The Red Cross and the Third Reich: On the Failure of Help*, 2006, by Christine Rütten. One of Walter Benjamin's last letters was to Burckhardt, 25 July 1940, seeking refuge in Switzerland.

17 AS letter to Klaus Mann, 21 May 1937, *Wir werden es schon zuwege bringen, das Leben*, p. 155.

18 'Bei Studenten in vier Ländern', *Insel Europa: Reportagen und Feuilletons 1930–1942*, pp. 156–7.

19 AS, 'The Ascension of the Khan Tengri', text in English, p. 1. SLA.

20 AS, *Lorenz Saladin: Ein Leben für die Berge*, p. 19.

21 Saladin described himself as '*1905 Verdingt zu den Bauern*'. Roland Begert's 2008 novel *Lange Jahre fremd*, about children used in industry after the war, as well as the 2012 film *Der Verdingbub* (The Foster Boy) drew much needed attention to children as cheap labour. In 2013 the Swiss government officially apologized for this historic exploitation.

22 AS, 'A Life for the Mountains', text in English, p. 1. SLA.

23 Saladin had a frost-bitten hand which turned gangrenous. He cut off part of the flesh, which led to blood poisoning.

24 AS, 'A Life for the Mountains', text in English, p. 1. SLA. The photographs, augmented by a further trove brought from Moscow by Robert Steiner and Emil Zopfi, are held in the Swiss Alpine Museum in Bern.

25 See Alexis Schwarzenbach's review of Annemarie's photographs in *Republik*, 29

September 2020. https://www.republik.ch/2020/09/29/was-will-ich-erfahren -etwas-wesentliches.

26 Klaus Mann's long letter to Annemarie, 21 February 1938, Klaus Mann Archive. MLM. Annemarie's reply, [18 March 1938], *Wir werden es schon zuwege bringen, das Leben*, pp. 162–5.

27 AS letter to Klaus Mann, 18 March 1938, *Wir werden es schon zuwege bringen, das Leben*, p. 165.

28 Klaus Mann, 18 March 1937, *Tagebücher*.

29 Anthony Heilbut cited in Sherill Tippins, *February House*, p. 46.

30 'Ein Paar Schuhe fallen in den Inn', *Insel Europa: Reportagen und Feuilletons 1930–1942*, p. 204.

31 AS, 'Österreich gründlich verändert', *Luzerner Tagblatt*, 27 April 1938; 'Fahrt durch das "befreite" Österreich', *Insel Europa*, p. 181.

32 AS, 'Massenverhaftungen im österreichischen Offizierkorps – Nationalsozialismus ohne Maske?', *Insel Europa*, p. 190.

33 Hubert Butler, 'The Kagran Gruppe', in *The Children of Drancy*, p. 198.

34 AS, 'Österreich gründlich verändert', *Luzerner Tagblatt*, 27 April 1938; 'Fahrt durch das "befreite" Österreich', *Insel Europa*, p. 181.

35 Ibid.

36 AS letter to Klaus Mann, [14 May 1938], *Wir werden es schon zuwege bringen, das Leben*, p. 166.

37 AS letter to Klaus Mann, [22 May 1938], Klaus Mann Archive. MSM.

38 AS to Renée Schwarzenbach-Wille, 25 May 1938. 190.8. Schwarzenbach Archives. ZBZ.

39 Klaus Mann, 1 June 1938, *Tagebücher*.

40 Medical history 44/5563, Annemarie Clarac-Schwarzenbach 11 July–4 August 1938, Ludwig Binswanger estate, Tubingen University Archives. Cited in Alexis Schwarzenbach, *Die Geborene*, pp. 332–3.

41 Alexis Schwarzenbach, *Die Geborene*, p. 333.

42 Klaus Mann, 22 July 1938, *Tagebücher*.

43 Klaus Mann, 1 June 1938, *Tagebücher*.

44 'Die von Binswanger entwichene Annemarie.' Thomas Mann, Sunday 14 August 1938, *Tagebücher*.

45 'Zu Tische AMS verödeter Engel.' Thomas Mann, Friday 9 September 1938, *Tagebücher*.

46 AS letter to Anita Forrer, 12 September 1938. SLA.

47 AS letter to Anita Forrer, 20 September 1938. SLA.

48 AS letter to Anita Forrer, 16 November 1938. SLA.

49 See her final letter to Claude Bourdet, 21 November 1938, *Lettres à Claude Bourdet 1931–1938*, p. 102.

50 AS letter to Klaus Mann, end of January 1939, *Wir werden es schon zuwege bringen, das Leben*, p. 173.

51 Ibid.

52 Ruth Yorck von Wartenburg and Karl Vollmoeller correspondence, 1 February 1939, Karl Vollmoeller Archive. DLA.

53 Christopher Isherwood, *Christopher and his Kind*, p. 338.

54 Renée Schwarzenbach-Wille to Suzanne Öhman-Schwarzenbach, 3 March 1939. Cited in Alexis Schwarzenbach, *Die Geborene*, p. 343.

55 Alexis Schwarzenbach, *Die Geborene*, pp. 345–6.

56 Ella Maillart, *The Cruel Way*, p. 73.

57 Duff Hart-Davis, *Peter Fleming: A Biography*, p. 135.

58 AS letter to Alfred Wolkenberg, 4 January 1939, cited in *All the Roads Are Open: The Afghan Journey*, Afterword by Roger Perret, p. 124.

59 AS letter to Klaus Mann, end of January 1939, *Wir werden es schon zuwege bringen, das Leben*, p. 173.

60 AS letter to Ella Maillart, Easter Sunday [9 April] 1939, *Alle Wege sind offen*, p. 242.

61 Ella Maillart, *The Cruel Way*, p. 1. Maillart disguises Annemarie behind the name Christina throughout – for the sake of clarity I have restored it.

62 Ibid., pp. 2–3.

63 AS photo caption: '*Letzte Stunde in der Schweiz: Halt am Simplon*', June 1939. Original in English. SLA.

64 '… mir eine Chance zu geben, die einer Reifeprüfung gleicht.' AS to Erika Mann, June 14 [1939], *Wir werden es schon zuwege bringen, das Leben*, p. 87.

65 Rebecca West, *Black Lamb and Grey Falcon* (1942); Nicolas Bouvier, *The Way of the World* (1963); Dervla Murphy, *Full Tilt: Ireland to India with a Bicycle* (1965).

66 Ella Maillart, *The Cruel Way*, p. 14.

67 Ibid., p. 17.

68 Ibid., p. 18.

69 Ibid., p. 62.

70 AS, *All the Roads Are Open*, pp. 9–10.

71 Ella Maillart, *The Cruel Way*, p. 14.

72 Ibid., p. 33.

73 AS to Erika Mann, June 14 [1939], *Wir werden es schon zuwege bringen, das Leben*, pp. 87–8.

74 Ella Maillart, *The Cruel Way*, p. 199.

75 Gertrude Bell, *Persian Pictures*, p. 182.

76 AS, *All the Roads Are Open*, p. 15.

77 Ella Maillart, *The Cruel Way*, p. 49.

78 Ibid., p. 75.

79 Ibid., pp. 81–2.

80 Ibid., p. 85.

81 AS, *All the Roads Are Open*, p. 26.

82 AS, 'Der Monat des Friedens', *National-Zeitung*, 5 February 1940.

83 Ella Maillart, *The Cruel Way*, p. 89.
84 AS, 'Der Monat des Friedens', *National-Zeitung*, 5 February 1940.
85 Ella Maillart, *The Cruel Way*, p. 162.
86 Ibid., p. 92.
87 Ibid., p. 112.
88 Jane Dieulafoy (1851–1916), French archaeologist in Persia, was one of the first Western travellers to dress as a male in order to pass incognito in Muslim society.
89 Ella Maillart, *The Cruel Way*, p. 117.
90 Andreas Tobler, '*Warum man ihnen keine Wahl ließ*', Sonntagszeitung.ch, 24 January 2021.
91 AS, 'Der Tschador', *Auf der Schattenseite*, pp. 233–5.
92 AS letter to Florianna Storrer-Madelung, 29 February 1938 [misdated?]. Storrer Archive. SLA.
93 AS, 'Aktuelles Afghanistan', in *Mitteilung der Ostschweizerischen Geographisch-Kommerziellen Gesellschaft* (Hueber & Co., 1940).
94 Ella Maillart, *The Cruel Way*, p. 194.
95 Ibid., p. 174.
96 Ibid., p. 193.
97 AS to Anita Forrer, 24 August 1939, *Alle Wege sind offen*, 2021 edition, p. 254.
98 AS, Kabul diary, 27/28 August, 1939, Carole Bonstein Archive, Geneva. See Dominique Laure Miermont's note on the transcribing and bowdlerization of this text, *Annemarie Schwarzenbach ou le mal d'Europe*, pp. 395–6.
99 AS, Kabul Diary, 30 August 1939, Carole Bonstein Archive, Geneva.
100 AS, 'Mobilisiert in Kabul', *National-Zeitung*, 1 December 1939. SLA.
101 AS, Kabul Diary, midnight, 2 September 1939, Carole Bonstein Archive, Geneva.
102 Ella Maillart, *The Cruel Way*, p. 197.
103 AS, Kabul Diary, 30 September 1939, Carole Bonstein Archive, Geneva.
104 Dominique Laure Miermont, *Annemarie Schwarzenbach ou le mal d'Europe*, p. 271.
105 AS, Kabul Diary, 25 October 1939, Carole Bonstein Archive, Geneva.
106 See Roger Perret's Afterword to *Alle Wege sind offen*, 2021 edition, p. 320.
107 AS, *All the Roads Are Open*, p. 45.
108 Ibid., p. 75.
109 Ibid., p. 107.
110 AS letter to Ella Maillart, 3 December 1939, Fonds Ella Maillart, Bibliothèque de Genève.
111 Dated 11 December 1938. SLA.
112 In Seamus Heaney's translation 'there are tears at the heart of things'. Seamus Heaney, Introduction to *The Redress of Poetry: Oxford Lectures*, 2002, p. xv.
113 Ella Maillart, *The Cruel Way*, p. 202.
114 AS, *All the Roads Are Open*, pp. 113–14.

115 AS, 'Der Brand des Orazio', *National-Zeitung*, 26 January 1940 and in *Auf der Schattenseite*, p. 246.
116 AS, 'Nach Westen', *Auf der Schattenseite*, p. 255.
117 Anna Seghers, *Transit*, translated by Margot Bettauer Dembo (New York: New York Review Books, 2013), p. 178.
118 'All these tribes are assembled as democratically as the old Swiss cantons.' AS, 'Die Grenzen Afghanistans', *Zürcher Illustrierte*, 29 November 1939. SLA. See also 'Afghanistan, die Schweiz Asiens', *Zürcher Illustrierte*, 2 May 1940, and numerous other articles on the subject.
119 AS letters to Otto Kleiber, 20 December 1939 and 23 July 1940, Otto Kleiber Archive. BUL.

9. Running on Empty

1 Alexis Schwarzenbach, *Die Geborene*, p. 353.
2 Clara Wille-von Bismarck, *Tagebuch*. 160.1. Schwarzenbach Archives. ZBZ.
3 See Regina Dieterle's *Nachwort* in Annemarie Schwarzenbach, *Auf der Schattenseite*, pp. 326–9.
4 'Und musste once and for good Schluss mit einem guten Teil Vergangenheit machen', AS to Klaus Mann, 18 January 1940, *Wir werden es schon zuwege bringen, das Leben*, p. 174.
5 Later she was recruited to the OSS – Office of Strategic Services – forerunner of the CIA. See Andreas Tobler, 'Warum man ihnen keine Wahl ließ', *Sonntagszeitung*, 21 January 2021.
6 Margot von Opel in conversation with Areti Georgiadou, Lichtenstein 1992, cited in *Das Leben zerfetzt sich mir*, p. 73.
7 Report in the Zurich City Archive, 19 April 1940, Dossier Paula H. Struck/ Wieland/v. Opel, Handler Hauptmann Meyer, V.E. c. 63. Cited in Alexis Schwarzenbach, *Die Geborene*, p. 351.
8 Renée Schwarzenbach-Wille to Suzanne Öhman-Schwarzenbach, 20 April 1940, Schwarzenbach Archives. ZBZ.
9 *New York Times*, 26 April 1940.
10 FBI Files on Fritz von Opel (US Department of Justice), 1940. 195.3. Schwarzenbach Archives. ZBZ.
11 AS, 'Nach Westen', *Auf der Schattenseite*, p. 258. Translated by Padraig Rooney as 'Westward Ho!' in *Transnational Literature*, Vol. 13, Oct 2021.
12 Selina Hastings, *Sybille Bedford: An Appetite for Life*, p. 121.
13 AS, 'Amerikanisches Tagebuch: die Weltausstellung', *Auf der Schattenseite*, p. 259.
14 AS, 'The Auto-da-Fé of the Mind' in Joseph Roth, *What I Saw: Reports from Berlin 1920–1933*, p. 207.
15 AS, 'Amerikanisches Tagebuch: die Weltausstellung', *Auf der Schattenseite*, p. 260.
16 AS, 'Im Plaza Hotel', *National-Zeitung*, 1 August 1940.

17 FBI Files on Fritz von Opel (US Department of Justice), 1940. 195.3. Schwarzenbach Archives. ZBZ.

18 See Alexander Stephan, *'Communazis': FBI Surveillance of German Emigré Writers* (Yale: Yale University Press, 2000).

19 Thomas Mann, *Tagebücher 1940–1943*.

20 Klaus Mann, 30 May 1940, *Tagebücher*.

21 AS letter to Ella Maillart, 15 June 1940, SLA.

22 Dominique Laure Miermont, *Annemarie Schwarzenbach ou le mal d'Europe*, p. 294.

23 Alfred Schwarzenbach, 'Im Flugzeug von New York nach der Schweiz', *NZZ*, 17/18 July 1940.

24 AS letter to Ella Maillart, 15 June 1940. SLA.

25 AS letter to Klaus Mann, 23 July 1940, *Wir werden es schon zuwege bringen, das Leben*, p. 178.

26 Developed in the US in 1934 and first used as competition enhancement in 1936 at the Berlin Olympic Games.

27 Margot von Opel letter to Busy Bodmer, 19 January 1941, cited in Miermont, *Annemarie Schwarzenbach ou le mal d'Europe*, p. 299.

28 Cited in Sherill Tippins, *February House*, p. 5.

29 Annemarie Schwarzenbach, 'Carson McCullers', *Auf der Schattenseite*, p. 265. See also my translation, 'Carson McCullers in 1940', AGNI 84, Boston University, 2016.

30 Virginia Spencer Carr, *The Lonely Hunter*, p. 100.

31 Klaus Mann, 12 June 1940, *Tagebücher*.

32 Carson McCullers, *Illumination and Night Glare*, p. 21.

33 '[S]he chose, nevertheless, to make of her husband what she wished him to be.' Virginia Spencer Carr, *The Lonely Hunter*, p. 75.

34 Carson McCullers, *Illumination and Night Glare*, p. 22.

35 AS, 'Carson McCullers', *Auf der Schattenseite*, p. 263.

36 AS letter to Robert Linscott, 23 August [1940], Robert Newton Linscott Archive, Washington University in St. Louis.

37 AS, 'Carson McCullers', *Auf der Schattenseite*, pp. 264–5.

38 Ibid., p. 265.

39 AS, 'The Fine People of Georgia' / 'Fabrikschlote und feine Leute in Georgia', *A-Z Arbeiter Zeitung* [*Basler Arbeiter Zeitung*], 19–20 April 1938. *Jenseits von New York*.

40 Virginia Spencer Carr, *The Lonely Hunter*, p. 87.

41 'The pieces I've written over the past few days are undistinguished, except perhaps for a good one on Carson McCullers (who wrote me a lovely letter, but her book can only be called good within certain limits)' AS letter to Klaus Mann, 21 June 1940, *Wir werden es schon zuwege bringen, das Leben*, p. 177.

42 AS, 'Carson McCullers', *Auf der Schattenseite*, p. 264.

43 Carson McCullers, *Illumination and Night Glare*, p. 6.

44 Sherill Tippins, *February House*, p. 22.

45 AS letter to Klaus Mann, 21 June 1940, *Wir werden es schon zuwege bringen, das Leben*, pp. 176–7.

46 Carson McCullers letter to Schwarzenbach, cited in *Auf der Schattenseite*, pp. 265–6. See Rooney, 'Carson McCullers in 1940', *Agni*, no. 84 (2016) pp. 69–74.

47 AS letter to Klaus Mann, 23 July 1940, *Wir werden es schon zuwege bringen, das Leben*, p. 179.

48 AS, 'Summer Days on Nantucket', *Thurgauer Zeitung*, 7 September 1940.

49 FBI Files on Fritz von Opel (US Department of Justice), 22 July 1940. 195.3. Schwarzenbach Archives. ZBZ.

50 Margot von Opel letter to Marie-Louise Bodmer, 19 January 1941, Marie-Louise Bodmer-Preiswerk Archive. Private collection, Luzern.

51 AS, 'Der Krater der Tiere', *Afrikanische Schriften*, p. 118.

52 AS letter to Otto Kleiber, July 23 1940. Otto Kleiber Archive. BUL.

53 AS letter to Klaus Mann, 23 July 1940, *Wir werden es schon zuwege bringen, das Leben*, pp. 178–9.

54 AS, *Alle Wege sind offen*.

55 AS, 'Im Plaza Hotel', *National-Zeitung*, 1 August 1940.

56 AS letter to Florianna Storrer-Madelung, 5 August 1940. Storrer Archive. SLA.

57 AS letter to Otto Kleiber, 15 September 1940. Otto Kleiber Archive, BUL.

58 Letter from Busy Bodmer to AS, 21 August 1940, cited in Miermont, *Annemarie Schwarzenbach ou le mal d'Europe*, p. 307.

59 Klaus Mann, 26 September 1940, *Tagebücher*.

60 Carson McCullers, *Illumination and Night Glare*, p. 30.

61 Carson McCullers, 'Brooklyn is my Neighborhood', *Vogue*, 1 March 1941.

62 Richard Wright reviewing *The Heart is a Lonely Hunter*, *New Republic*, 5 August 1940.

63 AS, '*The Great Dictator*: Charlie Chaplins neuer Film', *Die Weltwoche*, 4 April 1941; *Auf der Schattenseite*, p. 281.

64 Virginia Spencer Carr, *The Lonely Hunter*, p. 102.

65 Klaus Mann, *The Turning Point*, p. 335.

66 Klaus Mann, 19 October 1940, *Tagebücher*.

67 21 November. President Roosevelt had moved the celebration one week earlier to the third Thursday in November.

68 Sherill Tippins, *February House*, pp. 110–11.

69 The writer, photographer and documentary filmmaker Erica Andersen (1914–1976).

70 Freddy [Alfred] Schwarzenbach to Hans Schwarzenbach, 28 November 1940. Cited in Alexis Schwarzenbach, *Die Geborene*, pp. 258–9.

71 Death notice of Blythewood founder Dr. William Herbert Wiley, *New York Times*, 8 November 1936.

72 Blythewood opened in 1890 and was demolished in the 1960s. 'Glimpses of Blythewood' on Points group blog: https://pointshistory.com/2011/06/21/glimpses-of-blythewood/

73 Alexis Schwarzenbach reproduces Annemarie's letter in facsimile in *Auf der Schwelle des Fremden*, pp. 346–7.

74 Ruth Landshoff-Yorck, 'Annemarie', unpublished typescript. HGARC.

75 Alfred Wolkenberg was born in Vienna in 1911 and immigrated to the United States in 1939. In 1948 he founded Alva Studios of Long Island City, NY, which produced sculpture replicas.

76 Charles Linsmayer, *Annemarie Schwarzenbach*, p. 154.

77 Carson McCullers, *Illumination and Night Glare*, p. 34.

78 Alfred Wolkenberg interview with Roger Perret, 11 September 1986. Roger Perret Archive.

79 Jenn Shapland, *My Autobiography of Carson McCullers*, p. 71. Copyright constraints compelled Shapland to paraphrase important passages.

80 Ibid., p.79.

81 Carson McCullers letter to Robert Linscott, [1941?], Robert Newton Linscott Archive. WU.

82 Carson McCullers, *Illumination and Night Glare*, Introduction, p. xix.

83 AS letter to Klaus Mann, 28 January 1941, *Wir werden es schon zuwege bringen, das Leben*, p. 186.

84 Ibid.

85 Now given a makeover as the New York-Presbyterian Westchester Behavioral Health Center.

86 AS letter to Klaus Mann, 28 January 1941, *Wir werden es schon zuwege bringen, das Leben*, p. 186.

87 AS unpublished letter to Alfred Wolkenberg, [16 January 1941]. Roger Perret Archive.

88 Klaus Mann, 26 January 1941, *Tagebücher*, p. 88.

89 Margot von Opel letter to Marie-Louise Bodmer, 21 March 1941, Marie-Louise Bodmer-Preiswerk archive, Private papers, Luzern. Cited in Charles Linsmayer, *Annemarie Schwarzenbach*, p. 142.

90 '*Ich war ja seit Monaten halb tobsüchtig.*' AS unpublished letter to Alfred Wolkenberg, [16 January 1941]. Roger Perret Archive.

91 In English in the text.

92 AS unpublished letter to Alfred Wolkenberg, [16 January 1941]. Roger Perret Archive.

93 AS letter to Klaus Mann, 28 January 1941, *Wir werden es schon zuwege bringen, das Leben*, p. 186.

94 Alfred [Freddy] Schwarzenbach to Hans Schwarzenbach, 28 November 1940, Carole Bonstein Archive, Geneva.

95 AS, 'Amerikanische Ereignisse: 4. Umstellung auf Rüstungsindustrie'. SLA.

96 AS letter to Klaus Mann, 28 January 1941, *Wir werden es schon zuwege bringen, das Leben*, p. 187.
97 AS note to Dr. Kleiber attached to the typescript of 'Jahreswechsel in U.S.A.' SLA.
98 Cited in Alexis Schwarzenbach, *Die Geborene*, p. 361.
99 Robert O. Paxton, *Vichy France: Old Guard and New Order 1940–1944*, pp. 115–16.
100 AS letter to Carson McCullers, September 1941. UTA.
101 Carson McCullers letter, 13 June 1942, Annemarie Schwarzenbach Archive. SLA.
102 Margot von Opel letter to Klaus Mann, 15 November 1942, Klaus Mann Archive. MLM.
103 AS, 'White Plains' / 'Die weissen Ebenen', *National-Zeitung*, 7 August 1941. English translation by Padraig Rooney in *Waxwing Literary Journal*, Issue XXIII, Spring 2021.
104 Ibid.

10. Heart of Darkness

1 'Annemarie', a text in English by Ruth Landshoff-Yorck. HGARC.
2 AS letter to Ella Maillart, 23 March 1941. SLA.
3 AS letter to Ella Maillart, 2 August 1941. SLA.
4 AS, 'Offener Himmel über Lissabon…', *Thurgauer Zeitung*, 10 April 1941.
5 AS letter to Carl Jacob Burckhardt, 17 February 1941, *Annemarie Schwarzenbach: Analysen und Erstdrucke*, p. 263. She sounded the same note to Busy Budmer on arrival in Lisbon three days earlier: 'I'm not a deserter, and I'd very much like to prove it now.' AS letter to Busy Budmer, 14 February 1941, cited in Dominique Laure Miermont, *Annemarie Schwarzenbach ou le mal d'Europe*, p. 326.
6 Historiography moves with the times: '*Anpassung oder Widerstand*' – accommodation or resistance; for today's historians *Handlungsspielräume* – wiggle room. Gregor Spulher, 'Vom Weltkrieg zum Holocaust', in *Grenzfälle: Basel 1933–1945* (Basel: Christoph Merian Verlag und Historisches Museum Basel, 2020), p. 19.
7 Hubert Butler, 'The Invader Wore Slippers', *Escape from the Anthill*, p. 104.
8 Patrick Moser, 'Die Basler Chemie und der Nationalsozialismus', in *Grenzfälle: Basel 1933–1945*, p. 94.
9 Ibid., p. 98.
10 Thomas Maissen, 'Einleitende Gedanken zur Ausstellung', in *Grenzfälle: Basel 1933–1945*, p. 14.
11 Alexis Schwarzenbach, *Die Geborene*, p. 362.
12 AS letter to Ella Maillart, 23 March 1941. SLA.
13 '… hat Mama, mir "verboten", in die Schweiz zu reisen …' AS letter to Hans Schwarzenbach, 28 April [1942]. 201.2. Schwarzenbach Archives. ZBZ.
14 AS letter to Ella Maillart, 23 March 1941. SLA.

15 'Tout en développant des qualités peut-être héroïques', AS letter to Ella Maillart, 23 March 1941. SLA.

16 AS letter to Carson McCullers, 20 March 1942. UTA.

17 AS letter to Carson McCullers, 10 April 194. UTA.

18 AS letter to Ella Maillart, 23 March 1941. SLA.

19 Clara Wille-von Bismarck diary, 10 April 1941. 106.3. Schwarzenbach Archives. ZBZ.

20 AS, 'Kleine Reise durch Frankreich', *National-Zeitung*, 29 April 1941, *Insel Europa: Reportagen und Feuilletons 1930–1942*, p. 219.

21 AS, 'Schiffs-Tagebuch II', *Afrikanische Schriften*, p. 25.

22 Ibid.

23 In 2021 the German government formally recognized this colonial-era genocide.

24 AS, 'Schiffs-Tagebuch III', *Afrikanische Schriften*, p. 27.

25 At the turn of the century, São Tomé and Principe accounted for a third of Africa's production of the cocoa bean.

26 AS, 'Irgendwo in Französisch Westafrika', *Afrikanische Schriften*, pp. 78–9.

27 AS, letter in English to Erika Mann, June 1941. MLM.

28 André Gide, *Travels in the Congo*, translated by Dorothy Bussy, p. 9.

29 AS, 'Kleines Kongo-Tagebuch II: Auf einem Flussdampfer', *Afrikanische Schriften*, p. 104.

30 AS letter in English to Erika Mann, June 1941. MLM.

31 'Les origines de Radio-Brazzaville', interview with Pierre Bernard, *Espoir*, no. 54, March 1986.

32 AS letter in English to Erika Mann, June 1941. MLM.

33 Ibid.

34 '… *da man an höherer Stelle nicht damit einverstanden schien…*' AS, 'Beim Verlassen Afrikas I', *Afrikanische Schriften*, p. 126.

35 See the war diary of Sgt. Gaston Eve, who travelled this route six months after Annemarie. http://www.gastoneve.org.uk/pointenoire.html.

36 AS letter to Busy Bodmer, 14 June 1941. SLA.

37 AS letter to Carson McCullers, 3 October 1941. UTA.

38 See Swiss State Archives / *Schweizer Bundesarchiv*, Bern, Dossier Clarac-Schwarzenbach, Anna Marie, 25 August 1941 to 20 January 1942, Vol. 445. With thanks to Andreas Tobler for this indication. See also 'Nachwort', *Das Wunder des Baums*, pp. 253–4.

39 AS, 'Kleines Kongo-Tagebuch II: Auf einem Flussdampfer', *Afrikanische Schriften*, p. 105.

40 AS, 'Kleines Kongo-Tagebuch IV: Das Bild des Kongo', *Afrikanische Schriften*, p. 110.

41 AS letter in English to Erika Mann, 17 July 1941. MLM.

42 AS, 'Begegnung mit dem Dschungel', *Afrikanische Schriften*, p. 99.

43 AS, 'Die Niederlagen', *Afrikanische Schriften*, p. 84.

44 André Gide, *Travels in the Congo*, p. 12.

45 Miners in Elisabethville went on strike in December 1941, in the course of which approximately seventy, including their leader, Léonard Mpoyi, were shot dead in a stadium by soldiers under orders from the Governor of Katanga, Amour Maron.

46 Aimé Césaire, *Discours sur le Colonialisme*, p. 12.

47 AS letter to Carson McCullers, 29 July 1941. UTA.

48 André Gide, *Travels in the Congo*, p. 44.

49 AS letter to Ella Maillart, 2 August 1941. SLA.

50 AS, 'Der Belgische Kongo und der Krieg', *Afrikanische Schriften*, p. 114. Agreements had been signed to export Congolese copper to the United States and to Britain during the war. See David Northrup's *Beyond the Bend in the River: African Labour in Eastern Zaire 1865–1940* and Robert Paxton's *Vichy France: Old Guard and New Order 1940–1944*, p. 376.

51 Adam Hochschild, *King Leopold's Ghost* (Boston: Mariner Books, 1998), p. 279.

52 Florence Gillet, 'La "Mission" Cauvin: La propagande coloniale du gouvernement belge aux États-Unis pendant la Seconde Guerre mondiale', *Cahiers d'histoire du temps présent*, no. 15, 2005.

53 AS, 'Reise-Notizen IV: Der Strom', *Afrikanische Schriften*, p. 63.

54 AS, 'Reise-Notizen V: Der Äquator-Wald', *Afrikanische Schriften*, p. 69.

55 AS letter to Carson McCullers, 3 October 1941. UTA.

56 Yet another old colonial duffer: 'We must fight them until their absolute submission has been obtained, or their complete extermination … Inform the natives that if they cut another single vine, I will exterminate them to the last man.' Hochschild, *King Leopold's Ghost*, pp. 228–9.

57 AS letter to Ella Maillart, 21 November 1941. SLA.

58 Ibid.

59 'The forests here are associations.' Gide anticipated Colin Tudge's *The Secret Life of Trees* (London: Allen Lane, 2005).

60 Joseph Conrad, *Heart of Darkness*, p. 43.

61 AS, 'Beim Verlassen Afrikas II', *Afrikanische Schriften*, p. 133.

62 AS letter to Ella Maillart, 1 February 1942. SLA.

63 Elisabetha Wilhelmina Zeuner, 1852–1942. AS, 'Beim Verlassen Afrikas VI', *Afrikanische Schriften*, p. 150.

64 AS, 'Beim Verlassen Afrikas VIII', *Afrikanische Schriften*, p. 154.

65 AS, *Das Wunder des Baums*, p. 24.

66 AS letter to Ella Maillart, 14 March 1942. SLA.

67 And to her mother as well: 'Und täglich denke ich an jenes andere Leben wie an ein verlorenes Paradies' AS to Renée, 23 May 1908 [1942]. 190.8. Schwarzenbach Archives. ZBZ.

68 Michel-Rolph Trouillot, *Silencing the Past*, p. 49.

69 AS letter to Ella Maillart, 23 March 1941. SLA.

70 John Latouche and André Cauvin, *Congo*, p. 191.

71 Raoul Peck, *Exterminate All the Brutes, pace* Sven Lindqvist.

72 'Annemarie', unpublished text by Ruth Landshoff-Yorck, pp. 24–5. Ruth Landshoff-Yorck Archives. HGARC. The whereabouts of the bust are unknown.

73 AS letter to Hans Schwarzenbach, 28 April 1942. 201.2. Schwarzenbach Archives. ZBZ.

74 Margret Boveri letter to Gert Reiss, 23 July 1942, cited in Fähnders and Rohlf, *Annemarie Schwarzenbach: Analysen und Erstdrucke*, p. 288.

75 AS letter to Margret Boveri, 12 June 1942, Fähnders and Rohlf, *Annemarie Schwarzenbach: Analysen und Erstdrucke*, p. 290.

76 Charly Clerc letter to AS, 8 July 1942, Schwarzenbach Archive. SLA.

77 Anita Forrer to Marie Dagmar Maillart, 28 August 1943, Carole Bonstein Archive, Geneva.

78 Marie-Louise Lüscher, 'Erinnerungen an Annemarie Schwarzenbach', *Schweizer Frauenblatt*, July–August 1988. Cited in Dominique Laure Miermont, *Annemarie Schwarzenbach ou le mal d'Europe*, p. 358.

79 Robert O. Paxton, *Vichy France: Old Guard and New Order 1940–1944*, Introduction to the 2001 edition, pp. xiii and 46.

80 Germaine Krull, *La vie mène la danse*, p. 291.

81 See *Annemarie Schwarzenbach: Schweizerin und Rebellin*, documentary (2000): 'My account of circumstances then remains profoundly true, at least as far as I am concerned.'

82 AS letter to Busy Bodmer, 7 June 1942. SLA.

83 AS letter to Florianna Storrer-Madelung, 11 June 1942. Storrer Archive. SLA.

84 See Clarac's ('Saint-Ours') *'Amours du Poète'*: '*Joies, ô joies que j'ai cueillies sur tant de corps / Joies du feu, de velours, de soie / Joies achetées, vendues, mendier, / Frôlées, / Volées aux lèvres de l'adolescent…' Carnet de passage d'un pèlerin d'ailleurs*, p. 39.

85 Claude Clarac letter to Busy Bodmer, 4 December 1942. Cited in Dominique Laure Miermont, *Annemarie Schwarzenbach ou le mal d'Europe*, p. 381.

86 AS, 'Marokkanische Erntezeit', *National-Zeitung*, 18 June 1942; *Auf der Schattenseite*, p. 313.

87 AS, 'Eine Mondnacht in der Chella', *Afrikanische Schriften*, p. 172.

88 Alexis Schwarzenbach, *Die Geborene*, p. 373.

89 Details of Annemarie's medical treatment based on communications between Dr. Oscar Forel of Prangins and Dr. Paul Gut who took over Annemarie's case in St. Moritz, 26 and 29 October 1942. 190.8. Schwarzenbach Archives. ZBZ. Further details in Charles Linsmayer, *Annemarie Schwarzenbach*, pp. 180–5.

90 Claude Clarac letter to Ella Maillart, 18 February 1944, Carol Bonstein Archive, Geneva.

91 AS letter to Annigna Godly, 15 October 1942. 190.8. Schwarzenbach Archives. ZBZ. Reproduced in facsimile in *Auf der Schwelle des Fremden*, p. 383.

92 Cited in Dominique Laure Miermont, *Annemarie Schwarzenbach ou le mal d'Europe*, p. 372.

93 AS to Mabel Zuppinger, 19 October 1942. 190.8. Schwarzenbach Archives. ZBZ.

94 Alexis Schwarzenbach, *Die Geborene*, p. 380.

95 Dr. Gut letter to Dr. Hämmerli, 5 November 1942. 190.8. Schwarzenbach Archives. ZBZ.

96 Charles Linsmayer takes his cue from Dr. Gut's description of this treatment as 'amounting to "euthanasia"'. Linsmayer, *Annemarie Schwarzenbach*, p. 187. Dominique Laure Miermont does not comment on the rights or wrongs of Annemarie's treatment. Miermont, *Annemarie Schwarzenbach ou le mal d'Europe*, p. 373. Areti Georgiadou gives a cursory account. Georgiadou, *Das Leben zerfetzt sich mir*, pp. 223–5. Alexis Schwarzenbach provides family reactions to Forel's and Renée's handling of the case. Alexis Schwarzenbach, *Die Geborene*, pp. 384–6. In his biography of Annemarie, he too cites Dr. Gut's treatment as 'amounting to "euthanasia"', *Auf der Schwelle des Fremdens*, p. 402.

97 Alexis Schwarzenbach, *Die Geborene*, p. 386.

98 '*Annemarie auf dem Totenbett*', scr F RS V 60, Renée Schwarzenbach-Wille Archives. ZBZ.

99 Dominique Laure Miermont, *Annemarie Schwarzenbach ou le mal d'Europe*, p. 378.

100 '… *wie eine Kerze, die in einer Flamme schwindet.*' Gerhard Spinner, eulogy for Annemarie Schwarzenbach, 18 November 1942. 191.1. Schwarzenbach Archives. ZBZ.

101 Alice Bodmer letter to Marie-Louise Bodmer, 19 November 1942, cited in Charles Linsmayer, *Annemarie Schwarzenbach*, p. 189.

102 Carl Seelig, *Tages-Anzeiger*, 18 November 1942. Annemarie Schwarzenbach Archive. SLA.

103 Manuel Gasser, *Weltwoche*, 20 November 1942. Annemarie Schwarzenbach Archive. SLA.

104 Klaus Mann, *Der Wendepunkt* (1952).

105 'A Tree, A Rock, A Cloud', *Harper's Bazaar*, November 1942. Collected in *Ballad of a Sad Café* (1951).

106 Carson McCullers, *Illumination and Night Glare*, pp. 35–6.

107 Diaries of Ella Maillart, 17 and 22 February 1943, Easter 1948, Fonds Ella Maillart, Bibliothèque de Genève.

108 Margot von Opel letter to Klaus Mann, 15 November 1942, Klaus Mann Archive. MLM. Original in English.

109 Anita Forrer letter to Ella Maillart, 3 November 1943, Annemarie Schwarzenbach Archive. SLA. Original in English.

110 Foreword to Areti Georgiadou, *Das Leben zerfetzt sich mir*, p. 8.

111 Clara Wille letter to Anita Forrer, 25 September 1943, cited in Charles Linsmayer, *Annemarie Schwarzenbach*, p. 130 and in Alexis Schwarzenbach, *Die Geborene*, p. 391.

112 Alexis Schwarzenbach, *Die Geborene*, p. 392.

113 'Dream Vision'/'*Traumgesicht*', Sonnet LXIII, Albrecht Haushofer. My translation.

114 'Burned Books'/'*Verbrannte Bücher*', Sonnet XLIII, Albrecht Haushofer. My translation, first published in *Poetry Ireland Review*, no. 142, Spring 2024.

Bibliography

Archives

BUL: Otto Kleiber Archive, Basel University Library, Basel.

Carl Burckhardt Archive, Basel University Library, Basel.

DLA: Karl Vollmoeller Archive, Deutsches Literaturarchiv Marbach, Marbach am Neckar.

HGARC: Ruth Landshoff-Yorck Archive, Howard Gottlieb Archival Research Center, Boston University.

MLM: Erika Mann Archive, Monascenia Library, Munich.

Klaus Mann Archive, Monascenia Library, Munich.

Emmy Krüger Archive, Monascenia Library, Munich.

SLA: Annemarie Schwarzenbach Archive, Swiss Literary Archives, Bern.

Ernst Merz Archive, Swiss Literary Archives, Bern.

Niklaus Meienberg Archive, Swiss Literary Archives, Bern.

Storrer Archive, Swiss Literary Archives, Bern.

UTA: Carson McCullers Archive, Harry Ransom Humanities Research Center, University of Texas at Austin.

WU: Robert Newton Linscott Archive, Washington University in St. Louis.

ZBZ: Zentralbibliothek Zürich: Alexis Schwarzenbach Sammlung comprising Schwarzenbach family archives as well as Renée Schwarzenbach-Wille's photograph collection.

Beachy, Robert, *Gay Berlin: Birthplace of a Modern Identity* (New York: Knopf, 2014).

Bedford, Sybille, *Aldous Huxley: Volume 1, 1894–1939* (London: Collins, 1973).

Bell, Gertrude, *A Woman in Arabia: The Writings of the Queen of the Desert*, edited and introduced by Georgian Howell (New York: Penguin Books, 2015).

Bell, Gertrude, *Persian Pictures: From the Mountains to the Sea* (London: Tauris Parke, 2014).

Bell, Gertrude, *The Letters of Gertrude Bell, Volume 1* (London: Ernest Benn, 1927).

Benstock, Shari, *Women of the Left Bank: Paris 1900–1940* (London: Virago Press, 1987).

Blubacher, Thomas, '"Der Schock War Gewaltig": Carson McCullers schreibt Ruth Landshoff-Yorck über Annemarie Schwarzenbach', *Sinn und Form*, 5/2019.

Blubacher, Thomas, *Die vielen Leben der Ruth Landshoff-Yorck* (Berlin: Insel Verlag, 2015).

Breslauer, Marianne, *Bilder meines Lebens: Erinnerungen* (Wadenswil: Nimbus, 2012).

Breslauer, Marianne, *Photographien 1927–1937* (Berlin: Nationalgalerie, 1989).

Bürger, Jan, et al., *Im Schattenreich der wilden Zwanziger: Fotografien von Karl Vollmoeller aus dem Nachlass von Ruth Landshoff-Yorck* (Marbach am Neckar: Deutsche Schillergesellschaft, 2017).

Carr, Virginia Spencer, *The Lonely Hunter: A Biography of Carson McCullers* (Athens, GA: University of Georgia Press, 2003).

Castle, Terry, *The Apparitional Lesbian* (New York: Columbia University Press, 1993).

Césaire, Aimé, *Discours sur le Colonialisme* (Paris: Présence Africaine, 1955).

Clarac, Claude ('Saint-Ours'), *Carnet de Passage d'un Pèlerin d'Ailleurs* (Nantes: Petit Véhicule, 1994).

Conrad, Joseph, *Heart of Darkness*, edited by Robert Kimbrough (New York: Norton, 1988).

Esch, Kirsten, *Science and Crime*, documentary film (Berlin and Munich: Filmbüro-Süd, 2018).

Fähnders, Walter and Rohlf, Sabine, eds., *Annemarie Schwarzenbach: Analysen und Erstdrucke* (Bielefeld: Aisthesis Verlag, 2008).

Fanon, Frantz, *Black Skins, White Masks*, translated by Charles Lam Markmann (London: Paladin, 1970).

Gay, Peter, *Weimar Culture: The Outsider as Insider* (New York: W.W. Norton, 2001).

Georgiadou, Areti, *'Das Leben zerfetzt sich mir in tausend Stücke': Annemarie Schwarzenbach: eine Biographie* (Frankfurt: Campus Verlag, 1996).

Gide, André, *The Counterfeiters*, translated by Dorothy Bussy (New York: Random House, 1973).

Gide, André, *Travels in the Congo*, translated by Dorothy Bussy (London: Penguin Books, 1986).

Goode, James F., *Negotiating for the Past: Archaeology, Nationalism, and Diplomacy in the Middle East, 1919–1941* (Austin, TX: University of Texas Press, 2007).

Gordon, Mel, *Voluptuous Panic: The Erotic World of Weimar Berlin* (Venice, CA: Feral House, 2000).

Haffner, Herbert, *Furtwängler* (Berlin: Parthas, 2003).

Hart-Davis, Duff, *Peter Fleming: A Biography* (London: Jonathan Cape, 1974).

Hastings, Selina, *Sybille Bedford: An Appetite for Life* (London: Chatto & Windus, 2020).

Heilbut, Anthony, *Thomas Mann: Eros and Literature* (New York: Knopf, 1996).

Hemingway, Ernest, *The Sun Also Rises* (New York: Scribner, 1996).

Historisches Museum Basel, *Grenzfälle: Basel 1933–1945* (Basel: Christoph Merian Verlag & Historisches Museum Basel, 2020).

Ilg, Paul, *Der Starke Mann* (Frauenfeld: Huber & Co., 1917).

Isenberg, Noah, ed., *Weimar Cinema: An Essential Guide to Classic Films of the Era* (New York: Columbia University Press, 2008).

Isherwood, Christopher, *Goodbye to Berlin* (London: Penguin Books, 1974).

Jasanoff, Maya, *The Dawn Watch: Joseph Conrad in a Global World* (New York: Penguin Press, 2017).

Kessler, Harry Graf, *Das Tagebuch, Vol. 8: 1923–1926*, edited by Angela Reinthal et al. (Stuttgart: Klett-Cotta, 2009).

Kracauer, Siegfried, *The Mass Ornament: Weimar Essays*, translated, edited, and with an introduction by Thomas Y. Levin (Cambridge, MA: Harvard University Press, 1995).

Krull, Germaine, *Germaine Krull: The Monte Carlo Years* (Montreal: The Montreal Museum of Fine Arts, 2006).

Krull, Germaine, *La vie mène la danse* (Paris: Éditions Textuel, 2019).

Kuzniar, Alice A., *The Queer German Cinema* (Stanford, CA: Stanford University Press, 2000).

Landshoff-Yorck, Ruth, *Das Mädchen mit wenig PS: Feuilletons aus den zwanziger Jahren* (Berlin: Aviva, 2015).

Landshoff-Yorck, Ruth, *Roman einer Tänzerin* (Berlin: Aviva, 2002).

Latouche, John and Cauvin, André, *Congo* (New York: Willow, White & Co., 1948).

Lavizzari, Alexandra, *Fast eine Liebe: Annemarie Schwarzenbach und Carson McCullers* (Berlin: Ebersbach, 2008).

Lawrence, D.H., *Twilight in Italy* (London: Barrie & Jenkins, 1990).

Leininger, Raymond and Nicole, *La route sans borne* (Paris: J. Susse, 1947).

Lindqvist, Sven, *'Exterminate All the Brutes'*, translated by Joan Tate (London: Granta Books, 2018).

Linsmayer, Charles, *Annemarie Schwarzenbach: Ein Kapitel tragische Schweizer Literaturgeschichte* (Frauenfeld: Huber Verlag, 2008).

Maillart, Ella K., *The Cruel Way: Switzerland to Afghanistan in a Ford, 1939* (Chicago: University of Chicago Press, 2013).

Mann, Erika, *Blitze überm Ozean: Aufsätze, Reden, Reportagen*, edited by Irmela von der Lühe and Uwe Naumann (Reinbek bei Frankfurt: Rowohlt, 2000).

Mann, Erika, *Briefe und Antworten 1922–1950* (Munich: dtv Literatur, 1988).

Mann, Erika, *Mein Vater, der Zauberer* (Reinbek bei Frankfurt: Rowohlt, 1996).

Mann, Klaus, *Die neuen Eltern: Aufsätze, Reden, Kritiken 1924–1933*, edited by Uwe Naumann and Michel Toteberg (Reinbek bei Frankfurt: Rowohlt, 1992).

Mann, Klaus, *Flucht in den Norden* (Reinbek bei Frankfurt: Rowohlt, 2003).

Mann, Klaus, *Speed; Die Erzählungen aus dem Exil* (Reinbek bei Hamburg: Rowohlt, 1990).

Mann, Klaus, *Tagebücher 1931–1949*, online at Monacensia im Hildebrandhaus, Munich. https://www.monacensia-digital.de/mann/nav/classification/13486.

Mann, Klaus, *The Turning Point* (Princeton: Marcus Wiener Publishers, 2014).

Mann, Klaus, *Treffpunkt im Unendlichen* (Munich: Edition Spangenberg, 1992).

McCormick, Richard W., 'Coming Out of the Uniform', in *Weimar Cinema: an Essential Guide to Classic Films of the Era*, edited by Noah Isenberg (New York: Columbia University Press, 2008).

McCullers, Carson, *Illumination & Night Glare: The Unfinished Autobiography of Carson McCullers*, edited by Carlos L. Dews (Madison: University of Wisconsin Press, 1999).

McCullers, Carson, *Stories, Plays & Other Writings*, edited by Carlos L. Dews (New York: Library of America, 2017).

Meyer, Adele, *Lila Nächte: Die Damenklubs im Berlin der Zwanziger Jahre* (Berlin: Ed. Lit. Europe, 1994).

Miermont, Dominique Laure, *Annemarie Schwarzenbach ou le mal d'Europe* (Paris: Payot, 2004).

Miller, Neil, *Out of the Past: Gay and Lesbian History from 1869 to the Present* (New York: Vintage Books, 1995).

Paxton, Robert O., *Vichy France: Old Guard and New Order 1940–1944* (New York: Columbia University Press, 2001).

Persky, Stan, *Then We Take Berlin: Stories from the Other Side of Europe* (Toronto: Knopf, 1995).

Pritchett, V.S., *At Home and Abroad* (London: Chatto & Windus, 1990).

Pühl, Eberhard, *Annemarie Schwarzenbach in Rheinsberg* (Oldenburg: Isensee Verlag, 2019).

Rich, B. Ruby, 'From Repressive Tolerance to Erotic Liberation: *Girls in Uniform*', in Sandra Frieden et al., *Gender and German Cinema, volume 2* (Oxford: Berg, 1993), pp. 61–96.

Richter, Maren, *'Aber ich habe mich nicht entmutigen lassen': Marie Daelen – Ärztin und Gesundheitspolitikerin im 20. Jahrhundert* (Gottingen: Wallstein Verlag, 2019).

Roth, Joseph, *Reports from a Parisian Paradise: Essays from France 1925–1939*, translated by Michael Hofmann (New York: W.W. Norton, 2003).

Roth, Joseph, *What I Saw: Reports from Berlin 1920–1933*, translated with an introduction by Michael Hofmann (London: Granta Books, 2003).

Savigneau, Josyane, *Carson McCullers: A Life* (London: The Women's Press, 2001).

Schwarzenbach, Alexis, *Auf der Schwelle des Fremden: Das Leben der Annemarie Schwarzenbach* (Munich: Collection Rolf Heyne, 2011).

Schwarzenbach, Alexis, *Die Geborene: Renée Schwarzenbach-Wille und ihre Familie* (Zurich: Scheidegger & Spiess, 2004).

Schwarzenbach, Annemarie, *Afrikanische Schriften*, edited by Sofie Decock, Walter Fähnders and Uta Schaffers (Zurich: Chronos Verlag, 2012).

Schwarzenbach, Annemarie. *Alle Wege sind offen: Die Reise nach Afghanistan 1939/1940*, edited by Roger Perret (Basel: Lenos Verlag, 2021).

Schwarzenbach, Annemarie. *All the Roads Are Open*, translated by Isabel Fargo Cole (Calcutta: Seagull Books, 2011).

Schwarzenbach, Annemarie. *Auf der Schattenseite: Ausgewählte Reportagen, Feuilletons und Fotografien 1933–1942*, edited by Regina Dieterle and Roger Perret (Basel: Lenos Verlag, 1990).

Schwarzenbach, Annemarie. *An den äussersten Flüssen des Paradieses*, edited by Roger Perret (Basel: Lenos Verlag, 2016).

Schwarzenbach, Annemarie. *Bei diesem Regen: Erzählungen* (Basel: Lenos Verlag, 1989).

Schwarzenbach, Annemarie. *Das Buch von der Schweiz, Süd und Ost* (Munich: Piper Verlag, 1932).

Schwarzenbach, Annemarie. *Das Wunder des Baums* (Zurich: Chronos Verlag, 2011).

Schwarzenbach, Annemarie. *Death in Persia*, translated by Lucy Renner Jones (Calcutta: Seagull Books, 2013).

Schwarzenbach, Annemarie. *Eine Frau zu sehen* (Zurich: Kein & Aber, 2008).

Schwarzenbach, Annemarie. *Freunde um Bernhard* (Basel: Lenos Verlag, 1998).

Schwarzenbach, Annemarie. *Jenseits von New York: Reportagen und Fotografien 1936–1938*, edited by Roger Perret (Basel: Lenos Verlag, 2018).

Schwarzenbach, Annemarie. *La Quête du Réel*, edited and translated by Dominique Laure Miermont and Nicole Le Bris (Paris: La Quinzaine Littéraire/Louis Vuitton, 2011).

Schwarzenbach, Annemarie. *Les Quarante Colonnes du souvenir* (Noville-sur-Mehaigne: Esperluète éditions, 2008).

Schwarzenbach, Annemarie. *Lettres à Claude Bourdet 1931–1938*, edited by Dominique Laure Miermont (Carouge-Genève: Éditions Zoé, 2008).

Schwarzenbach, Annemarie. *Lorenz Saladin: Ein Leben für die Berge*, edited by Robert Steiner and Emil Zopf (Basel: Lenos Verlag, 2007).

Schwarzenbach, Annemarie. *Lyric Novella*, translated by Lucy Renner Jones (Calcutta: Seagull Books, 2011).

Schwarzenbach, Annemarie. *Novelle lyrique*, translated by Emmanuelle Corté (Lagrasse: Verdier poche, 2016).

Schwarzenbach, Annemarie. *Orientreisen: Reportagen aus der Fremde* (Berlin: edition ebersbach, 2010).

Schwarzenbach, Annemarie. *Rives du Congo, Tétouan / Kongo-Ufer, Aus Tétouan*, translated by Dominique Laure Miermont (Noville-sur-Mehaigne: Esperluète éditions, 2005).

Schwarzenbach, Annemarie. *Tod in Persien* (Basel: Lenos Verlag, 1995).

Schwarzenbach, Annemarie. *Winter in Vorderasien* (Basel: Lenos Verlag, 2008).

Schwarzenbach, Annemarie, 'Wir werden es schon zuwege bringen, das Leben': Annemarie Schwarzenbach an Erika und Klaus Mann: Briefe 1930–1942, edited by Uta Fleischmann (Pfäffenweiler: Centaurus, 1993).

Schwarzenbach, Annemarie, Ella Maillart and Nicolas Bouvier, Unsterbliches Blau: Reisen nach Afghanistan / Bleu immortel: Voyages en Afghanistan (Zurich: Verlag Scheidegger & Spiess / Geneva: Éditions Zoé, 2003).

Segers, Anna, Transit, translated by Margot Bettauer Dembo (New York: NYRB, 2013).

Shapland, Jenn, My Autobiography of Carson McCullers (Portland: Tin House, 2020).

Spender, Stephen, The Temple (London: Faber & Faber, 1989).

Speyer, Wilhelm, Die Goldene Horde: Erzählung (Berlin: Rowohlt Verlag, 1931).

Speyer, Wilhelm, Sommer in Italien: Eine Liebesgeschichte (Berlin: Rowohlt Verlag, 1932).

Spotts, Frederic, Cursed Legacy: The Tragic Life of Klaus Mann (New Haven: Yale University Press, 2016).

Stark, Freya, Perseus in the Wind: A Life of Travel (London: Tauris Parke, 2013).

Steinert Borella, Sara, The Travel Narratives of Ella Maillart: (En)Gendering the Quest (New York: Peter Lang, 2006).

Sternheim, Thea, Tagebücher 1903–1971, 5 vols, edited by Thomas Ehrsam and Regula Wyss (Gottingen: Wallstein Verlag, 2011).

Tippins, Sherill, February House: The Story of W.H. Auden, Carson McCullers, Jane and Paul Bowles, Benjamin Britten, and Gypsy Rose Lee, Under One Roof in Wartime America (Boston: Houghton Mifflin, 2005).

Tobler, Andreas, '"Beteiligt sind wir alle": Annemarie Schwarzenbach und Die Sammlung', Wendepunkte – Tournants: Beiträge zur Klaus-Mann-Tagung aus Anlass seines 100. Geburtstages: Jahrbuch für Internationale Germanistik: Reihe A: Band 91 (Bern: Peter Lang, 2008).

Trouillot, Michel-Rolph, Silencing the Past: Power and the Production of History (Boston: Beacon Press, 1995).

Tworek, Elisabeth, Literarisches München zur Zeit von Thomas Mann: Von der Bohème zum Exil (Regensburg & Munich: Verlag Friedrich Pustet, 2016).

Wanner, Kurt and Breslauer, Marianne, Wo ich mich leichter fühle als anderswo: Annemarie Schwarzenbach und ihre Zeit in Graubünden (Maienfeld: Bündner Monatsblatt, 1997).

Weiss, Andrea, In the Shadow of the Magic Mountain: The Erika and Klaus Mann Story (Chicago: University of Chicago Press, 2008).

Welti, Francesco, Der Baron, die Kunst und das Nazigold (Frauenfeld: Verlag Huber, 2008).

Willems, Elvira, ed., Annemarie Schwarzenbach, Autorin – Reisende – Fotografin (Herbolzheim: Centaurus Verlag & Media, 1998).

Wittstock, Uwe, *February 1933: The Winter of Literature* (Cambridge: Polity, 2023).

Woods, Gregory, *Homintern: How Gay Culture Liberated the Modern World* (New Haven: Yale University Press, 2017).

Wrong, Michela, *In the Footsteps of Mr Kurtz: Living on the Brink of Disaster in the Congo* (London: Fourth Estate, 2000).

Zimmer, Nina and Waldmeier, Martin, eds., *Aufbruch ohne Ziel: Annemarie Schwarzenbach als Fotografin* (Zurich: Lars Müller Publishers, 2020).

Index